Y BLOOD

ILLUSTRATOR
KIYO KYUJYO

AUTHOR
SUNAO YOSHIDA

CHARACTER DESIGN
THORES
SHIBAMOTO

VOLUME THREE

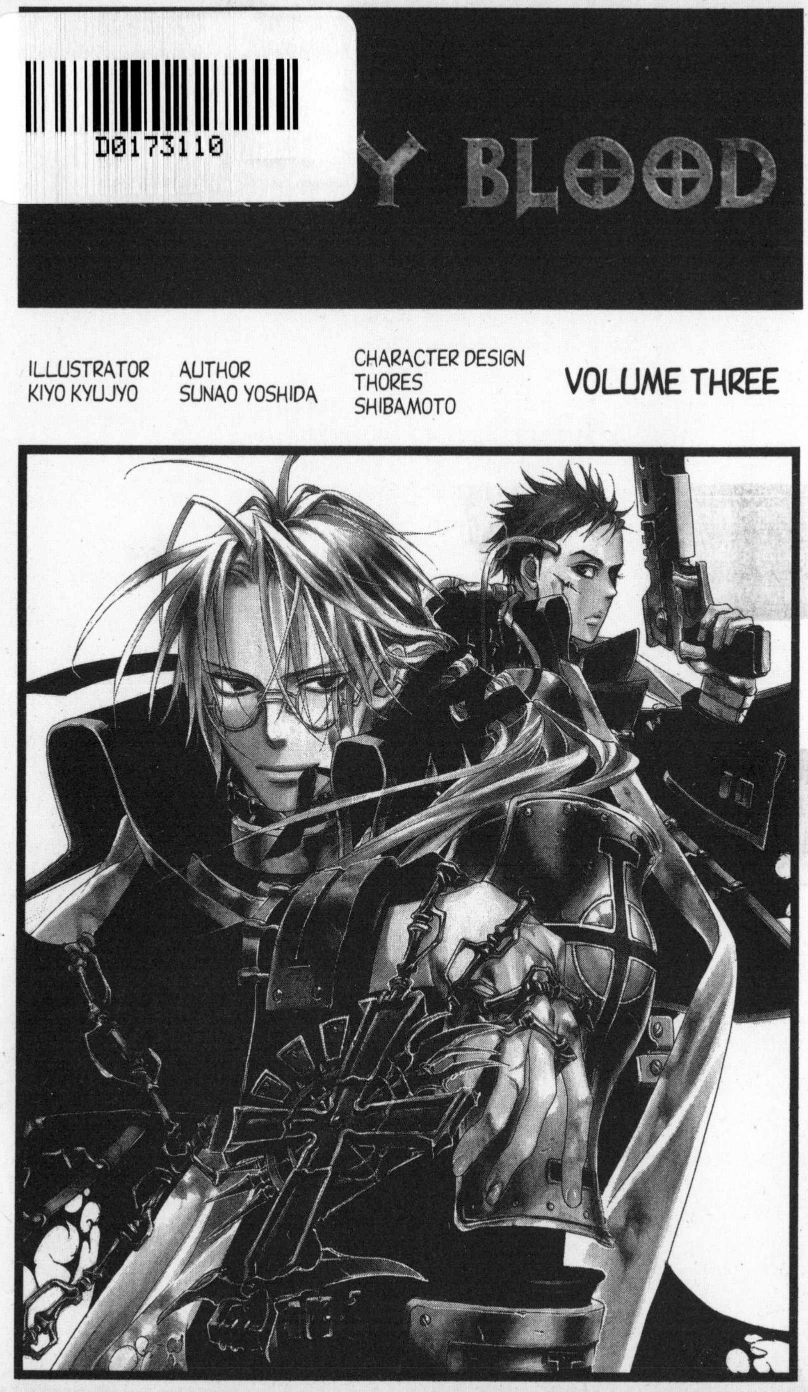

Trinity Blood Volume 3
Story By Sunao Yoshida
Art By Kiyo Kyujyo
Character Designs by Thores Shibamoto

Translation - Beni Axia Conrad
English Adaptation - Christine Boylan
Copy Editor - Stephanie Duchin
Retouch and Lettering - Star Print Brokers
Production Artist - Gavin Hignight
Graphic Designer - James Lee

Editor - Lillian Diaz-Przybyl
Digital Imaging Manager - Chris Buford
Pre-Production Supervisor - Erika Terriquez
Art Director - Anne Marie Horne
Production Manager - Elisabeth Brizzi
Managing Editor - Vy Nguyen
VP of Production - Ron Klamert
Editor-in-Chief - Rob Tokar
Publisher - Mike Kiley
President and C.O.O. - John Parker
C.E.O. and Chief Creative Officer - Stuart Levy

A **TOKYOPOP** Manga

TOKYOPOP Inc.
5900 Wilshire Blvd. Suite 2000
Los Angeles, CA 90036

E-mail: info@TOKYOPOP.com
Come visit us online at www.TOKYOPOP.com

TRINITY BLOOD Volume 3 © Kiyo KYUJYO 2005 © Sunao YOSHIDA 2005 First published in Japan in 2005 by KADOKAWA SHOTEN PUBLISHING CO., LTD., Tokyo. English translation rights arranged with KADOKAWA SHOTEN PUBLISHING CO., LTD., Tokyo through TUTTLE-MORI AGENCY, INC., Tokyo. English text copyright © 2007 TOKYOPOP Inc.

ISBN: 978-1-59816-676-7

First TOKYOPOP printing: July 2007
10 9 8 7 6 5 4 3 2 1
Printed in the USA

TRINITY BLOOD™

VOLUME 3

WRITTEN BY

SUNAO YOSHIDA

ILLUSTRATED BY

KIYO KYUJYO

TOKYOPOP®

HAMBURG // LONDON // LOS ANGELES // TOKYO

Characters & Story

THE STORY

Civilization has been destroyed by a catastrophe of epic proportions. Mankind is at war with vampires, an alien life form that appeared when the earth changed. Father Abel Nightroad, Sister Esther Blanchett and Tres Iquis are on the road to their safe harbor, the Vatican, battling vampires along the way. When they finally reach their destination, Rome...

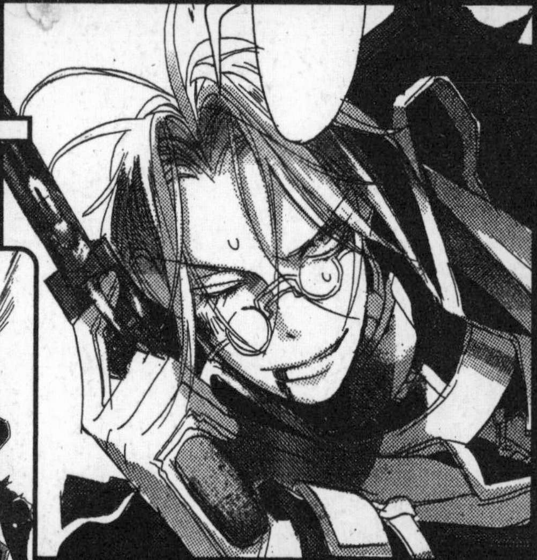

Abel Nightroad

An absentminded, destitute traveling priest from the Vatican's secret AX organization. His official title is AX enforcement officer. His job is to arrest law-breaking vampires. And he takes 13 lumps of sugar in his tea.

Becomes

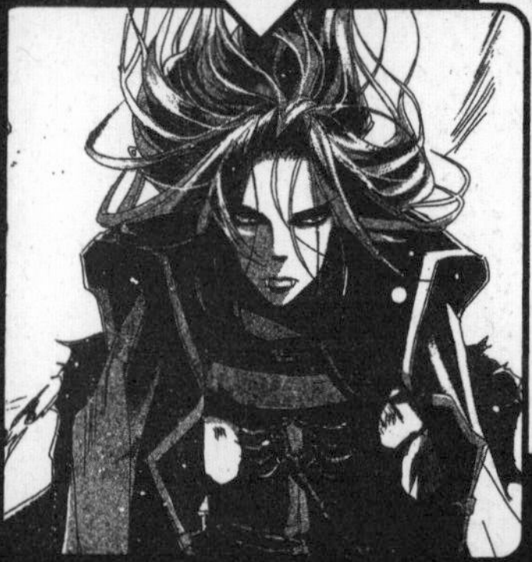

Crusnik

When Abel's threatened and left with no other means of escape, he transforms into a Crusnik, a mysterious vampire who drinks the blood of other vampires and possesses great power.

TRINITY BLOOD

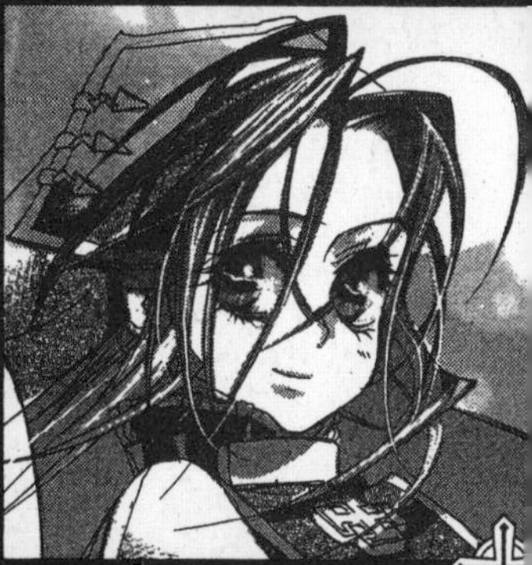

Tres Iqus

Like Abel, he is also an AX enforcement officer. His code name is "Gunslinger." He is a machine, rather than a human.

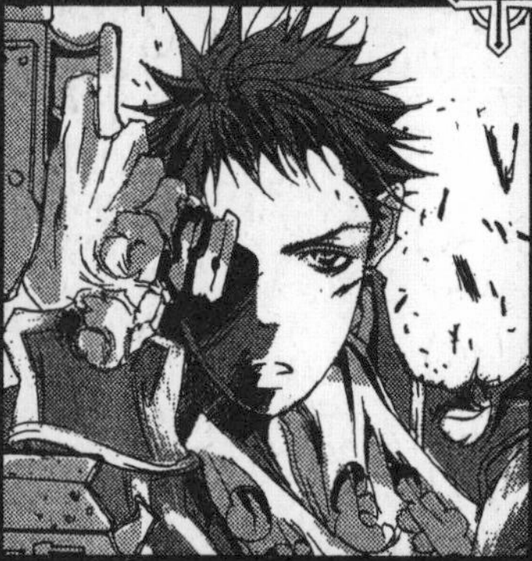

Esther Blanchett

A novice nun with a strong sense of justice. After she lost her church and friends in a battle with vampires, she chose action over despair and followed Abel when he said, "I am on your side."

Terminology

The Vatican

The Holy See–the ultra-nationalistic organizing body that backs humanity's side in the fight against the vampires. Its headquarters are in Rome.

Terran

The Short-Lived Race–the term vampires use in reference to humans.

Methuselah

The Long-Lived Race—the term vampires use in reference to themselves.

Vampire

Alien life forms that suddenly arrived after the Earth's catastrophe. They drink the blood of humans and have long lives and superhuman physical abilities.

CONTENTS

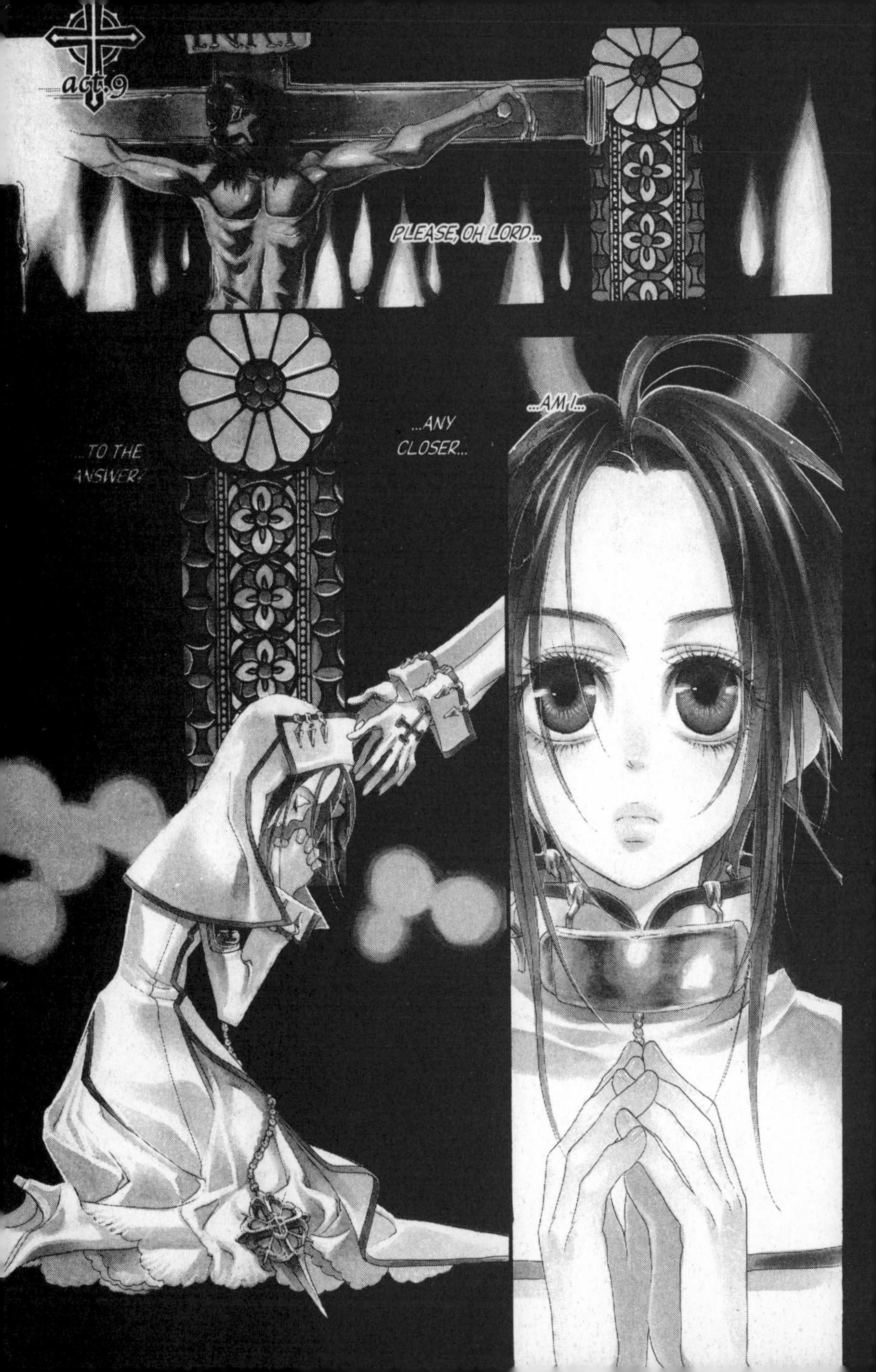
act.9
PLEASE, OH LORD...
...AM I...
...ANY CLOSER...
...TO THE ANSWER?

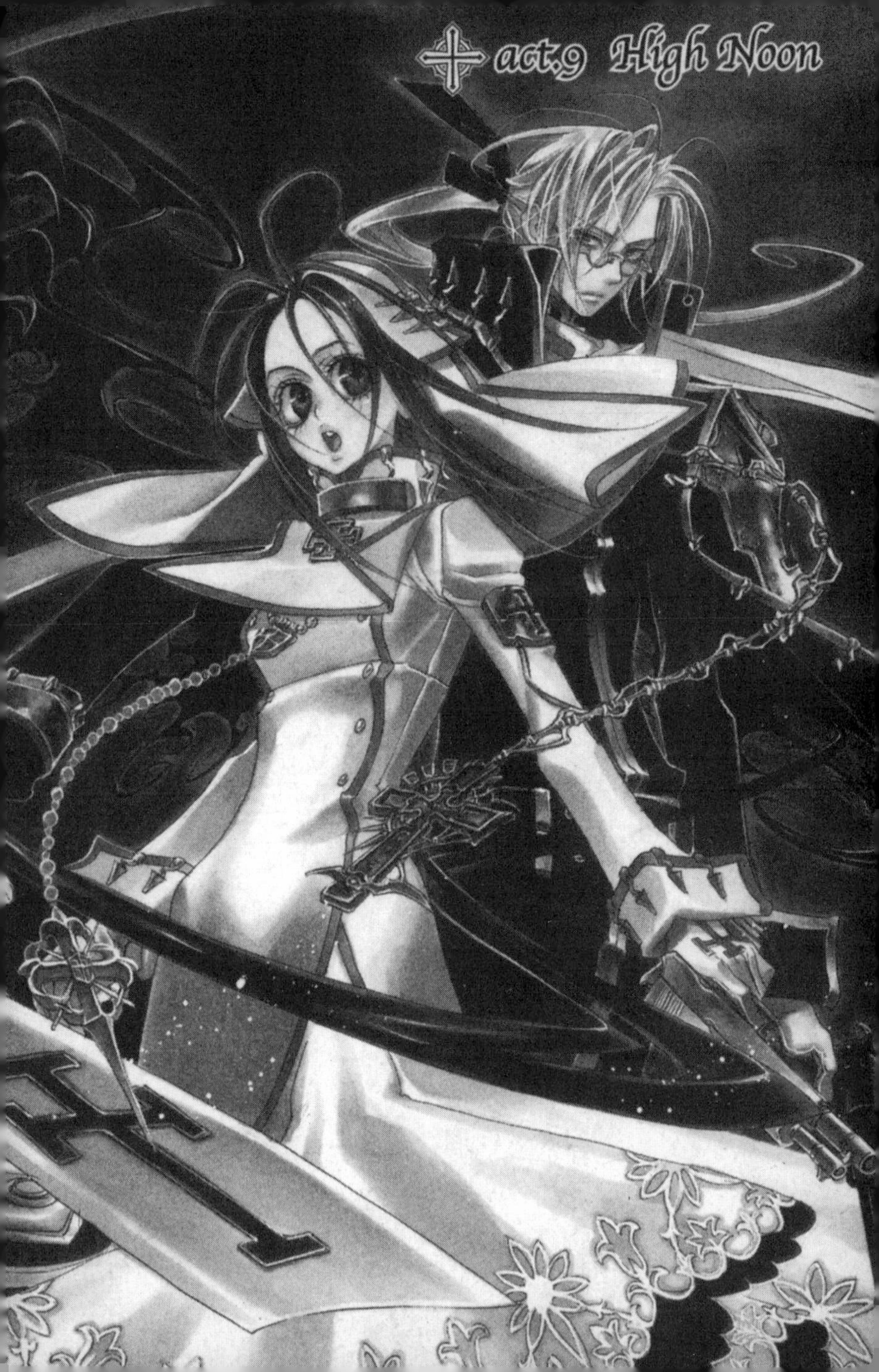
act.9 High Noon

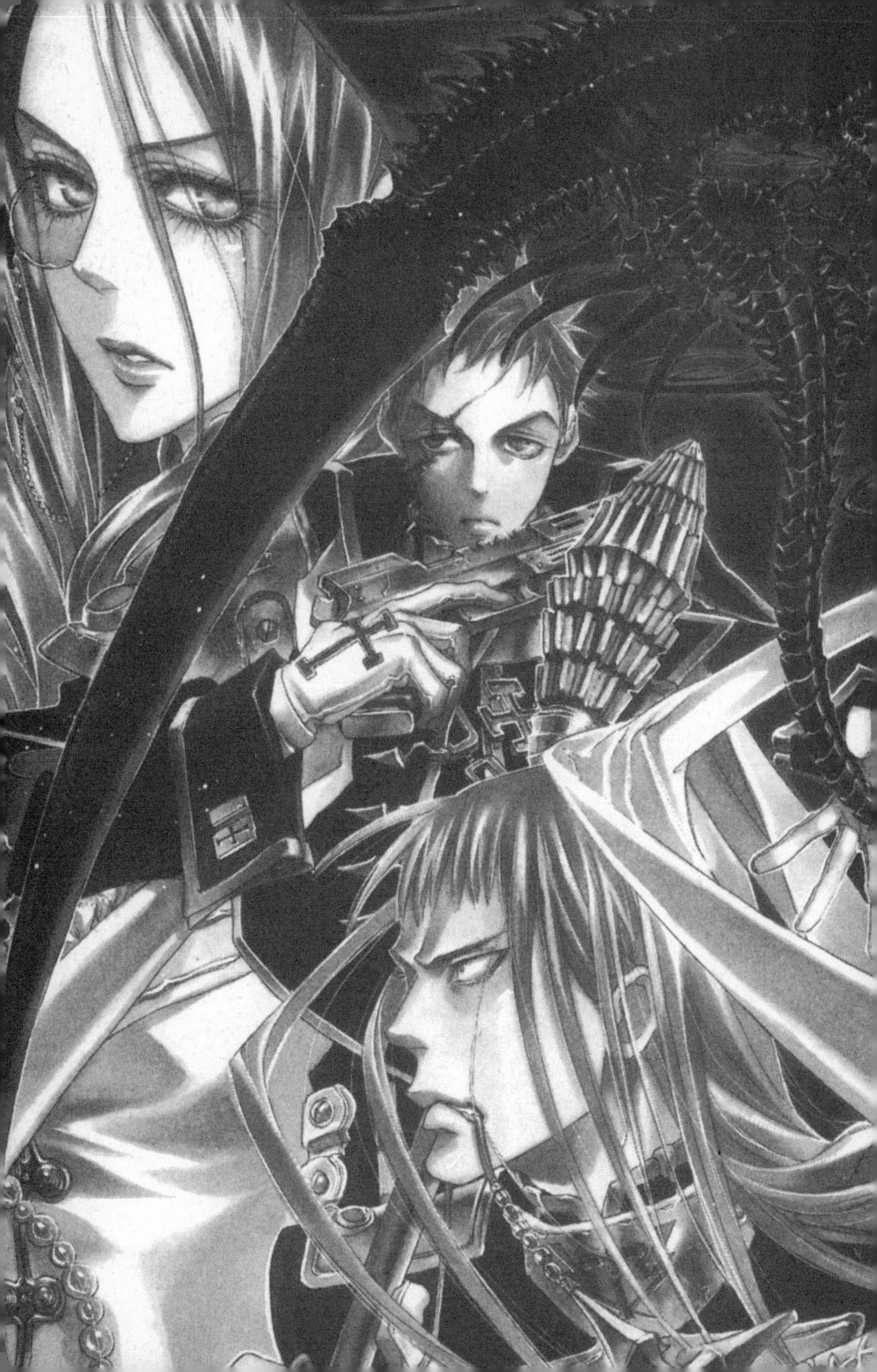

TRINITY BLOOD

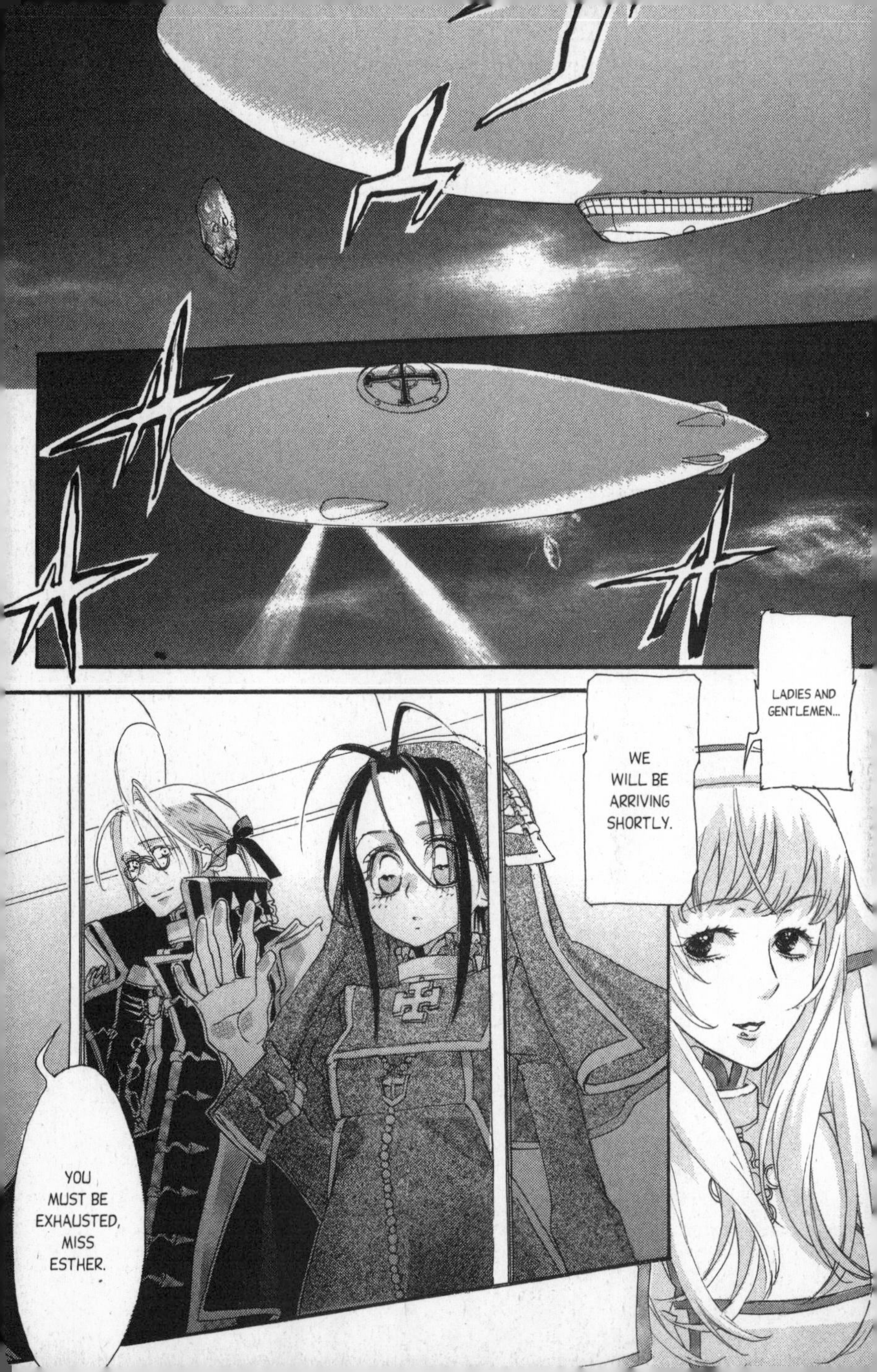
LADIES AND GENTLEMEN...
WE WILL BE ARRIVING SHORTLY.
YOU MUST BE EXHAUSTED, MISS ESTHER.

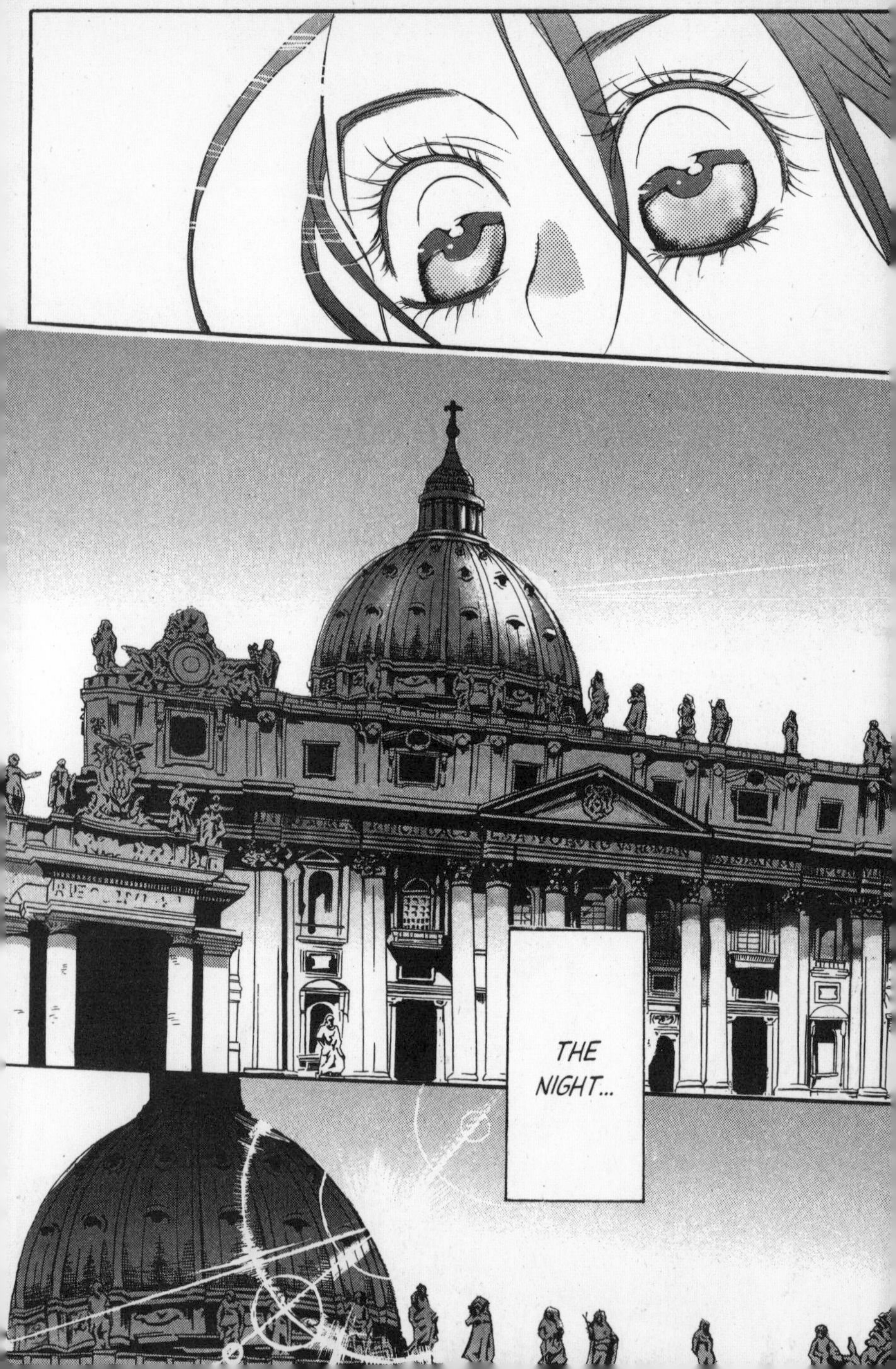
THE NIGHT...

...FADES
INTO
DAWN.

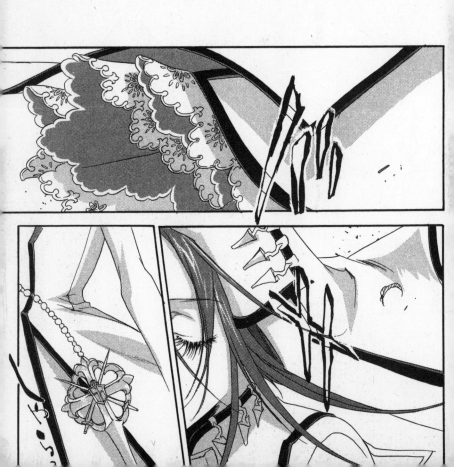

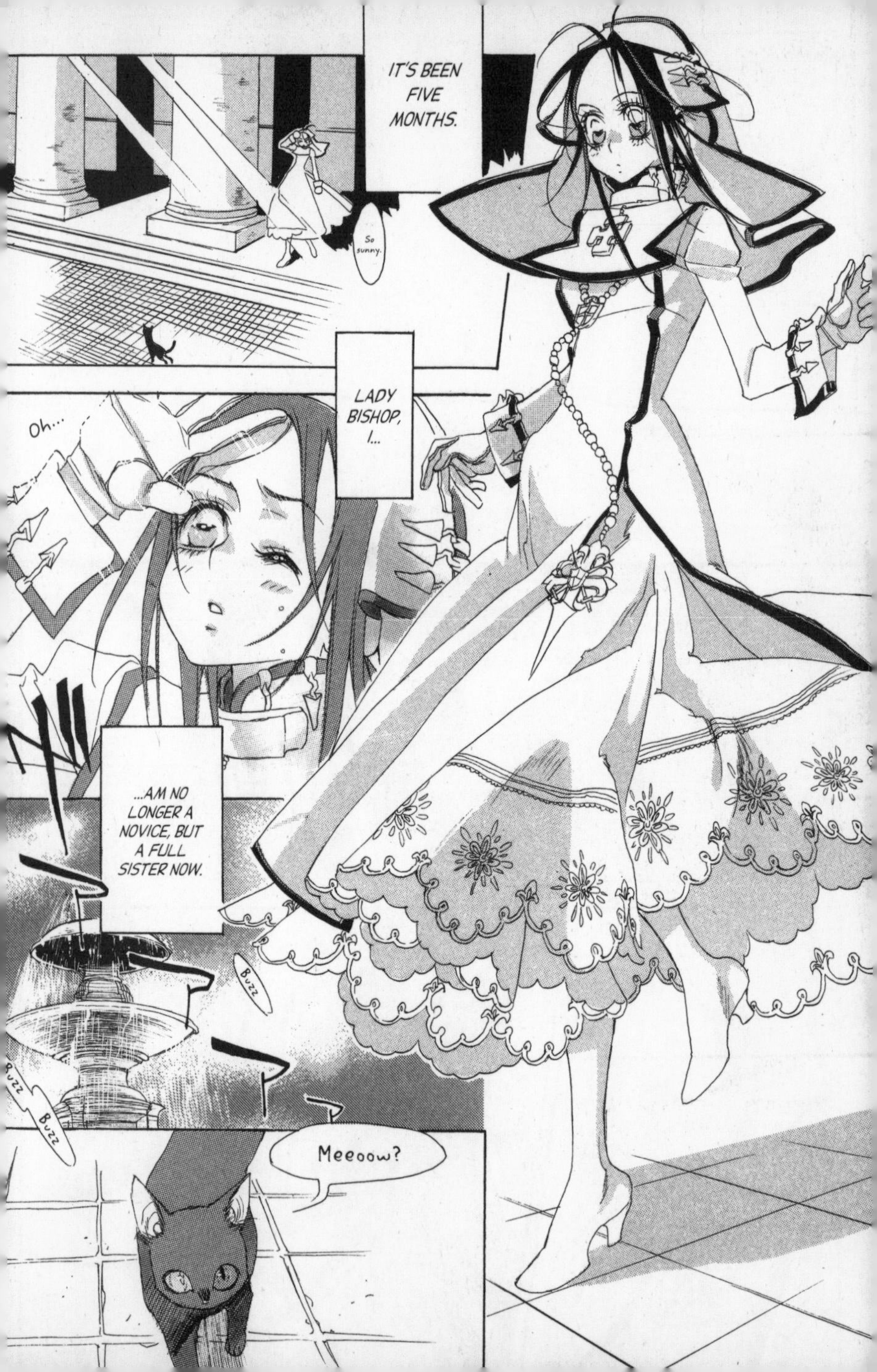
IT'S BEEN FIVE MONTHS.
LADY BISHOP, I...
...AM NO LONGER A NOVICE, BUT A FULL SISTER NOW.
So sunny.
Oh...
Buzz
Buzz
Buzz
Meeoow?

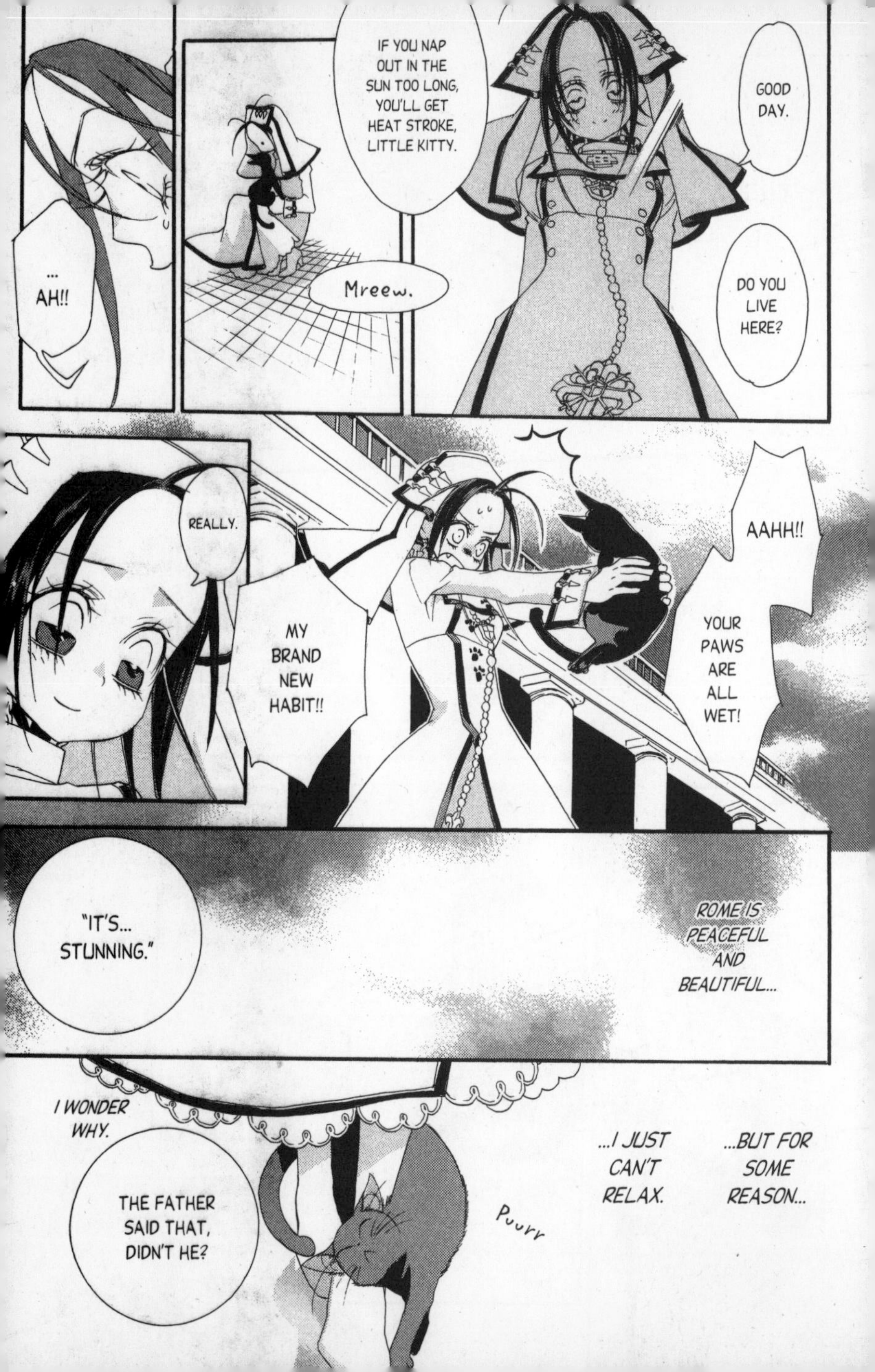
GOOD DAY.
DO YOU LIVE HERE?
IF YOU NAP OUT IN THE SUN TOO LONG, YOU'LL GET HEAT STROKE, LITTLE KITTY.
Mreeew.
... AH!!
AAHH!!
YOUR PAWS ARE ALL WET!
MY BRAND NEW HABIT!!
REALLY.
ROME IS PEACEFUL AND BEAUTIFUL...
"IT'S... STUNNING."
...BUT FOR SOME REASON...
...I JUST CAN'T RELAX.
I WONDER WHY.
Puurr
THE FATHER SAID THAT, DIDN'T HE?

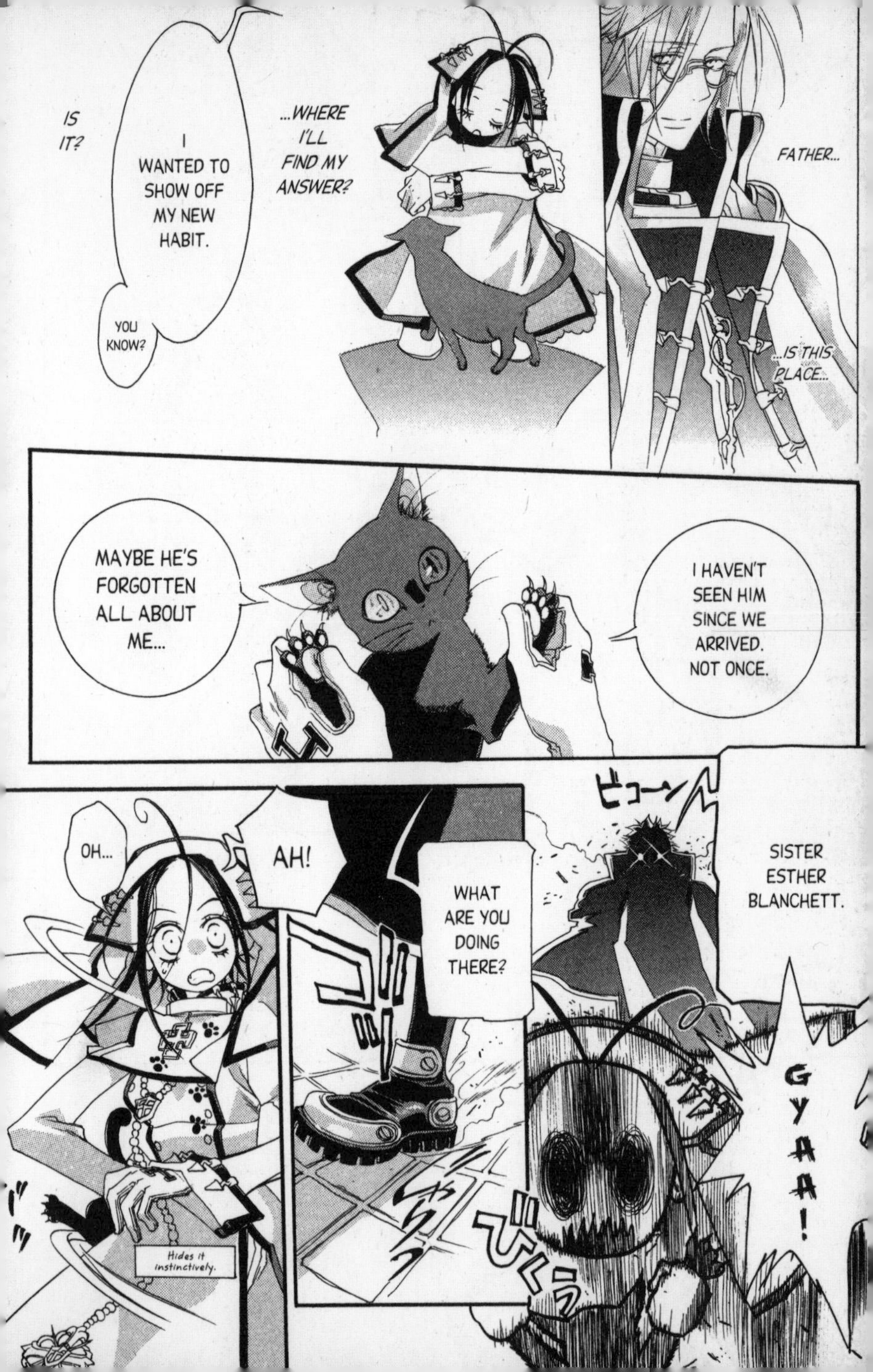
FATHER...
...IS THIS PLACE...
...WHERE I'LL FIND MY ANSWER?
IS IT?
I WANTED TO SHOW OFF MY NEW HABIT.
YOU KNOW?
I HAVEN'T SEEN HIM SINCE WE ARRIVED. NOT ONCE.
MAYBE HE'S FORGOTTEN ALL ABOUT ME...
SISTER ESTHER BLANCHETT.
ビコーン
WHAT ARE YOU DOING THERE?
GYAA!
AH!
OH...
Hides it instinctively.

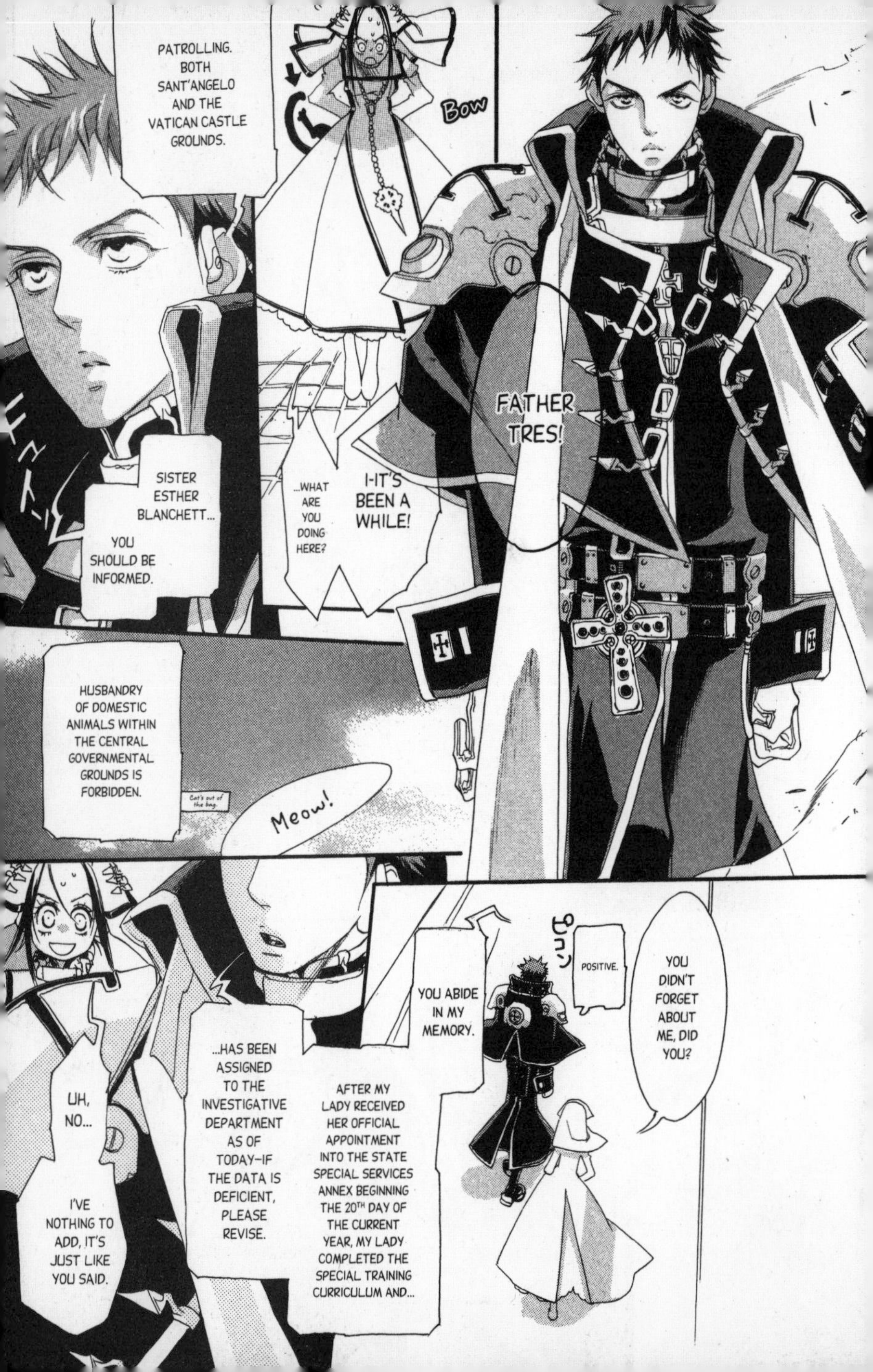
FATHER TRES!
Bow
I-IT'S BEEN A WHILE!
...WHAT ARE YOU DOING HERE?
PATROLLING. BOTH SANT'ANGELO AND THE VATICAN CASTLE GROUNDS.
SISTER ESTHER BLANCHETT... YOU SHOULD BE INFORMED.
HUSBANDRY OF DOMESTIC ANIMALS WITHIN THE CENTRAL GOVERNMENTAL GROUNDS IS FORBIDDEN.
Meow!
Cat's out of the bag.
YOU DIDN'T FORGET ABOUT ME, DID YOU?
ピコン
POSITIVE.
YOU ABIDE IN MY MEMORY.
AFTER MY LADY RECEIVED HER OFFICIAL APPOINTMENT INTO THE STATE SPECIAL SERVICES ANNEX BEGINNING THE 20TH DAY OF THE CURRENT YEAR, MY LADY COMPLETED THE SPECIAL TRAINING CURRICULUM AND...
...HAS BEEN ASSIGNED TO THE INVESTIGATIVE DEPARTMENT AS OF TODAY–IF THE DATA IS DEFICIENT, PLEASE REVISE.
UH, NO...
I'VE NOTHING TO ADD, IT'S JUST LIKE YOU SAID.

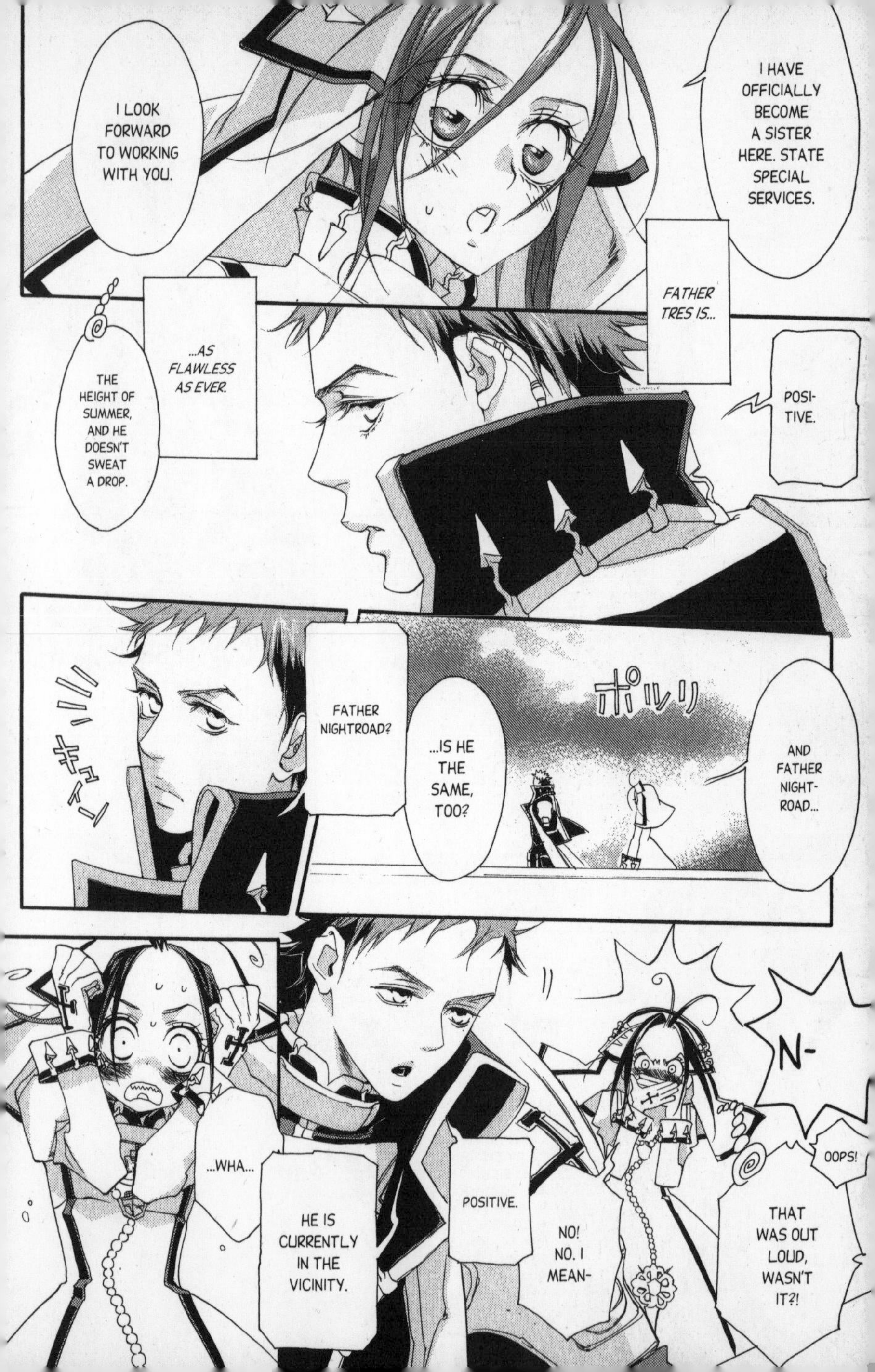
I HAVE OFFICIALLY BECOME A SISTER HERE. STATE SPECIAL SERVICES.
I LOOK FORWARD TO WORKING WITH YOU.
FATHER TRES IS...
POSI-TIVE.
...AS FLAWLESS AS EVER.
THE HEIGHT OF SUMMER, AND HE DOESN'T SWEAT A DROP.
AND FATHER NIGHT-ROAD...
ポルルリ
...IS HE THE SAME, TOO?
FATHER NIGHTROAD?
キュイーン
N-
OOPS!
THAT WAS OUT LOUD, WASN'T IT?!
NO! NO. I MEAN-
POSITIVE.
HE IS CURRENTLY IN THE VICINITY.
...WHA...

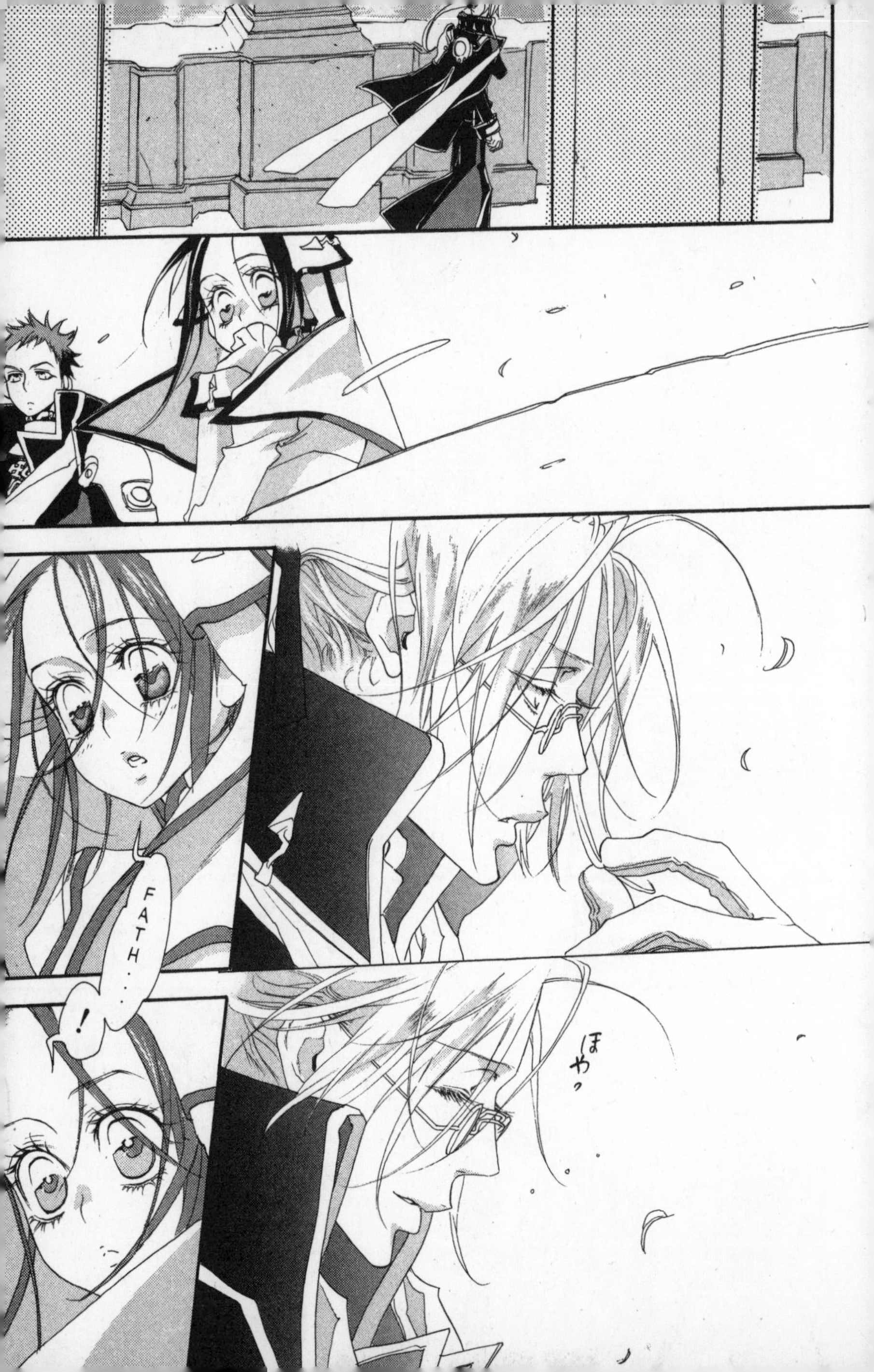
FATH...
!
ほやっ

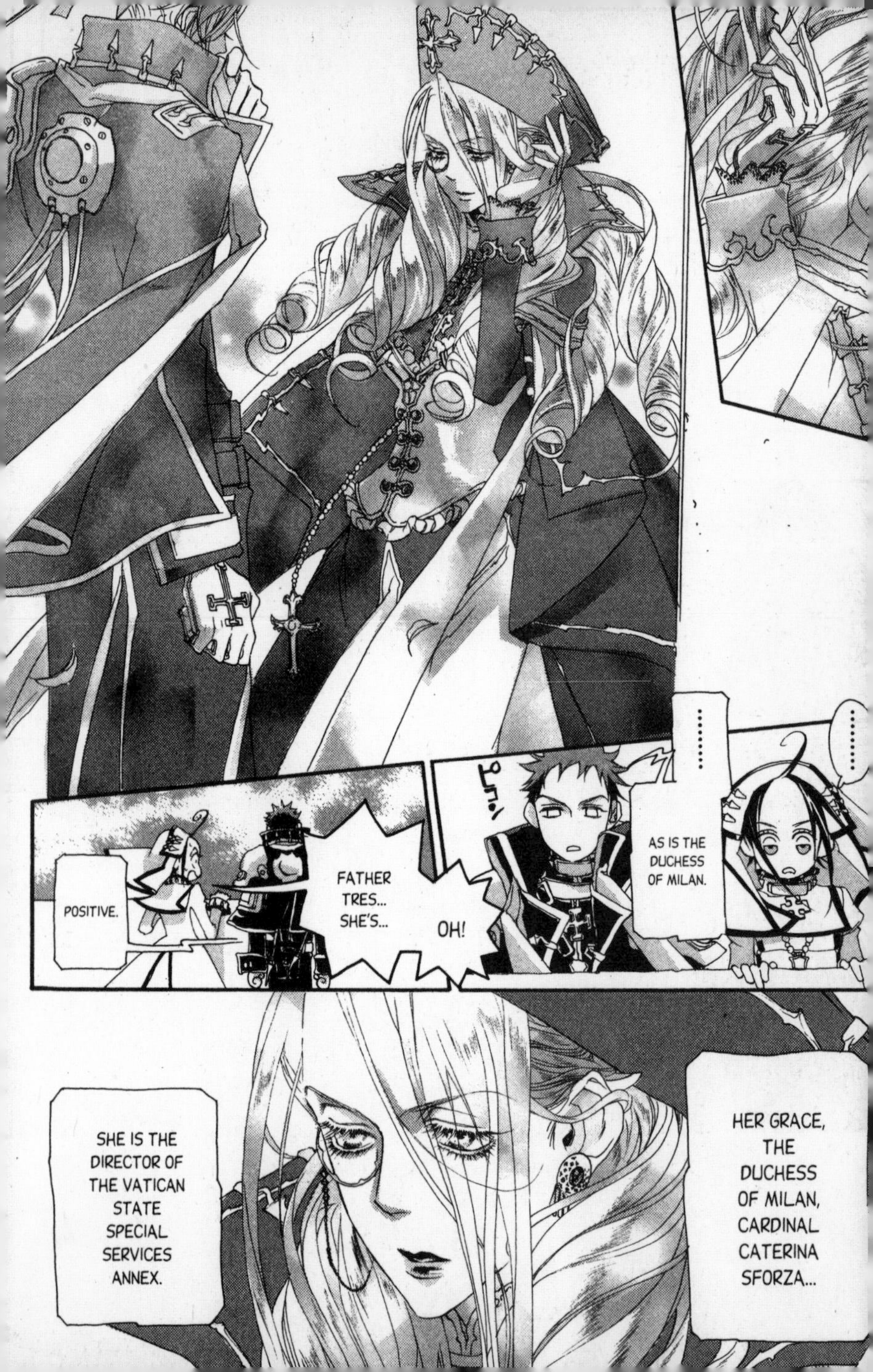
......
......
AS IS THE DUCHESS OF MILAN.
OH!
FATHER TRES... SHE'S...
POSITIVE.
HER GRACE, THE DUCHESS OF MILAN, CARDINAL CATERINA SFORZA...
SHE IS THE DIRECTOR OF THE VATICAN STATE SPECIAL SERVICES ANNEX.

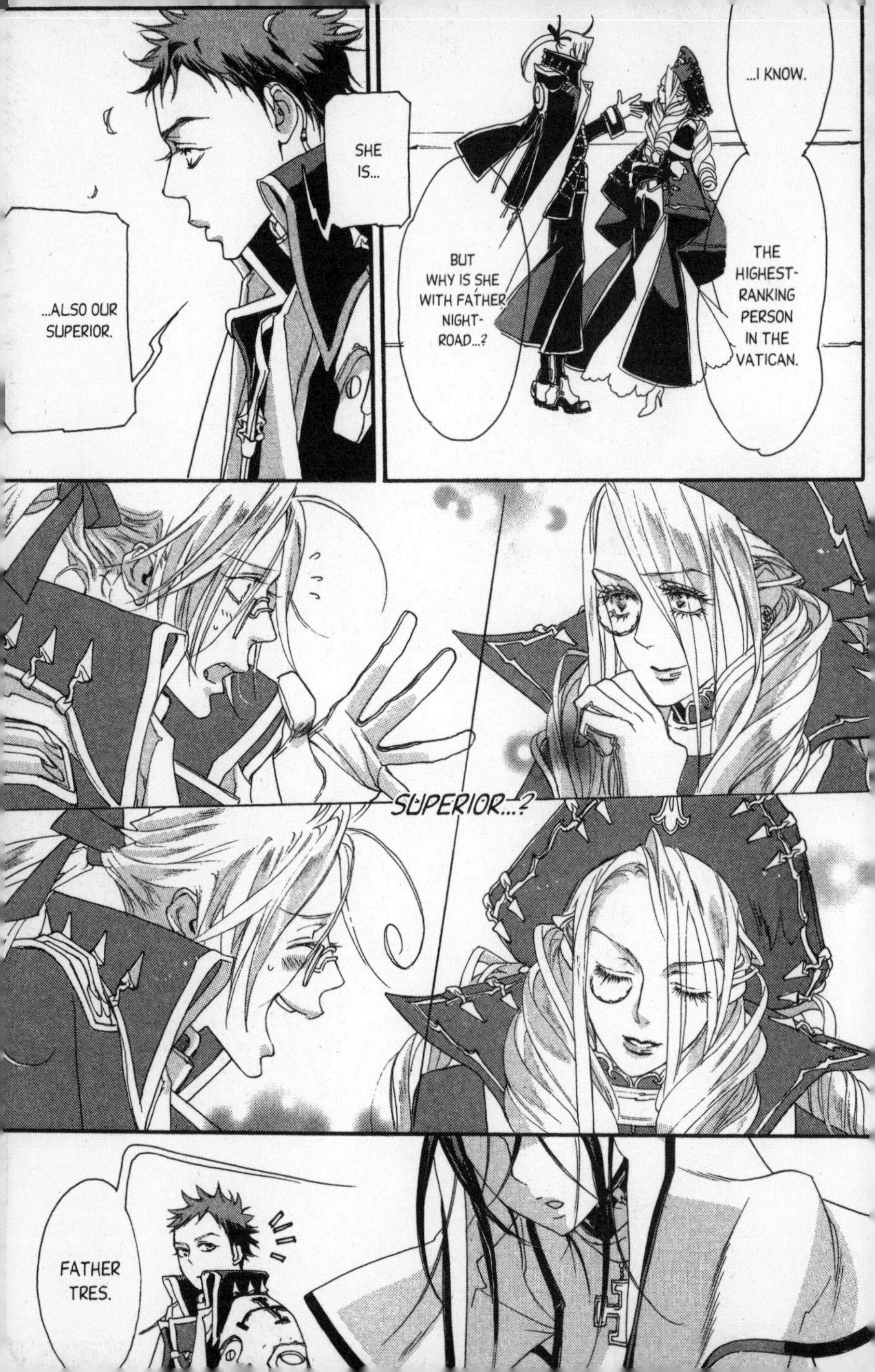
...I KNOW.
THE HIGHEST-RANKING PERSON IN THE VATICAN.
BUT WHY IS SHE WITH FATHER NIGHT-ROAD...?
SHE IS...
...ALSO OUR SUPERIOR.
SUPERIOR...?
FATHER TRES.

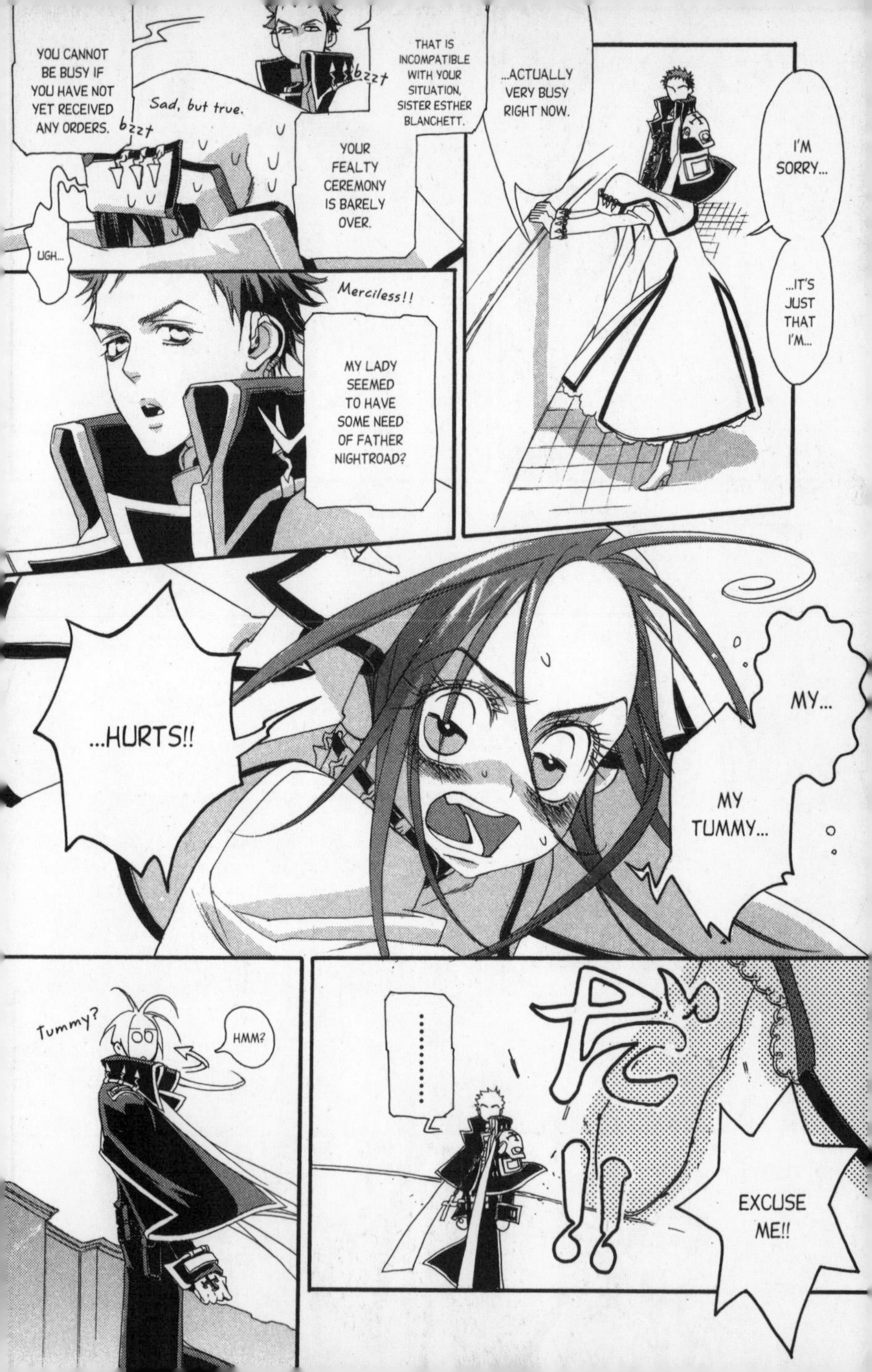
I'M SORRY...
...IT'S JUST THAT I'M...
...ACTUALLY VERY BUSY RIGHT NOW.
THAT IS INCOMPATIBLE WITH YOUR SITUATION, SISTER ESTHER BLANCHETT.
bzzt
YOUR FEALTY CEREMONY IS BARELY OVER.
YOU CANNOT BE BUSY IF YOU HAVE NOT YET RECEIVED ANY ORDERS.
bzzt
Sad, but true.
UGH...
Merciless!!
MY LADY SEEMED TO HAVE SOME NEED OF FATHER NIGHTROAD?
MY...
MY TUMMY...
...HURTS!!
EXCUSE ME!!
......
HMM?
Tummy?

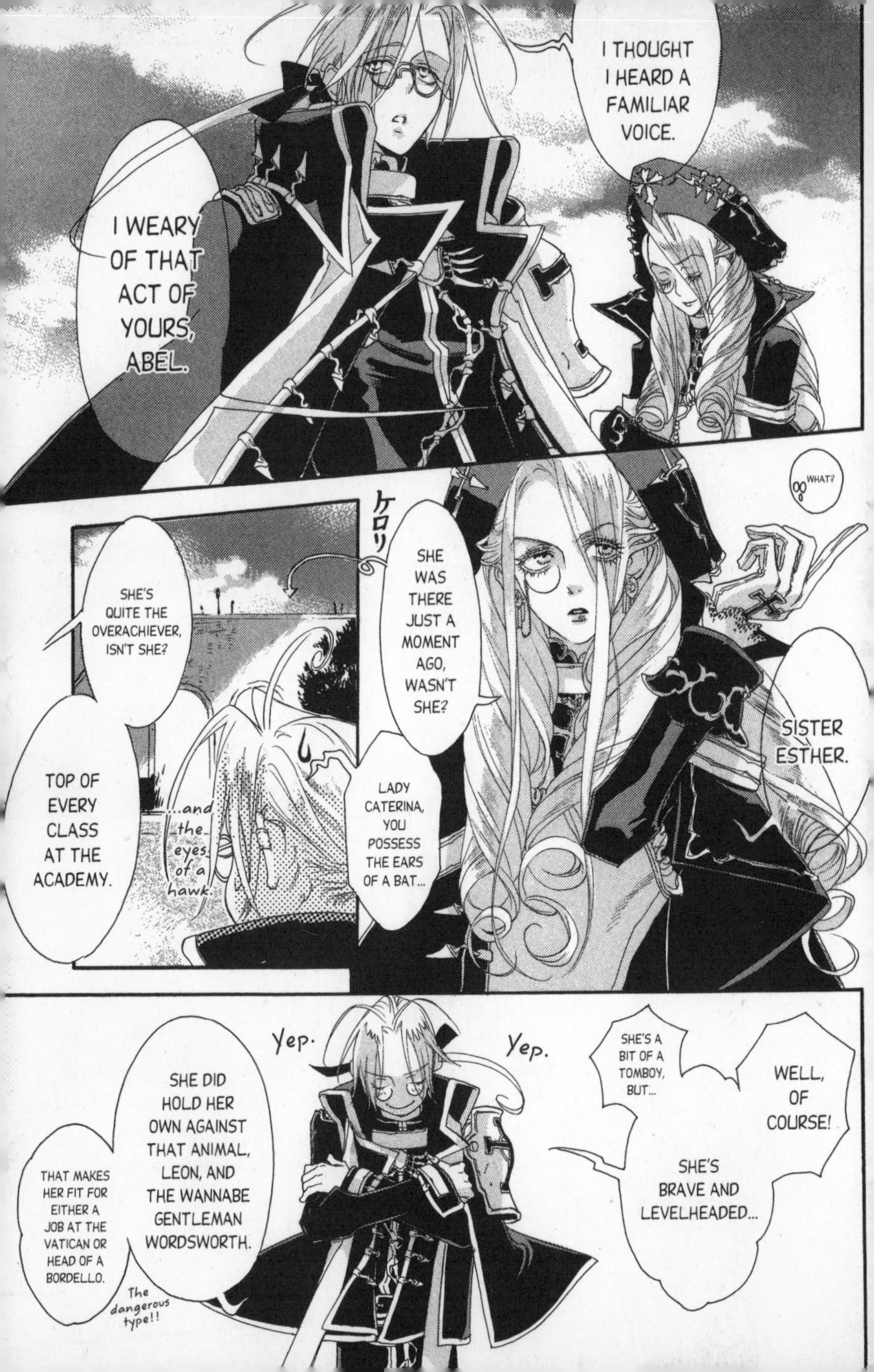
I THOUGHT I HEARD A FAMILIAR VOICE.
I WEARY OF THAT ACT OF YOURS, ABEL.
WHAT?
SISTER ESTHER.
ケロリ
SHE WAS THERE JUST A MOMENT AGO, WASN'T SHE?
LADY CATERINA, YOU POSSESS THE EARS OF A BAT...
SHE'S QUITE THE OVERACHIEVER, ISN'T SHE?
TOP OF EVERY CLASS AT THE ACADEMY.
...and the eyes of a hawk.
WELL, OF COURSE!
SHE'S A BIT OF A TOMBOY, BUT...
SHE'S BRAVE AND LEVELHEADED...
Yep.
Yep.
SHE DID HOLD HER OWN AGAINST THAT ANIMAL, LEON, AND THE WANNABE GENTLEMAN WORDSWORTH.
THAT MAKES HER FIT FOR EITHER A JOB AT THE VATICAN OR HEAD OF A BORDELLO.
The dangerous type!!

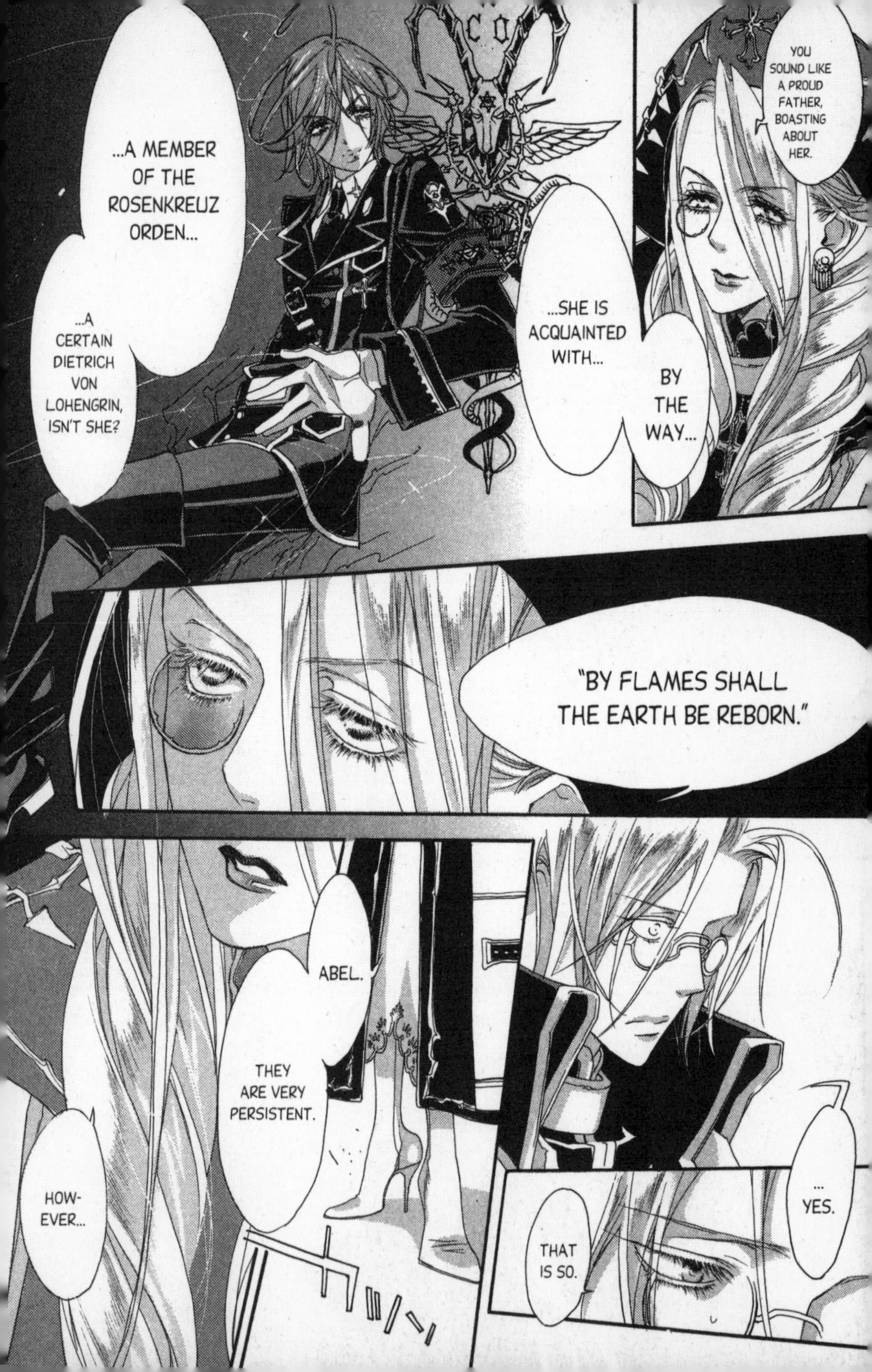
YOU SOUND LIKE A PROUD FATHER, BOASTING ABOUT HER.
BY THE WAY...
...SHE IS ACQUAINTED WITH...
...A MEMBER OF THE ROSENKREUZ ORDEN...
...A CERTAIN DIETRICH VON LOHENGRIN, ISN'T SHE?
"BY FLAMES SHALL THE EARTH BE REBORN."
... YES.
THAT IS SO.
ABEL.
THEY ARE VERY PERSISTENT.
HOW-EVER...

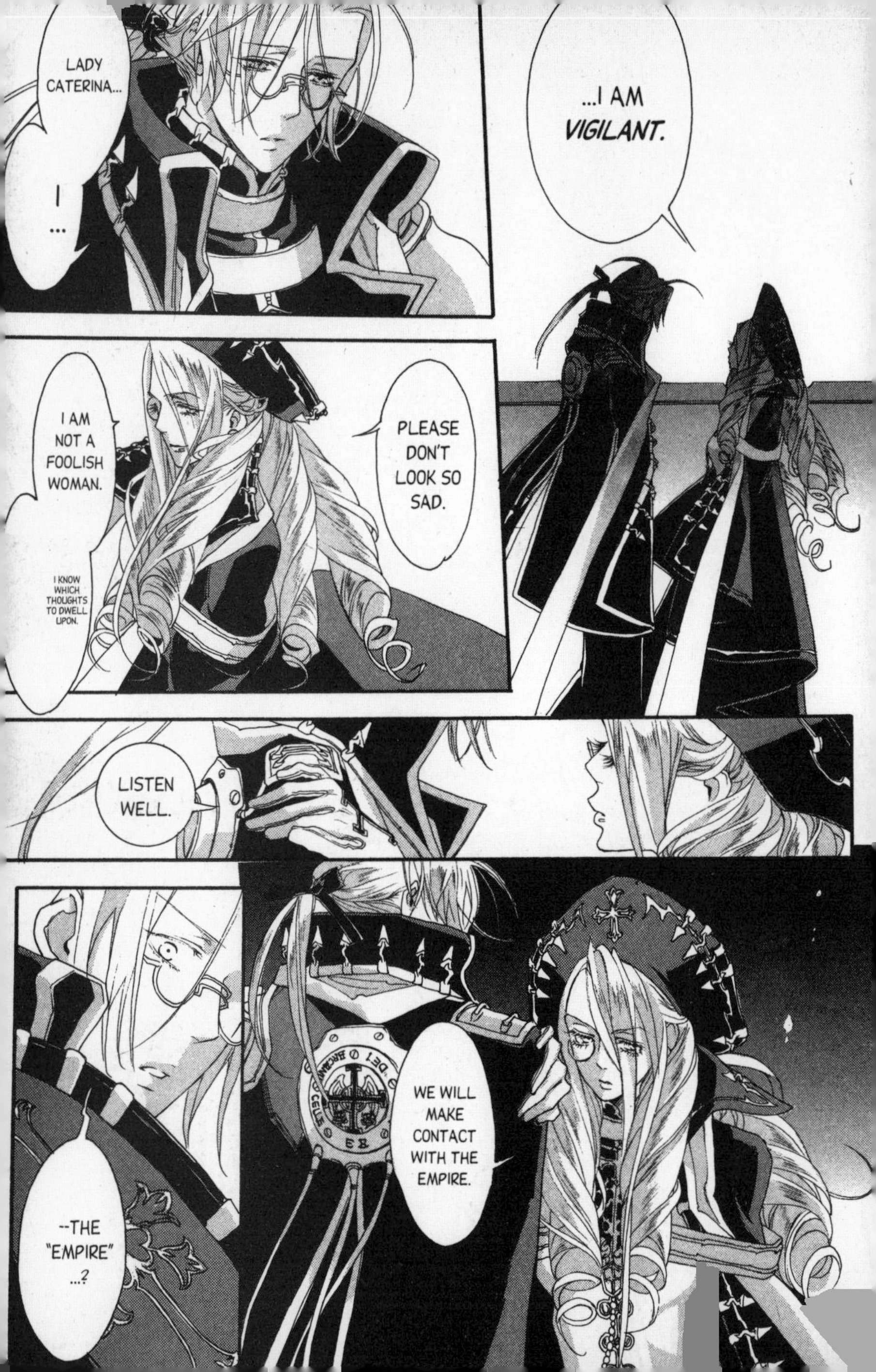
...I AM *VIGILANT.*
LADY CATERINA...
I ...
PLEASE DON'T LOOK SO SAD.
I AM NOT A FOOLISH WOMAN.
I KNOW WHICH THOUGHTS TO DWELL UPON.
LISTEN WELL.
WE WILL MAKE CONTACT WITH THE EMPIRE.
--THE "EMPIRE" ...?

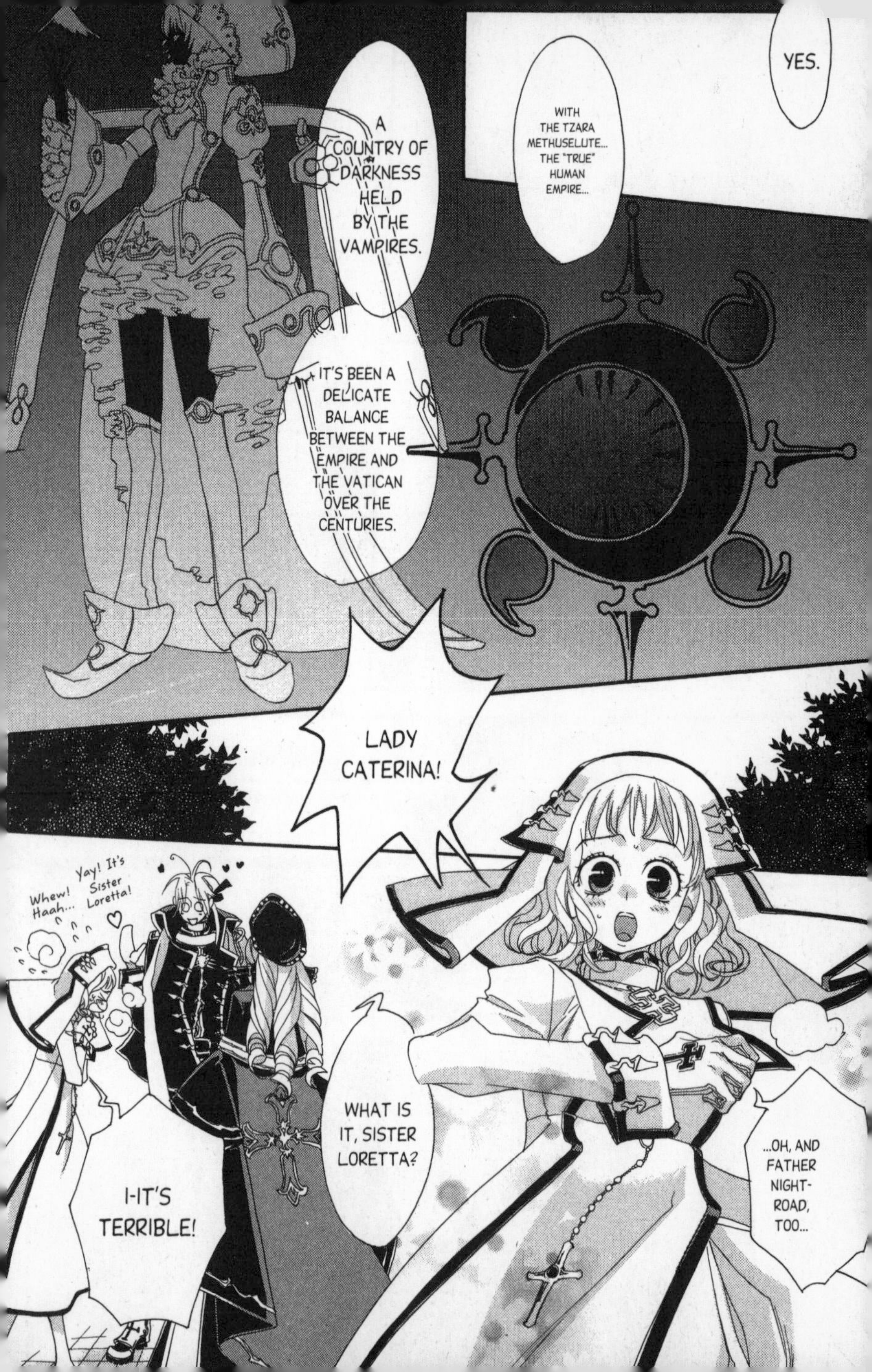
YES.
WITH THE TZARA METHUSELUTE... THE "TRUE" HUMAN EMPIRE...
A COUNTRY OF DARKNESS HELD BY THE VAMPIRES.
IT'S BEEN A DELICATE BALANCE BETWEEN THE EMPIRE AND THE VATICAN OVER THE CENTURIES.
LADY CATERINA!
...OH, AND FATHER NIGHT-ROAD, TOO...
WHAT IS IT, SISTER LORETTA?
I-IT'S TERRIBLE!
Yay! It's Sister Loretta!
Whew! Haah...

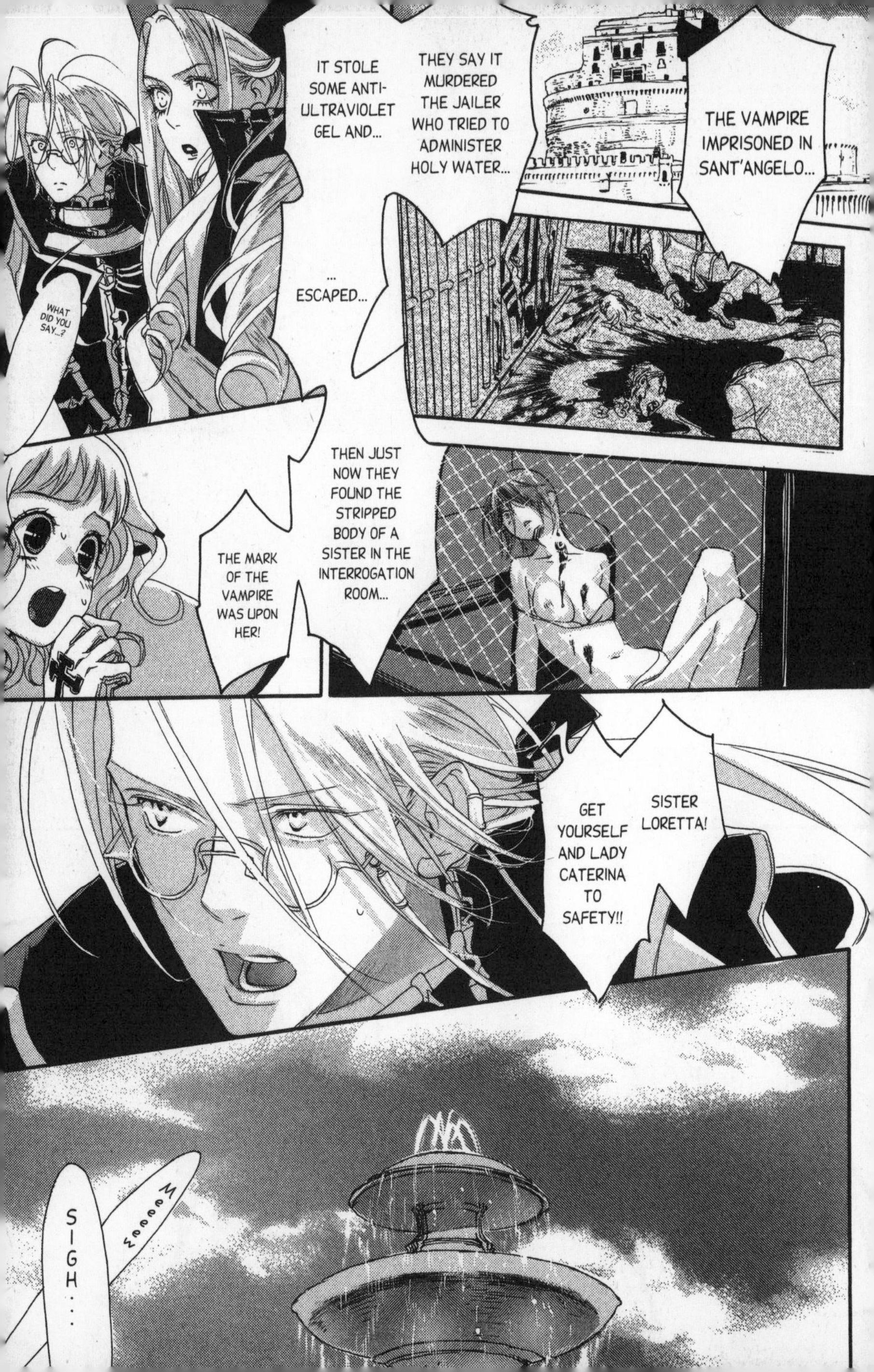
THE VAMPIRE IMPRISONED IN SANT'ANGELO...
THEY SAY IT MURDERED THE JAILER WHO TRIED TO ADMINISTER HOLY WATER...
IT STOLE SOME ANTI-ULTRAVIOLET GEL AND...
... ESCAPED...
WHAT DID YOU SAY...?
THEN JUST NOW THEY FOUND THE STRIPPED BODY OF A SISTER IN THE INTERROGATION ROOM...
THE MARK OF THE VAMPIRE WAS UPON HER!
SISTER LORETTA!
GET YOURSELF AND LADY CATERINA TO SAFETY!!
Meeeee
SIGH...

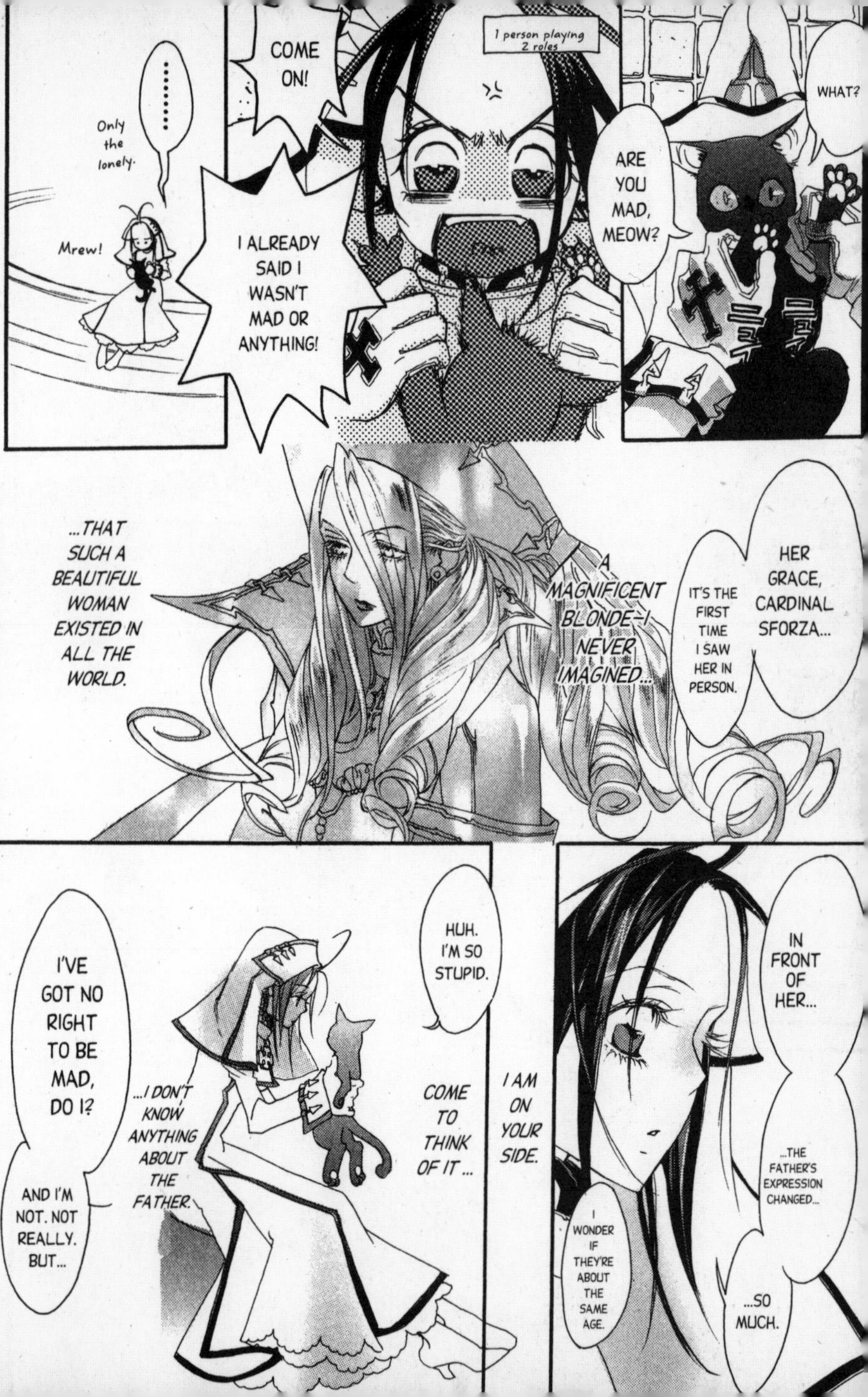
WHAT?
ARE YOU MAD, MEOW?
1 person playing 2 roles
COME ON!
I ALREADY SAID I WASN'T MAD OR ANYTHING!
....
Only the lonely.
Mrew!
HER GRACE, CARDINAL SFORZA...
IT'S THE FIRST TIME I SAW HER IN PERSON.
A MAGNIFICENT BLONDE—I NEVER IMAGINED...
...THAT SUCH A BEAUTIFUL WOMAN EXISTED IN ALL THE WORLD.
IN FRONT OF HER...
...THE FATHER'S EXPRESSION CHANGED...
...SO MUCH.
I WONDER IF THEY'RE ABOUT THE SAME AGE.
I AM ON YOUR SIDE.
HUH. I'M SO STUPID.
COME TO THINK OF IT...
...I DON'T KNOW ANYTHING ABOUT THE FATHER.
I'VE GOT NO RIGHT TO BE MAD, DO I?
AND I'M NOT. NOT REALLY. BUT...

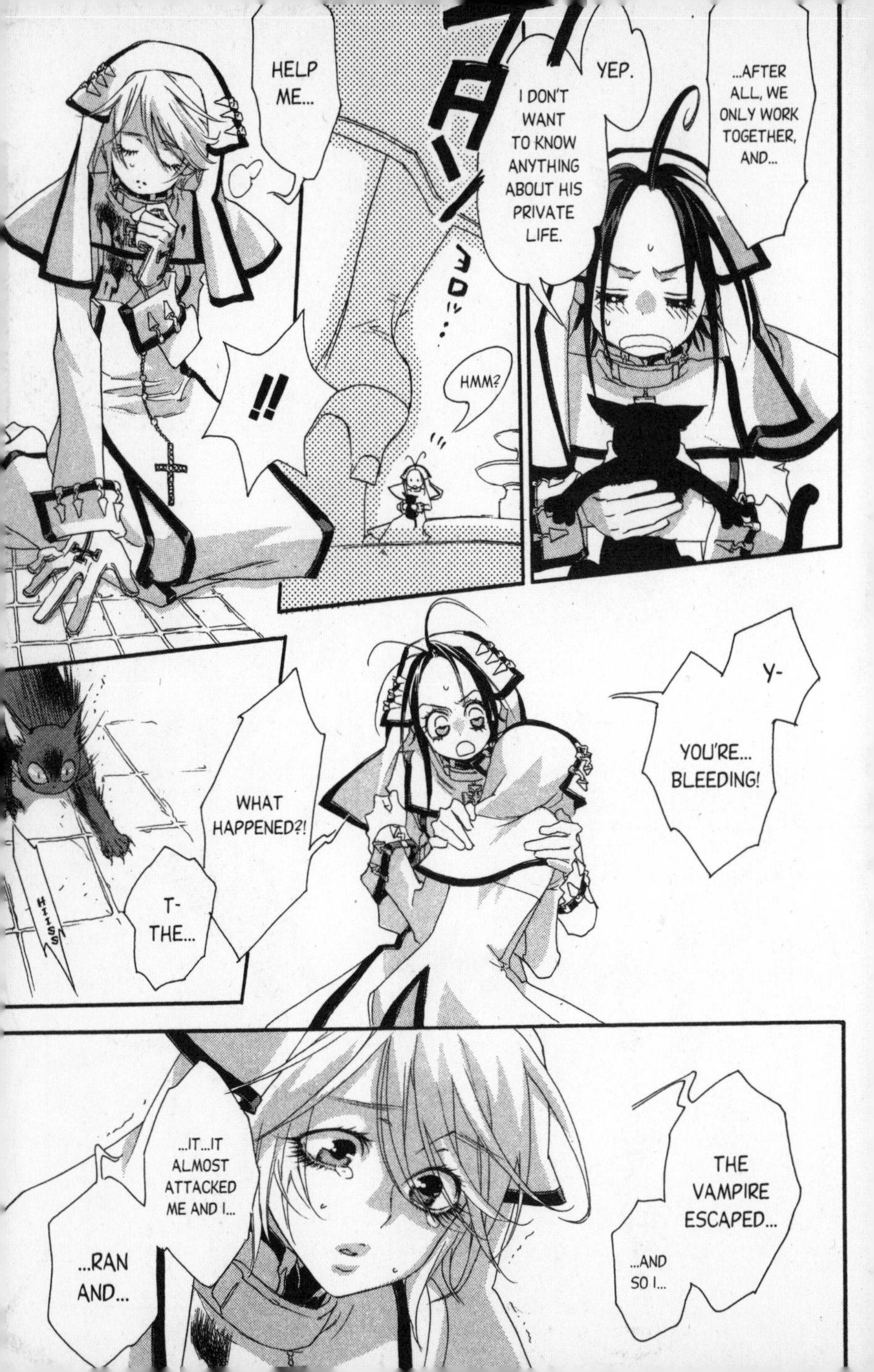
...AFTER ALL, WE ONLY WORK TOGETHER, AND...
YEP.
I DON'T WANT TO KNOW ANYTHING ABOUT HIS PRIVATE LIFE.
HMM?
HELP ME...
!!
Y-
YOU'RE... BLEEDING!
WHAT HAPPENED?!
T-
THE...
HIIISS
THE VAMPIRE ESCAPED...
...AND SO I...
...IT...IT ALMOST ATTACKED ME AND I...
...RAN AND...

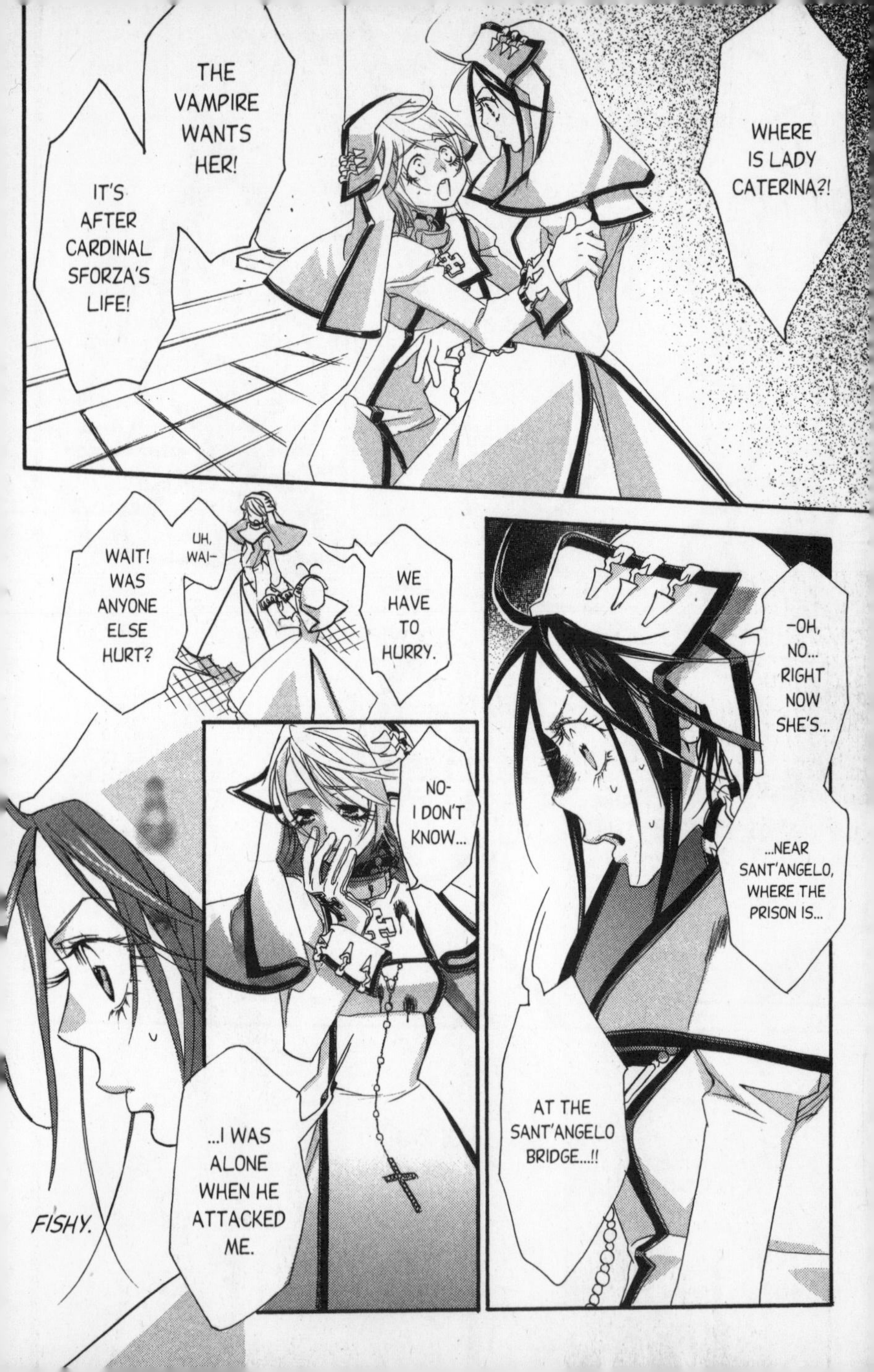
WHERE IS LADY CATERINA?!
THE VAMPIRE WANTS HER!
IT'S AFTER CARDINAL SFORZA'S LIFE!
-OH, NO... RIGHT NOW SHE'S...
...NEAR SANT'ANGELO, WHERE THE PRISON IS...
AT THE SANT'ANGELO BRIDGE...!!
WE HAVE TO HURRY.
UH, WAI-
WAIT! WAS ANYONE ELSE HURT?
NO- I DON'T KNOW...
...I WAS ALONE WHEN HE ATTACKED ME.
FISHY.

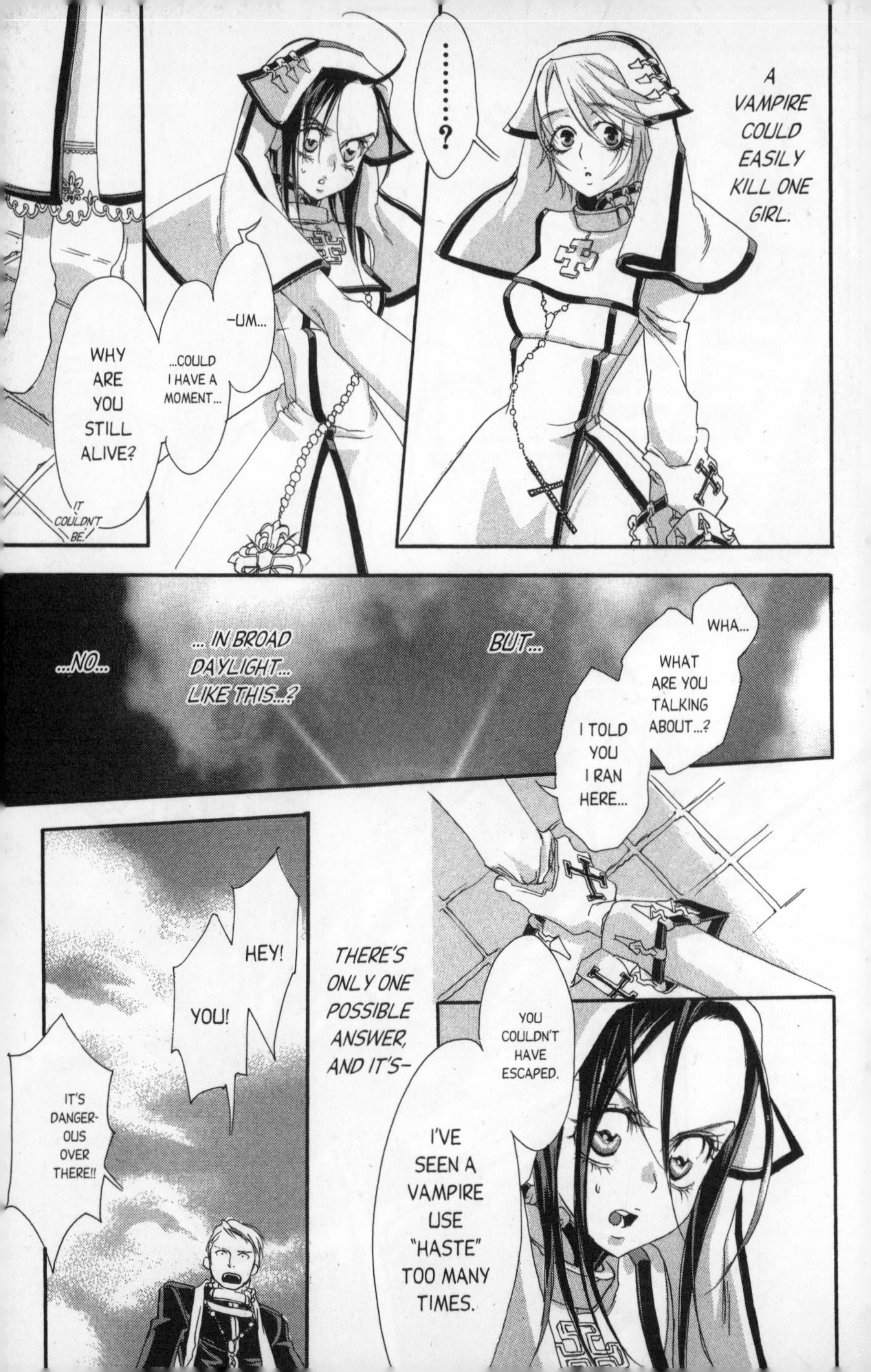
A VAMPIRE COULD EASILY KILL ONE GIRL.
......?
—UM...
...COULD I HAVE A MOMENT...
WHY ARE YOU STILL ALIVE?
IT COULDN'T BE.
WHA...
WHAT ARE YOU TALKING ABOUT...?
I TOLD YOU I RAN HERE...
BUT...
...IN BROAD DAYLIGHT... LIKE THIS...?
...NO...
YOU COULDN'T HAVE ESCAPED.
I'VE SEEN A VAMPIRE USE "HASTE" TOO MANY TIMES.
THERE'S ONLY ONE POSSIBLE ANSWER, AND IT'S—
HEY!
YOU!
IT'S DANGER-OUS OVER THERE!!

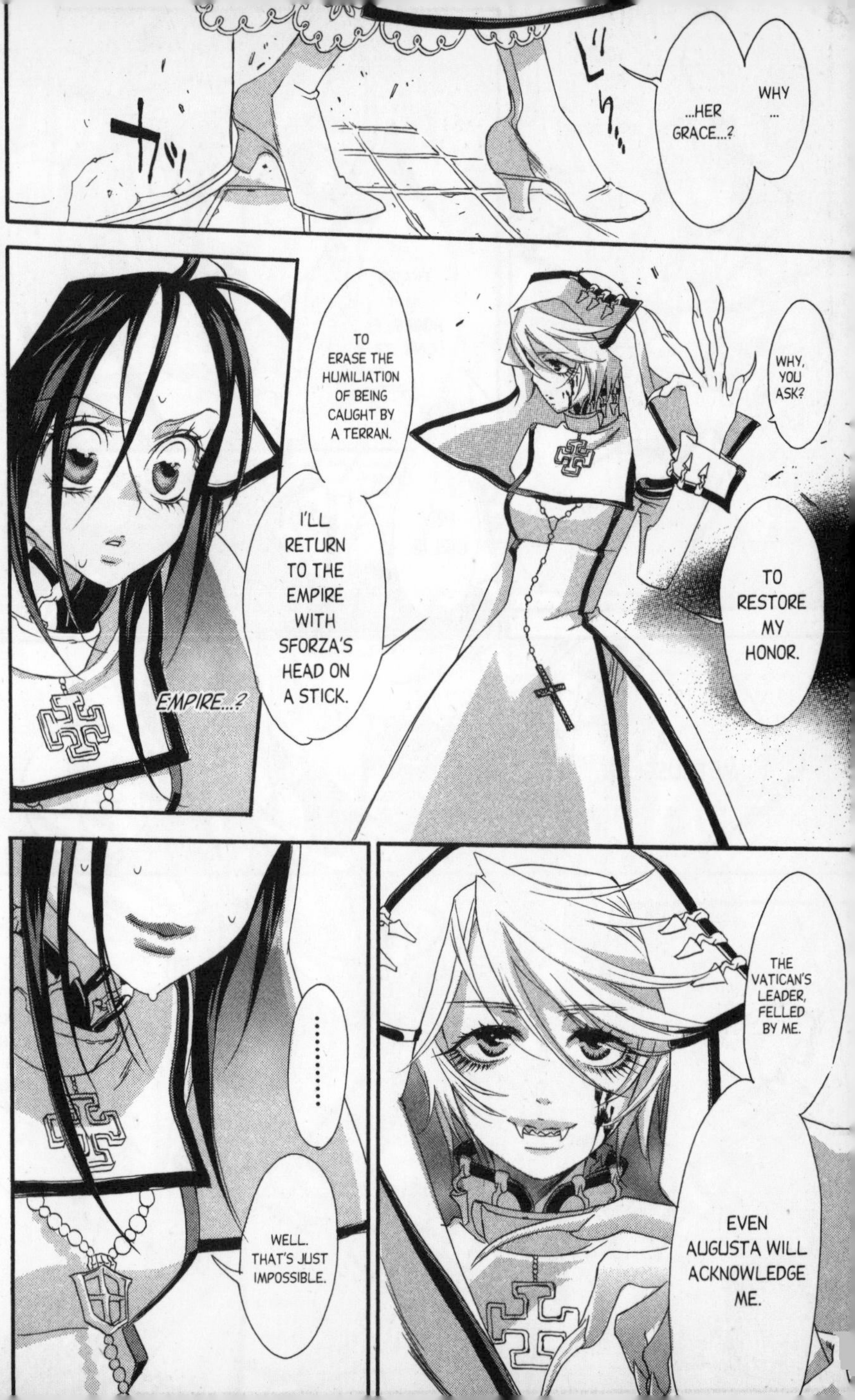
WHY ...
...HER GRACE...?
WHY, YOU ASK?
TO RESTORE MY HONOR.
TO ERASE THE HUMILIATION OF BEING CAUGHT BY A TERRAN.
I'LL RETURN TO THE EMPIRE WITH SFORZA'S HEAD ON A STICK.
EMPIRE...?
THE VATICAN'S LEADER, FELLED BY ME.
EVEN AUGUSTA WILL ACKNOWLEDGE ME.
....
WELL. THAT'S JUST IMPOSSIBLE.

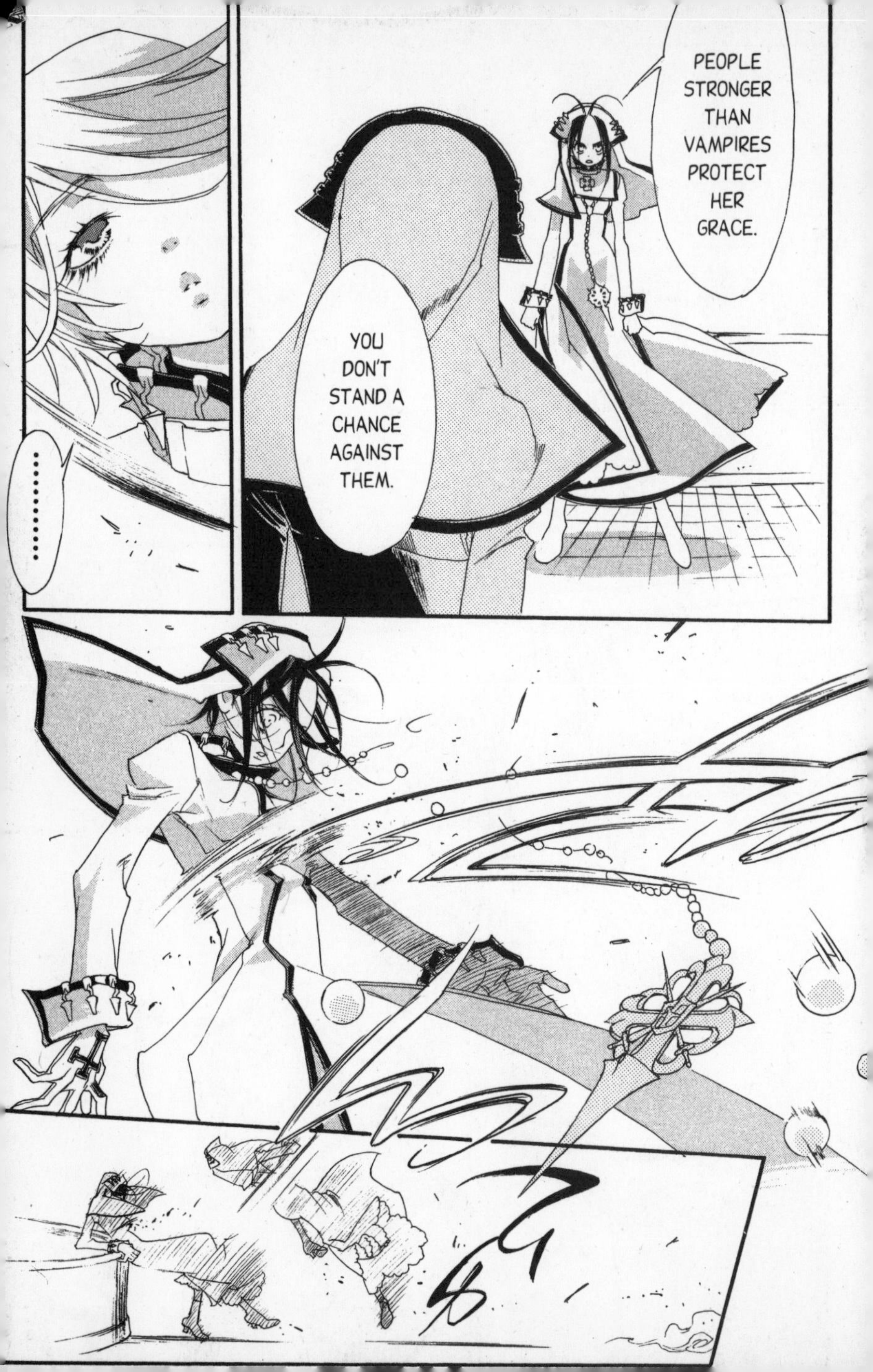
PEOPLE STRONGER THAN VAMPIRES PROTECT HER GRACE.
YOU DON'T STAND A CHANCE AGAINST THEM.
....

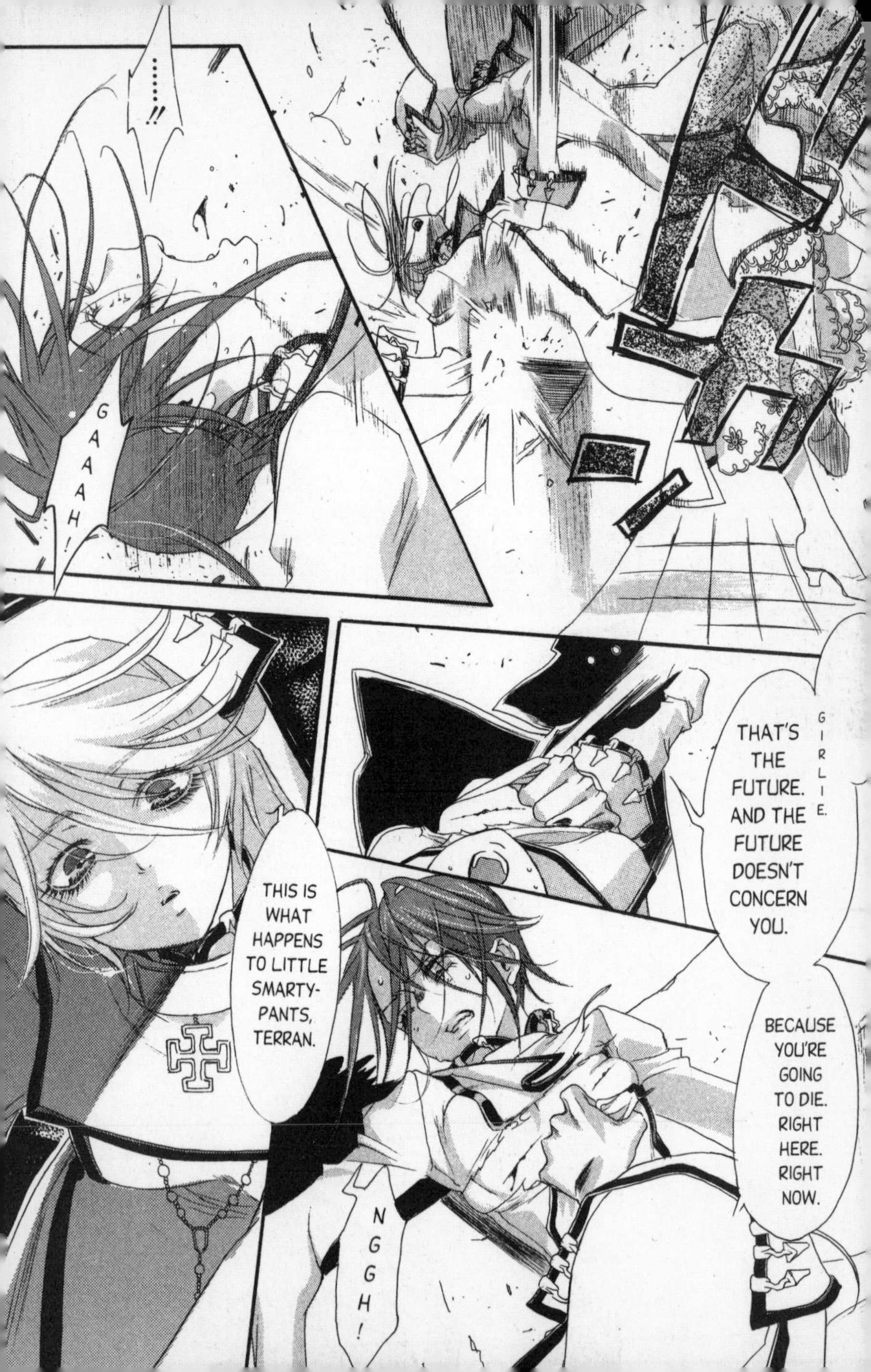
......!!
GAAAAH!
THAT'S THE FUTURE. AND THE FUTURE DOESN'T CONCERN YOU.
GIRLIE.
BECAUSE YOU'RE GOING TO DIE. RIGHT HERE. RIGHT NOW.
NGGH!
THIS IS WHAT HAPPENS TO LITTLE SMARTY-PANTS, TERRAN.

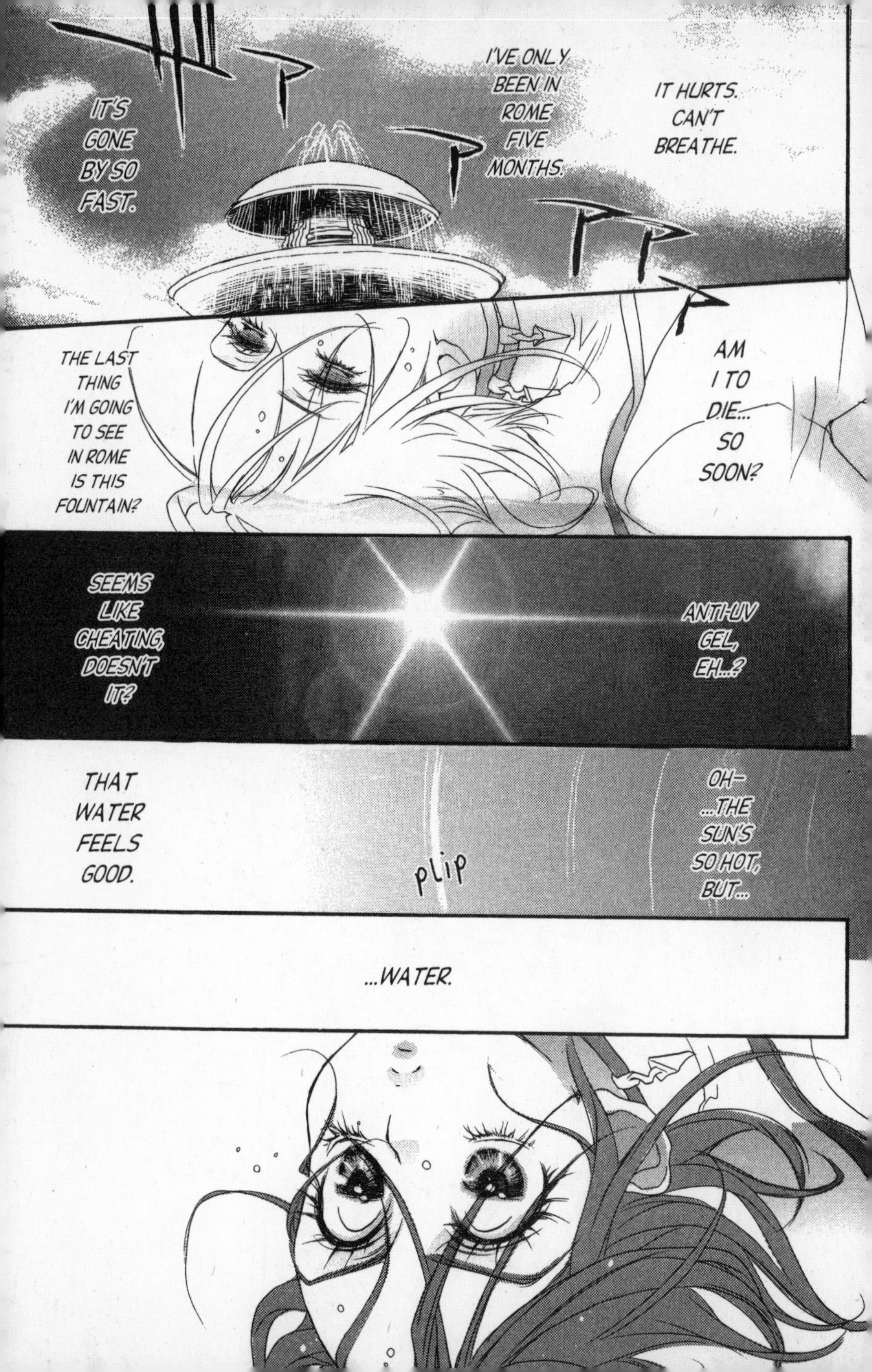
IT HURTS. CAN'T BREATHE.
I'VE ONLY BEEN IN ROME FIVE MONTHS.
IT'S GONE BY SO FAST.
AM I TO DIE... SO SOON?
THE LAST THING I'M GOING TO SEE IN ROME IS THIS FOUNTAIN?
ANTI-UV GEL, EH...?
SEEMS LIKE CHEATING, DOESN'T IT?
OH— ...THE SUN'S SO HOT, BUT...
plip
THAT WATER FEELS GOOD.
...WATER.

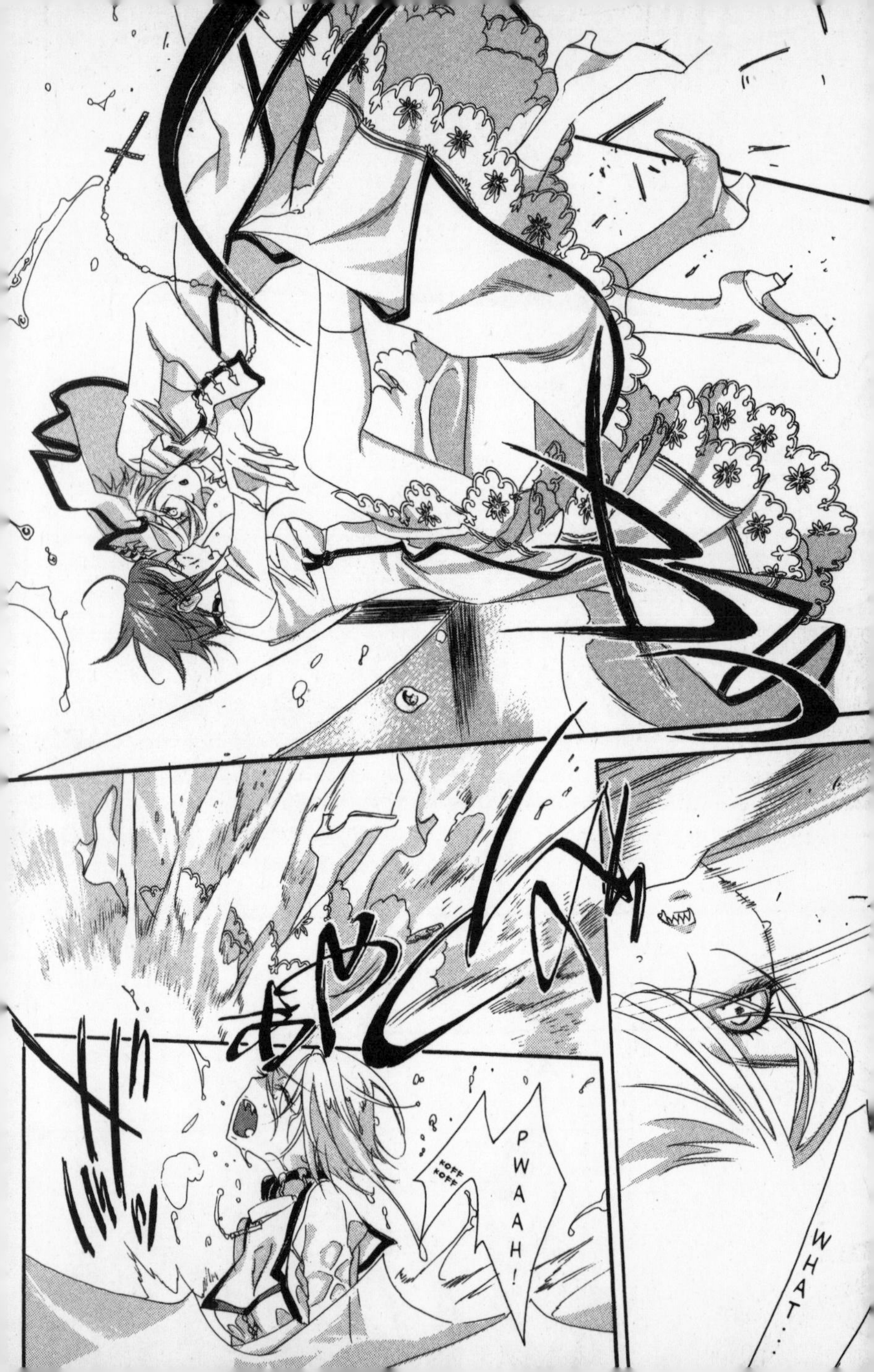
WHAT...
PWAAH!
KOFF KOFF

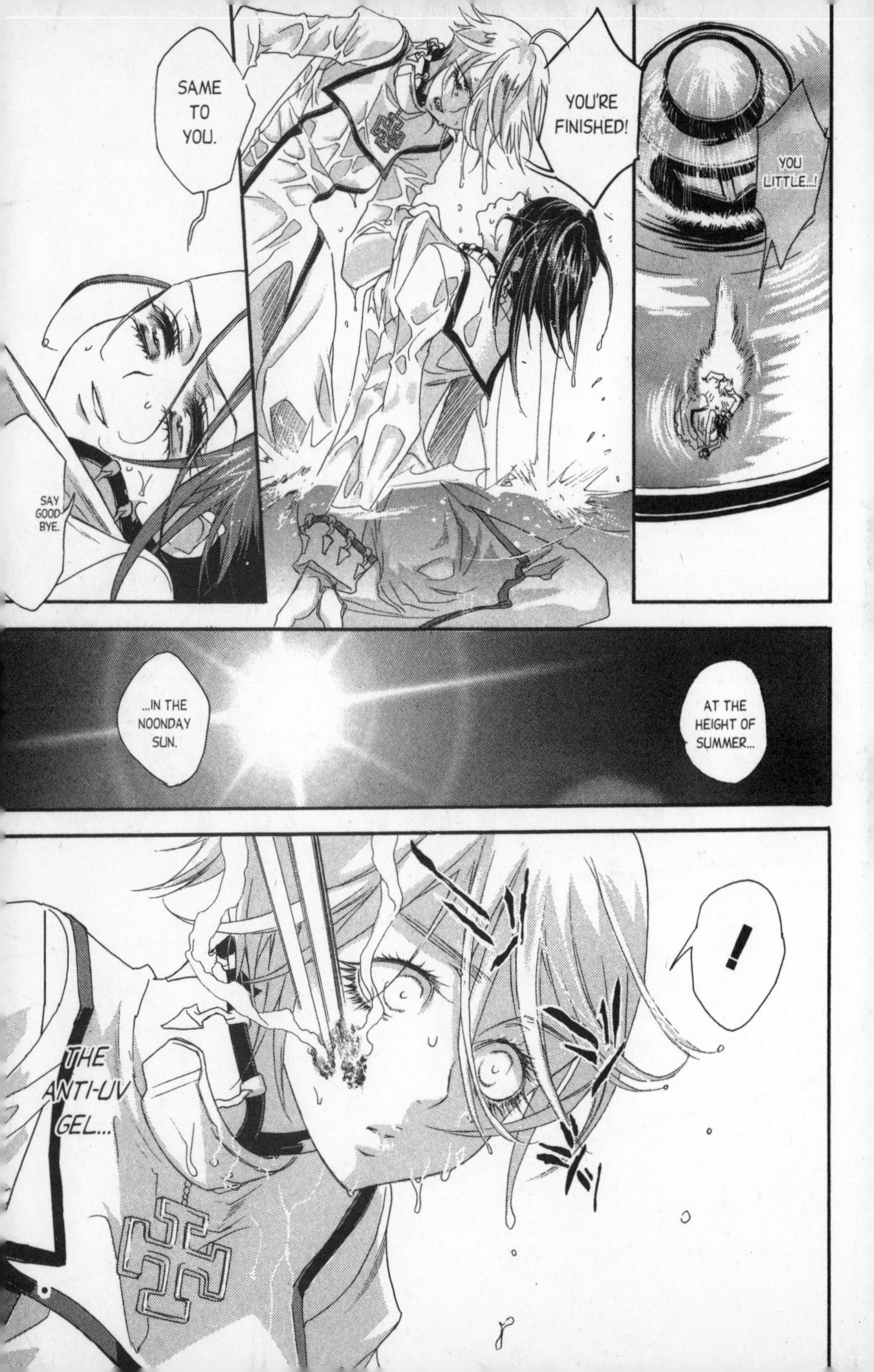
YOU LITTLE...!
YOU'RE FINISHED!
SAME TO YOU.
SAY GOOD-BYE.
AT THE HEIGHT OF SUMMER...
...IN THE NOONDAY SUN.
!
THE ANTI-UV GEL...

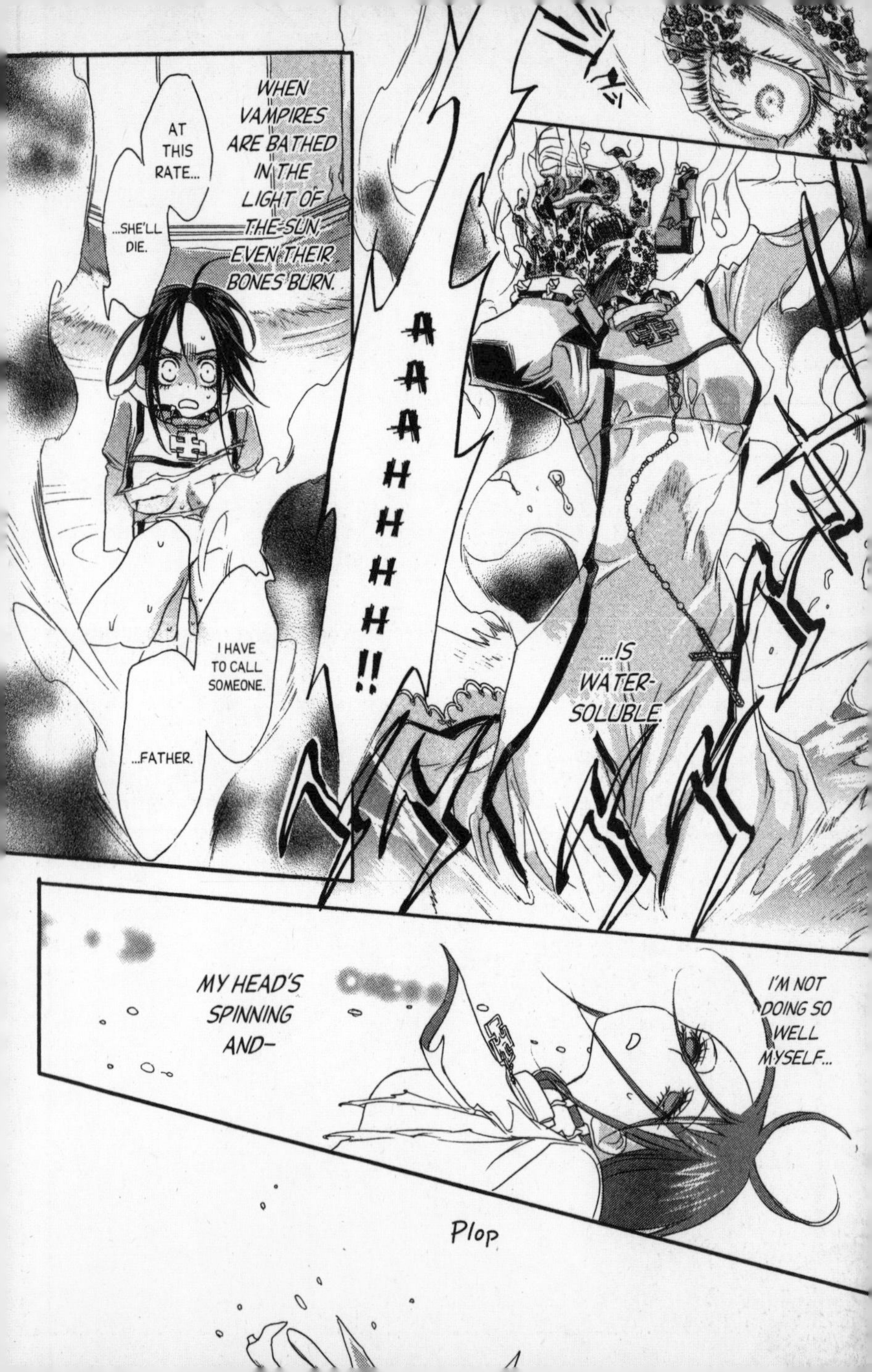
AAAHHHHH!!
...IS WATER-SOLUBLE.
WHEN VAMPIRES ARE BATHED IN THE LIGHT OF THE SUN, EVEN THEIR BONES BURN.
AT THIS RATE...
...SHE'LL DIE.
I HAVE TO CALL SOMEONE.
...FATHER.
I'M NOT DOING SO WELL MYSELF...
MY HEAD'S SPINNING AND–
Plop

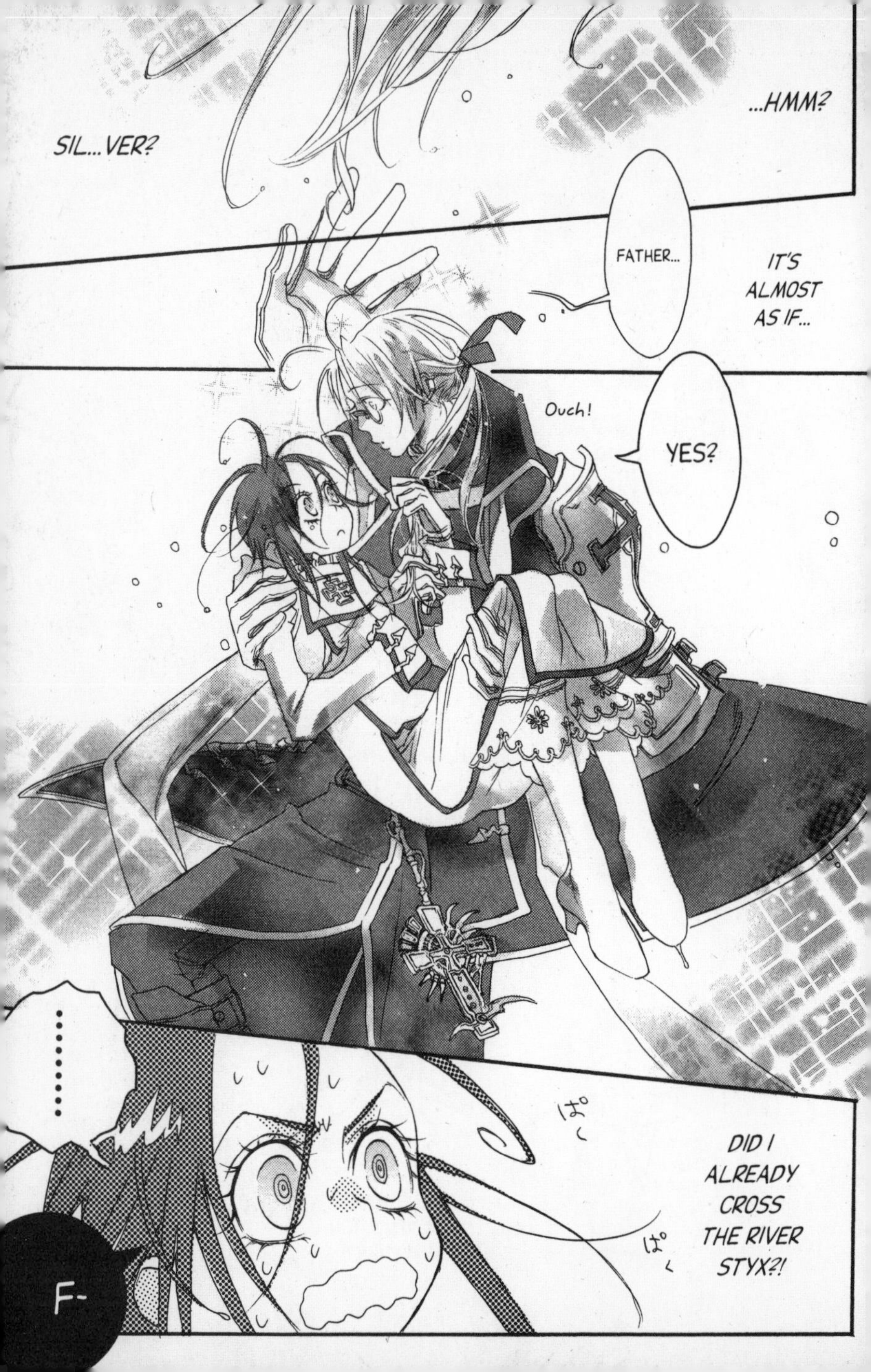

...HMM?
SIL...VER?
IT'S ALMOST AS IF...
FATHER...
YES?
Ouch!
DID I ALREADY CROSS THE RIVER STYX?!
ぱく
ぱく
......
F-

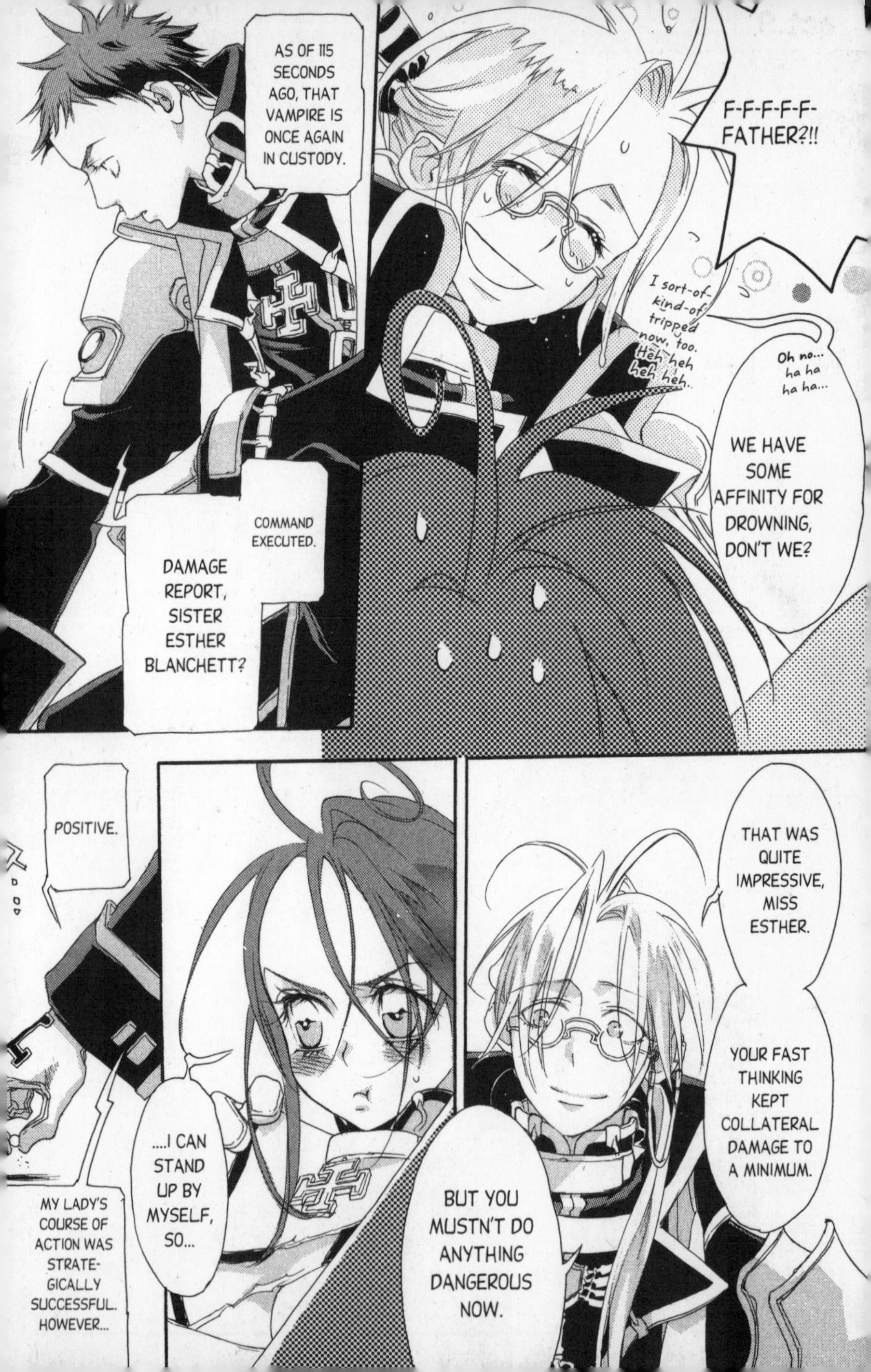

F-F-F-F-F-FATHER?!!
I sort-of-kind-of tripped now, too. Heh heh heh heh..
Oh no... ha ha ha ha...
WE HAVE SOME AFFINITY FOR DROWNING, DON'T WE?
AS OF 115 SECONDS AGO, THAT VAMPIRE IS ONCE AGAIN IN CUSTODY.
COMMAND EXECUTED.
DAMAGE REPORT, SISTER ESTHER BLANCHETT?
THAT WAS QUITE IMPRESSIVE, MISS ESTHER.
YOUR FAST THINKING KEPT COLLATERAL DAMAGE TO A MINIMUM.
BUT YOU MUSTN'T DO ANYTHING DANGEROUS NOW.
....I CAN STAND UP BY MYSELF, SO...
POSITIVE.
MY LADY'S COURSE OF ACTION WAS STRATE-GICALLY SUCCESSFUL. HOWEVER...

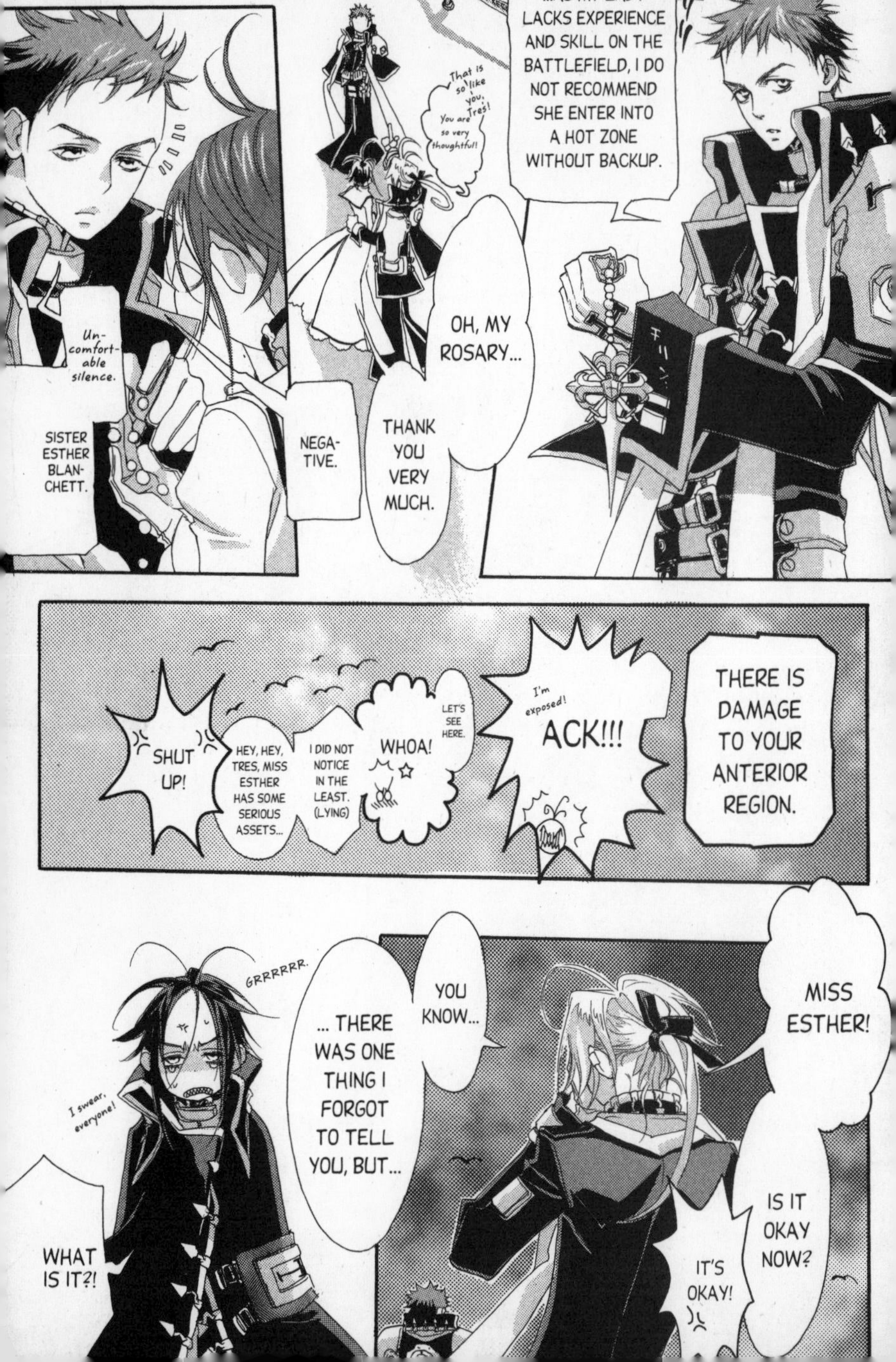
...AS MY LADY LACKS EXPERIENCE AND SKILL ON THE BATTLEFIELD, I DO NOT RECOMMEND SHE ENTER INTO A HOT ZONE WITHOUT BACKUP.
OH, MY ROSARY...
THANK YOU VERY MUCH.
That is so like you, Tres! You are so very thoughtful!
NEGA-TIVE.
Un-comfort-able silence.
SISTER ESTHER BLAN-CHETT.
THERE IS DAMAGE TO YOUR ANTERIOR REGION.
ACK!!!
I'm exposed!
LET'S SEE HERE.
WHOA!
I DID NOT NOTICE IN THE LEAST. (LYING)
HEY, HEY, TRES, MISS ESTHER HAS SOME SERIOUS ASSETS...
SHUT UP!
MISS ESTHER!
IS IT OKAY NOW?
IT'S OKAY!
YOU KNOW...
... THERE WAS ONE THING I FORGOT TO TELL YOU, BUT...
GRRRRRR.
I swear, everyone!
WHAT IS IT?!

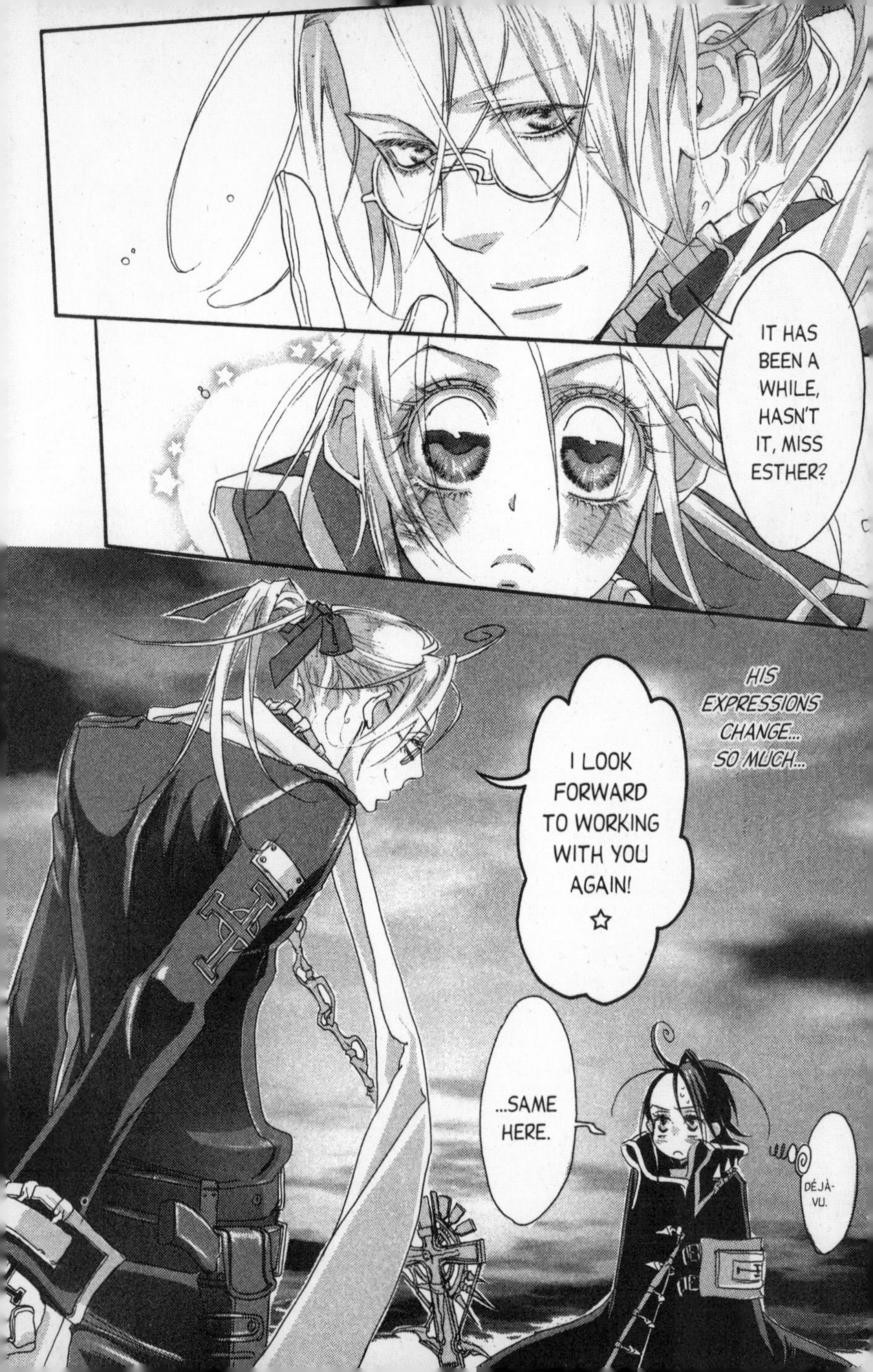
IT HAS BEEN A WHILE, HASN'T IT, MISS ESTHER?
HIS EXPRESSIONS CHANGE... SO MUCH...
I LOOK FORWARD TO WORKING WITH YOU AGAIN! ☆
...SAME HERE.
DÉJÀ-VU.

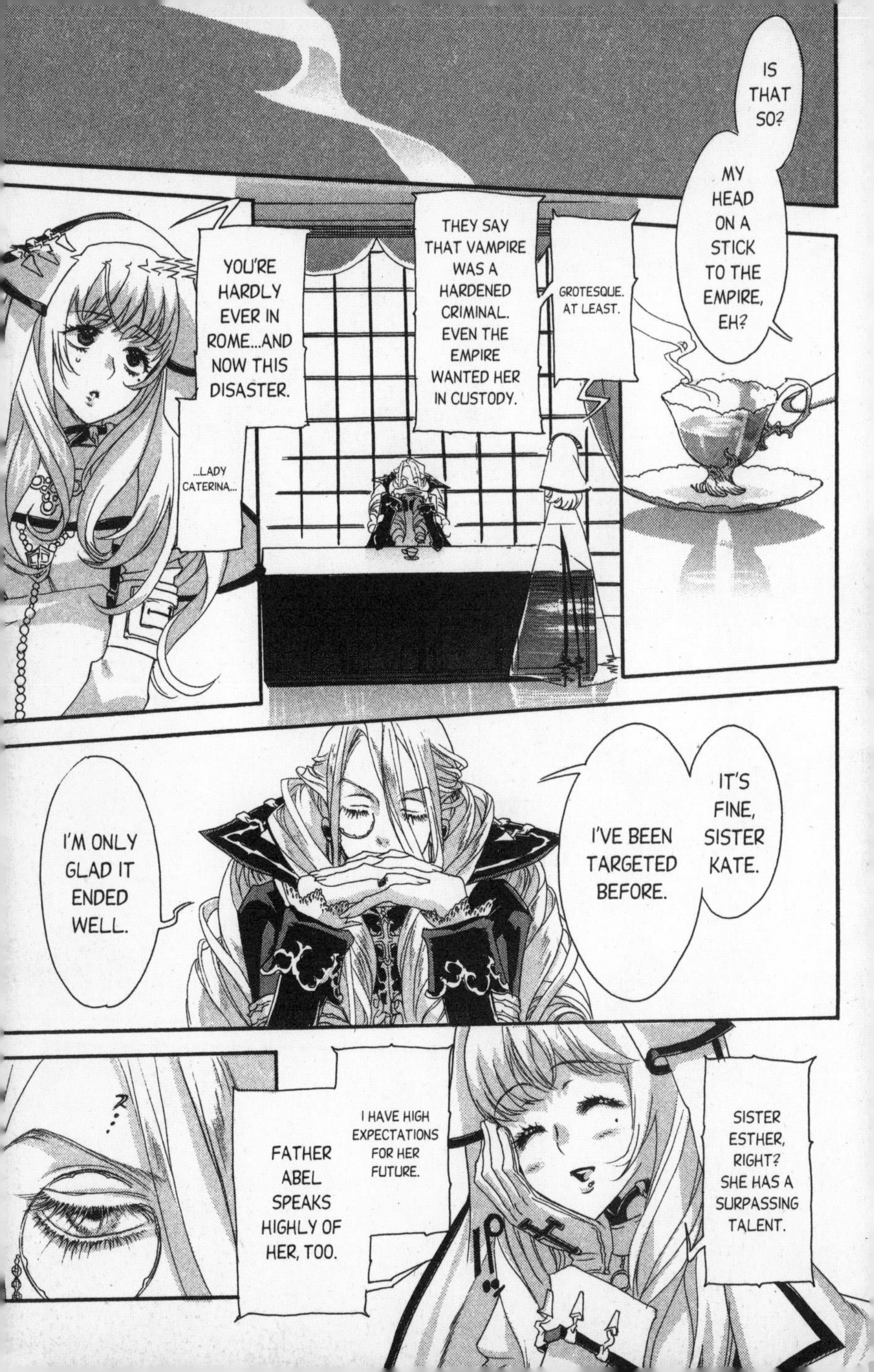
IS THAT SO?
MY HEAD ON A STICK TO THE EMPIRE, EH?
GROTESQUE. AT LEAST.
THEY SAY THAT VAMPIRE WAS A HARDENED CRIMINAL. EVEN THE EMPIRE WANTED HER IN CUSTODY.
YOU'RE HARDLY EVER IN ROME...AND NOW THIS DISASTER.
...LADY CATERINA...
IT'S FINE, SISTER KATE.
I'VE BEEN TARGETED BEFORE.
I'M ONLY GLAD IT ENDED WELL.
SISTER ESTHER, RIGHT? SHE HAS A SURPASSING TALENT.
I HAVE HIGH EXPECTATIONS FOR HER FUTURE.
FATHER ABEL SPEAKS HIGHLY OF HER, TOO.

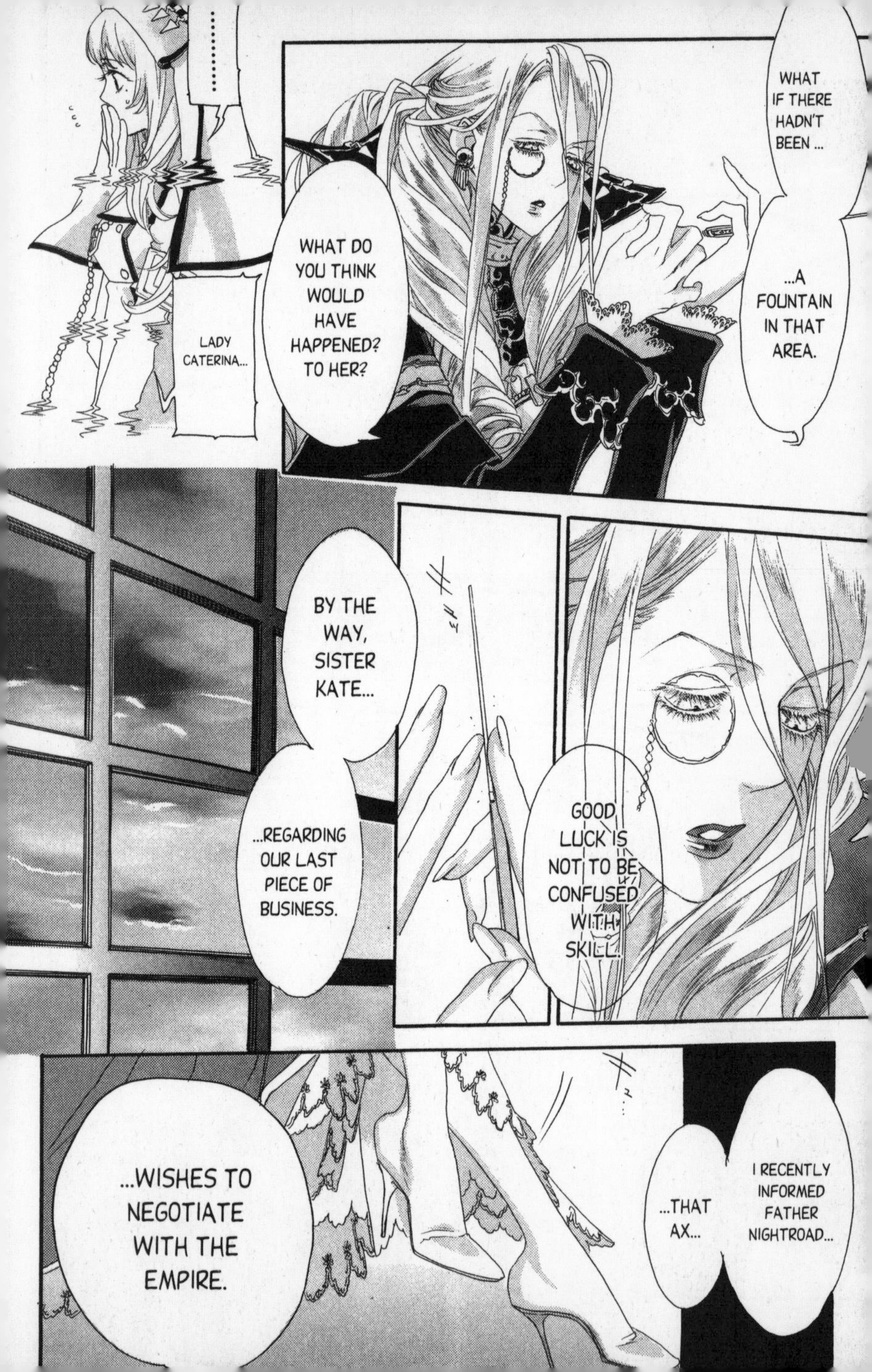
WHAT IF THERE HADN'T BEEN ...
...A FOUNTAIN IN THAT AREA.
WHAT DO YOU THINK WOULD HAVE HAPPENED? TO HER?
......
LADY CATERINA...
GOOD LUCK IS NOT TO BE CONFUSED WITH SKILL.
BY THE WAY, SISTER KATE...
...REGARDING OUR LAST PIECE OF BUSINESS.
I RECENTLY INFORMED FATHER NIGHTROAD...
...THAT AX...
...WISHES TO NEGOTIATE WITH THE EMPIRE.

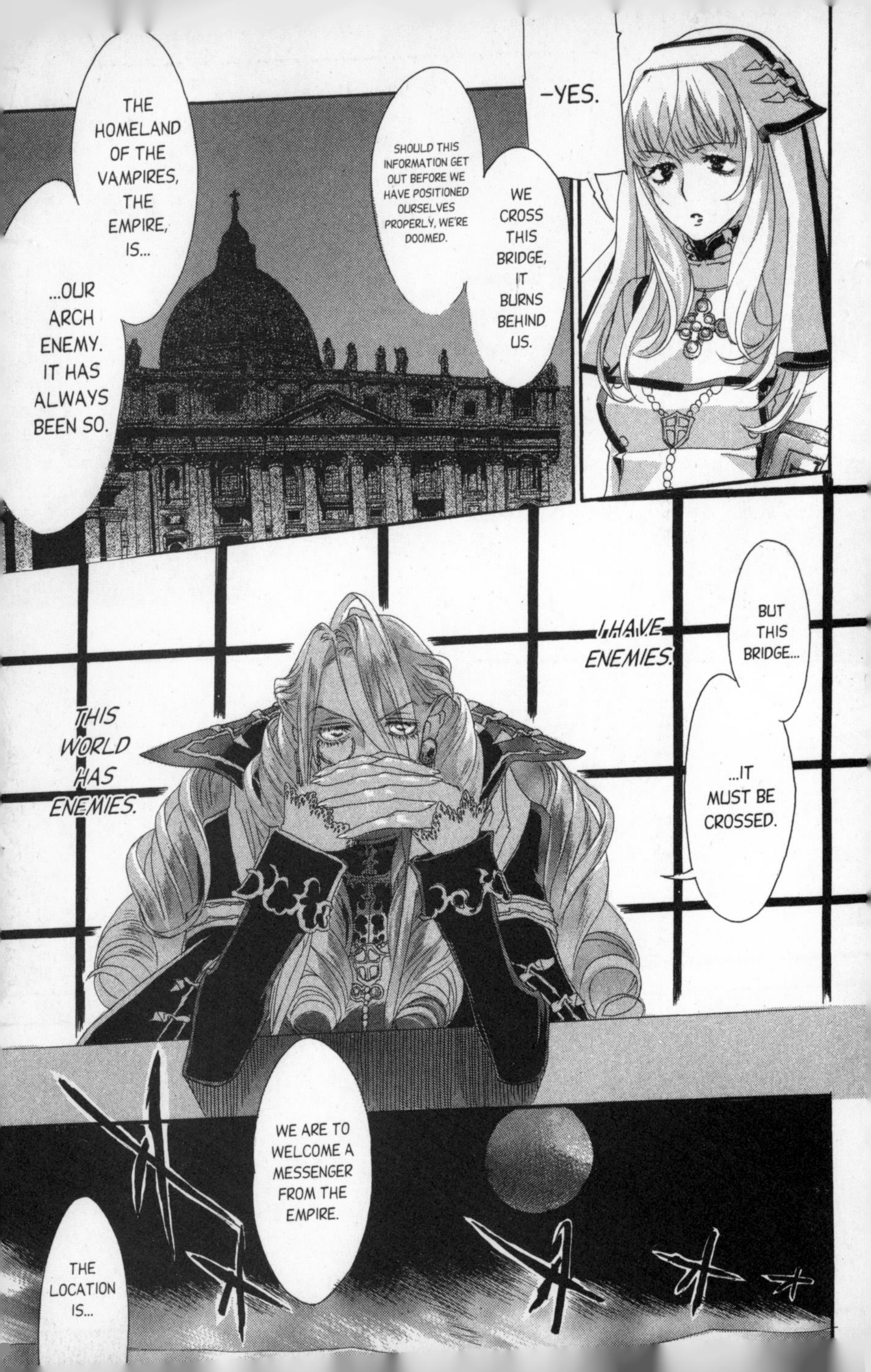
—YES.
THE HOMELAND OF THE VAMPIRES, THE EMPIRE, IS...
...OUR ARCH ENEMY. IT HAS ALWAYS BEEN SO.
SHOULD THIS INFORMATION GET OUT BEFORE WE HAVE POSITIONED OURSELVES PROPERLY, WE'RE DOOMED.
WE CROSS THIS BRIDGE, IT BURNS BEHIND US.
BUT THIS BRIDGE...
...IT MUST BE CROSSED.
I HAVE ENEMIES.
THIS WORLD HAS ENEMIES.
WE ARE TO WELCOME A MESSENGER FROM THE EMPIRE.
THE LOCATION IS...

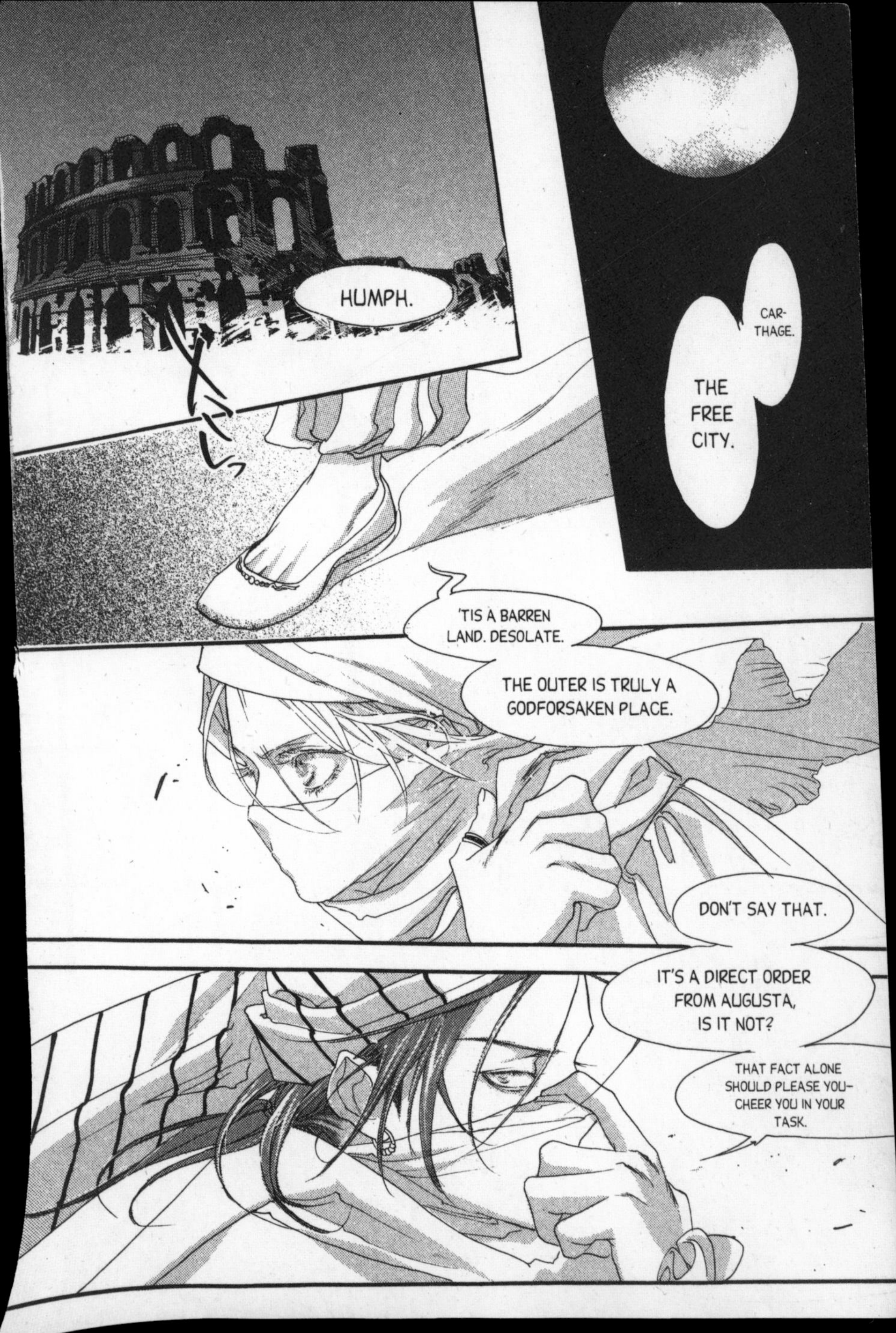

CAR-
THAGE.
THE
FREE
CITY.
HUMPH.
'TIS A BARREN
LAND. DESOLATE.
THE OUTER IS TRULY A
GODFORSAKEN PLACE.
DON'T SAY THAT.
IT'S A DIRECT ORDER
FROM AUGUSTA,
IS IT NOT?
THAT FACT ALONE
SHOULD PLEASE YOU—
CHEER YOU IN YOUR
TASK.

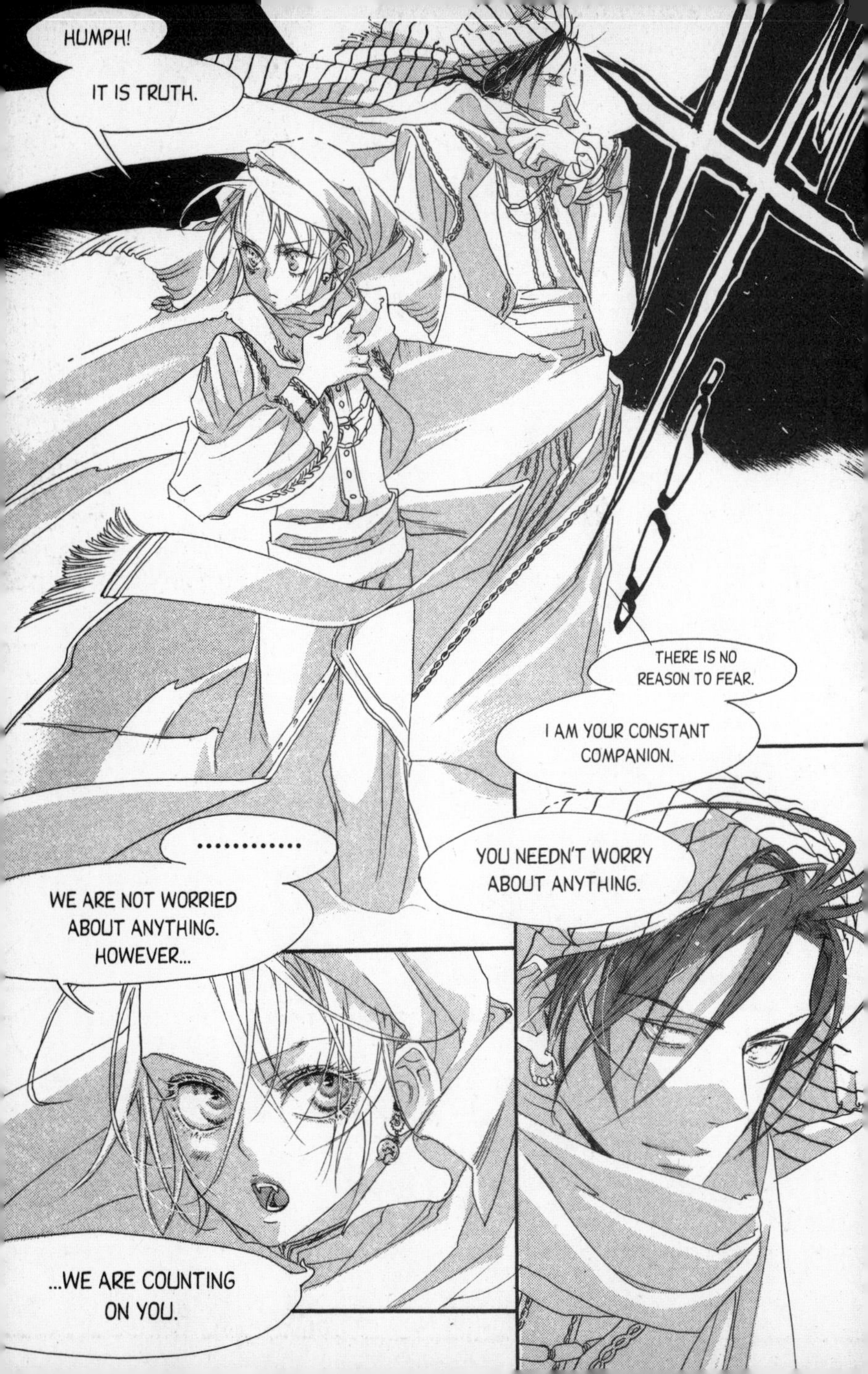
HUMPH!
IT IS TRUTH.
THERE IS NO REASON TO FEAR.
I AM YOUR CONSTANT COMPANION.
YOU NEEDN'T WORRY ABOUT ANYTHING.
....
WE ARE NOT WORRIED ABOUT ANYTHING. HOWEVER...
...WE ARE COUNTING ON YOU.

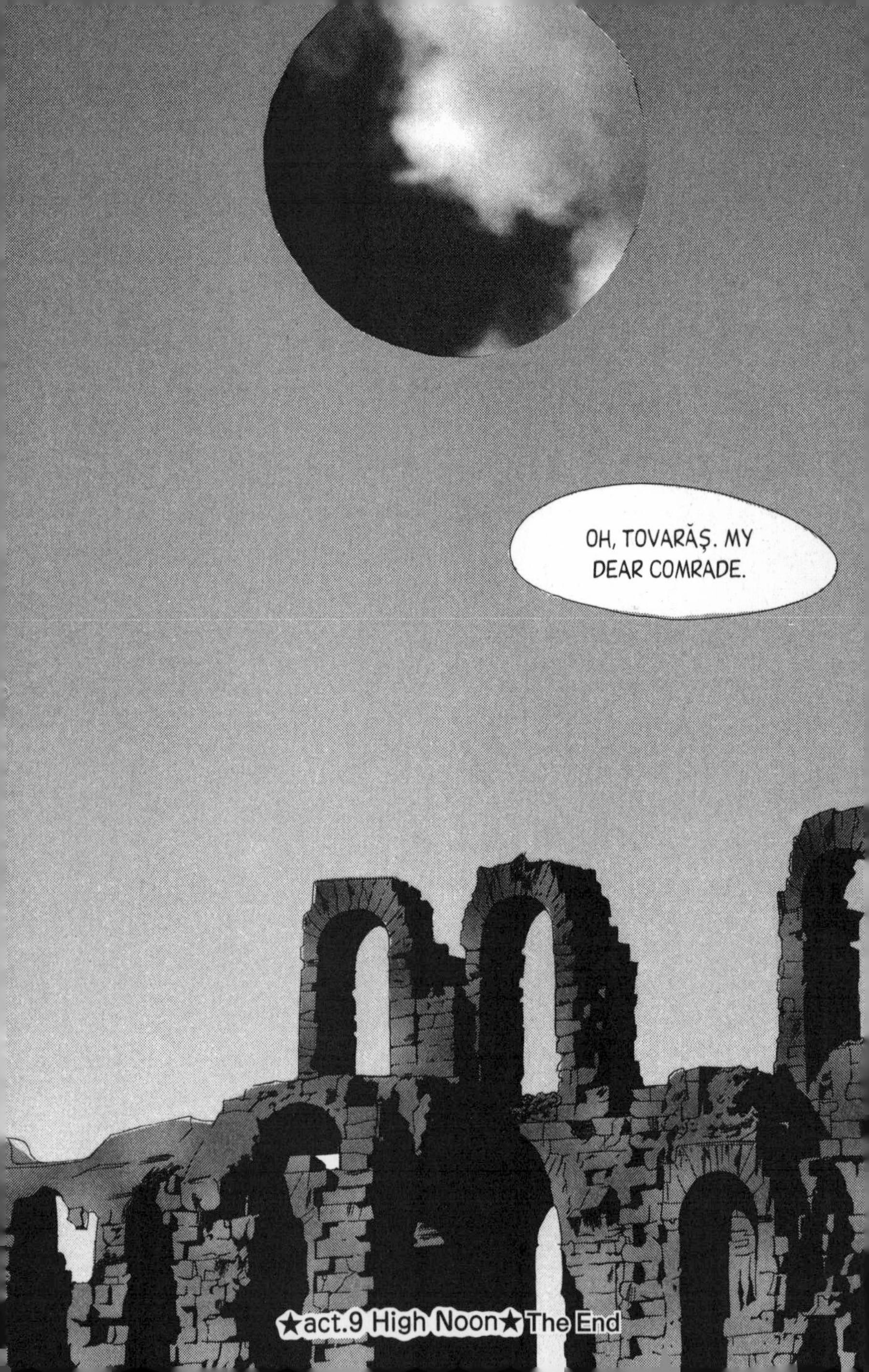
OH, TOVARĂȘ. MY DEAR COMRADE.
★act.9 High Noon★The End

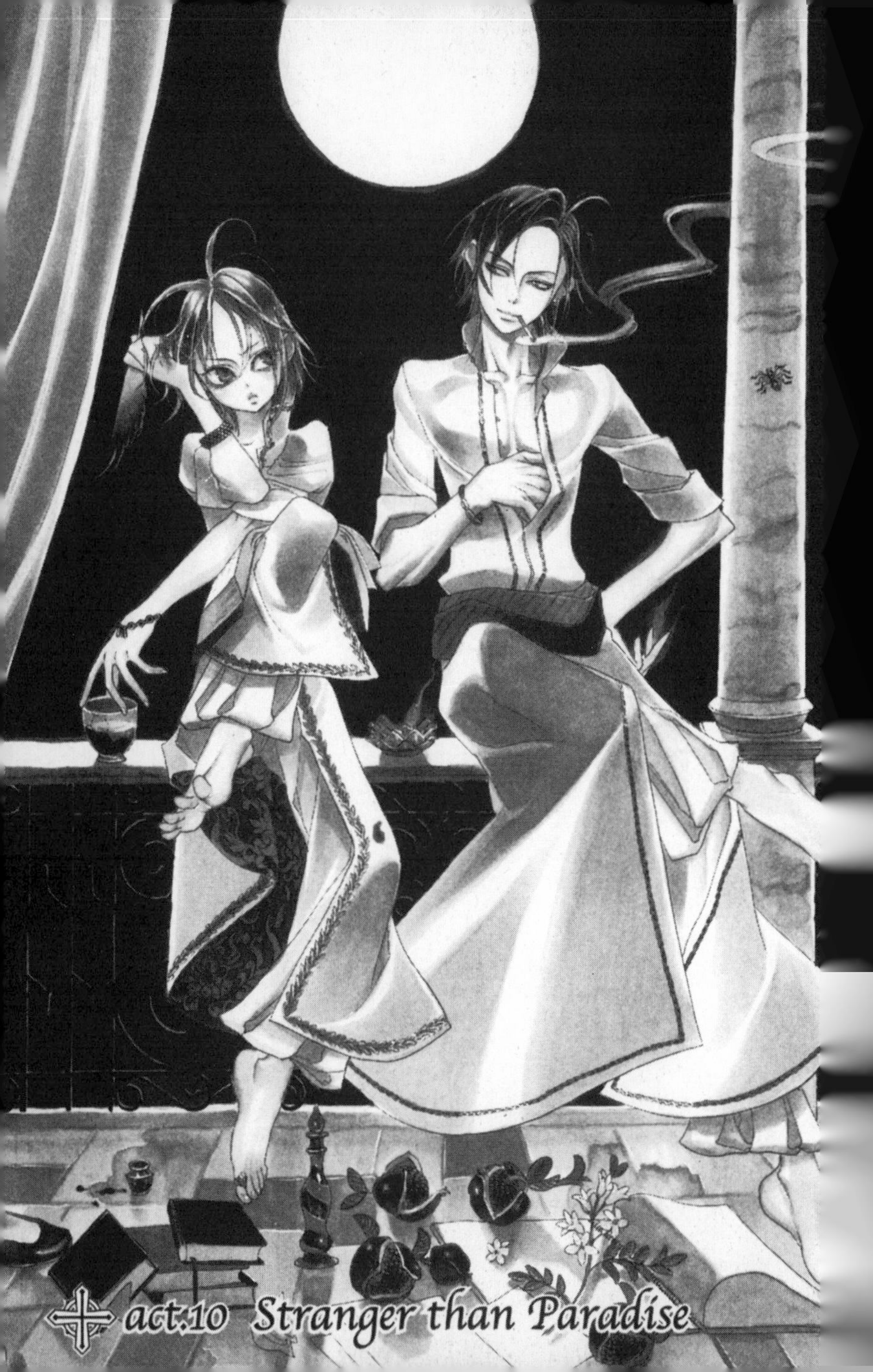
act.10 Stranger than Paradise

TRINITY BLOOD

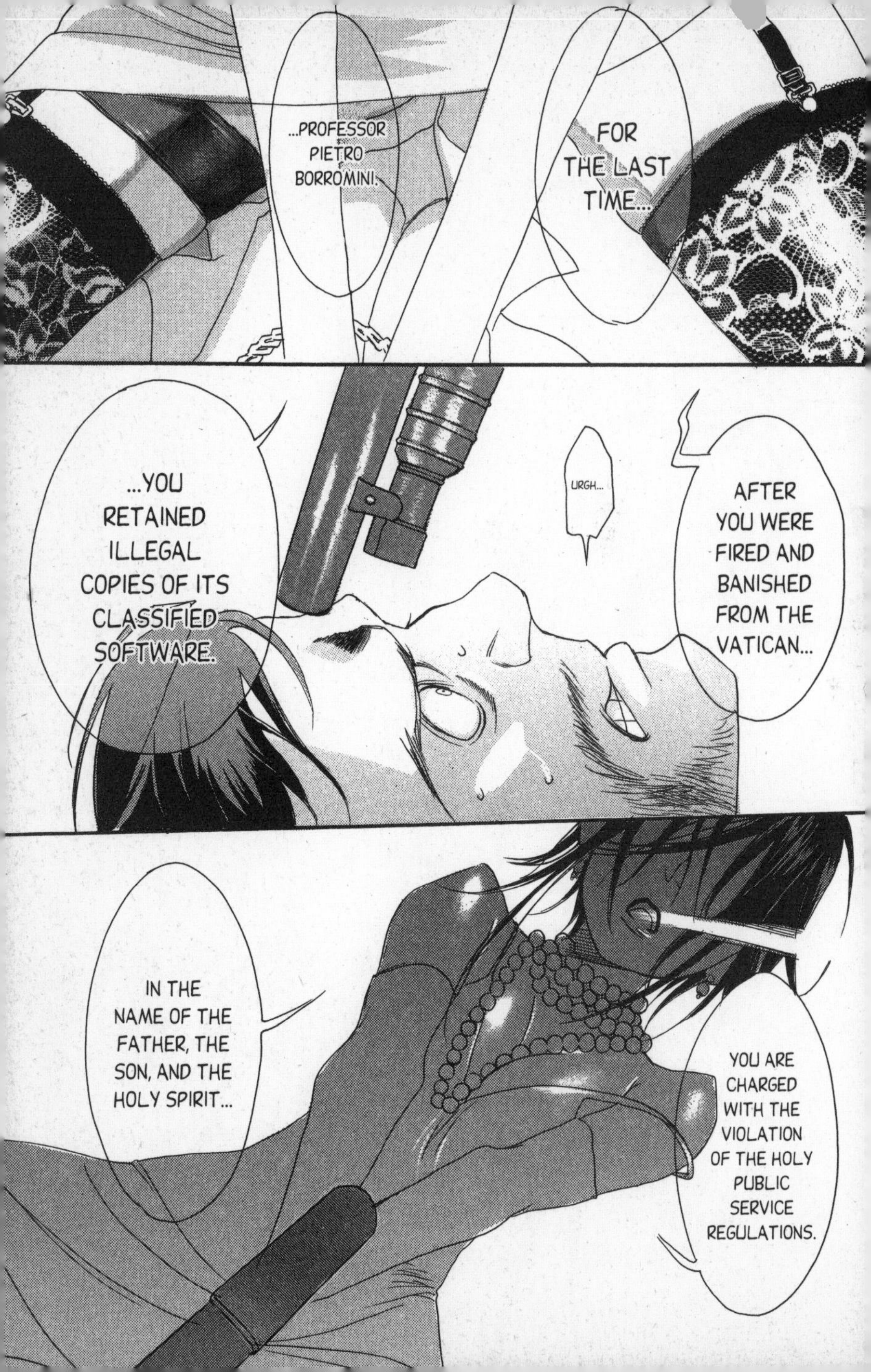
FOR THE LAST TIME...
...PROFESSOR PIETRO BORROMINI.
AFTER YOU WERE FIRED AND BANISHED FROM THE VATICAN...
URGH...
...YOU RETAINED ILLEGAL COPIES OF ITS CLASSIFIED SOFTWARE.
YOU ARE CHARGED WITH THE VIOLATION OF THE HOLY PUBLIC SERVICE REGULATIONS.
IN THE NAME OF THE FATHER, THE SON, AND THE HOLY SPIRIT...

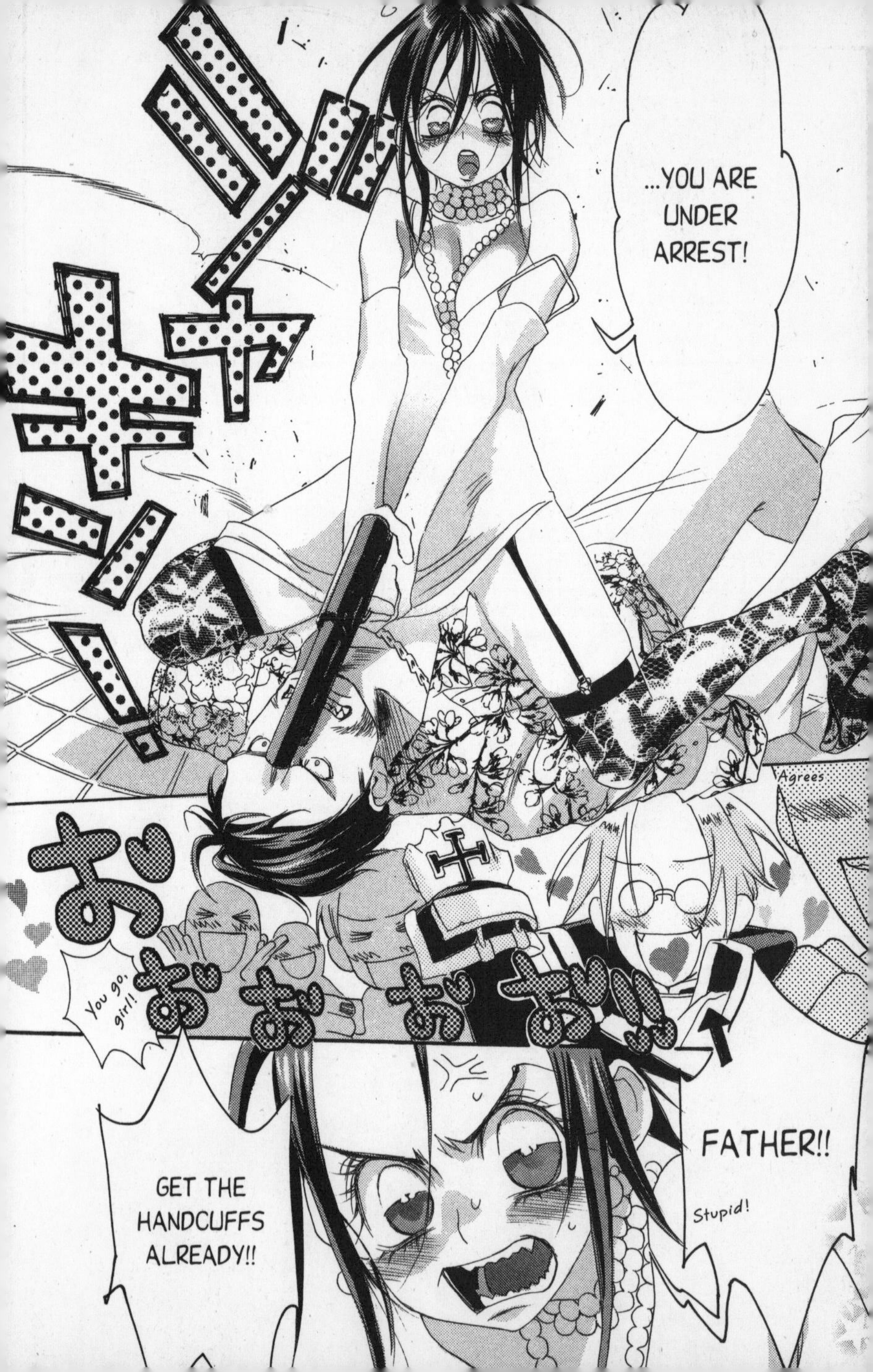
...YOU ARE UNDER ARREST!
Agrees
おおおおお!!
You go, girl!
FATHER!!
Stupid!
GET THE HANDCUFFS ALREADY!!

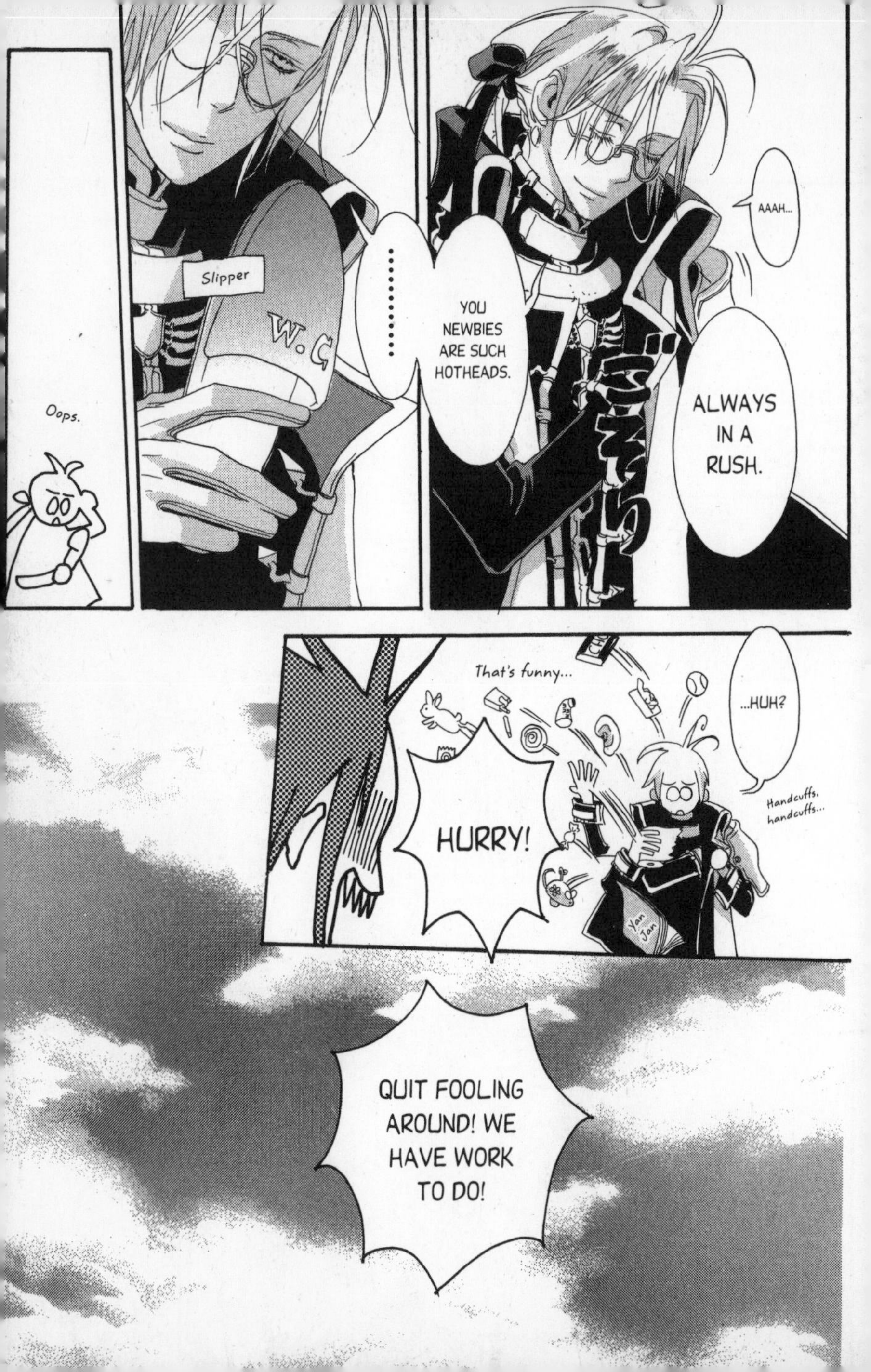
AAAH...
ALWAYS IN A RUSH.
YOU NEWBIES ARE SUCH HOTHEADS.
......
Slipper
W.C
Oops.
...HUH?
Handcuffs, handcuffs...
That's funny...
HURRY!
Yan Jan
QUIT FOOLING AROUND! WE HAVE WORK TO DO!

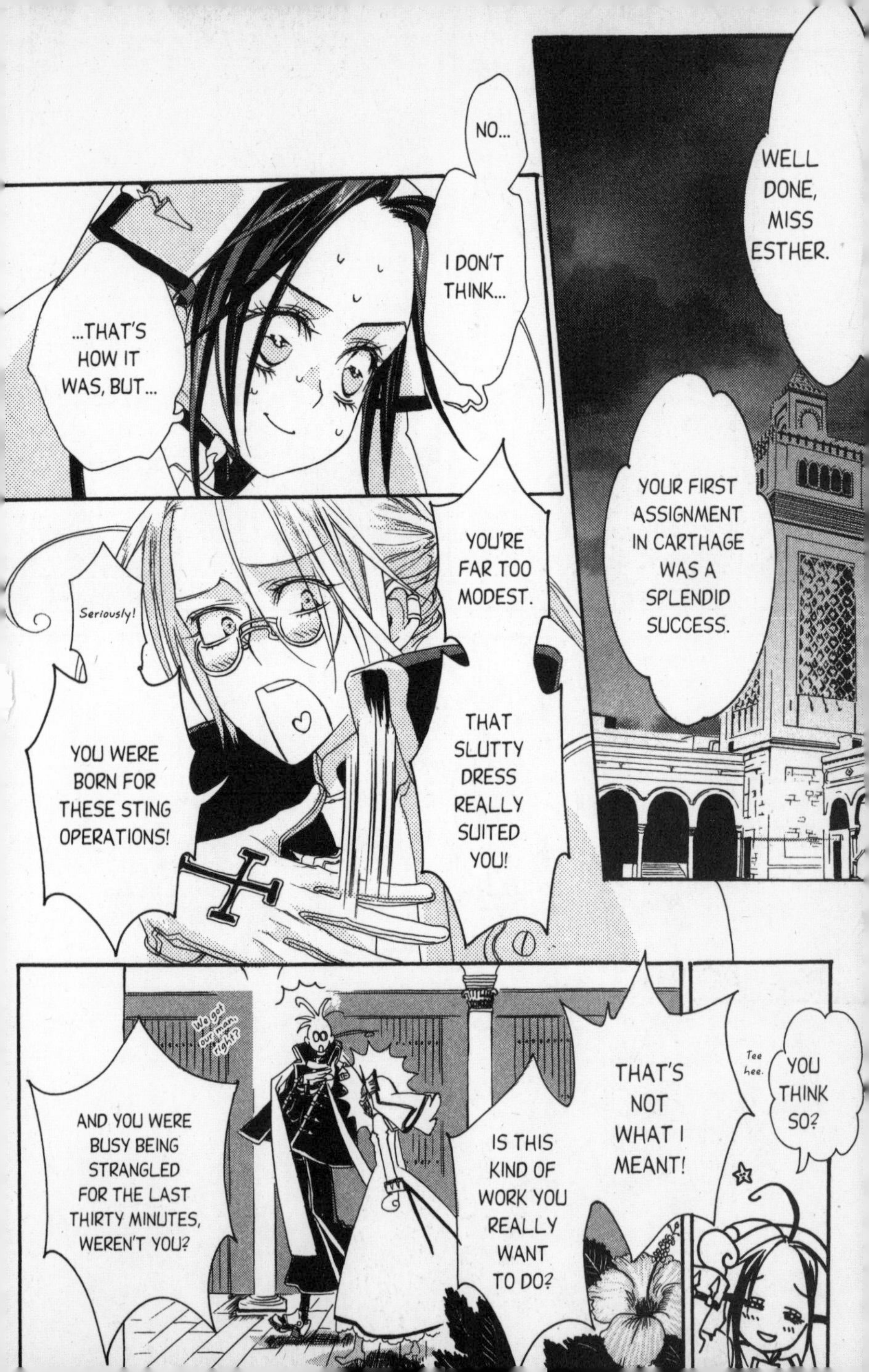
WELL DONE, MISS ESTHER.
YOUR FIRST ASSIGNMENT IN CARTHAGE WAS A SPLENDID SUCCESS.
NO...
I DON'T THINK...
...THAT'S HOW IT WAS, BUT...
YOU'RE FAR TOO MODEST.
THAT SLUTTY DRESS REALLY SUITED YOU!
Seriously!
YOU WERE BORN FOR THESE STING OPERATIONS!
Tee hee.
YOU THINK SO?
THAT'S NOT WHAT I MEANT!
IS THIS KIND OF WORK YOU REALLY WANT TO DO?
AND YOU WERE BUSY BEING STRANGLED FOR THE LAST THIRTY MINUTES, WEREN'T YOU?

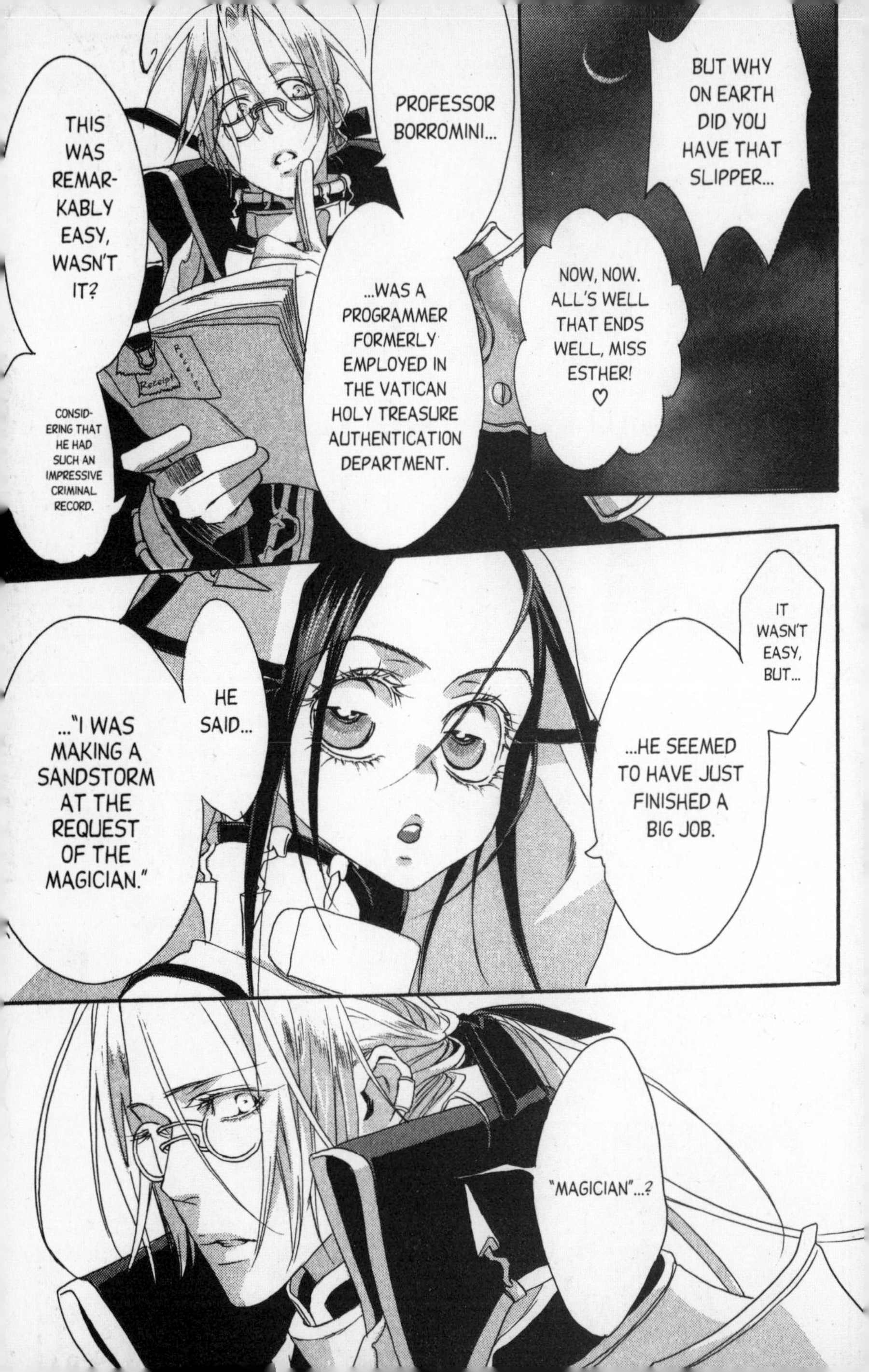
BUT WHY ON EARTH DID YOU HAVE THAT SLIPPER...
NOW, NOW. ALL'S WELL THAT ENDS WELL, MISS ESTHER! ♡
PROFESSOR BORROMINI...
...WAS A PROGRAMMER FORMERLY EMPLOYED IN THE VATICAN HOLY TREASURE AUTHENTICATION DEPARTMENT.
THIS WAS REMAR-KABLY EASY, WASN'T IT?
CONSID-ERING THAT HE HAD SUCH AN IMPRESSIVE CRIMINAL RECORD.
Receipt
IT WASN'T EASY, BUT...
...HE SEEMED TO HAVE JUST FINISHED A BIG JOB.
HE SAID...
..."I WAS MAKING A SANDSTORM AT THE REQUEST OF THE MAGICIAN."
"MAGICIAN"...?

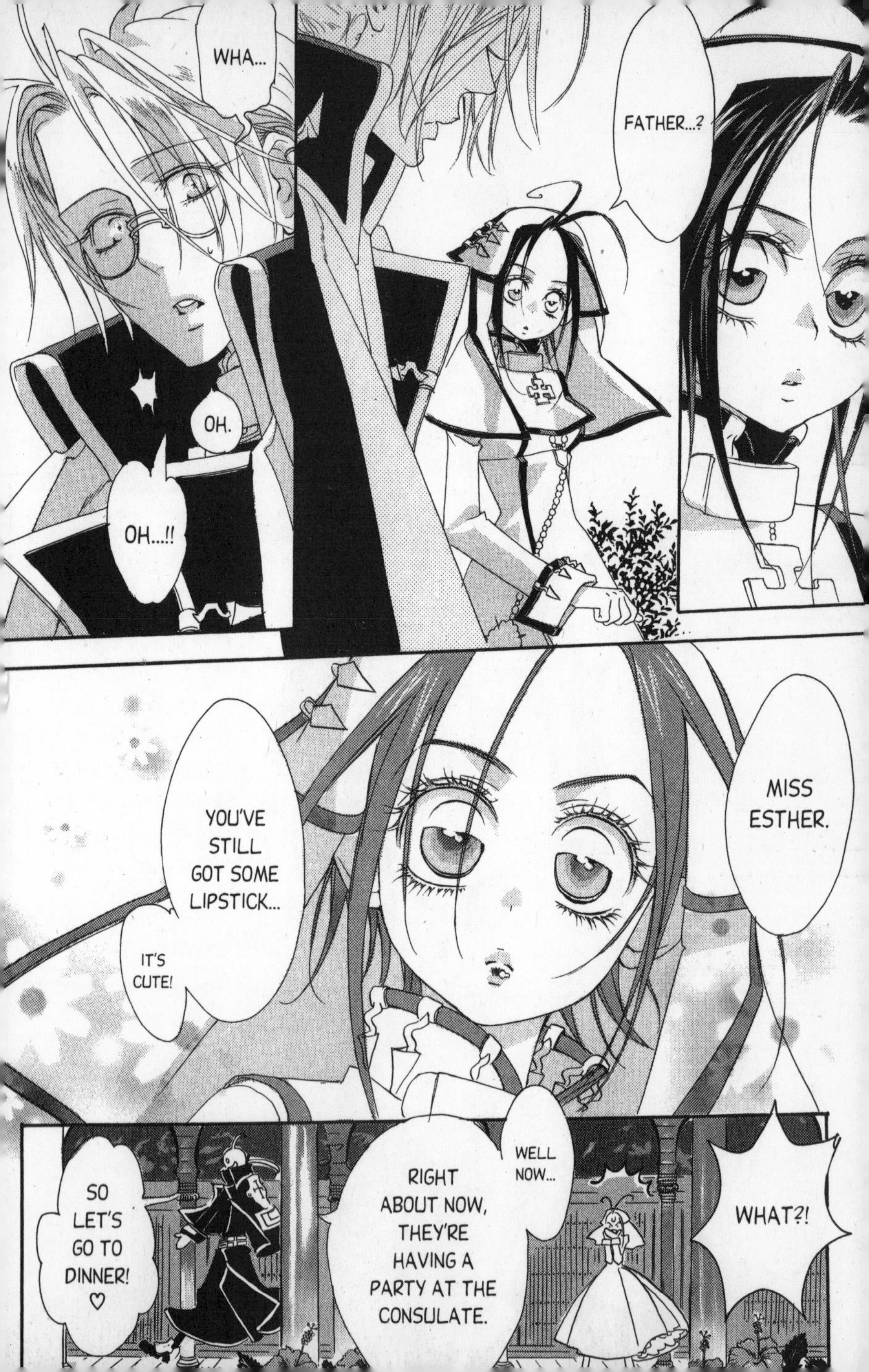
FATHER...?
WHA...
OH.
OH...!!
MISS ESTHER.
YOU'VE STILL GOT SOME LIPSTICK...
IT'S CUTE!
WHAT?!
WELL NOW...
RIGHT ABOUT NOW, THEY'RE HAVING A PARTY AT THE CONSULATE.
SO LET'S GO TO DINNER! ♡

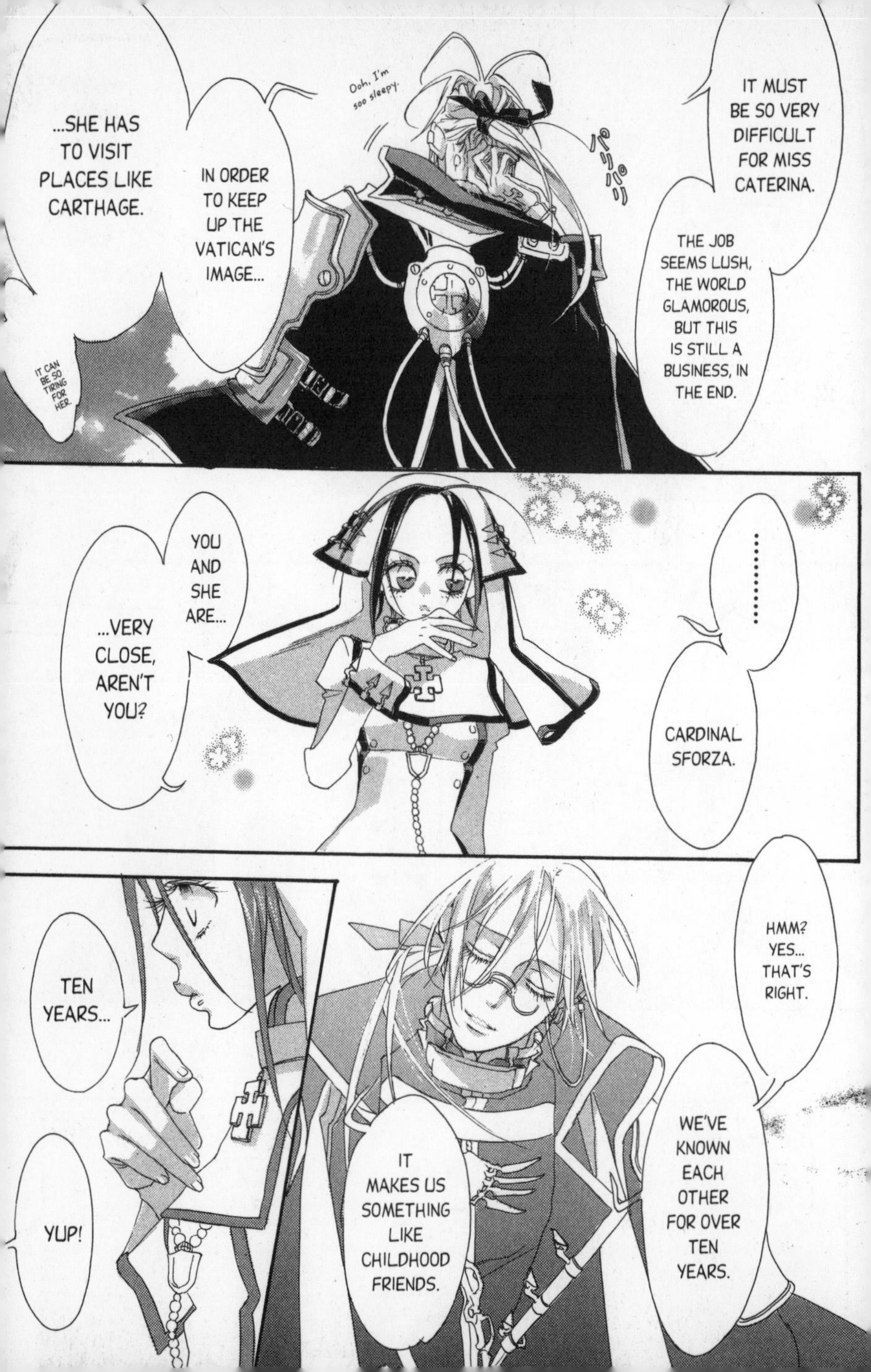
IT MUST BE SO VERY DIFFICULT FOR MISS CATERINA.
THE JOB SEEMS LUSH, THE WORLD GLAMOROUS, BUT THIS IS STILL A BUSINESS, IN THE END.
Ooh, I'm soo sleepy.
IN ORDER TO KEEP UP THE VATICAN'S IMAGE...
...SHE HAS TO VISIT PLACES LIKE CARTHAGE.
IT CAN BE SO TIRING FOR HER.
......
CARDINAL SFORZA.
YOU AND SHE ARE...
...VERY CLOSE, AREN'T YOU?
HMM? YES... THAT'S RIGHT.
WE'VE KNOWN EACH OTHER FOR OVER TEN YEARS.
IT MAKES US SOMETHING LIKE CHILDHOOD FRIENDS.
TEN YEARS...
YUP!

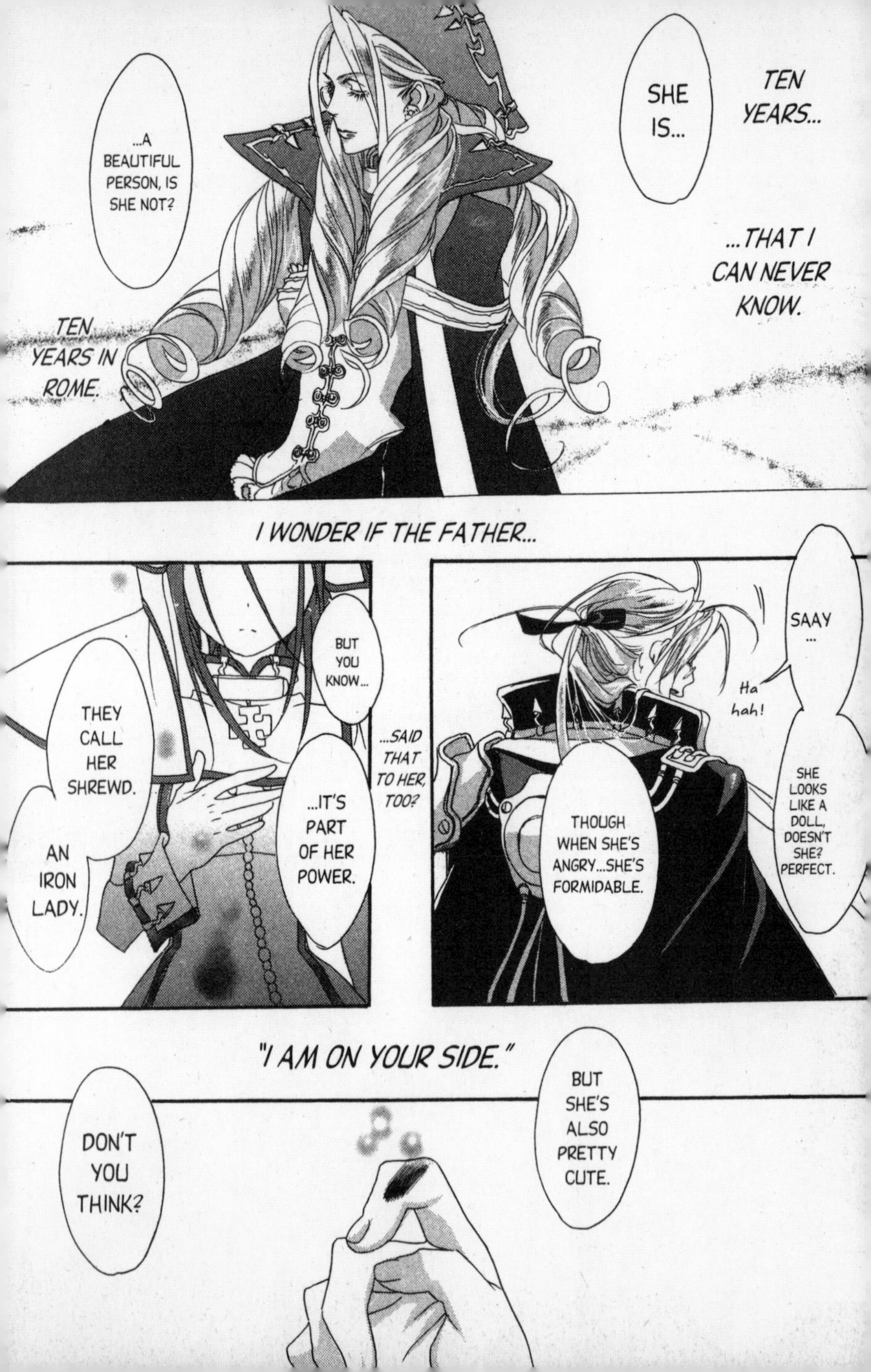
TEN YEARS...
SHE IS...
...A BEAUTIFUL PERSON, IS SHE NOT?
...THAT I CAN NEVER KNOW.
TEN YEARS IN ROME.
I WONDER IF THE FATHER...
SAAY...
Ha hah!
SHE LOOKS LIKE A DOLL, DOESN'T SHE? PERFECT.
THOUGH WHEN SHE'S ANGRY...SHE'S FORMIDABLE.
...SAID THAT TO HER, TOO?
THEY CALL HER SHREWD.
AN IRON LADY.
BUT YOU KNOW...
...IT'S PART OF HER POWER.
"I AM ON YOUR SIDE."
BUT SHE'S ALSO PRETTY CUTE.
DON'T YOU THINK?

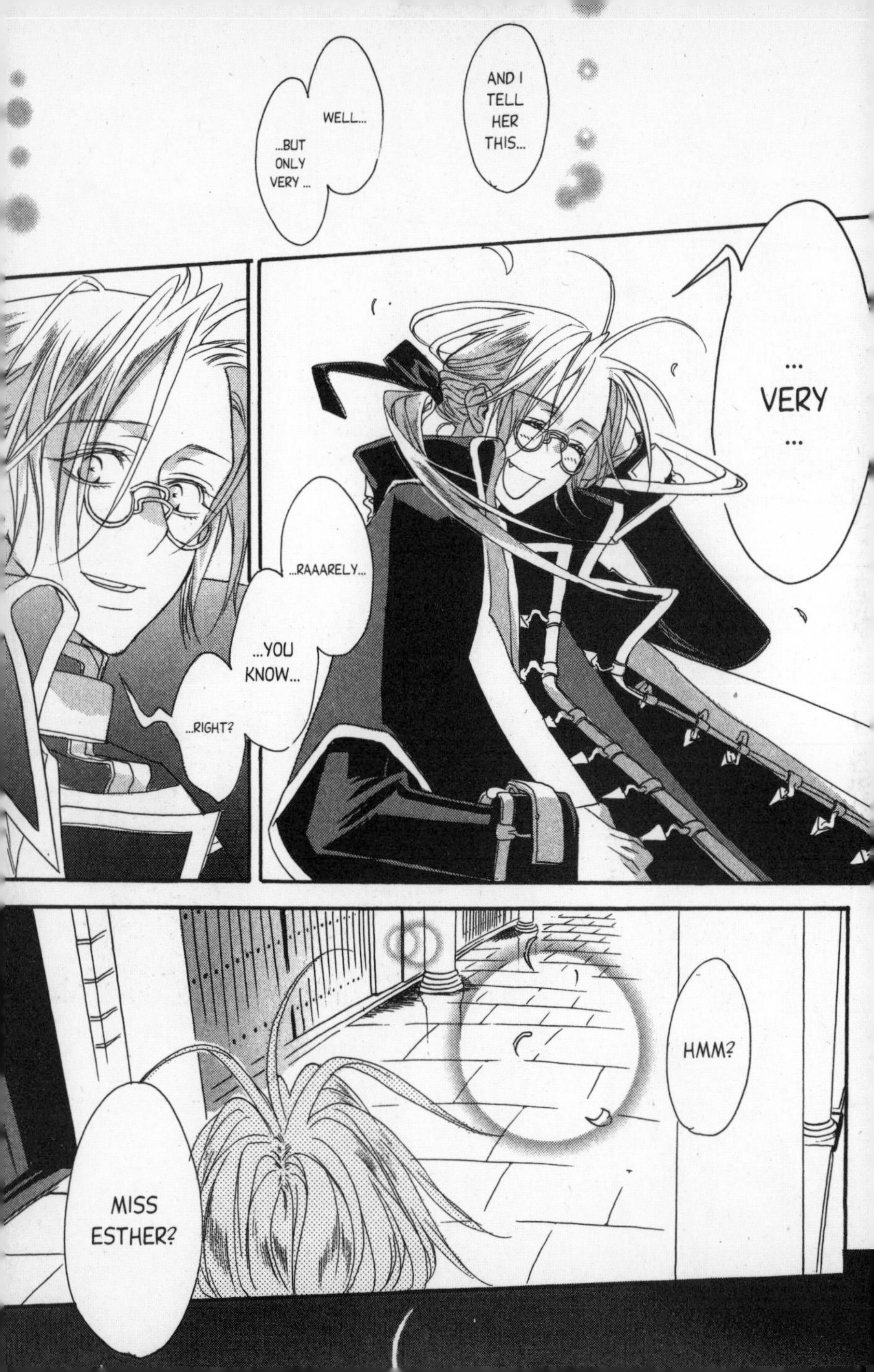
AND I TELL HER THIS...
WELL... ...BUT ONLY VERY ...
... VERY ...
...RAAARELY...
...YOU KNOW...
...RIGHT?
HMM?
MISS ESTHER?

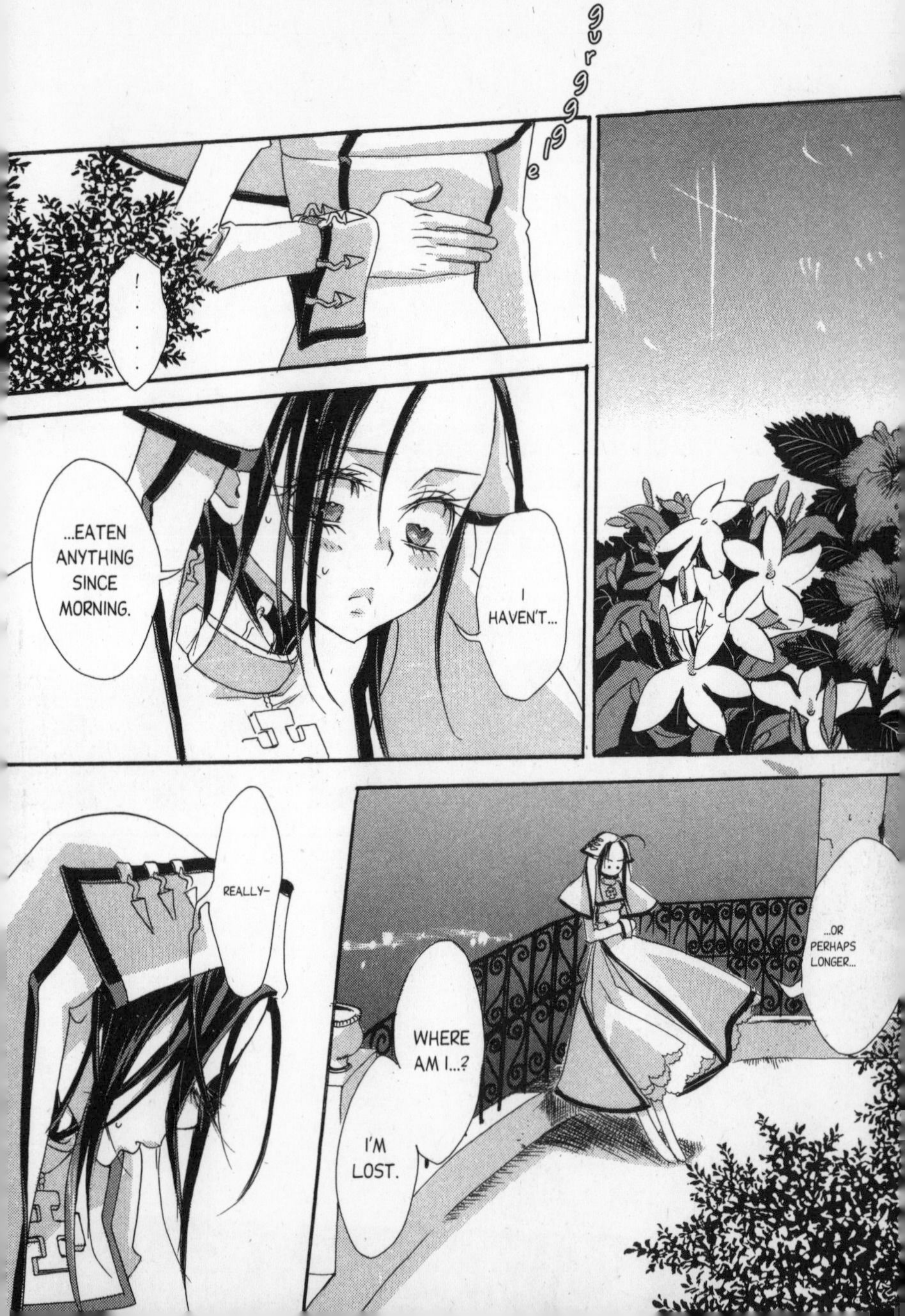
gurggle
!......
I HAVEN'T...
...EATEN ANYTHING SINCE MORNING.
...OR PERHAPS LONGER...
WHERE AM I...?
I'M LOST.
REALLY-

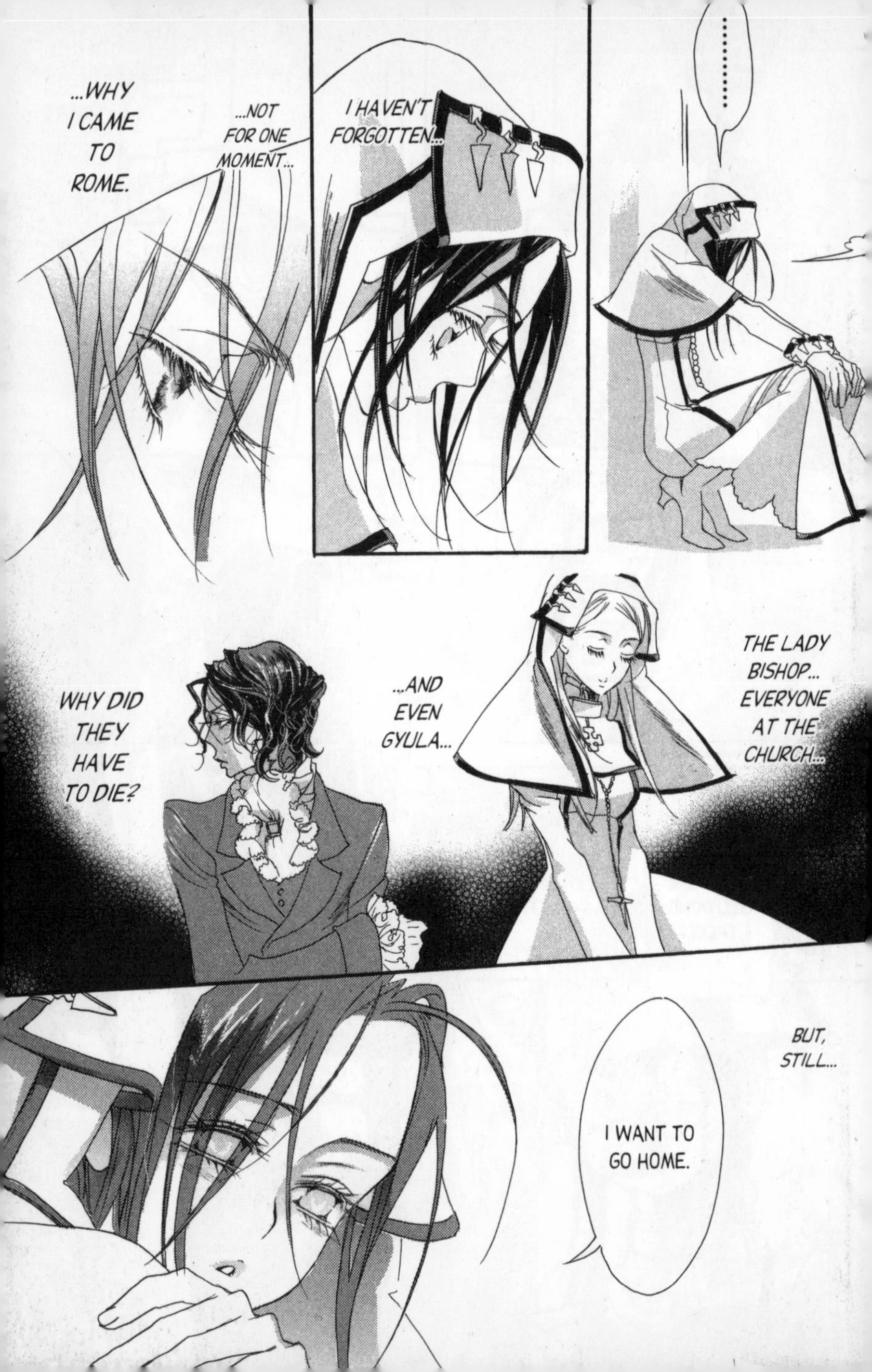
......
I HAVEN'T FORGOTTEN...
...NOT FOR ONE MOMENT...
...WHY I CAME TO ROME.
THE LADY BISHOP... EVERYONE AT THE CHURCH...
...AND EVEN GYULA...
WHY DID THEY HAVE TO DIE?
BUT, STILL...
I WANT TO GO HOME.

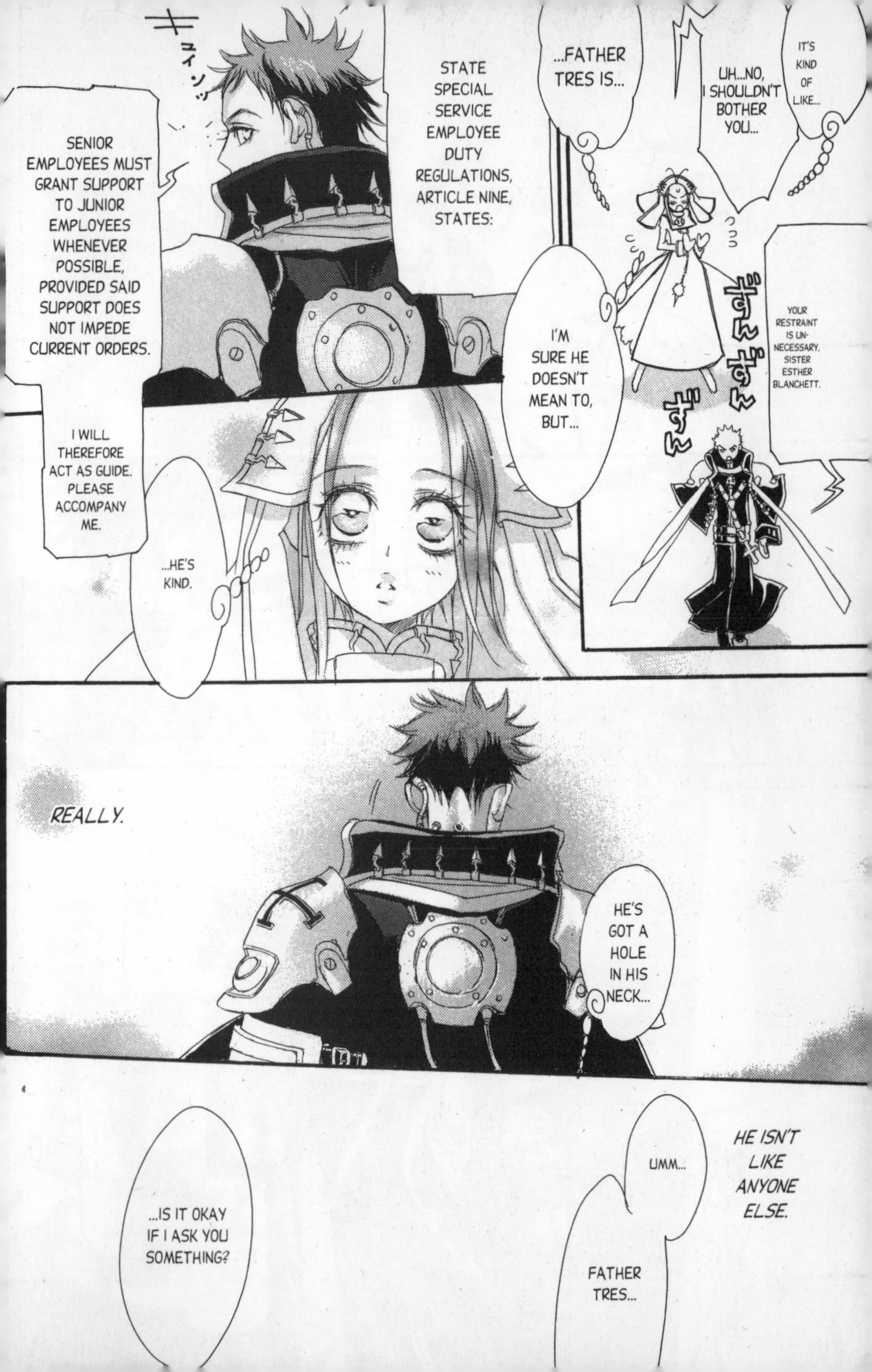
IT'S KIND OF LIKE...
UH...NO, I SHOULDN'T BOTHER YOU...
ずんずんずんずん
YOUR RESTRAINT IS UN-NECESSARY, SISTER ESTHER BLANCHETT.
...FATHER TRES IS...
I'M SURE HE DOESN'T MEAN TO, BUT...
STATE SPECIAL SERVICE EMPLOYEE DUTY REGULATIONS, ARTICLE NINE, STATES:
キュインッ
SENIOR EMPLOYEES MUST GRANT SUPPORT TO JUNIOR EMPLOYEES WHENEVER POSSIBLE, PROVIDED SAID SUPPORT DOES NOT IMPEDE CURRENT ORDERS.
I WILL THEREFORE ACT AS GUIDE. PLEASE ACCOMPANY ME.
...HE'S KIND.
HE'S GOT A HOLE IN HIS NECK...
REALLY.
HE ISN'T LIKE ANYONE ELSE.
UMM...
FATHER TRES...
...IS IT OKAY IF I ASK YOU SOMETHING?

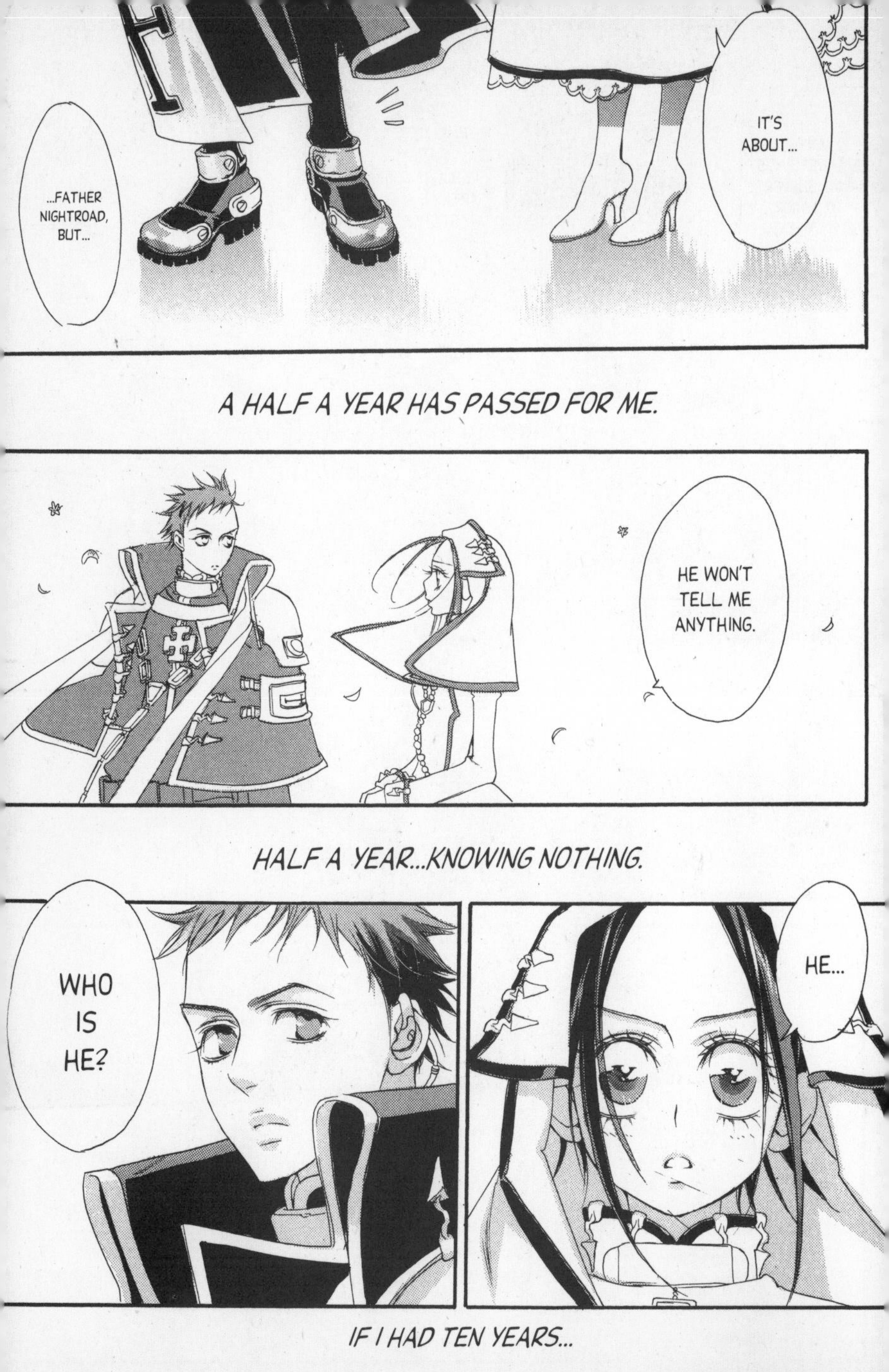
IT'S ABOUT...
...FATHER NIGHTROAD, BUT...
A HALF A YEAR HAS PASSED FOR ME.
HE WON'T TELL ME ANYTHING.
HALF A YEAR...KNOWING NOTHING.
HE...
WHO IS HE?
IF I HAD TEN YEARS...

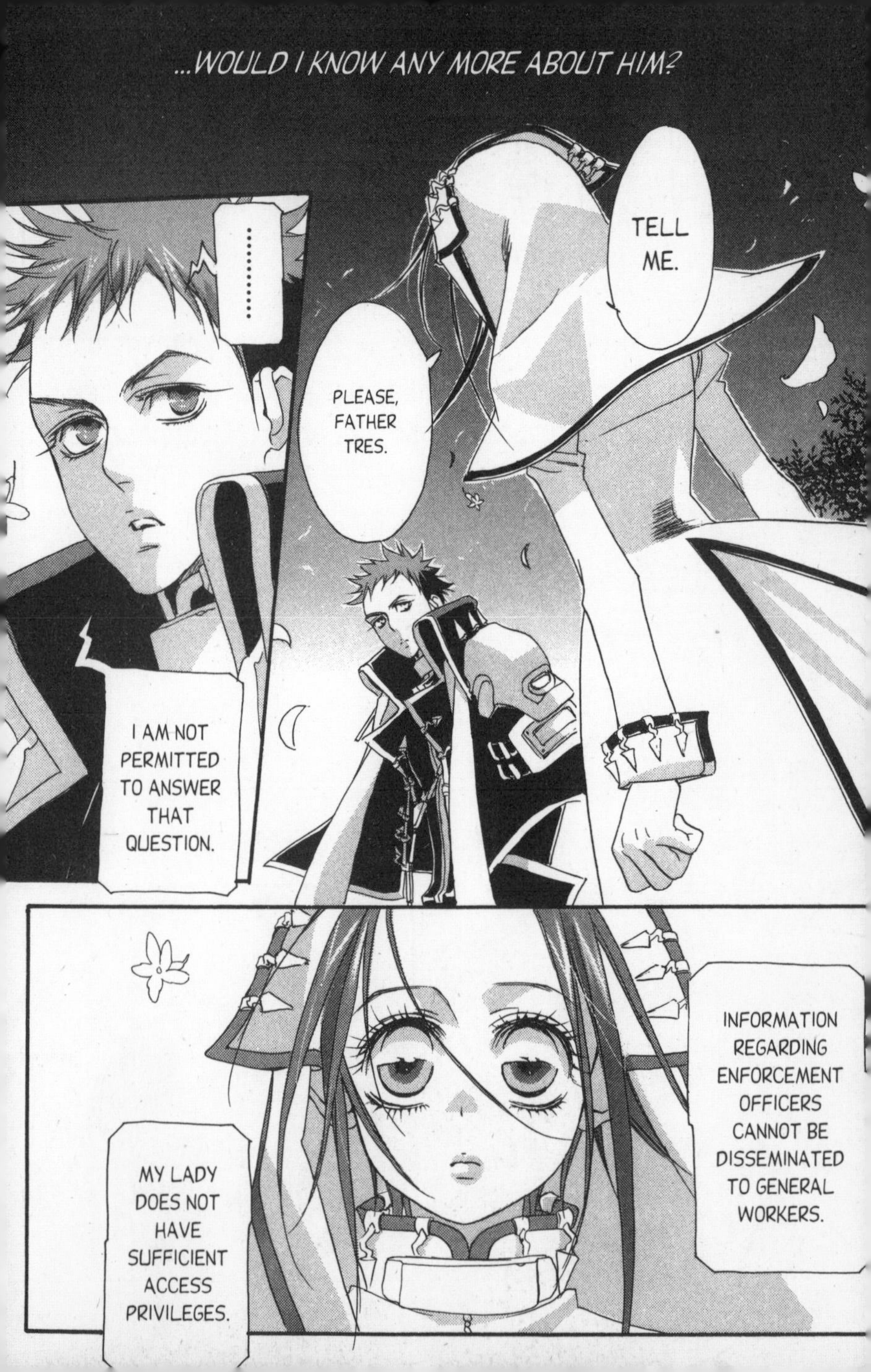
...WOULD I KNOW ANY MORE ABOUT HIM?
TELL ME.
PLEASE, FATHER TRES.
......
I AM NOT PERMITTED TO ANSWER THAT QUESTION.
INFORMATION REGARDING ENFORCEMENT OFFICERS CANNOT BE DISSEMINATED TO GENERAL WORKERS.
MY LADY DOES NOT HAVE SUFFICIENT ACCESS PRIVILEGES.

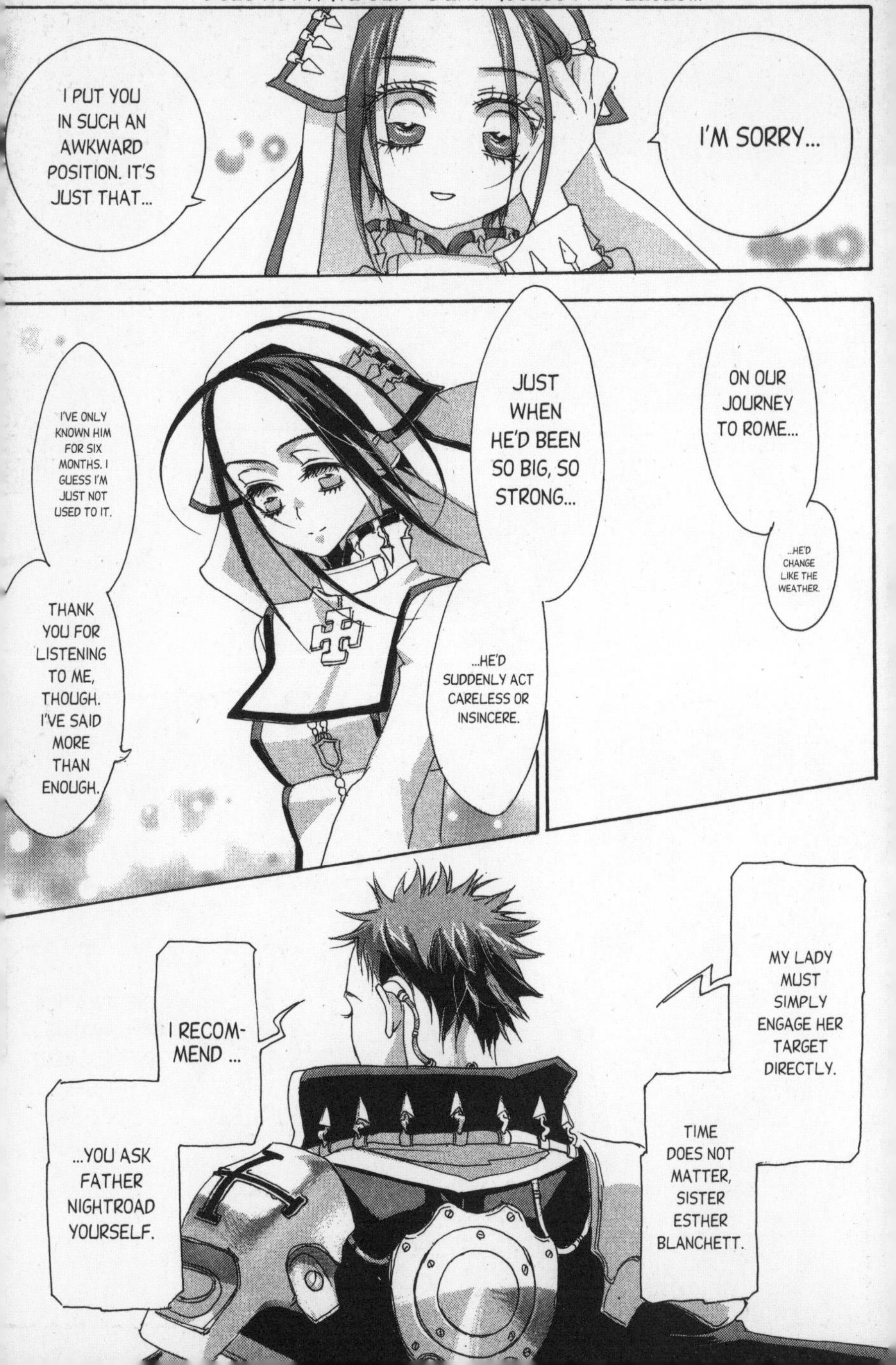
I'M SORRY...
I PUT YOU IN SUCH AN AWKWARD POSITION. IT'S JUST THAT...
ON OUR JOURNEY TO ROME...
...HE'D CHANGE LIKE THE WEATHER.
JUST WHEN HE'D BEEN SO BIG, SO STRONG...
...HE'D SUDDENLY ACT CARELESS OR INSINCERE.
I'VE ONLY KNOWN HIM FOR SIX MONTHS. I GUESS I'M JUST NOT USED TO IT.
THANK YOU FOR LISTENING TO ME, THOUGH. I'VE SAID MORE THAN ENOUGH.
MY LADY MUST SIMPLY ENGAGE HER TARGET DIRECTLY.
TIME DOES NOT MATTER, SISTER ESTHER BLANCHETT.
I RECOM-MEND ...
...YOU ASK FATHER NIGHTROAD YOURSELF.

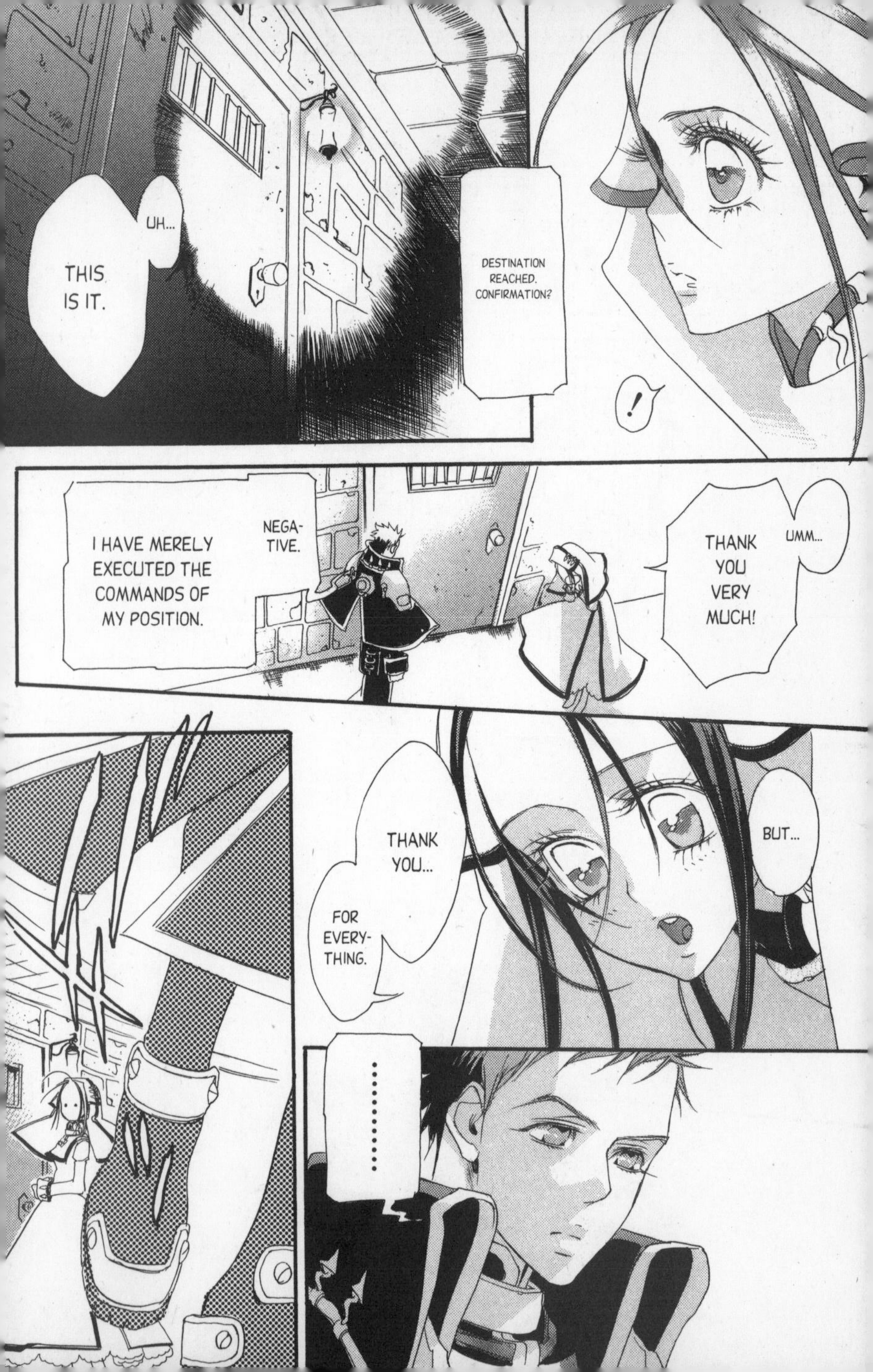
DESTINATION REACHED. CONFIRMATION?
!
UH...
THIS IS IT.
UMM...
THANK YOU VERY MUCH!
NEGA-TIVE.
I HAVE MERELY EXECUTED THE COMMANDS OF MY POSITION.
BUT...
THANK YOU...
FOR EVERY-THING.
......

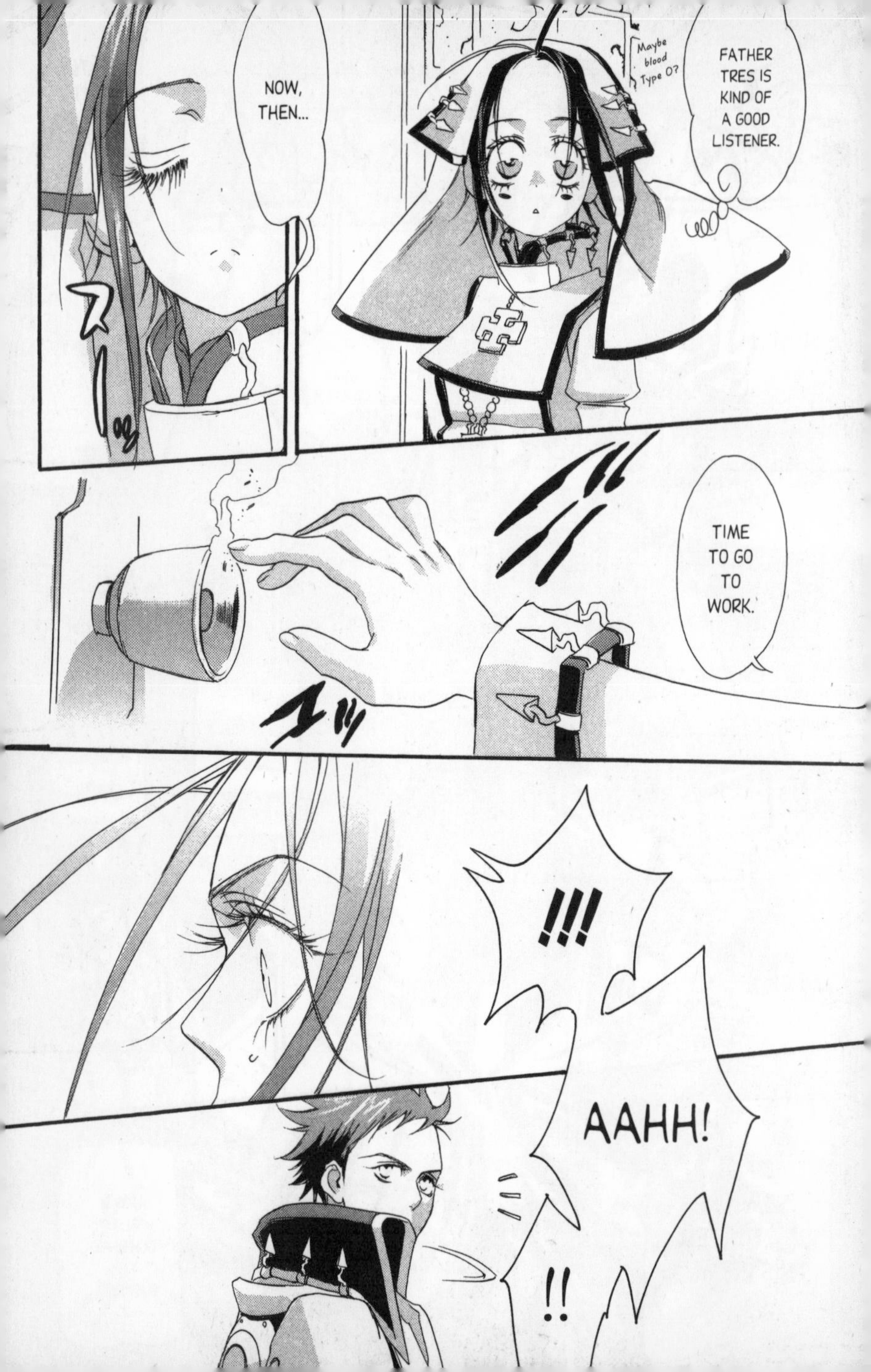
FATHER TRES IS KIND OF A GOOD LISTENER.
Maybe blood Type O?
NOW, THEN...
TIME TO GO TO WORK.
!!!
AAHH!
!!

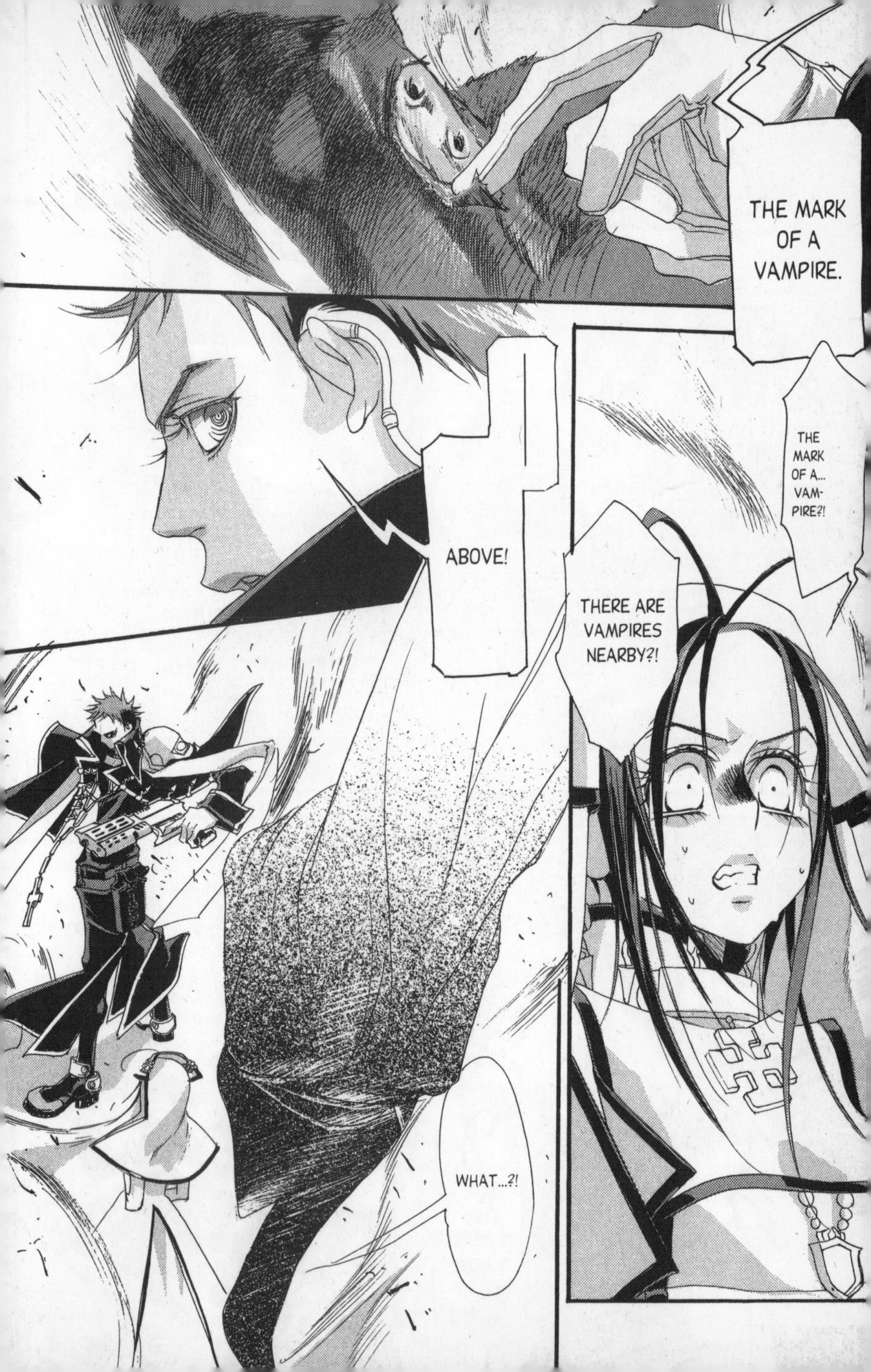
THE MARK OF A VAMPIRE.
THE MARK OF A... VAM-PIRE?!
THERE ARE VAMPIRES NEARBY?!
ABOVE!
WHAT...?!

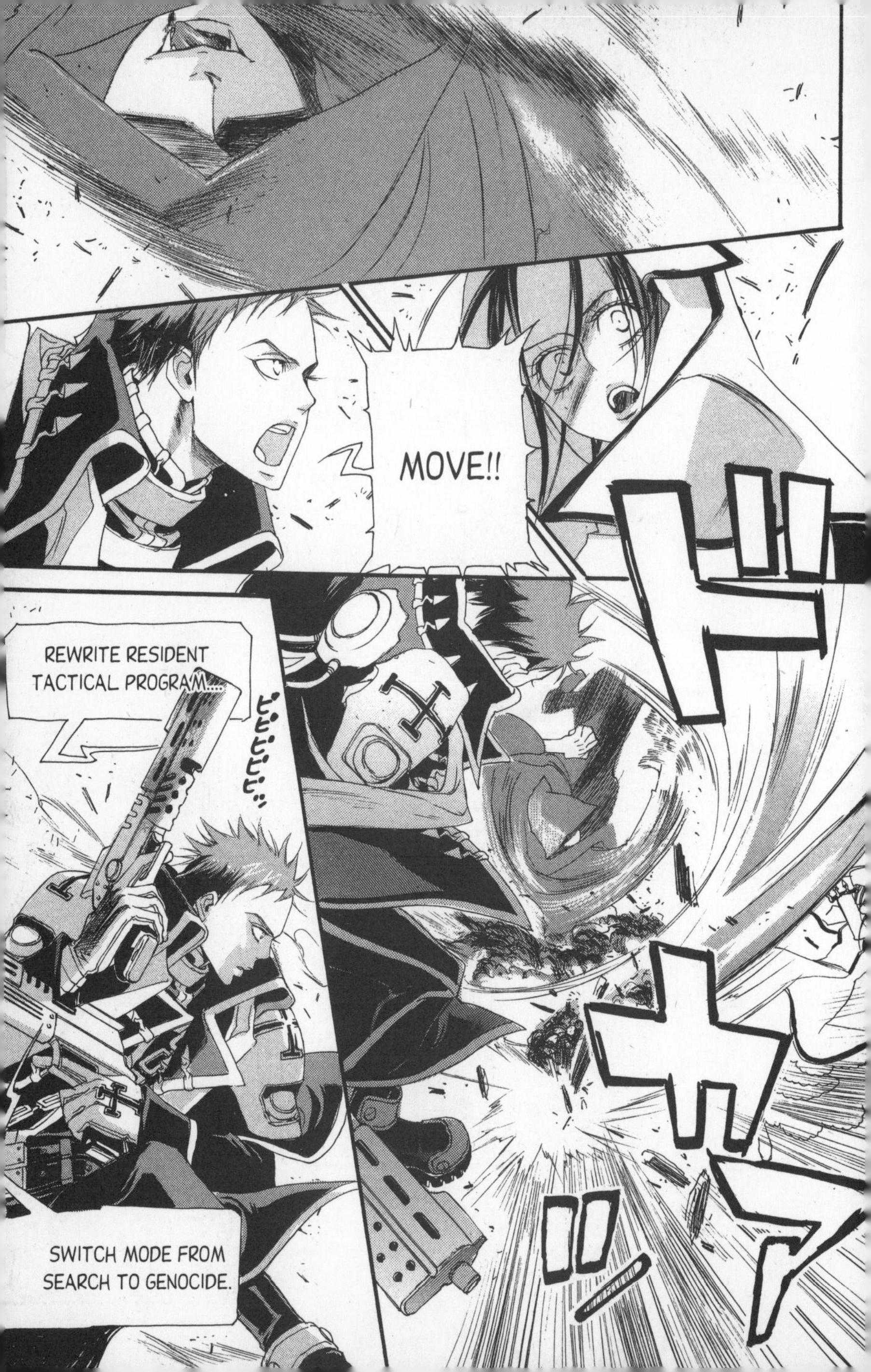
MOVE!!
REWRITE RESIDENT TACTICAL PROGRAM....
SWITCH MODE FROM SEARCH TO GENOCIDE.

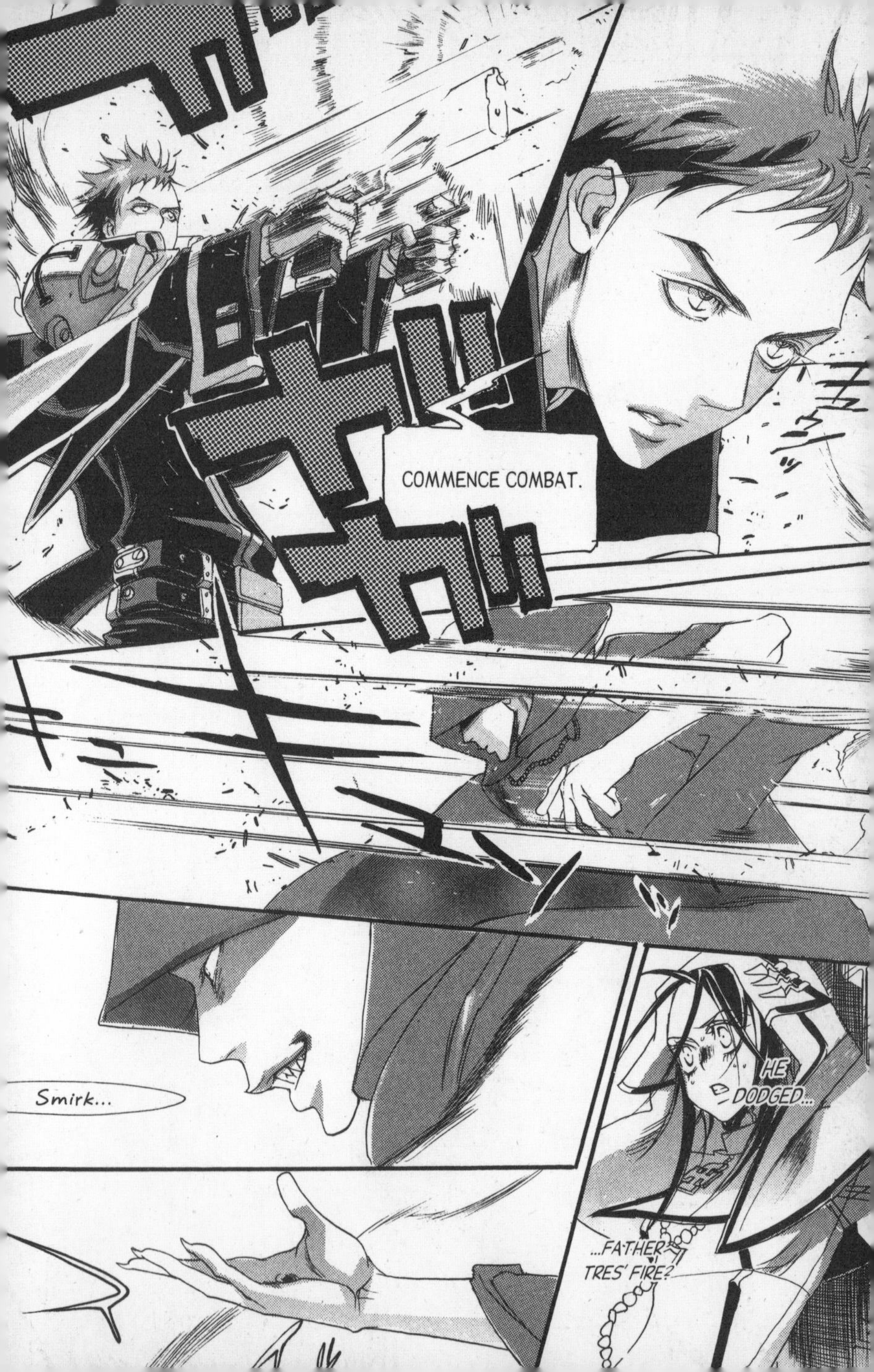
COMMENCE COMBAT.
HE DODGED...
...FATHER TRES' FIRE?
Smirk...

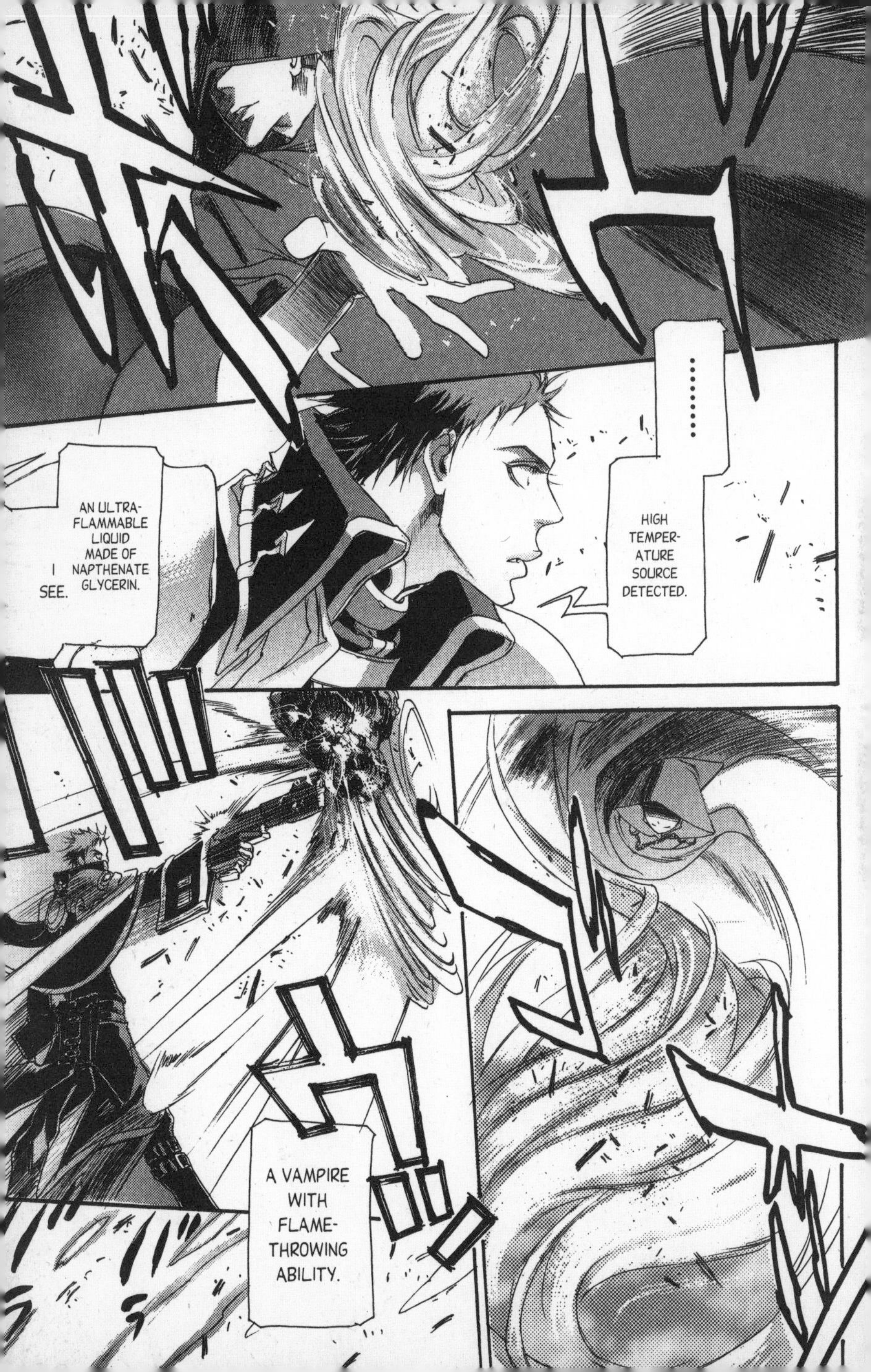
......
HIGH TEMPERATURE SOURCE DETECTED.
AN ULTRA-FLAMMABLE LIQUID MADE OF NAPTHENATE GLYCERIN.
I SEE.
A VAMPIRE WITH FLAME-THROWING ABILITY.

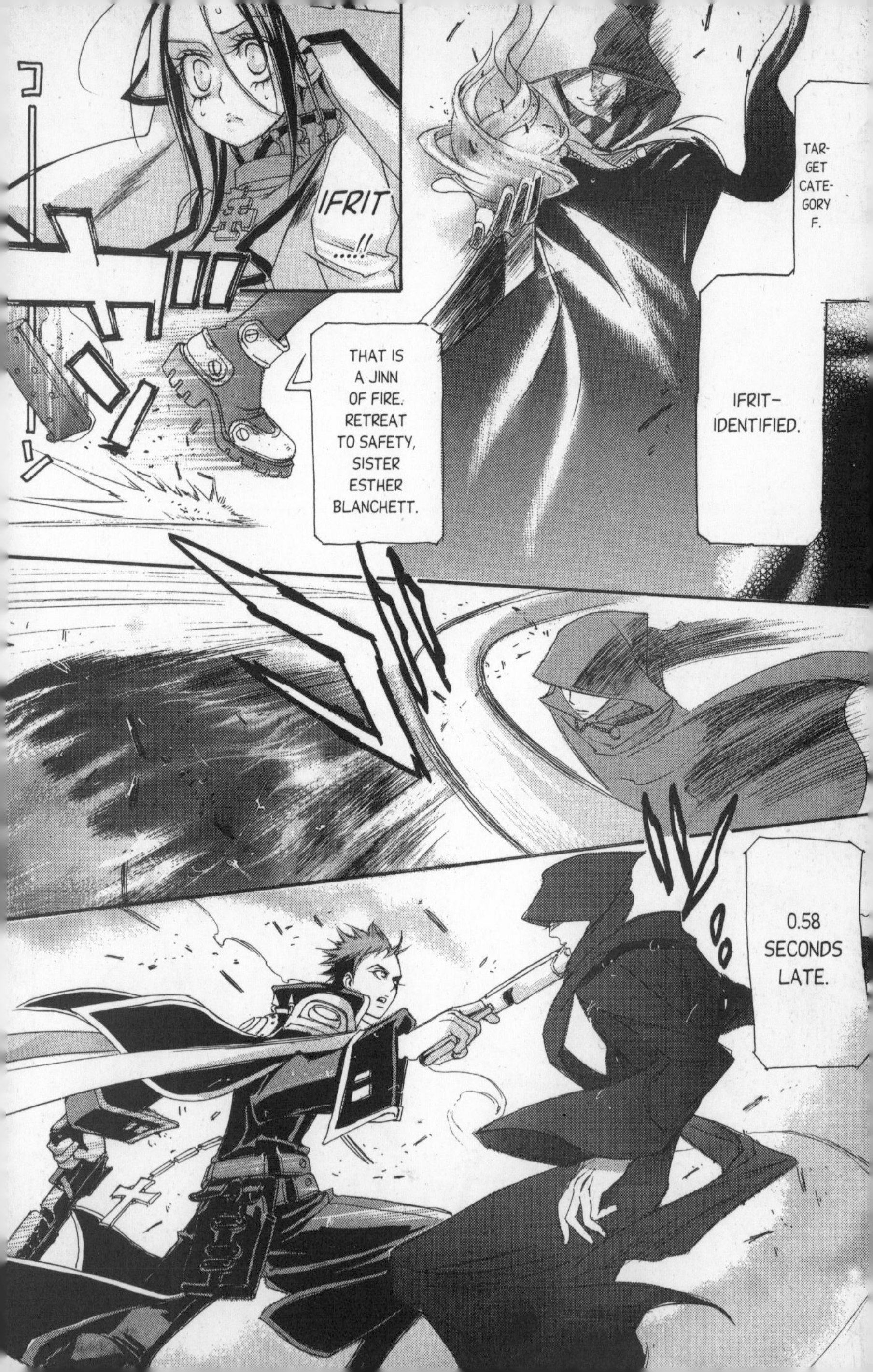
TARGET CATEGORY F.
IFRIT—IDENTIFIED.
THAT IS A JINN OF FIRE. RETREAT TO SAFETY, SISTER ESTHER BLANCHETT.
IFRIT
......!!
0.58 SECONDS LATE.

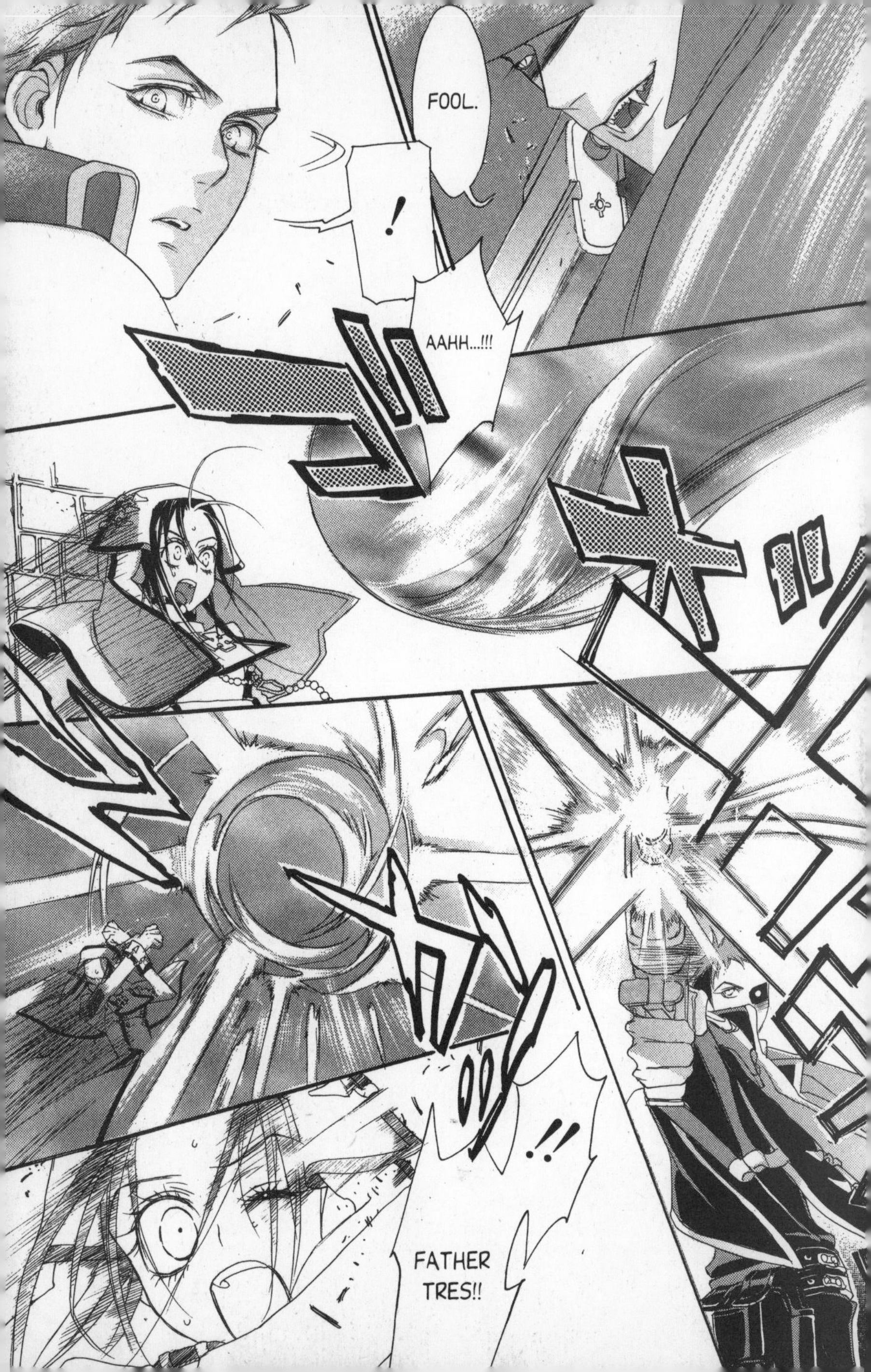
FOOL.
!
AAHH...!!!
!!
FATHER TRES!!

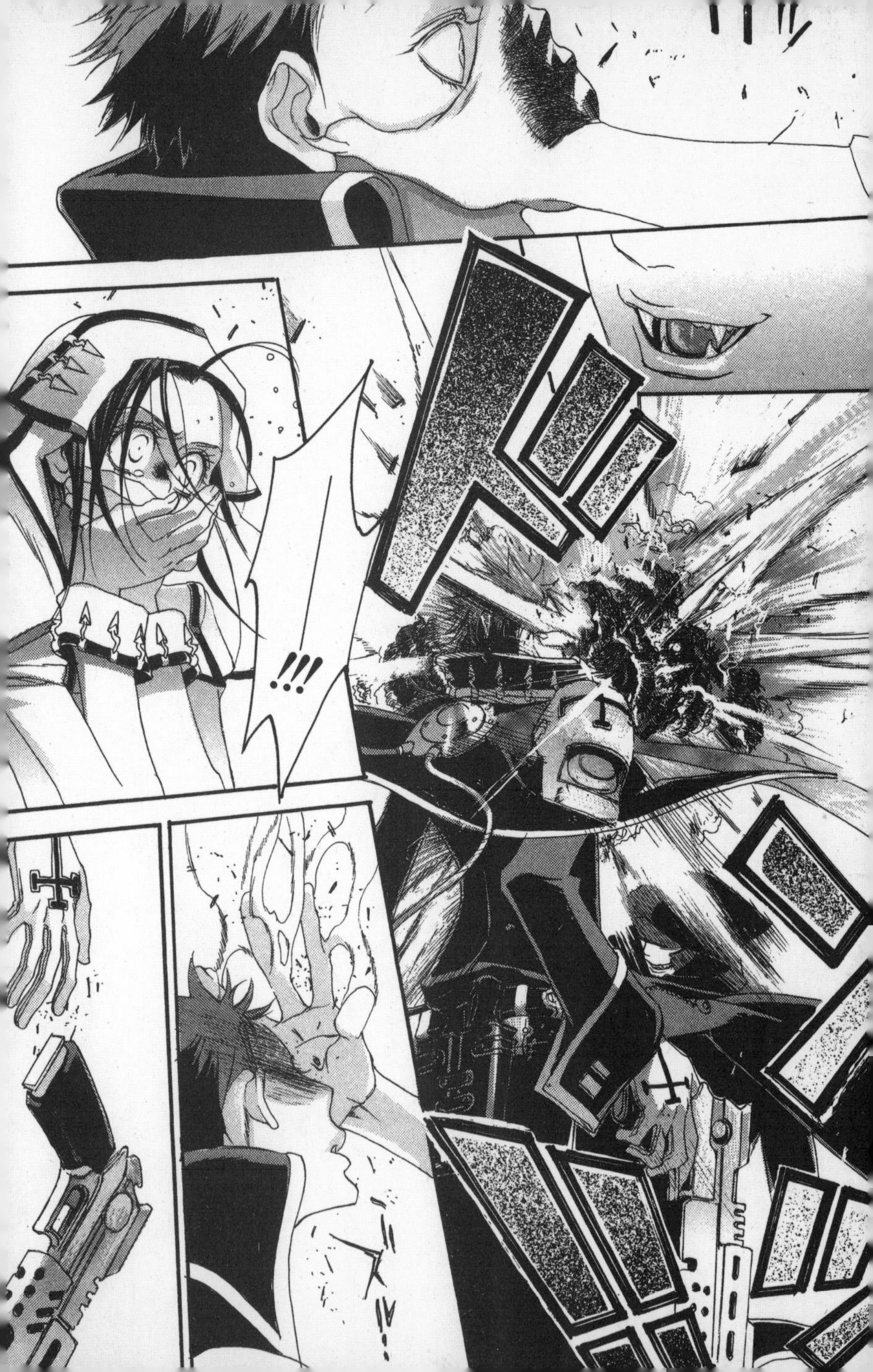
!!!

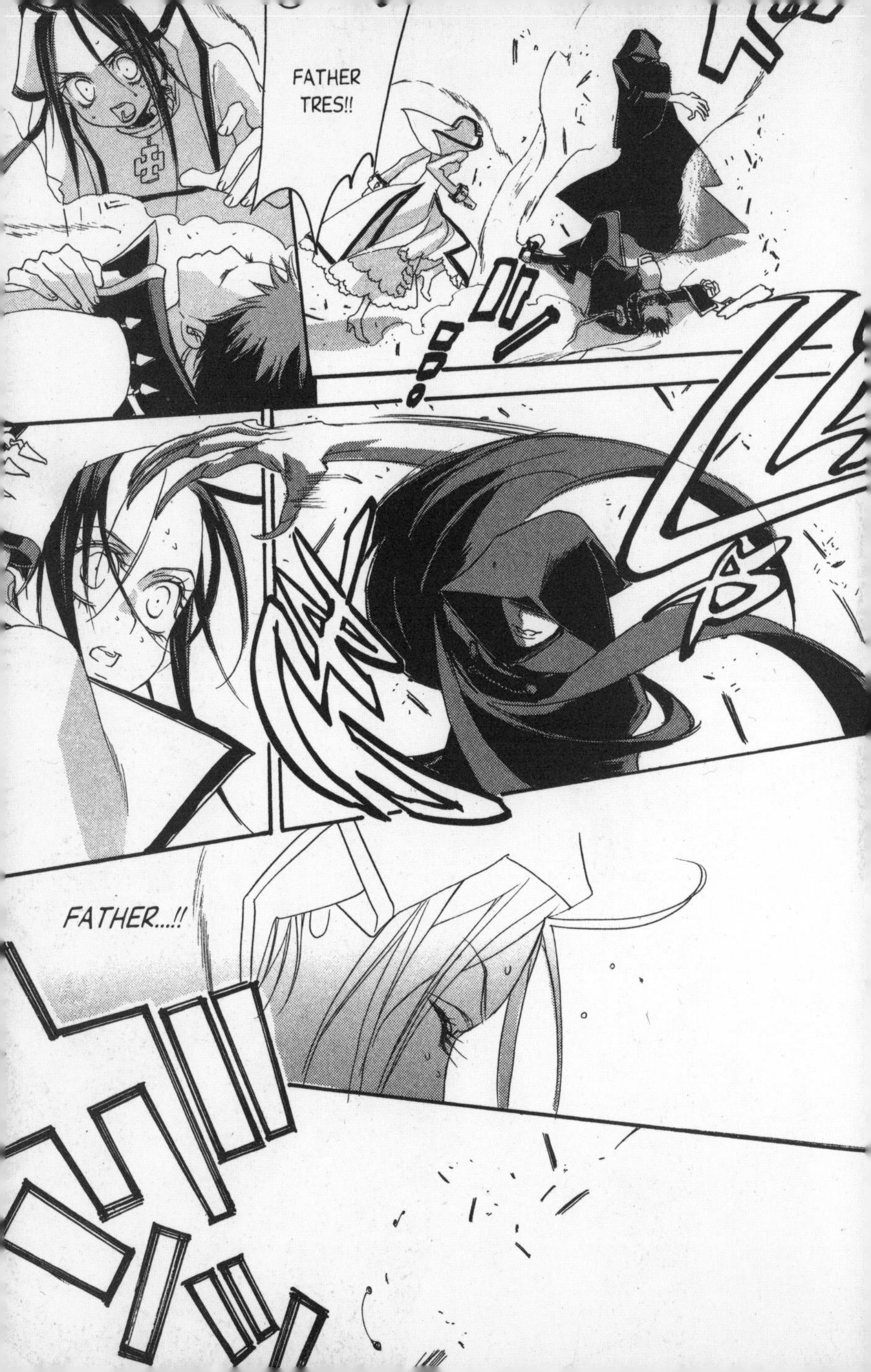
FATHER TRES!!
FATHER...!!

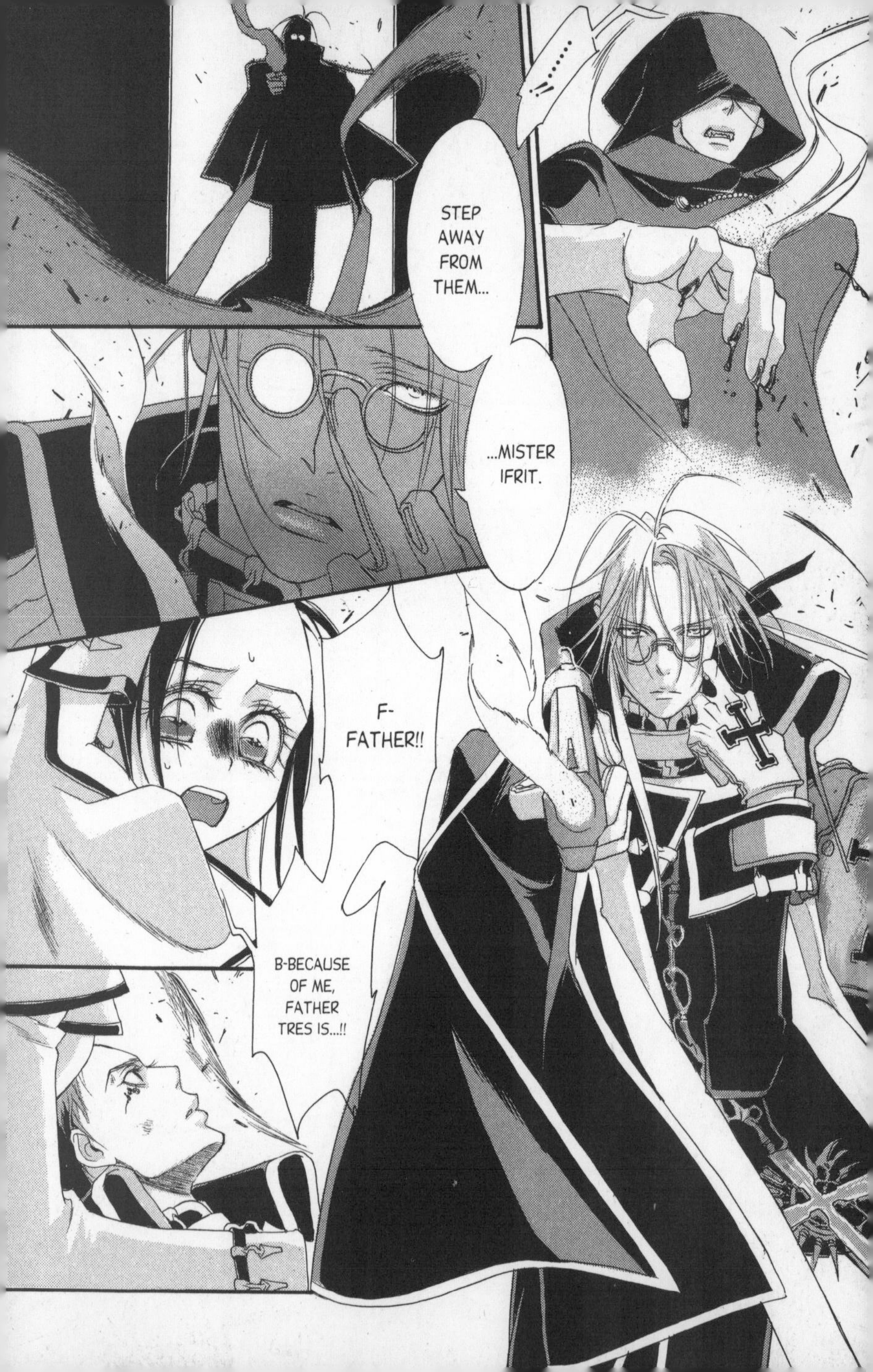
STEP AWAY FROM THEM...
...MISTER IFRIT.
F-FATHER!!
B-BECAUSE OF ME, FATHER TRES IS...!!

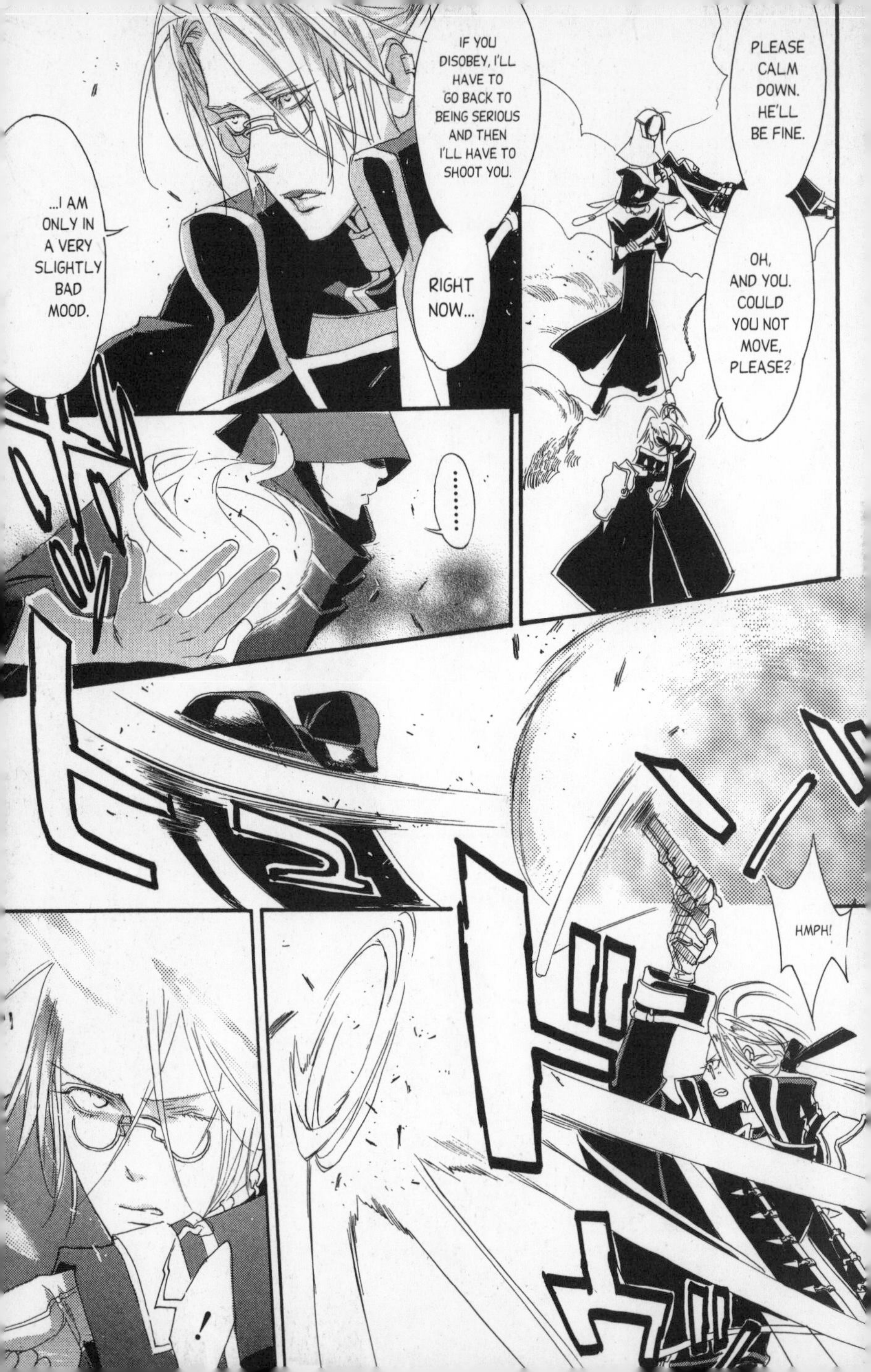
PLEASE CALM DOWN. HE'LL BE FINE.
OH, AND YOU. COULD YOU NOT MOVE, PLEASE?
IF YOU DISOBEY, I'LL HAVE TO GO BACK TO BEING SERIOUS AND THEN I'LL HAVE TO SHOOT YOU.
RIGHT NOW...
...I AM ONLY IN A VERY SLIGHTLY BAD MOOD.
....
HMPH!
!

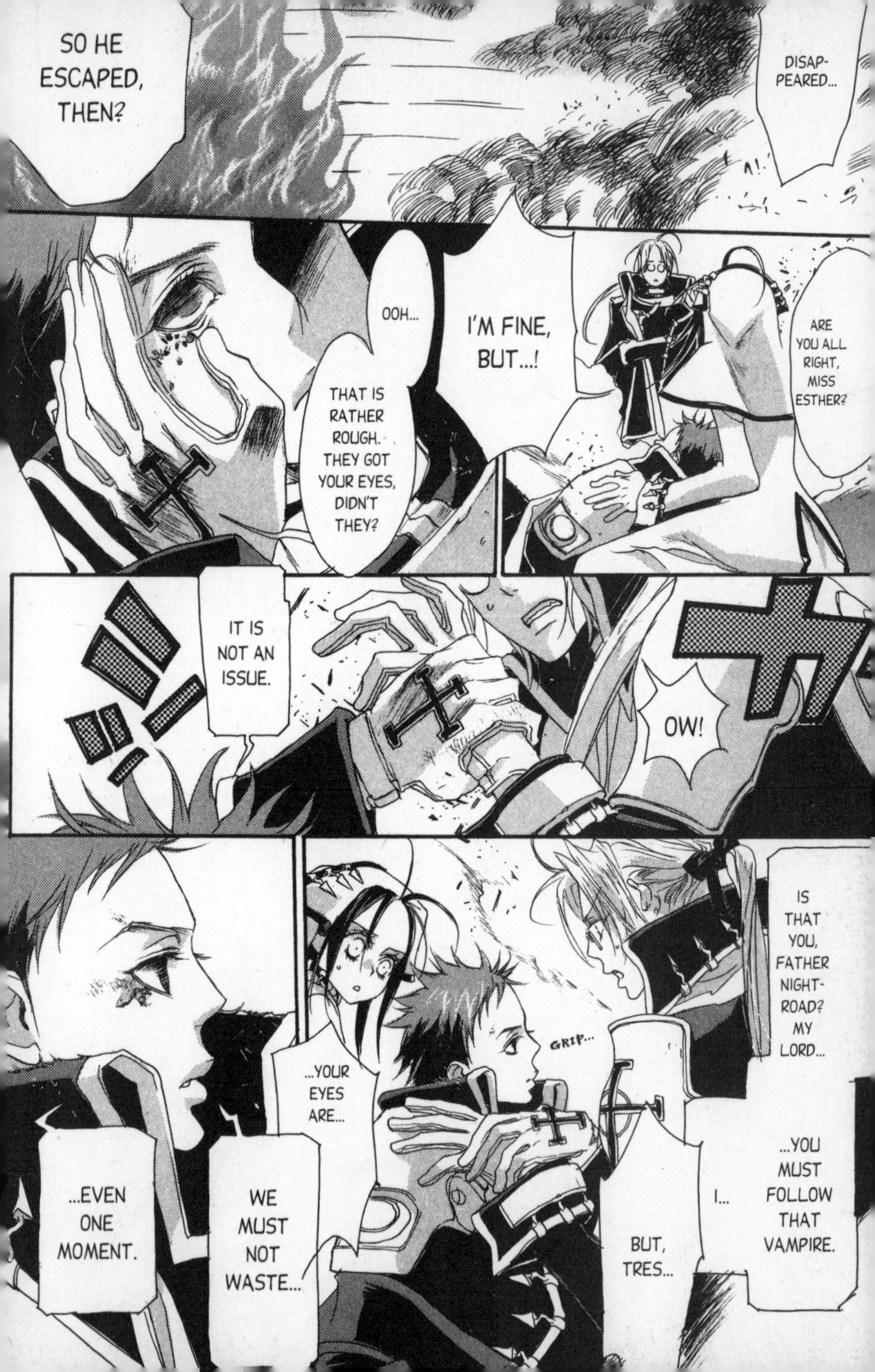
DISAP-PEARED...
SO HE ESCAPED, THEN?
ARE YOU ALL RIGHT, MISS ESTHER?
I'M FINE, BUT...!
OOH...
THAT IS RATHER ROUGH. THEY GOT YOUR EYES, DIDN'T THEY?
OW!
IT IS NOT AN ISSUE.
IS THAT YOU, FATHER NIGHT-ROAD? MY LORD...
...YOU MUST FOLLOW THAT VAMPIRE.
I...
BUT, TRES...
GRIP...
...YOUR EYES ARE...
WE MUST NOT WASTE...
...EVEN ONE MOMENT.

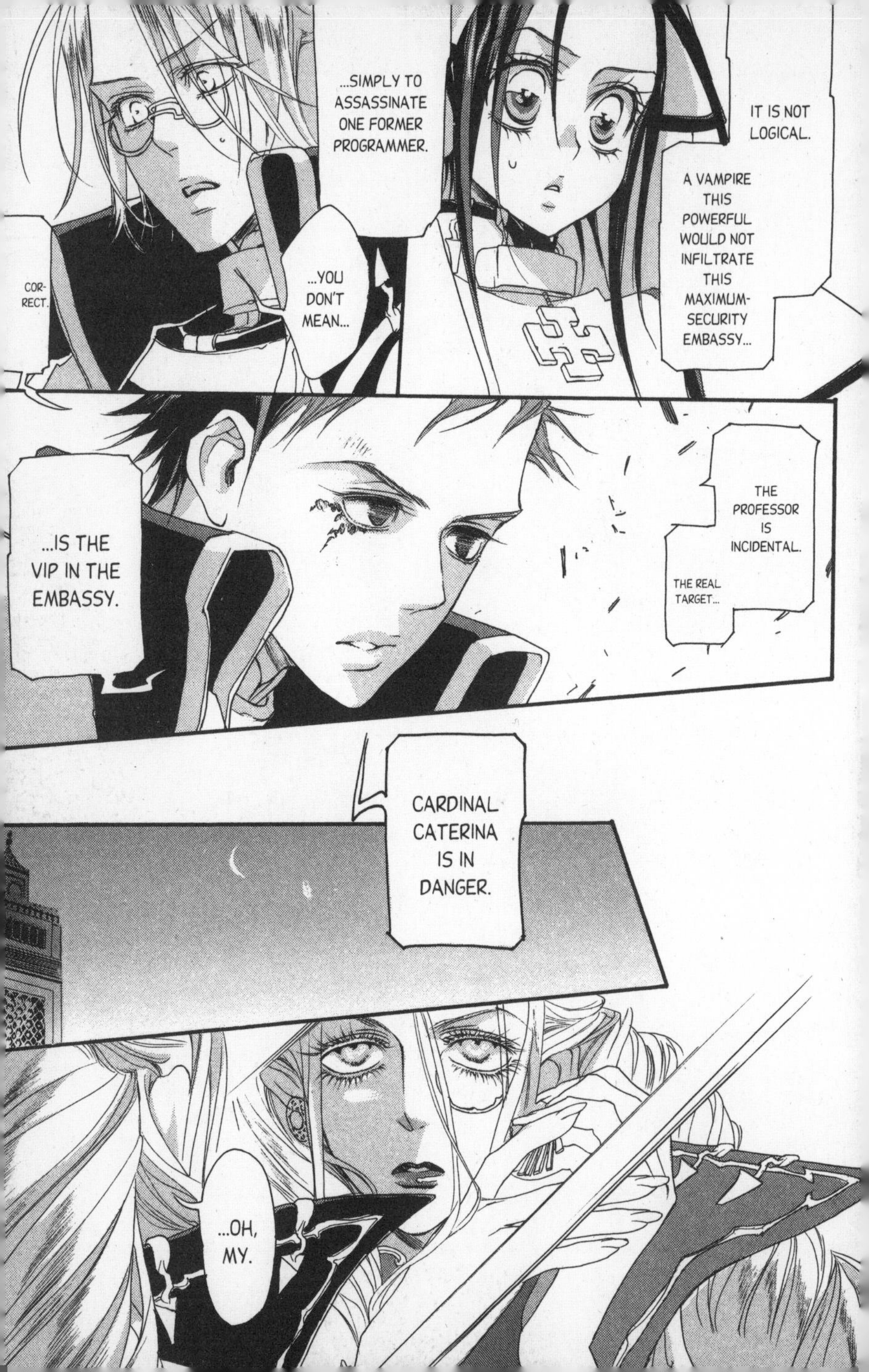
IT IS NOT LOGICAL.
A VAMPIRE THIS POWERFUL WOULD NOT INFILTRATE THIS MAXIMUM-SECURITY EMBASSY...
...SIMPLY TO ASSASSINATE ONE FORMER PROGRAMMER.
...YOU DON'T MEAN...
COR-RECT.
THE PROFESSOR IS INCIDENTAL.
THE REAL TARGET...
...IS THE VIP IN THE EMBASSY.
CARDINAL CATERINA IS IN DANGER.
...OH, MY.

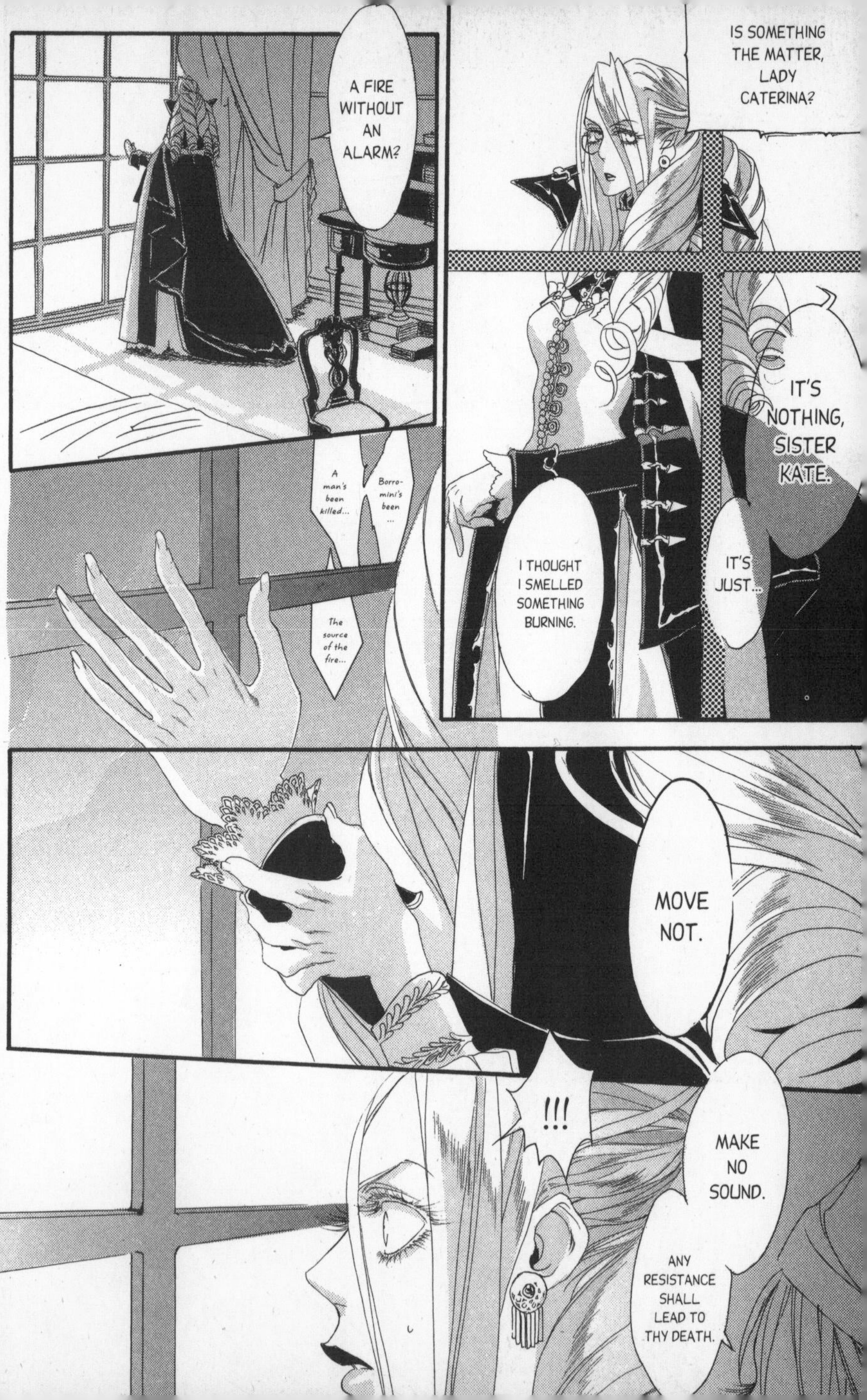
IS SOMETHING THE MATTER, LADY CATERINA?
IT'S NOTHING, SISTER KATE.
IT'S JUST...
I THOUGHT I SMELLED SOMETHING BURNING.
A FIRE WITHOUT AN ALARM?
Borromini's been ...
A man's been killed...
The source of the fire...
MOVE NOT.
!!!
MAKE NO SOUND.
ANY RESISTANCE SHALL LEAD TO THY DEATH.

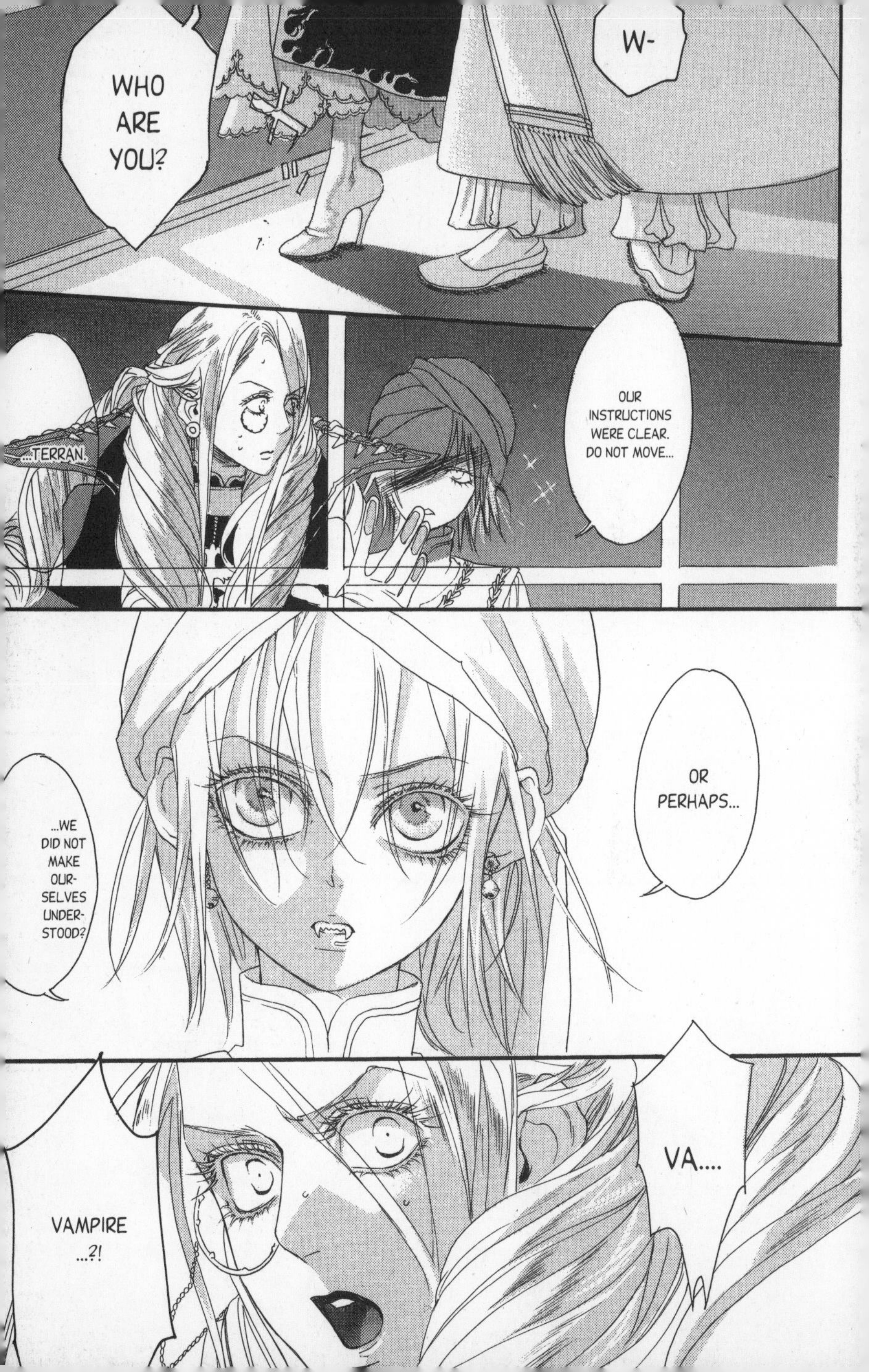
W-
WHO ARE YOU?
OUR INSTRUCTIONS WERE CLEAR. DO NOT MOVE...
...TERRAN.
OR PERHAPS...
...WE DID NOT MAKE OUR-SELVES UNDER-STOOD?
VA....
VAMPIRE ...?!

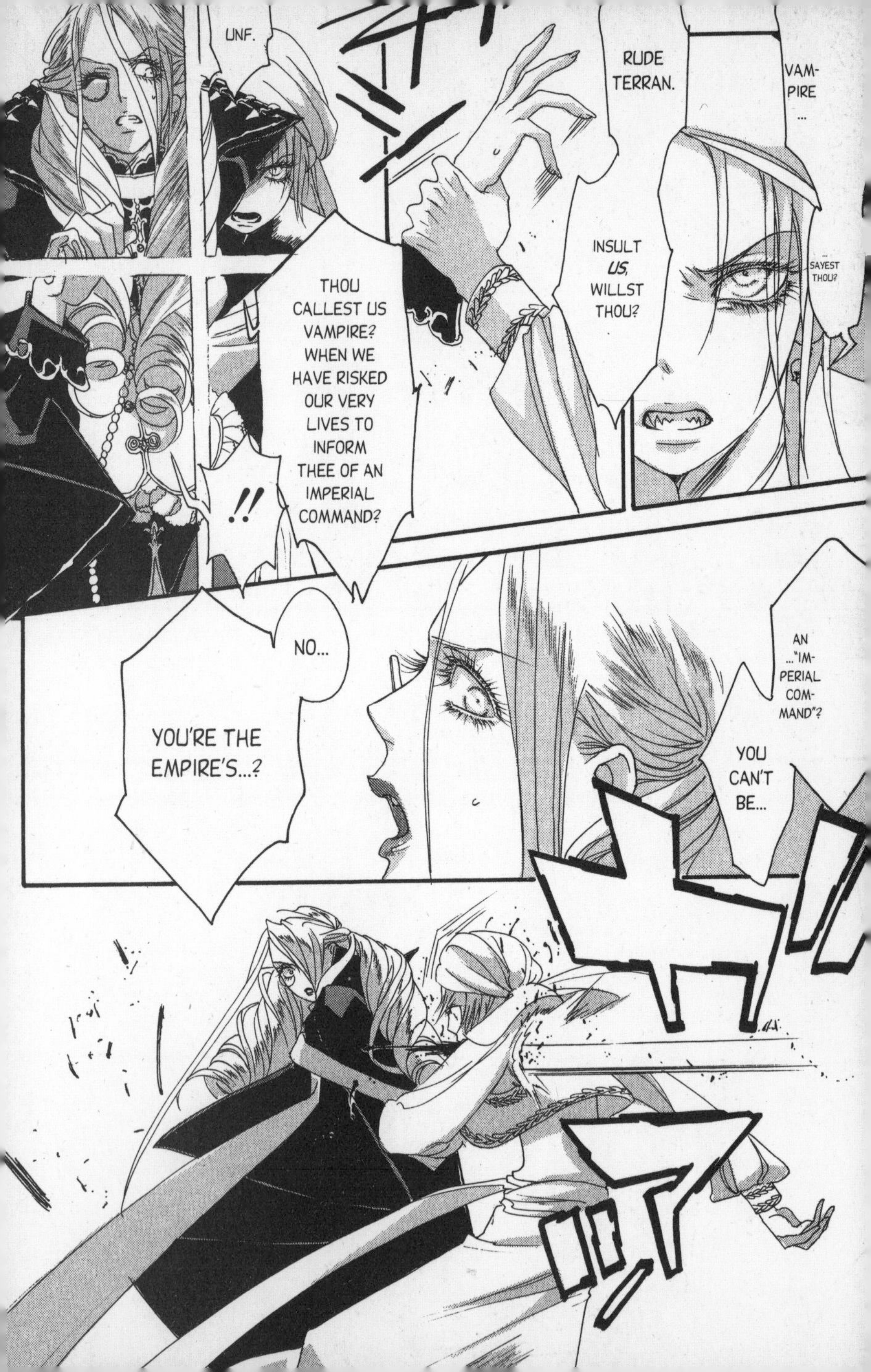
VAMPIRE...
RUDE TERRAN.
...SAYEST THOU?
INSULT *US*, WILLST THOU?
UNF.
THOU CALLEST US VAMPIRE? WHEN WE HAVE RISKED OUR VERY LIVES TO INFORM THEE OF AN IMPERIAL COMMAND?
!!
AN ..."IMPERIAL COMMAND"?
YOU CAN'T BE...
NO...
YOU'RE THE EMPIRE'S...?

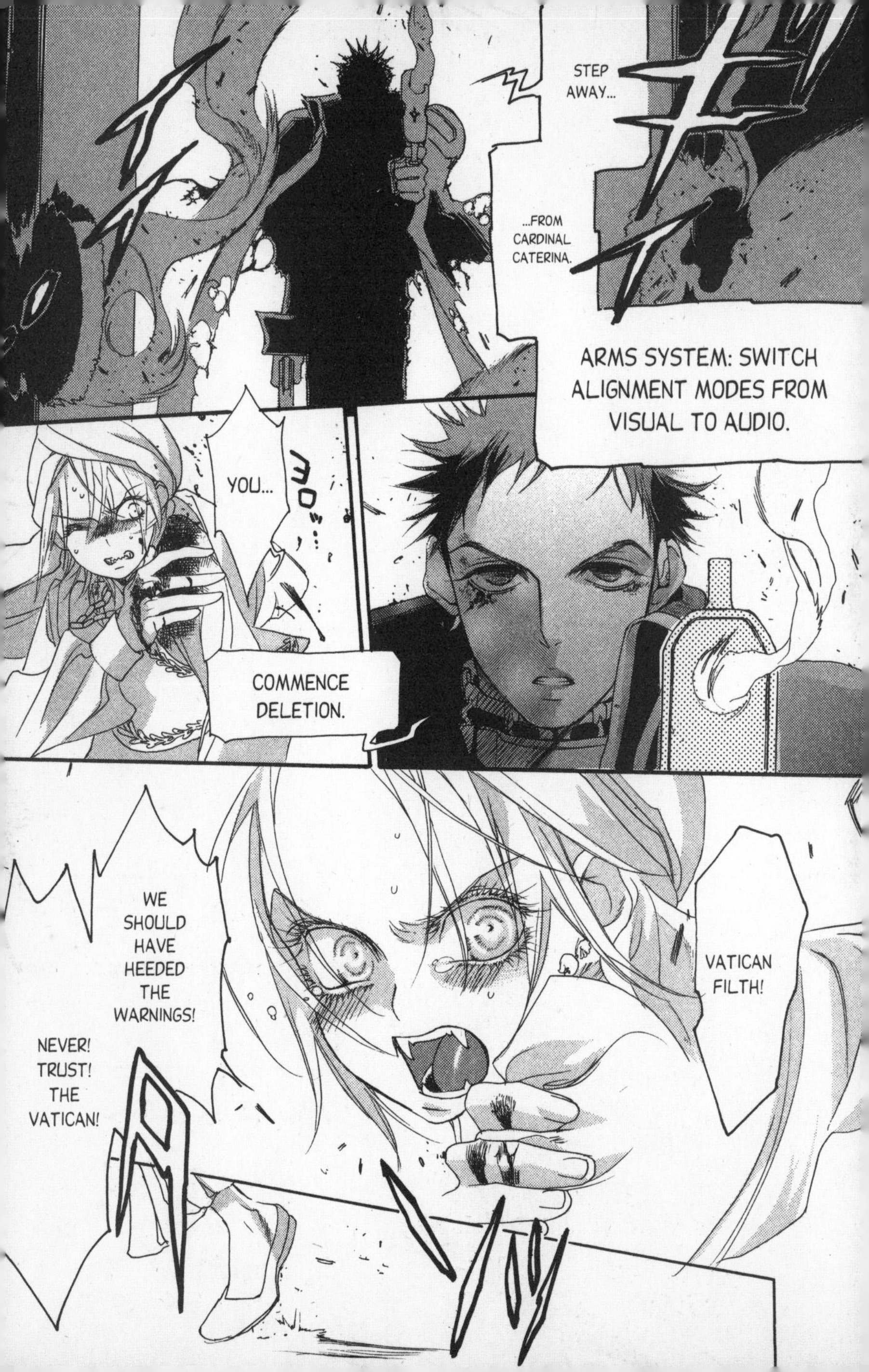
STEP AWAY...
...FROM CARDINAL CATERINA.
ARMS SYSTEM: SWITCH ALIGNMENT MODES FROM VISUAL TO AUDIO.
YOU...
COMMENCE DELETION.
VATICAN FILTH!
WE SHOULD HAVE HEEDED THE WARNINGS!
NEVER! TRUST! THE VATICAN!

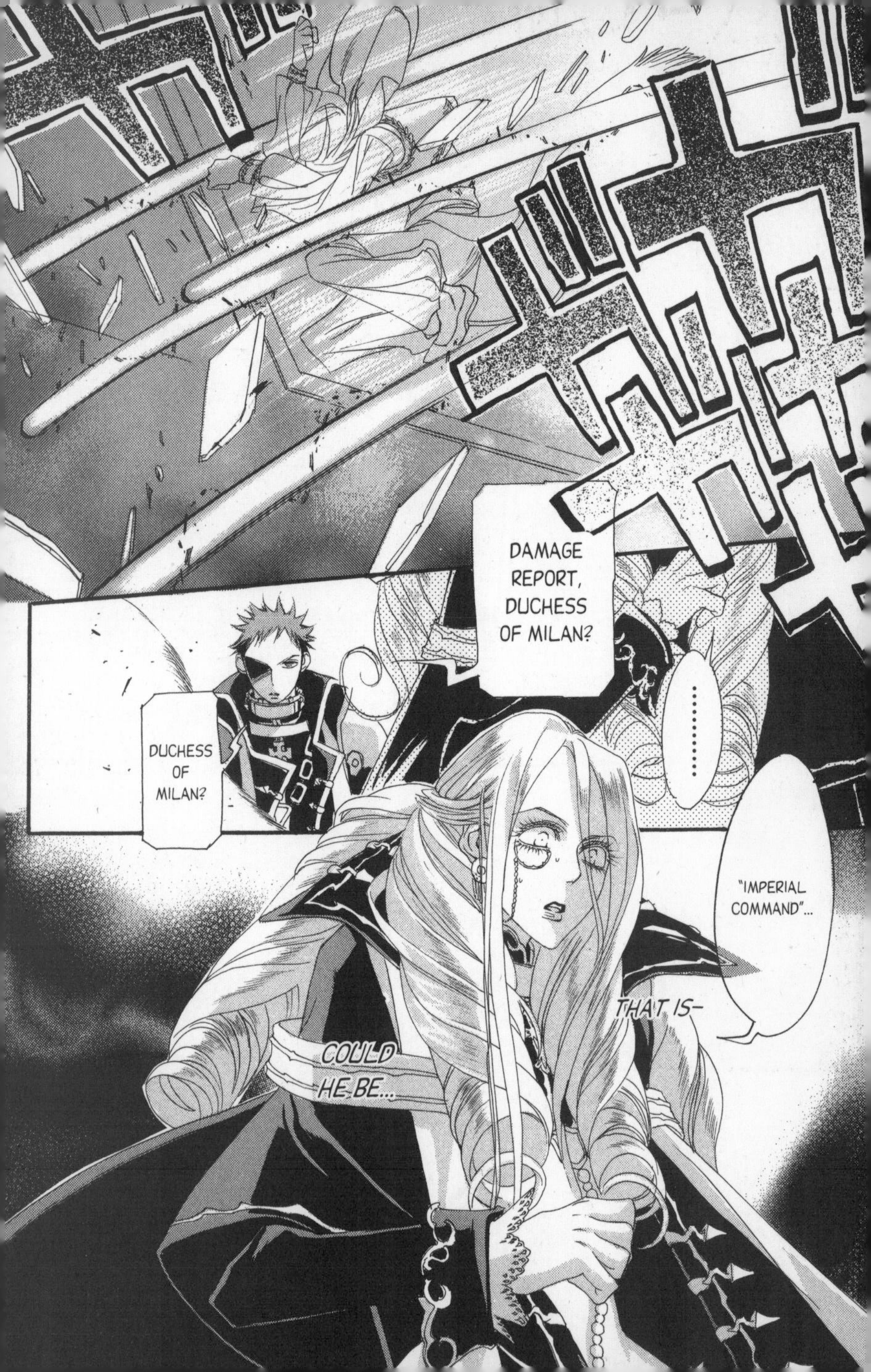
DAMAGE REPORT, DUCHESS OF MILAN?
....
DUCHESS OF MILAN?
"IMPERIAL COMMAND"...
THAT IS–
COULD HE BE...

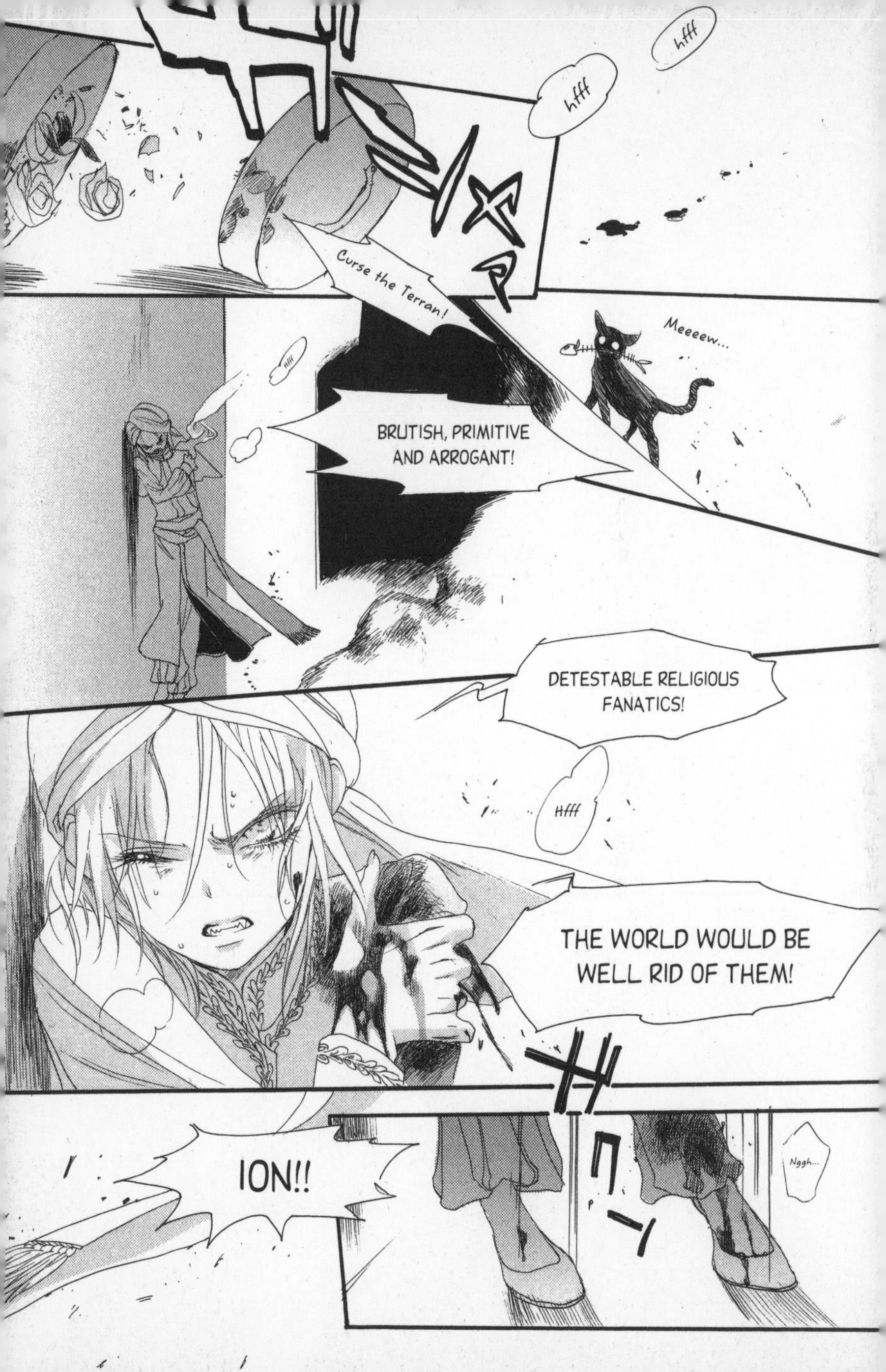
hfff
hfff
Curse the Terran!
Meeeew...
hfff
BRUTISH, PRIMITIVE AND ARROGANT!
DETESTABLE RELIGIOUS FANATICS!
Hfff
THE WORLD WOULD BE WELL RID OF THEM!
Nggh...
ION!!

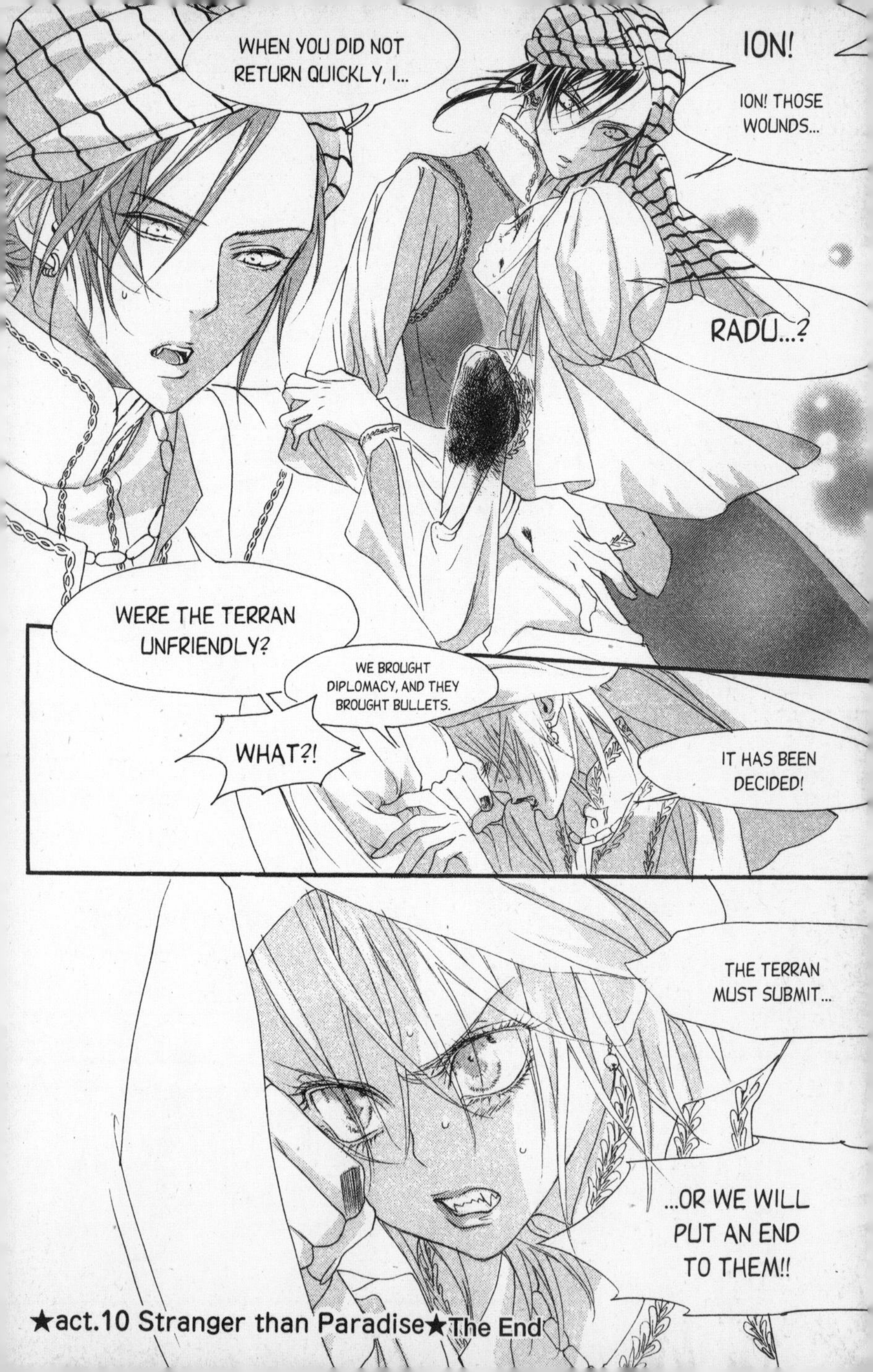
ION!
ION! THOSE WOUNDS...
RADU...?
WHEN YOU DID NOT RETURN QUICKLY, I...
WERE THE TERRAN UNFRIENDLY?
WE BROUGHT DIPLOMACY, AND THEY BROUGHT BULLETS.
WHAT?!
IT HAS BEEN DECIDED!
THE TERRAN MUST SUBMIT...
...OR WE WILL PUT AN END TO THEM!!
★act.10 Stranger than Paradise★The End

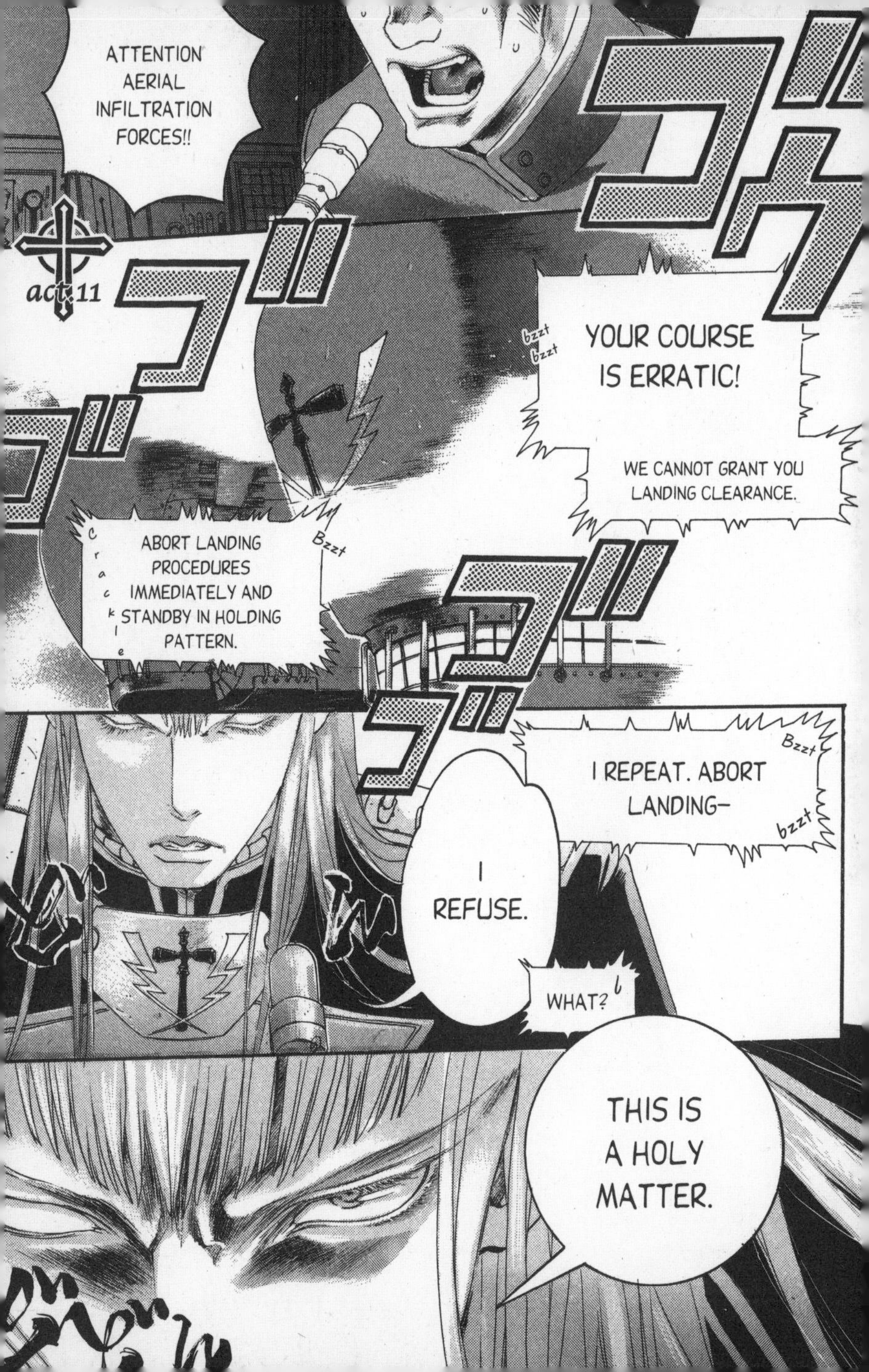
ATTENTION AERIAL INFILTRATION FORCES!!
act 11
bzzt bzzt
YOUR COURSE IS ERRATIC!
WE CANNOT GRANT YOU LANDING CLEARANCE.
Bzzt
crackle
ABORT LANDING PROCEDURES IMMEDIATELY AND STANDBY IN HOLDING PATTERN.
Bzzt
I REPEAT. ABORT LANDING–
bzzt
I REFUSE.
WHAT?
THIS IS A HOLY MATTER.

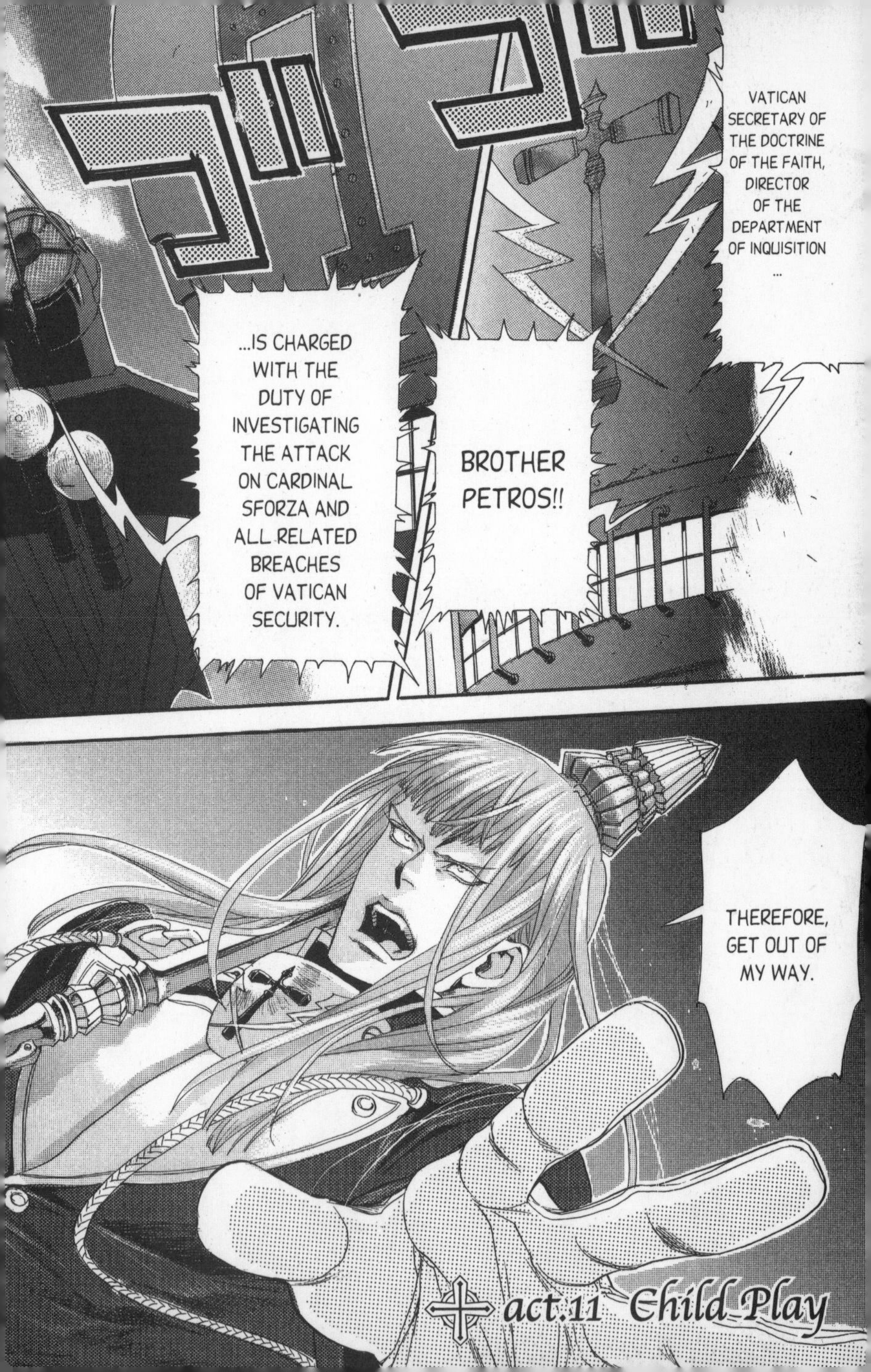
VATICAN SECRETARY OF THE DOCTRINE OF THE FAITH, DIRECTOR OF THE DEPARTMENT OF INQUISITION ...
BROTHER PETROS!!
...IS CHARGED WITH THE DUTY OF INVESTIGATING THE ATTACK ON CARDINAL SFORZA AND ALL RELATED BREACHES OF VATICAN SECURITY.
THEREFORE, GET OUT OF MY WAY.
act.11 Child Play

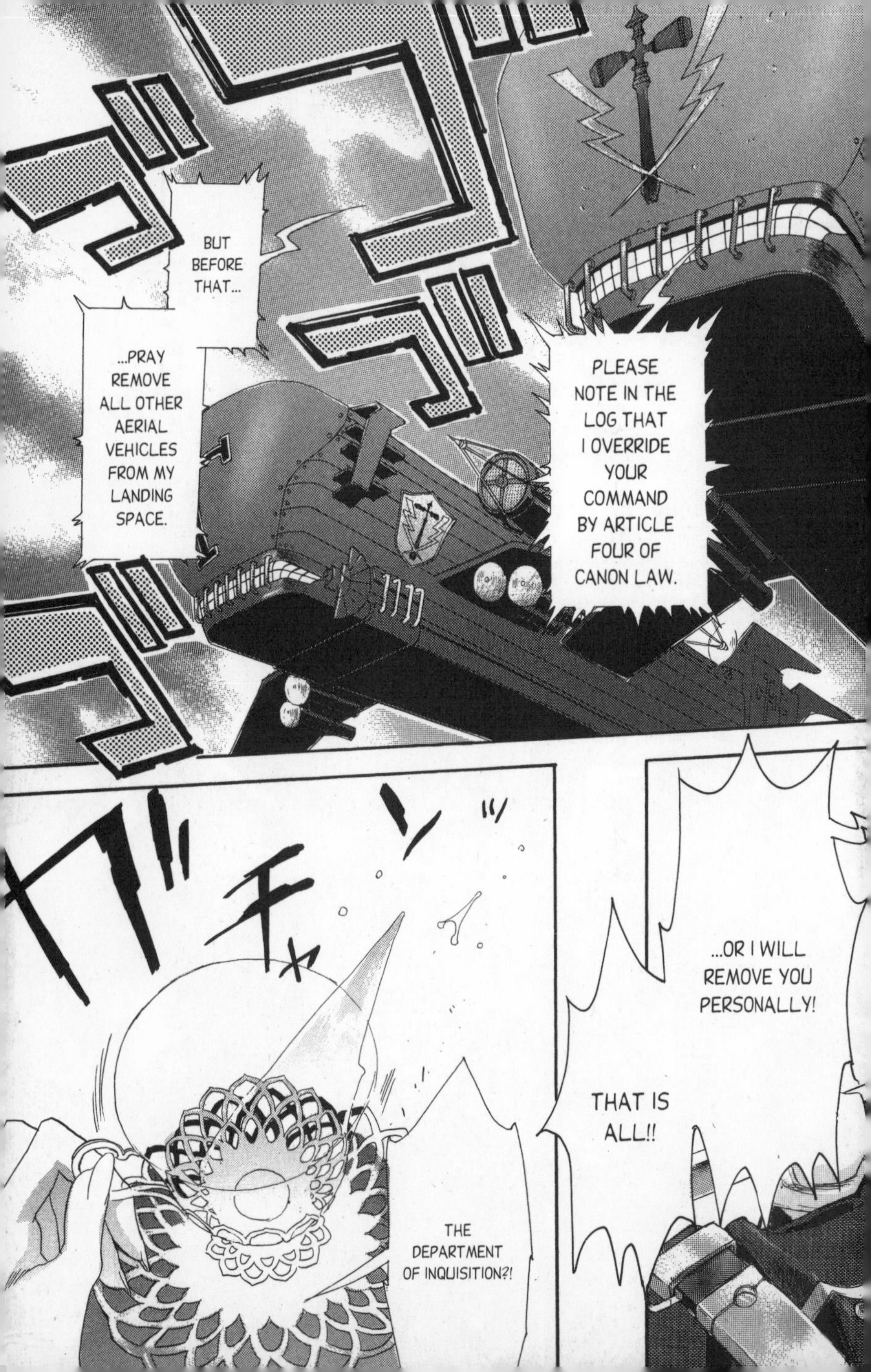
PLEASE NOTE IN THE LOG THAT I OVERRIDE YOUR COMMAND BY ARTICLE FOUR OF CANON LAW.
BUT BEFORE THAT...
...PRAY REMOVE ALL OTHER AERIAL VEHICLES FROM MY LANDING SPACE.
...OR I WILL REMOVE YOU PERSONALLY!
THAT IS ALL!!
ガチャン
THE DEPARTMENT OF INQUISITION?!

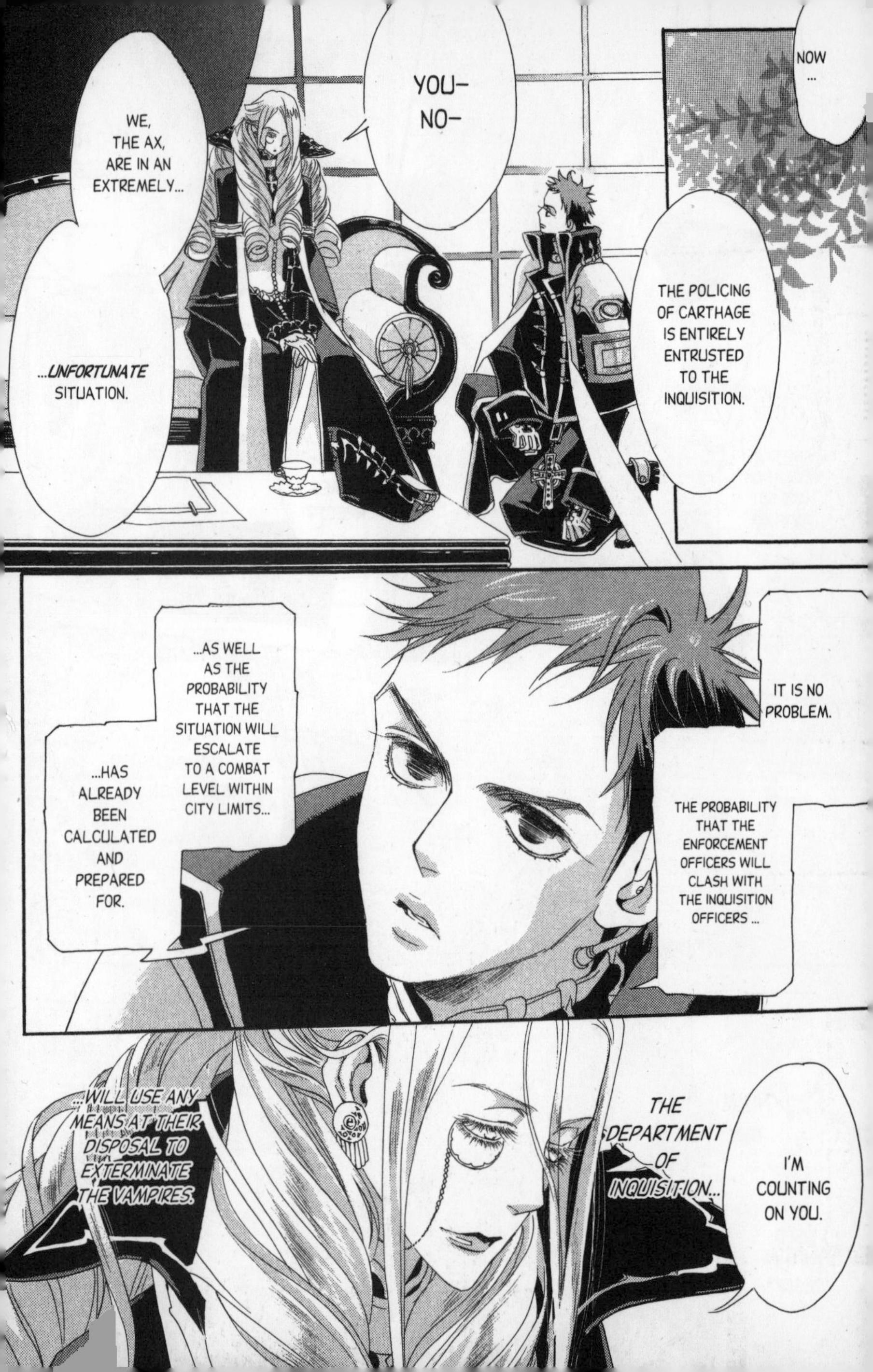
NOW ...
THE POLICING OF CARTHAGE IS ENTIRELY ENTRUSTED TO THE INQUISITION.
YOU— NO—
WE, THE AX, ARE IN AN EXTREMELY...
...*UNFORTUNATE* SITUATION.
IT IS NO PROBLEM.
THE PROBABILITY THAT THE ENFORCEMENT OFFICERS WILL CLASH WITH THE INQUISITION OFFICERS ...
...AS WELL AS THE PROBABILITY THAT THE SITUATION WILL ESCALATE TO A COMBAT LEVEL WITHIN CITY LIMITS...
...HAS ALREADY BEEN CALCULATED AND PREPARED FOR.
I'M COUNTING ON YOU.
THE DEPARTMENT OF INQUISITION...
...WILL USE ANY MEANS AT THEIR DISPOSAL TO EXTERMINATE THE VAMPIRES.

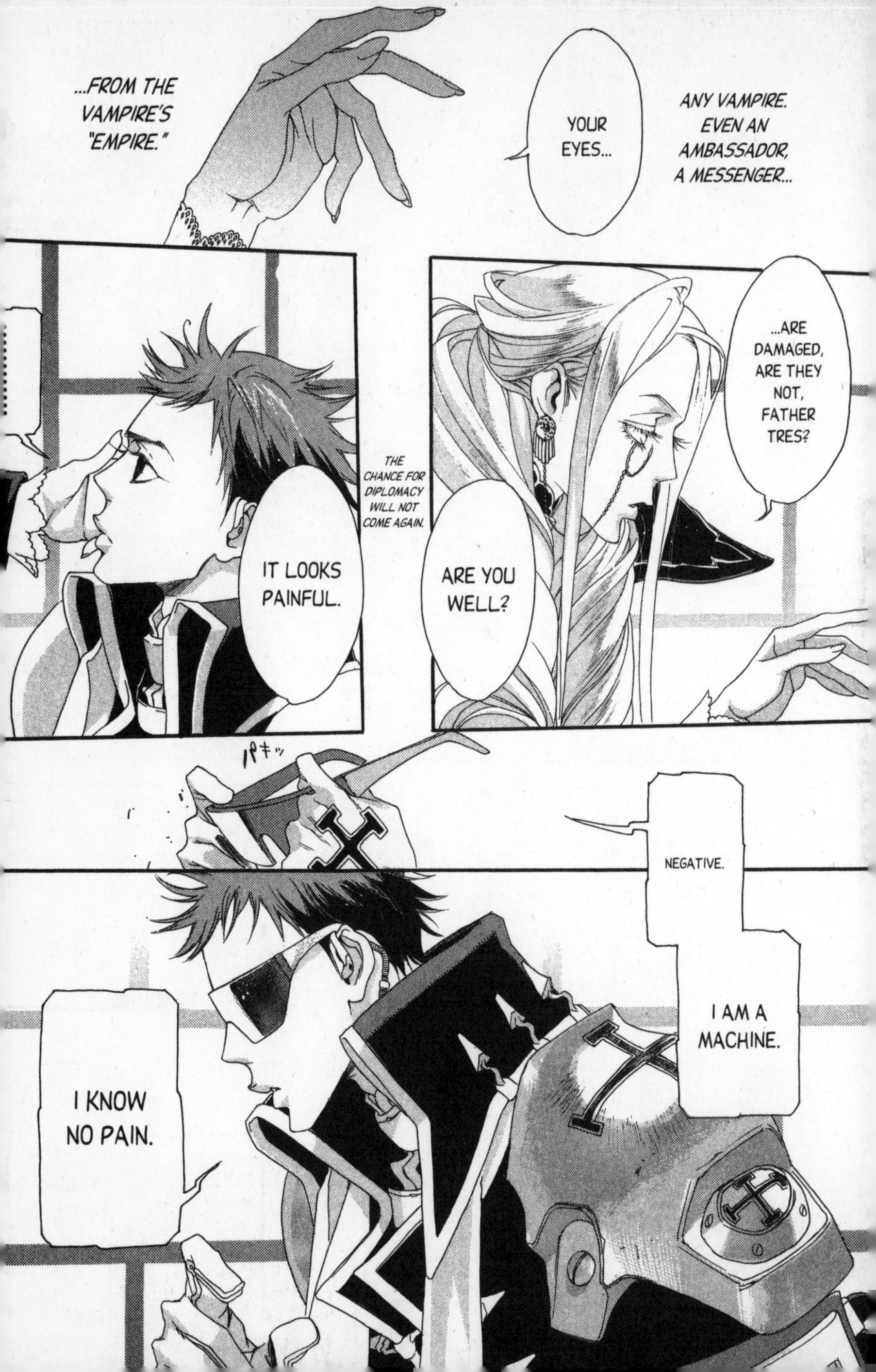
ANY VAMPIRE. EVEN AN AMBASSADOR, A MESSENGER...
YOUR EYES...
...FROM THE VAMPIRE'S "EMPIRE."
...ARE DAMAGED, ARE THEY NOT, FATHER TRES?
ARE YOU WELL?
THE CHANCE FOR DIPLOMACY WILL NOT COME AGAIN.
IT LOOKS PAINFUL.
パキッ
NEGATIVE.
I AM A MACHINE.
I KNOW NO PAIN.

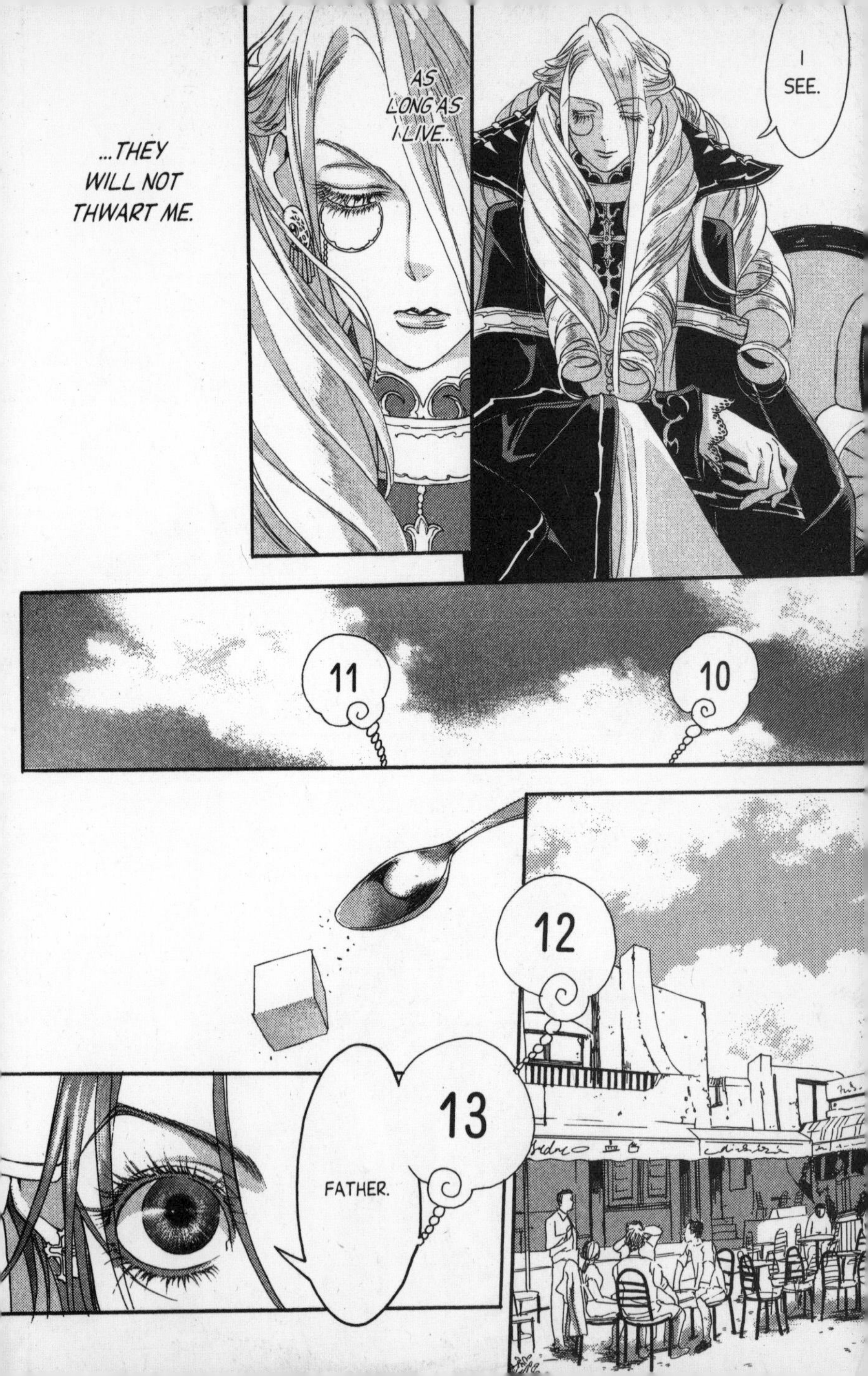
I SEE.
AS LONG AS I LIVE...
...THEY WILL NOT THWART ME.
10
11
12
13
FATHER.

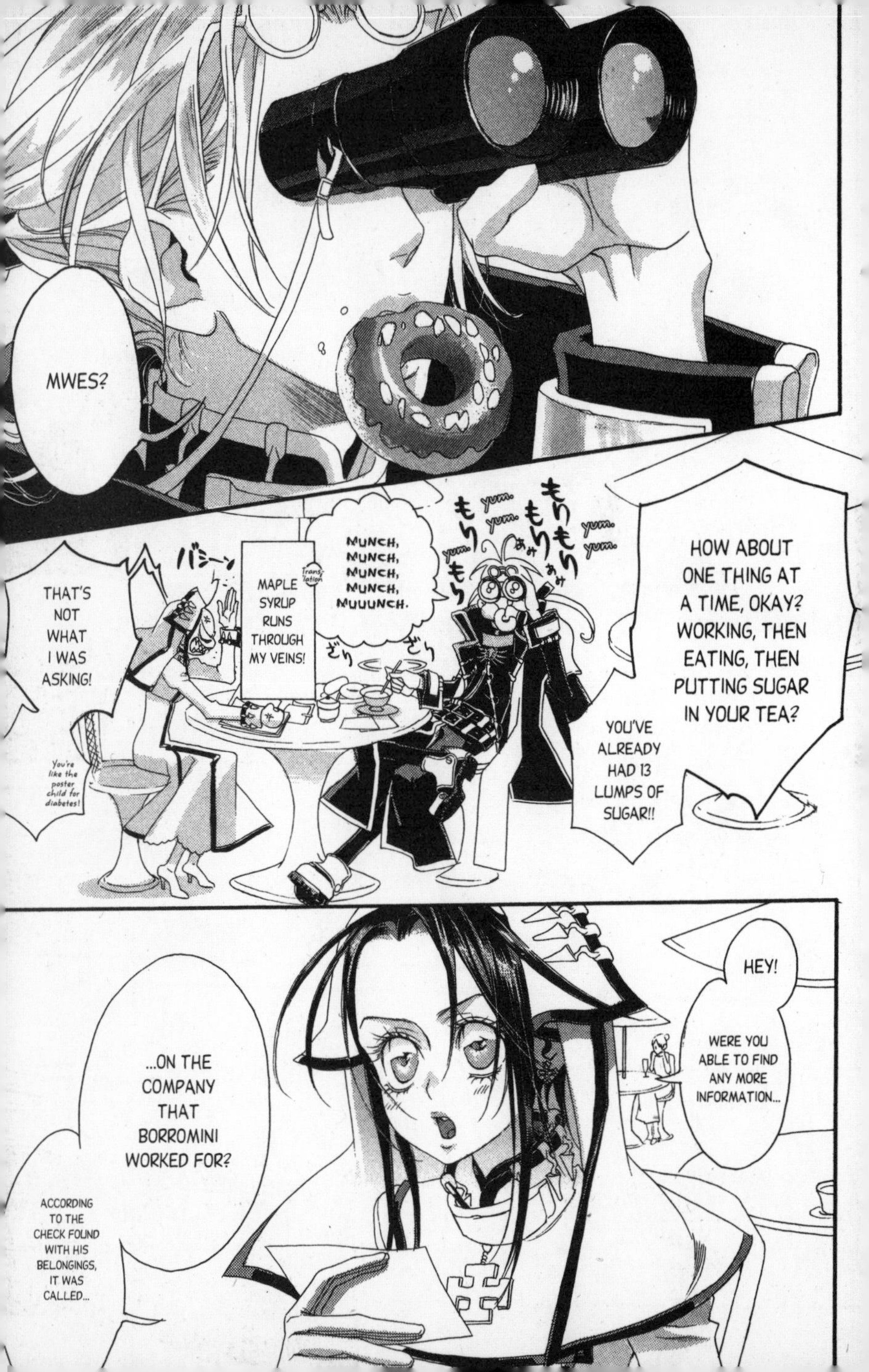
MWES?
HOW ABOUT ONE THING AT A TIME, OKAY? WORKING, THEN EATING, THEN PUTTING SUGAR IN YOUR TEA?
YOU'VE ALREADY HAD 13 LUMPS OF SUGAR!!
yum. yum.
yum. yum.
yum.
MUNCH, MUNCH, MUNCH, MUNCH, MUUUNCH.
Translation
MAPLE SYRUP RUNS THROUGH MY VEINS!
THAT'S NOT WHAT I WAS ASKING!
You're like the poster child for diabetes!
HEY!
WERE YOU ABLE TO FIND ANY MORE INFORMATION...
...ON THE COMPANY THAT BORROMINI WORKED FOR?
ACCORDING TO THE CHECK FOUND WITH HIS BELONGINGS, IT WAS CALLED...

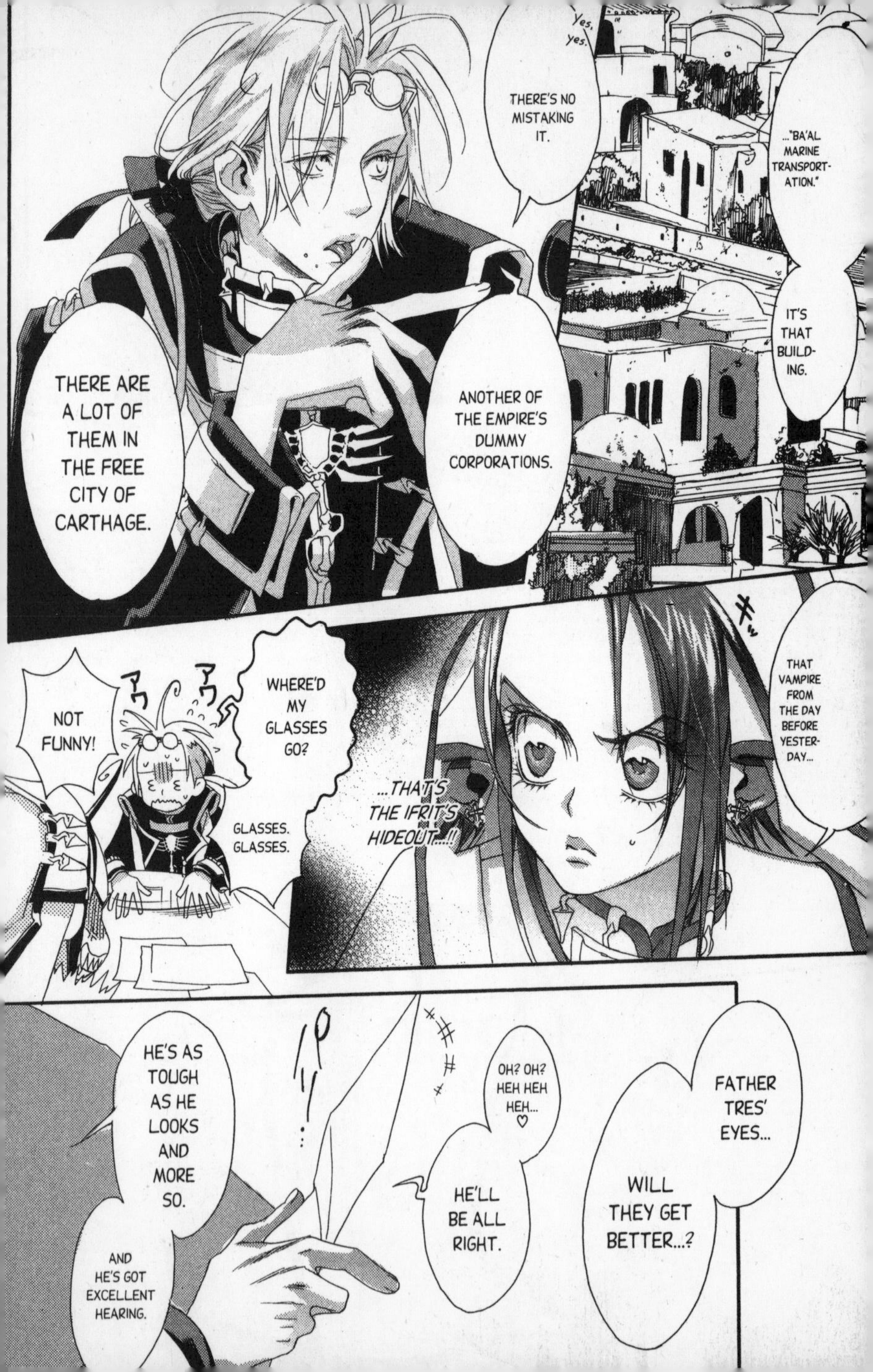
..."BA'AL MARINE TRANSPORTATION."
IT'S THAT BUILDING.
Yes, yes.
THERE'S NO MISTAKING IT.
ANOTHER OF THE EMPIRE'S DUMMY CORPORATIONS.
THERE ARE A LOT OF THEM IN THE FREE CITY OF CARTHAGE.
THAT VAMPIRE FROM THE DAY BEFORE YESTERDAY...
...THAT'S THE IFRIT'S HIDEOUT...!!
WHERE'D MY GLASSES GO?
NOT FUNNY!
GLASSES. GLASSES.
FATHER TRES' EYES...
WILL THEY GET BETTER...?
OH? OH? HEH HEH HEH... ♡
HE'LL BE ALL RIGHT.
HE'S AS TOUGH AS HE LOOKS AND MORE SO.
AND HE'S GOT EXCELLENT HEARING.

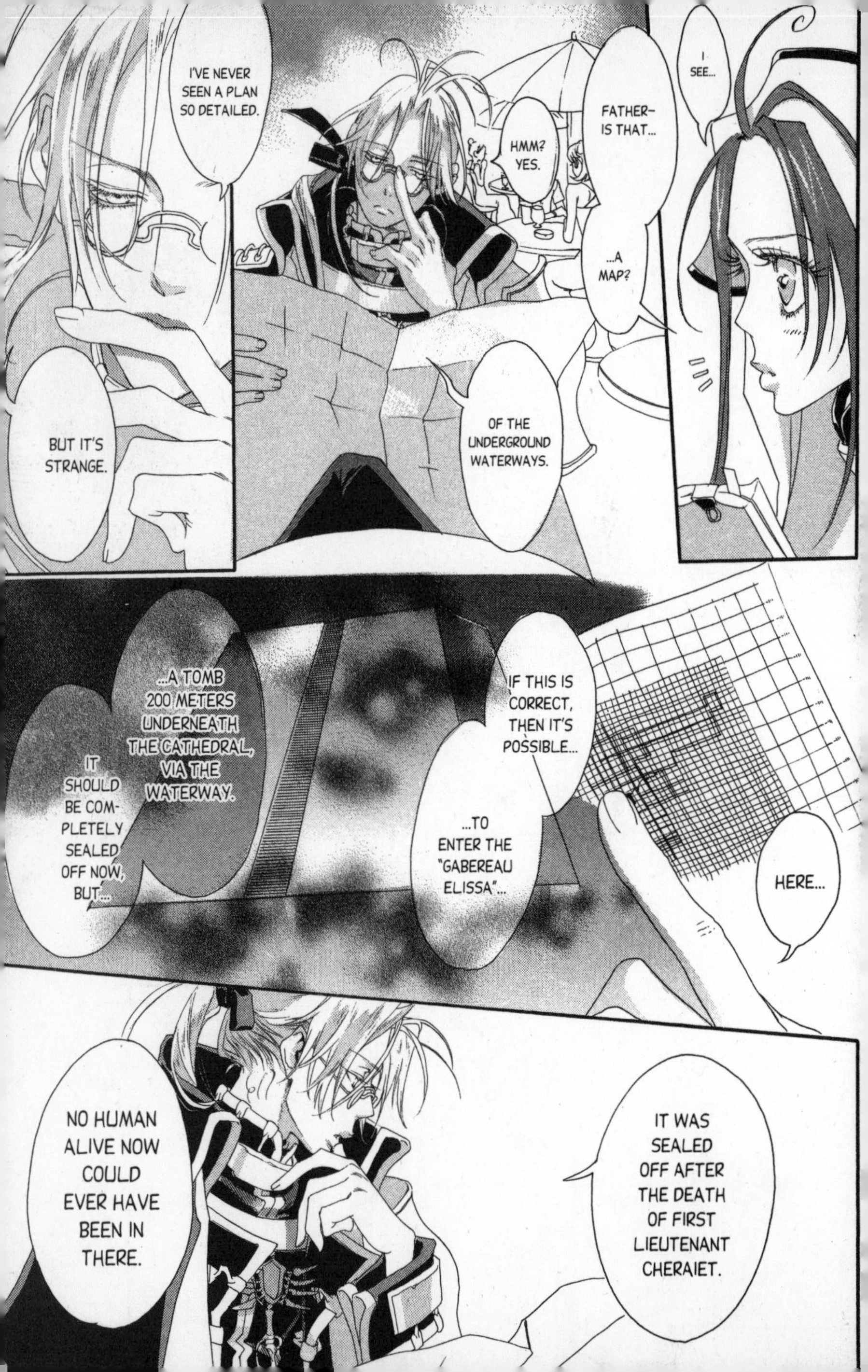
I SEE...
FATHER— IS THAT...
...A MAP?
HMM? YES.
OF THE UNDERGROUND WATERWAYS.
I'VE NEVER SEEN A PLAN SO DETAILED.
BUT IT'S STRANGE.
HERE...
IF THIS IS CORRECT, THEN IT'S POSSIBLE...
...TO ENTER THE "GABEREAU ELISSA"...
...A TOMB 200 METERS UNDERNEATH THE CATHEDRAL, VIA THE WATERWAY.
IT SHOULD BE COMPLETELY SEALED OFF NOW, BUT...
IT WAS SEALED OFF AFTER THE DEATH OF FIRST LIEUTENANT CHERAIET.
NO HUMAN ALIVE NOW COULD EVER HAVE BEEN IN THERE.

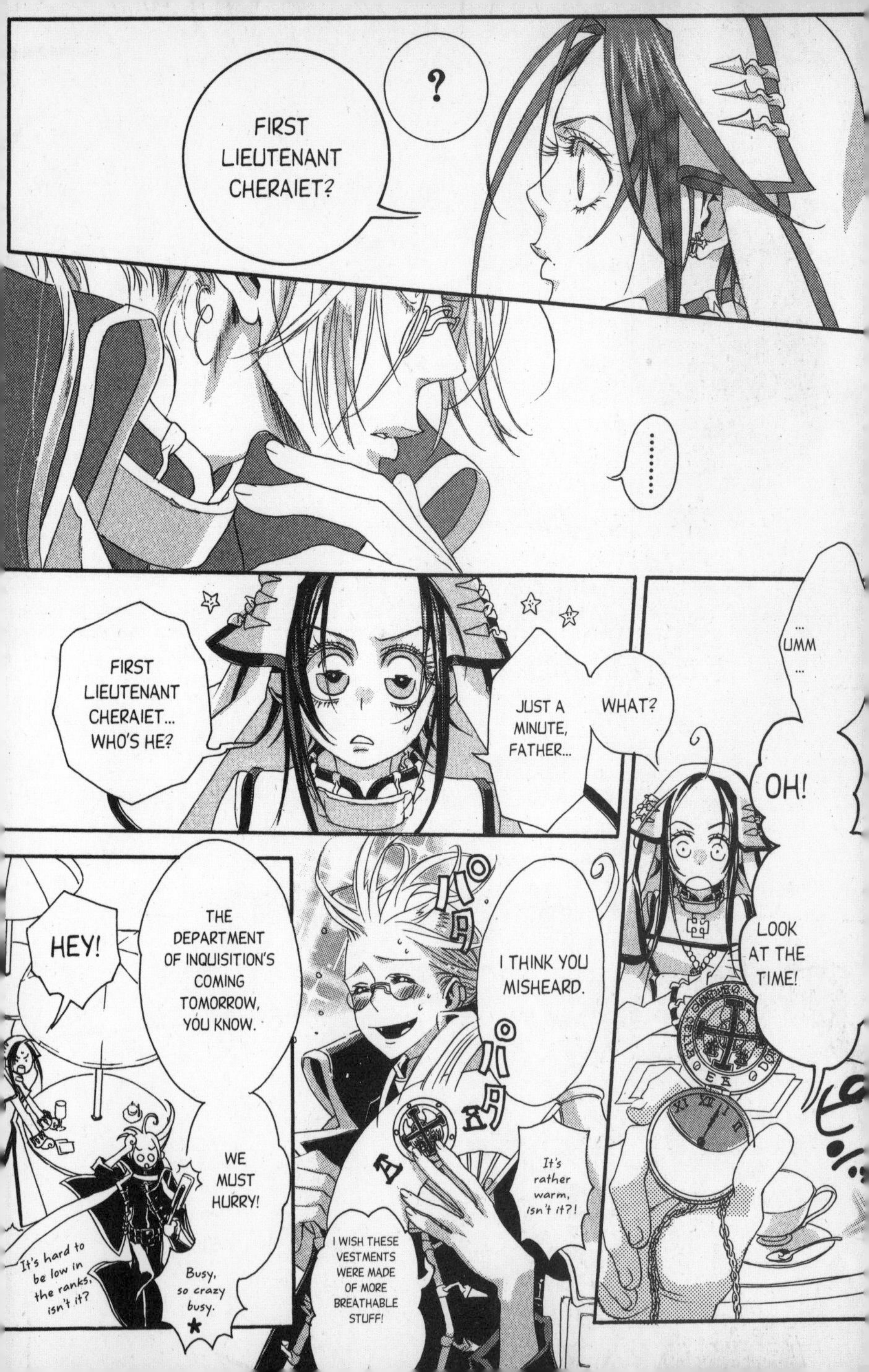
?
FIRST LIEUTENANT CHERAIET?
……
... UMM ...
OH!
LOOK AT THE TIME!
WHAT?
JUST A MINUTE, FATHER...
FIRST LIEUTENANT CHERAIET... WHO'S HE?
パタ
I THINK YOU MISHEARD.
パタ
It's rather warm, isn't it?!
I WISH THESE VESTMENTS WERE MADE OF MORE BREATHABLE STUFF!
THE DEPARTMENT OF INQUISITION'S COMING TOMORROW, YOU KNOW.
HEY!
WE MUST HURRY!
Busy, so crazy busy.
It's hard to be low in the ranks, isn't it?

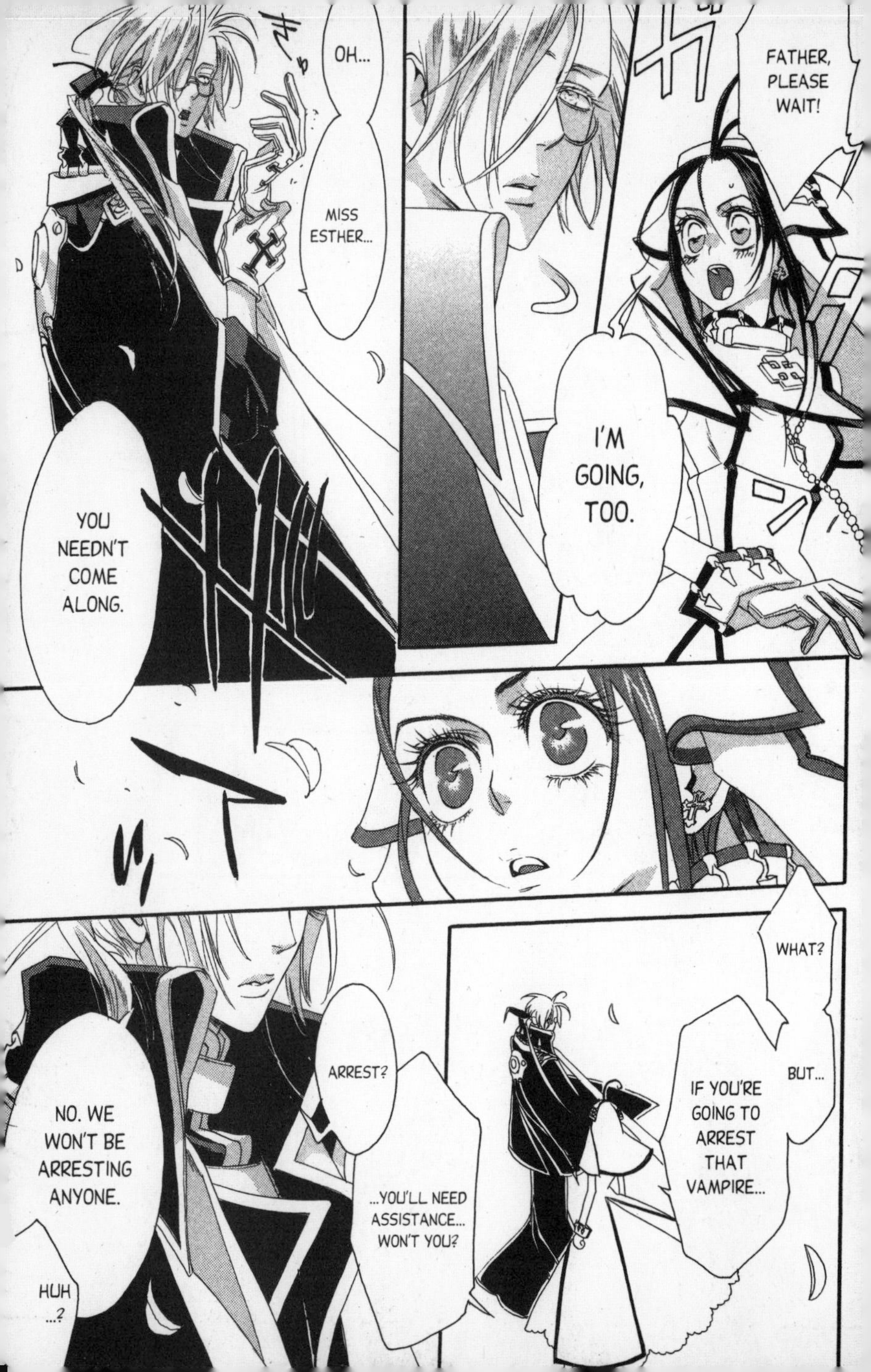
FATHER, PLEASE WAIT!
I'M GOING, TOO.
OH...
MISS ESTHER...
YOU NEEDN'T COME ALONG.
WHAT?
BUT...
IF YOU'RE GOING TO ARREST THAT VAMPIRE...
...YOU'LL NEED ASSISTANCE... WON'T YOU?
ARREST?
NO. WE WON'T BE ARRESTING ANYONE.
HUH...?

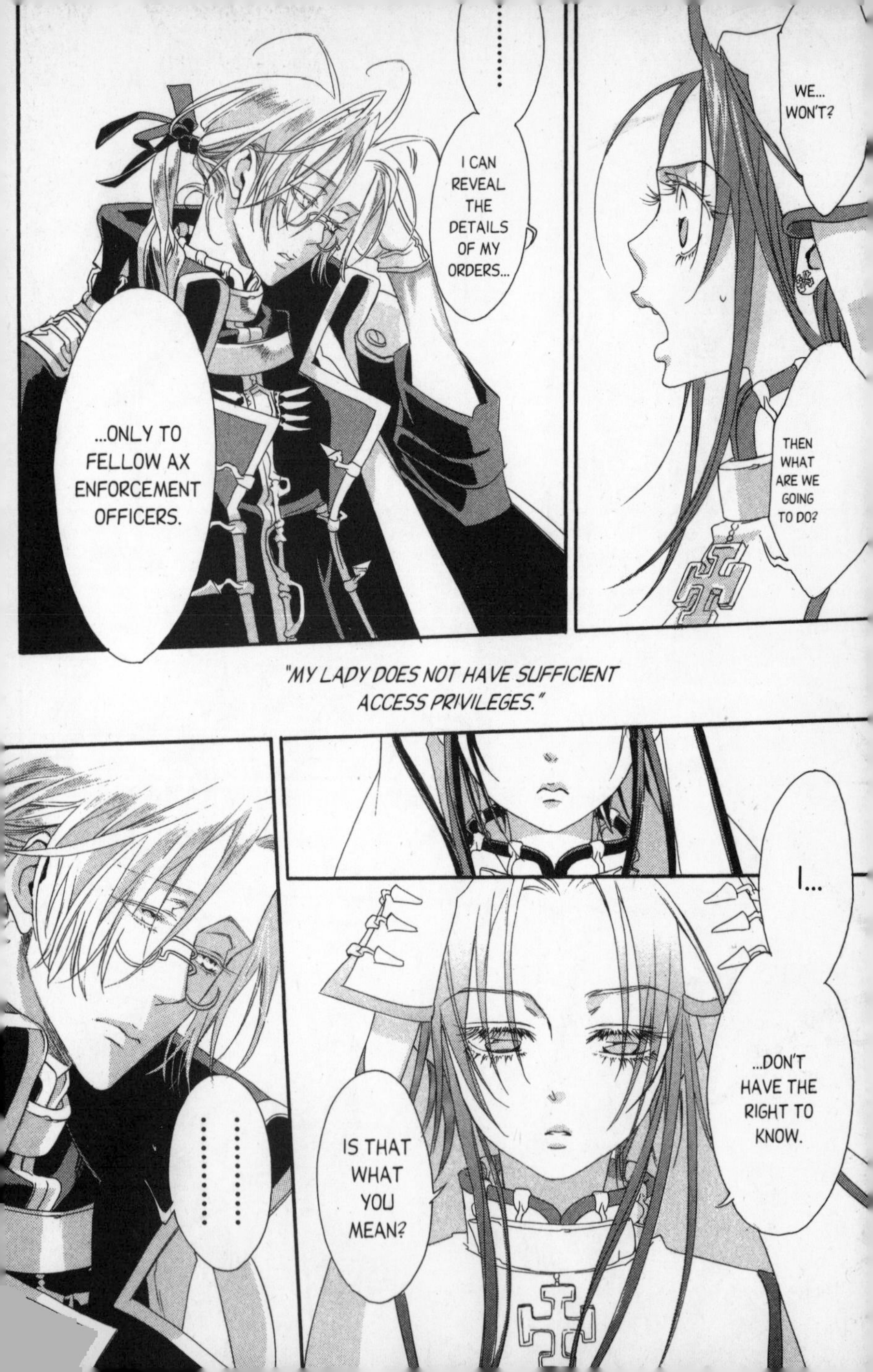
WE... WON'T?
THEN WHAT ARE WE GOING TO DO?
......
I CAN REVEAL THE DETAILS OF MY ORDERS...
...ONLY TO FELLOW AX ENFORCEMENT OFFICERS.
"MY LADY DOES NOT HAVE SUFFICIENT ACCESS PRIVILEGES."
I...
...DON'T HAVE THE RIGHT TO KNOW.
IS THAT WHAT YOU MEAN?
......

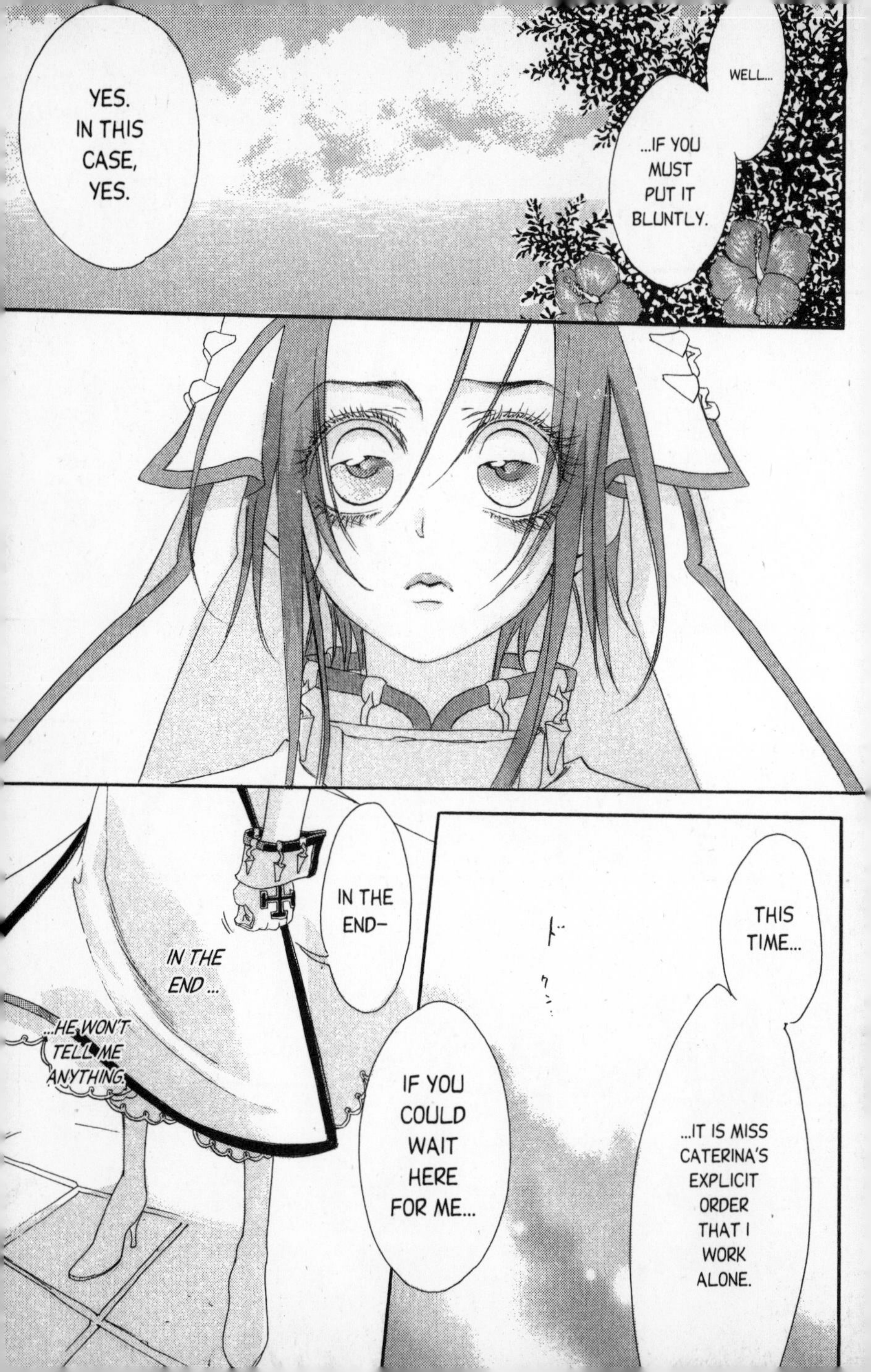
WELL...
...IF YOU MUST PUT IT BLUNTLY.
YES. IN THIS CASE, YES.
THIS TIME...
...IT IS MISS CATERINA'S EXPLICIT ORDER THAT I WORK ALONE.
IF YOU COULD WAIT HERE FOR ME...
IN THE END—
IN THE END ...
...HE WON'T TELL ME ANYTHING.

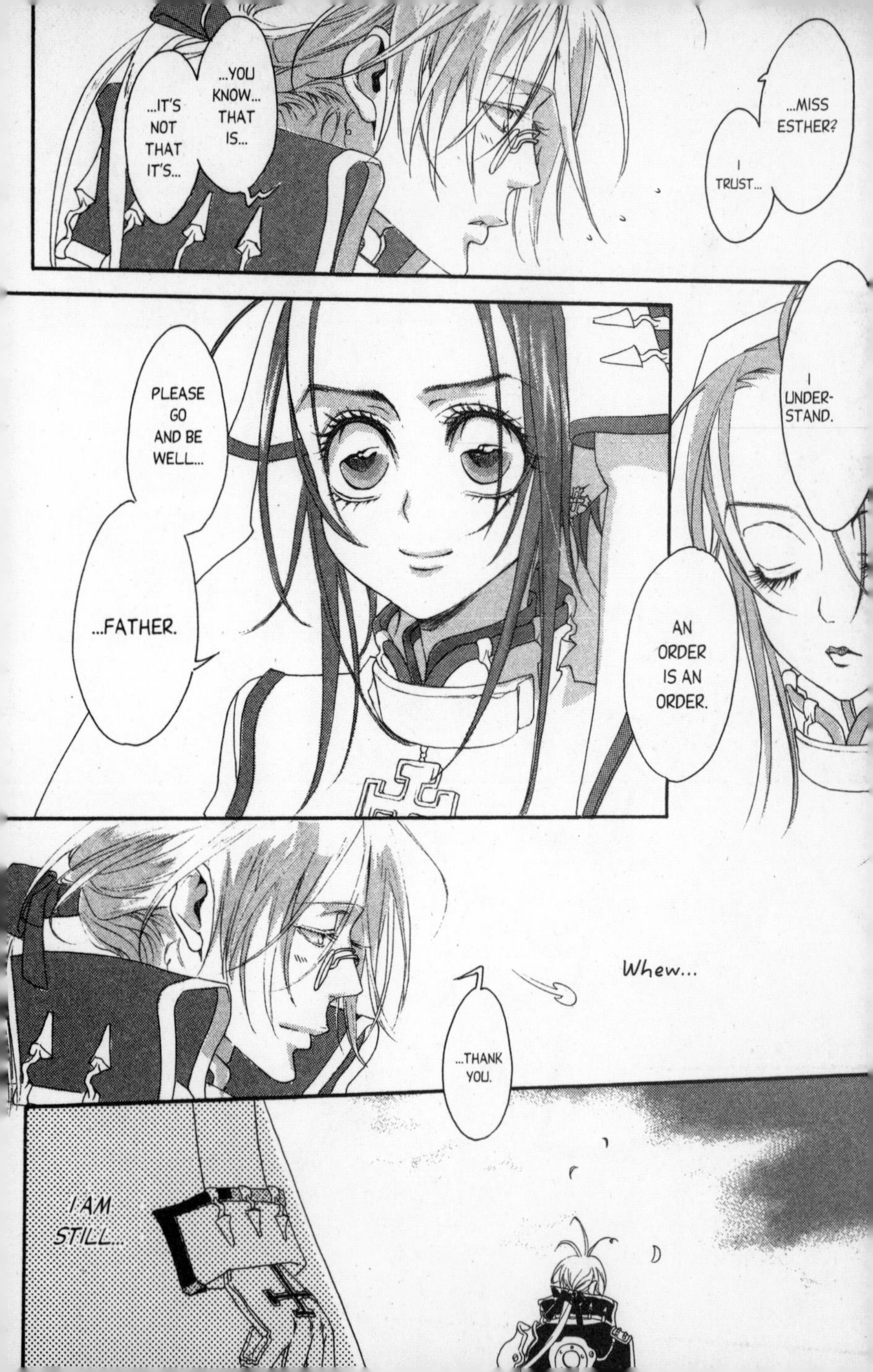
...MISS ESTHER?
I TRUST...
...YOU KNOW... THAT IS...
...IT'S NOT THAT IT'S...
I UNDER-STAND.
AN ORDER IS AN ORDER.
PLEASE GO AND BE WELL...
...FATHER.
Whew...
...THANK YOU.
I AM STILL...

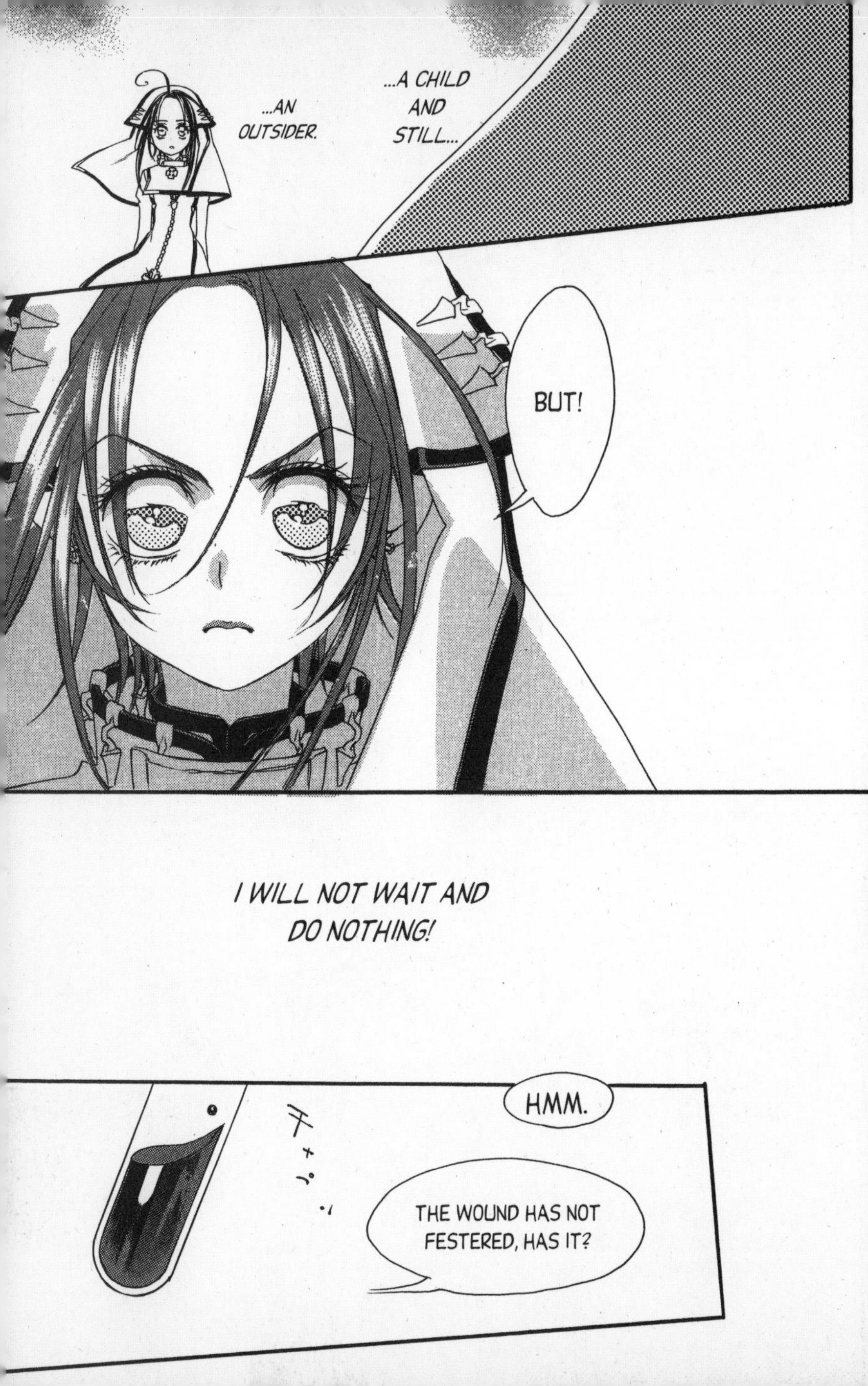
...A CHILD AND STILL...
...AN OUTSIDER.
BUT!
I WILL NOT WAIT AND DO NOTHING!
HMM.
THE WOUND HAS NOT FESTERED, HAS IT?

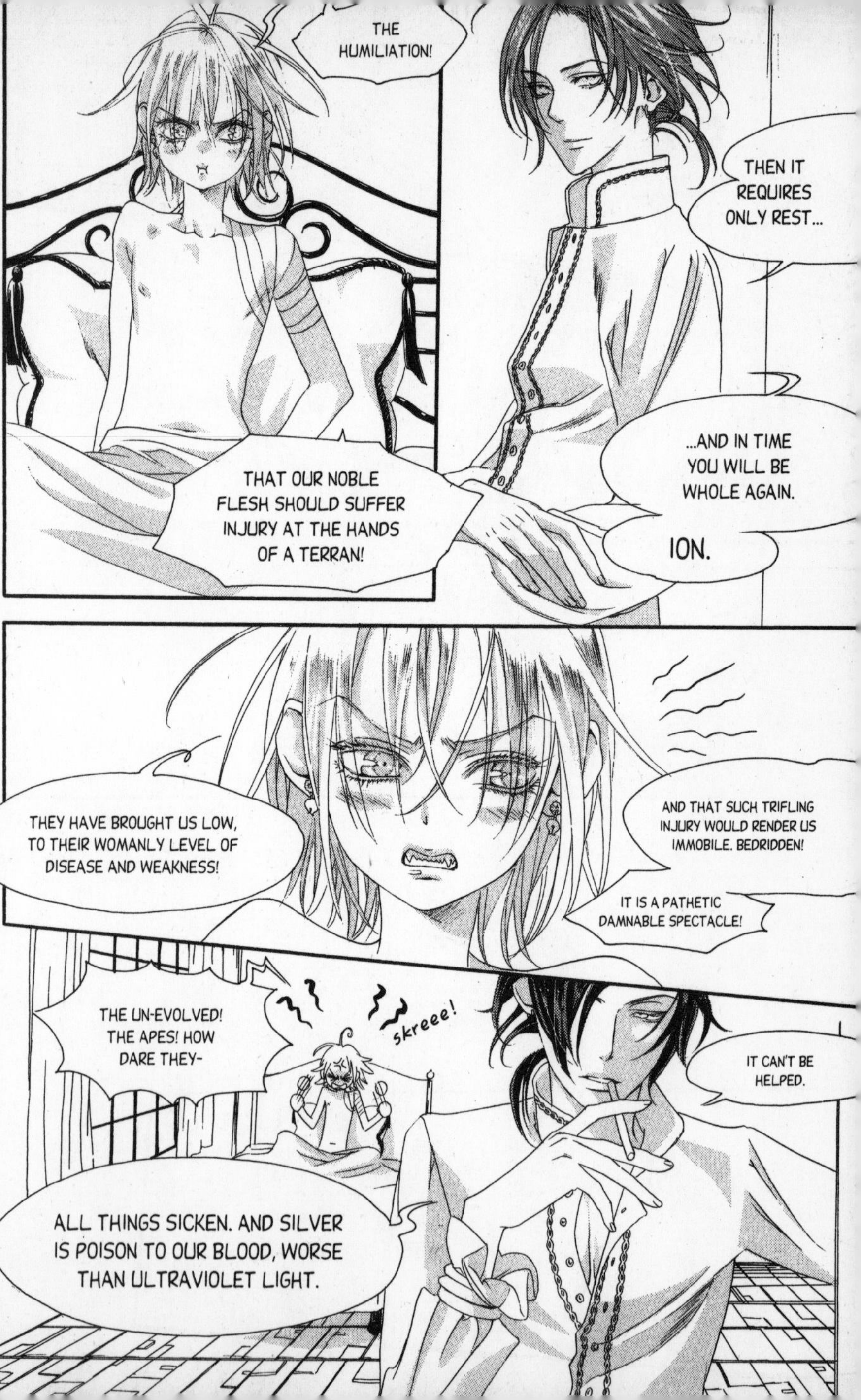
THE HUMILIATION!
THEN IT REQUIRES ONLY REST...
...AND IN TIME YOU WILL BE WHOLE AGAIN.
ION.
THAT OUR NOBLE FLESH SHOULD SUFFER INJURY AT THE HANDS OF A TERRAN!
AND THAT SUCH TRIFLING INJURY WOULD RENDER US IMMOBILE. BEDRIDDEN!
IT IS A PATHETIC DAMNABLE SPECTACLE!
THEY HAVE BROUGHT US LOW, TO THEIR WOMANLY LEVEL OF DISEASE AND WEAKNESS!
IT CAN'T BE HELPED.
skreee!
THE UN-EVOLVED! THE APES! HOW DARE THEY-
ALL THINGS SICKEN. AND SILVER IS POISON TO OUR BLOOD, WORSE THAN ULTRAVIOLET LIGHT.

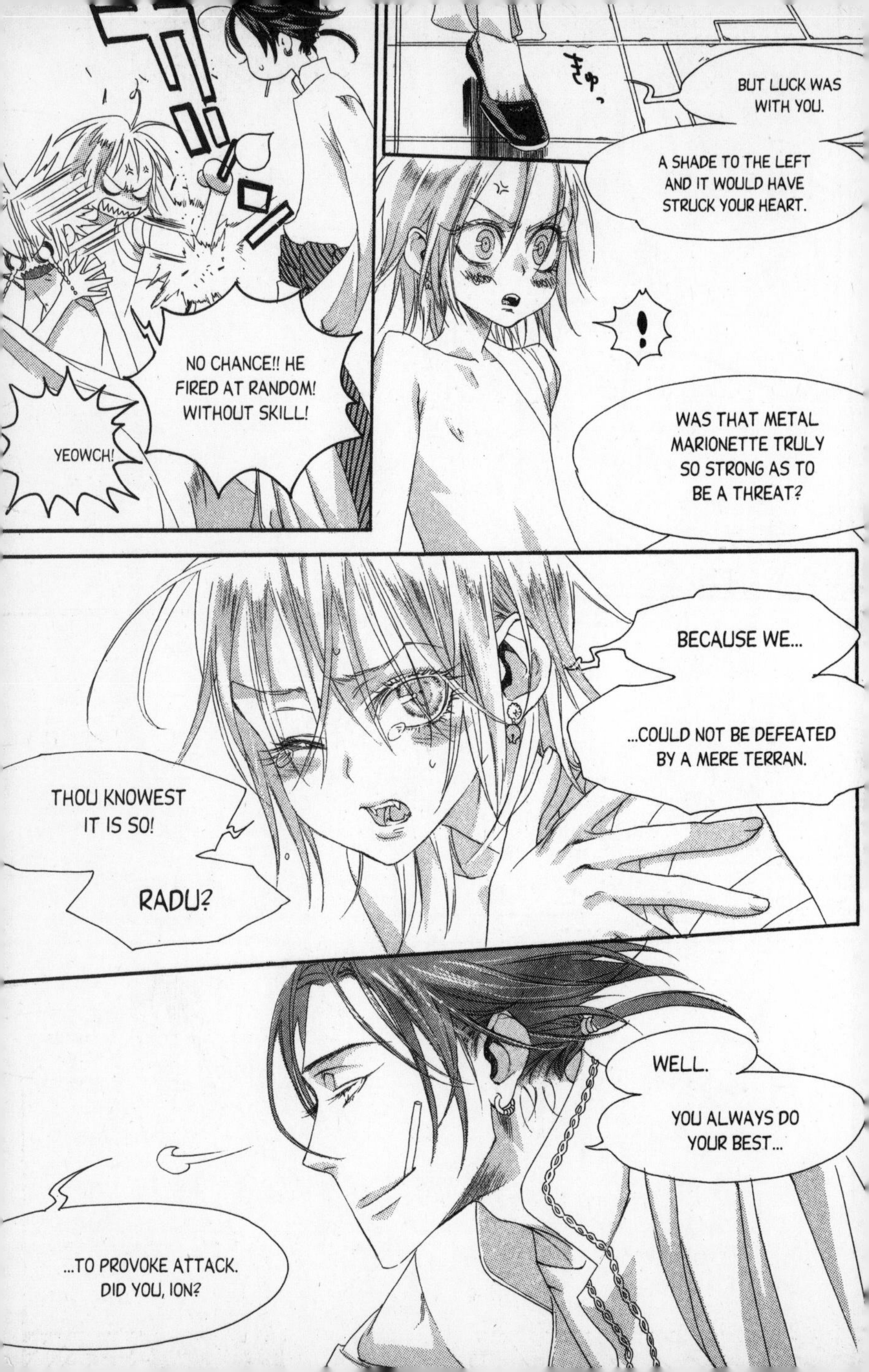
きゅっ
BUT LUCK WAS WITH YOU.
A SHADE TO THE LEFT AND IT WOULD HAVE STRUCK YOUR HEART.
!
WAS THAT METAL MARIONETTE TRULY SO STRONG AS TO BE A THREAT?
NO CHANCE!! HE FIRED AT RANDOM! WITHOUT SKILL!
YEOWCH!
BECAUSE WE...
...COULD NOT BE DEFEATED BY A MERE TERRAN.
THOU KNOWEST IT IS SO!
RADU?
WELL.
YOU ALWAYS DO YOUR BEST...
...TO PROVOKE ATTACK. DID YOU, ION?

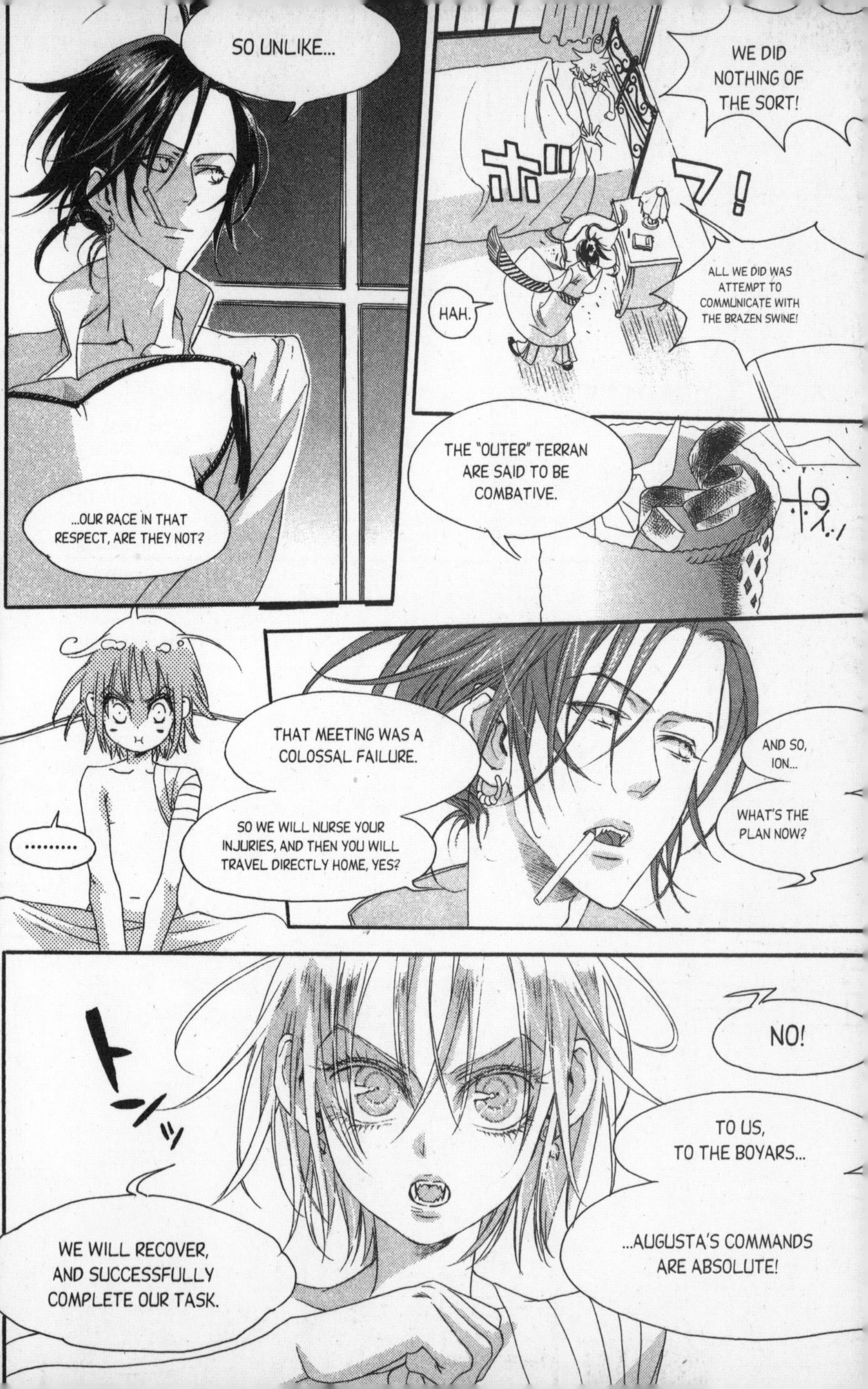
WE DID NOTHING OF THE SORT!
ALL WE DID WAS ATTEMPT TO COMMUNICATE WITH THE BRAZEN SWINE!
HAH.
THE "OUTER" TERRAN ARE SAID TO BE COMBATIVE.
SO UNLIKE...
...OUR RACE IN THAT RESPECT, ARE THEY NOT?
AND SO, ION...
WHAT'S THE PLAN NOW?
THAT MEETING WAS A COLOSSAL FAILURE.
SO WE WILL NURSE YOUR INJURIES, AND THEN YOU WILL TRAVEL DIRECTLY HOME, YES?
....
NO!
TO US, TO THE BOYARS...
...AUGUSTA'S COMMANDS ARE ABSOLUTE!
WE WILL RECOVER, AND SUCCESSFULLY COMPLETE OUR TASK.

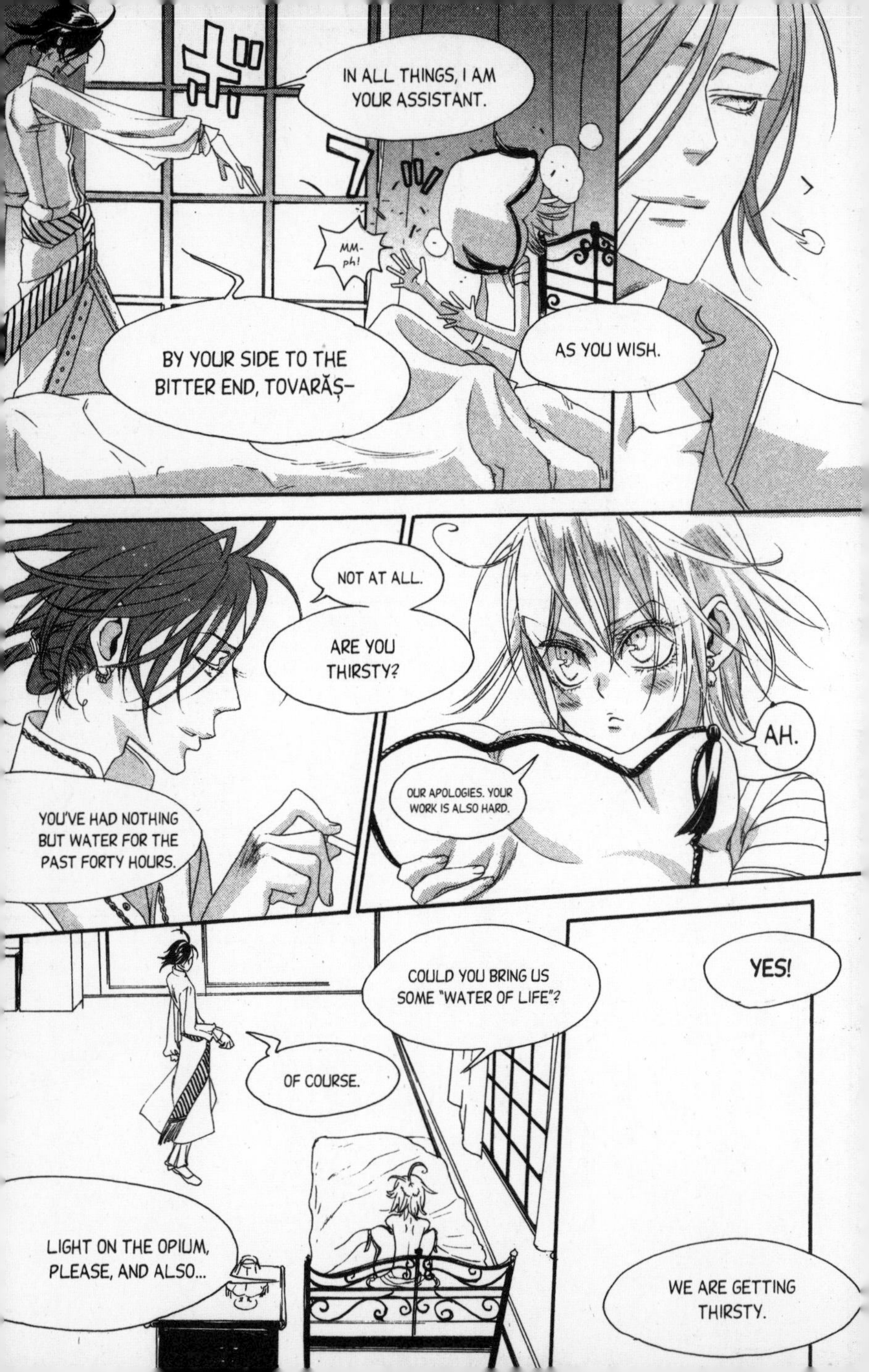
AS YOU WISH.
IN ALL THINGS, I AM YOUR ASSISTANT.
MM-ph!
BY YOUR SIDE TO THE BITTER END, TOVARĂȘ–
AH.
OUR APOLOGIES. YOUR WORK IS ALSO HARD.
NOT AT ALL.
ARE YOU THIRSTY?
YOU'VE HAD NOTHING BUT WATER FOR THE PAST FORTY HOURS.
YES!
WE ARE GETTING THIRSTY.
COULD YOU BRING US SOME "WATER OF LIFE"?
OF COURSE.
LIGHT ON THE OPIUM, PLEASE, AND ALSO...

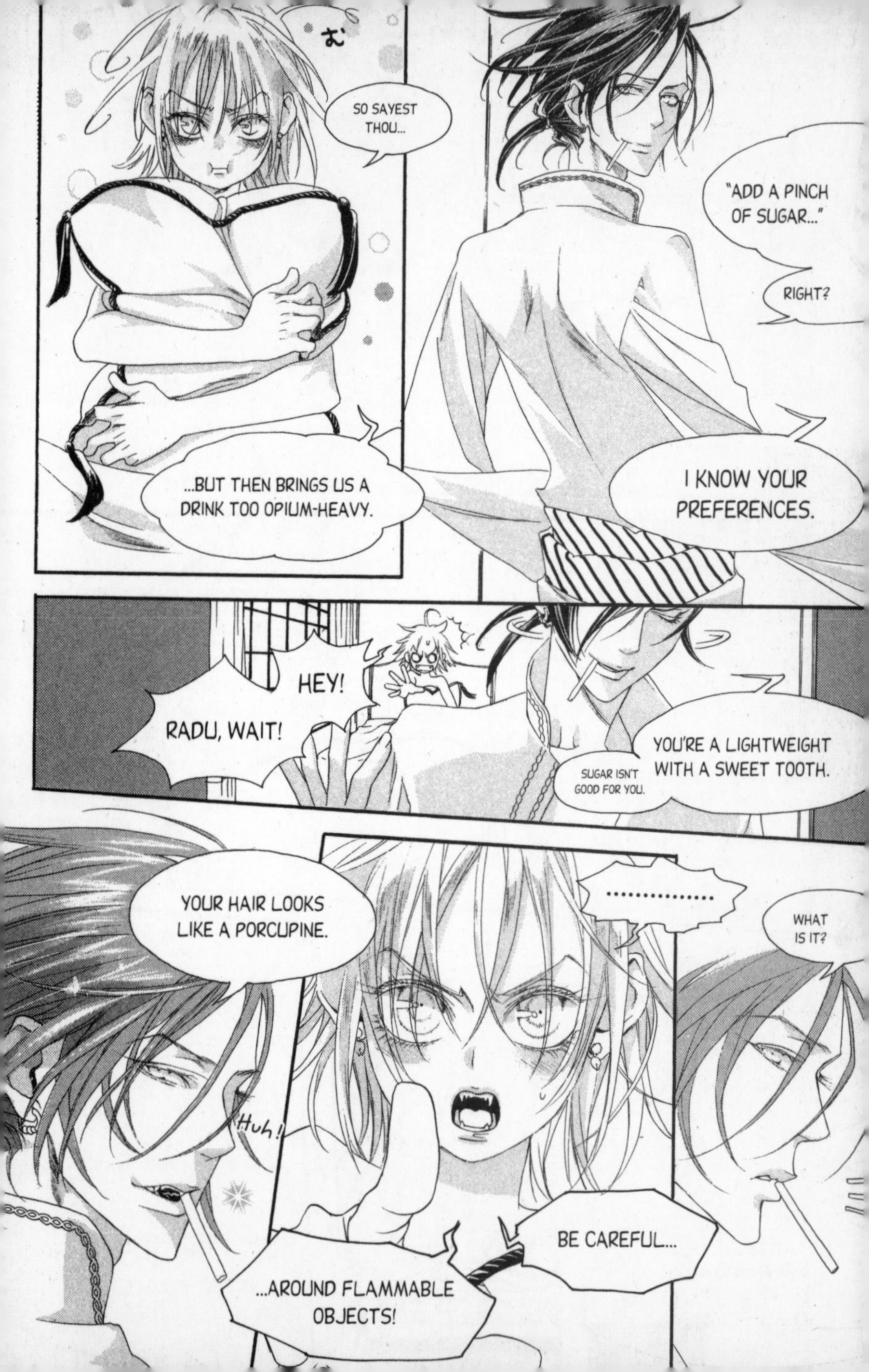
"ADD A PINCH OF SUGAR..."
RIGHT?
I KNOW YOUR PREFERENCES.
む
SO SAYEST THOU...
...BUT THEN BRINGS US A DRINK TOO OPIUM-HEAVY.
YOU'RE A LIGHTWEIGHT WITH A SWEET TOOTH.
SUGAR ISN'T GOOD FOR YOU.
HEY!
RADU, WAIT!
WHAT IS IT?
....
BE CAREFUL...
...AROUND FLAMMABLE OBJECTS!
YOUR HAIR LOOKS LIKE A PORCUPINE.
Huh!

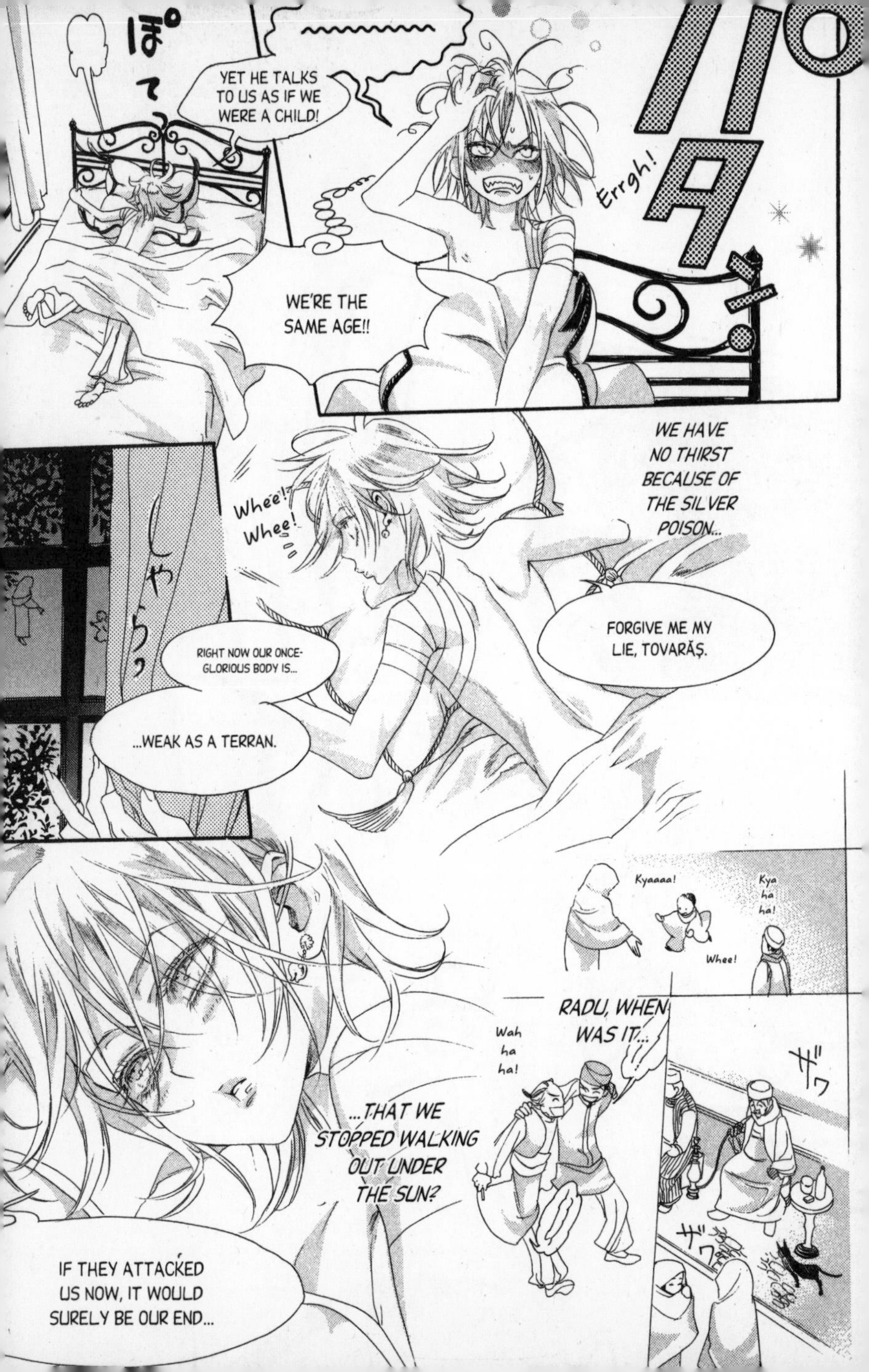
パタ
Errgh!
~~~~~~
YET HE TALKS TO US AS IF WE WERE A CHILD!
WE'RE THE SAME AGE!!
ぽて
WE HAVE NO THIRST BECAUSE OF THE SILVER POISON...
Whee! Whee!
FORGIVE ME MY LIE, TOVARĂȘ.
RIGHT NOW OUR ONCE-GLORIOUS BODY IS...
...WEAK AS A TERRAN.
しゃら
Kya ha ha!
Kyaaaa!
Whee!
ザワ
ザワ
RADU, WHEN WAS IT...
Wah ha ha!
...THAT WE STOPPED WALKING OUT UNDER THE SUN?
IF THEY ATTACKED US NOW, IT WOULD SURELY BE OUR END...
~~~~~~

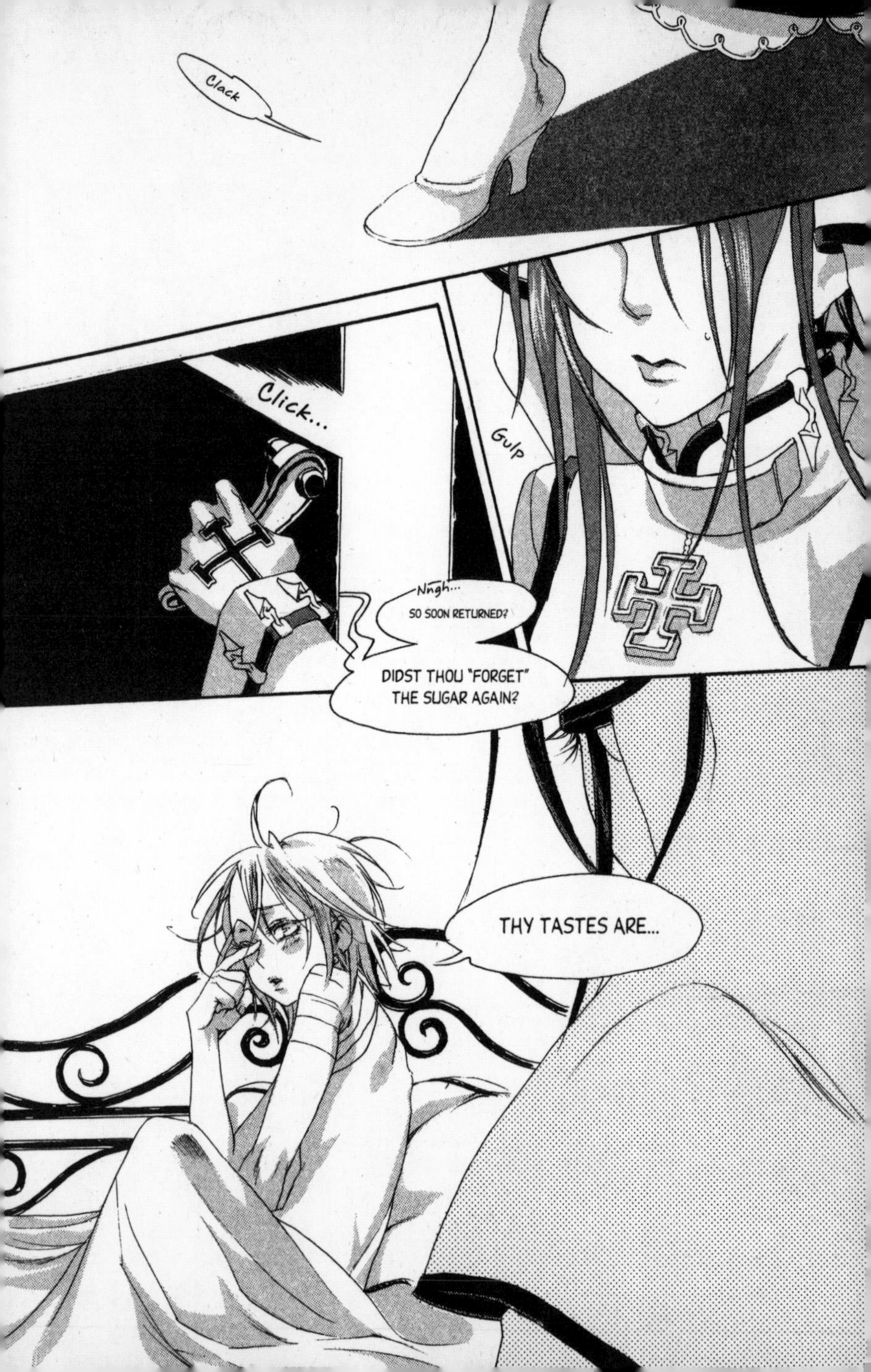

Clack
Gulp
Click...
Nngh...
SO SOON RETURNED?
DIDST THOU "FORGET" THE SUGAR AGAIN?
THY TASTES ARE...

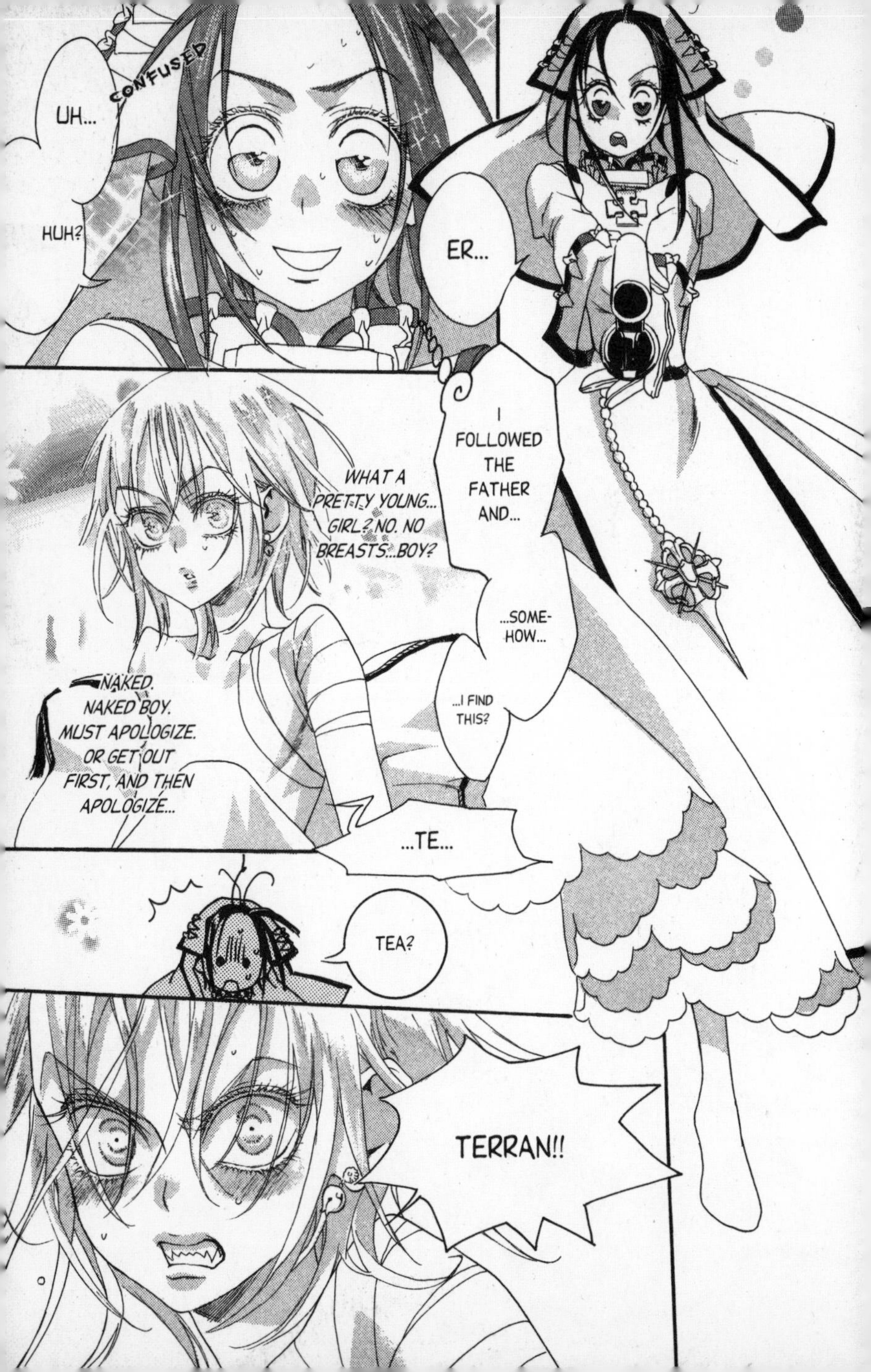
ER...
I FOLLOWED THE FATHER AND...
...SOME-HOW...
...I FIND THIS?
UH...
CONFUSED
HUH?
WHAT A PRETTY YOUNG... GIRL? NO. NO BREASTS...BOY?
NAKED. NAKED BOY. MUST APOLOGIZE. OR GET OUT FIRST, AND THEN APOLOGIZE...
...TE...
TEA?
TERRAN!!

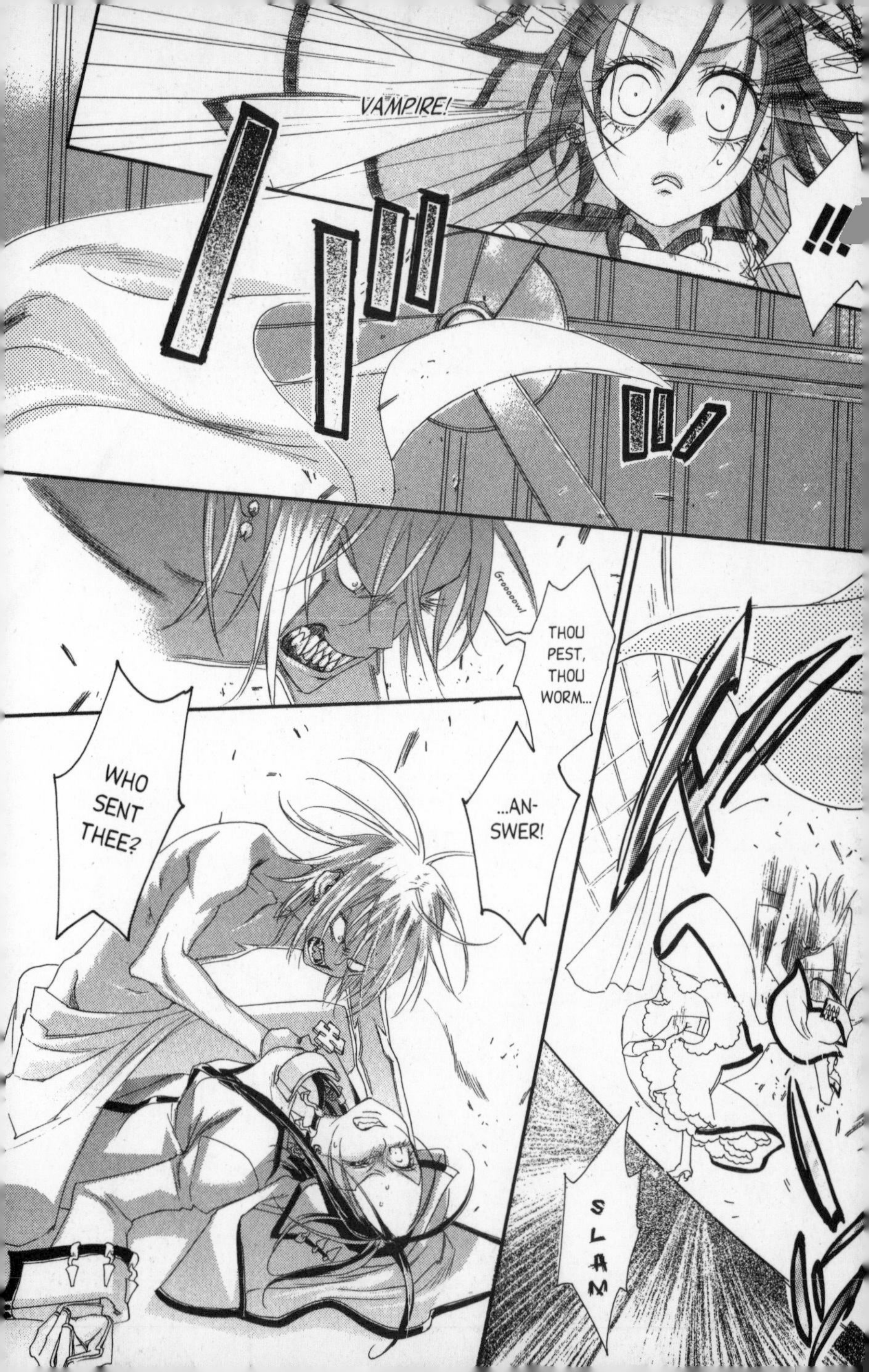
VAMPIRE!
!!
S L A M
Grooooowl
THOU PEST, THOU WORM...
...AN-SWER!
WHO SENT THEE?

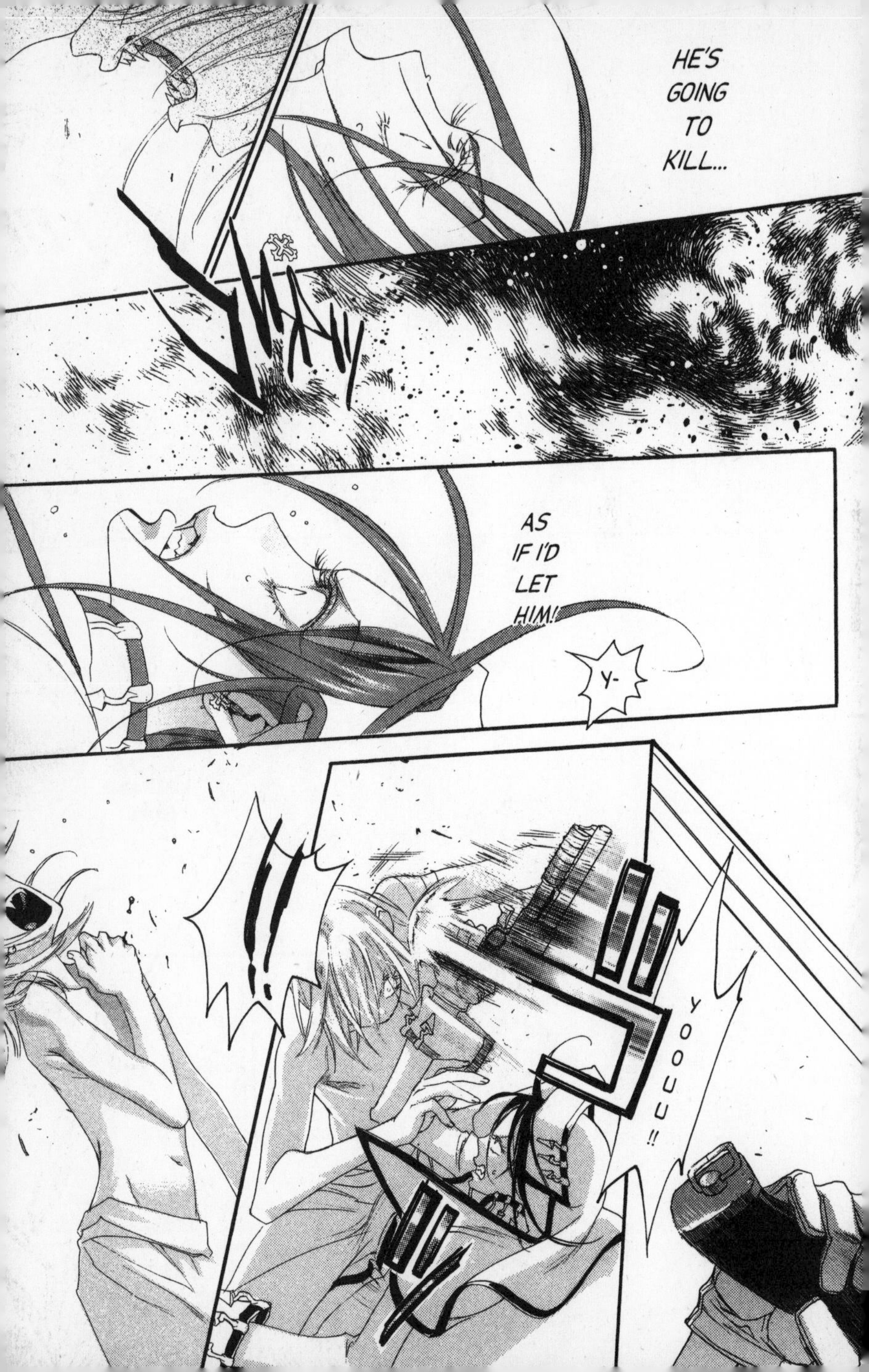
HE'S GOING TO KILL...
AS IF I'D LET HIM!
Y-
!!
YOOUUU!!

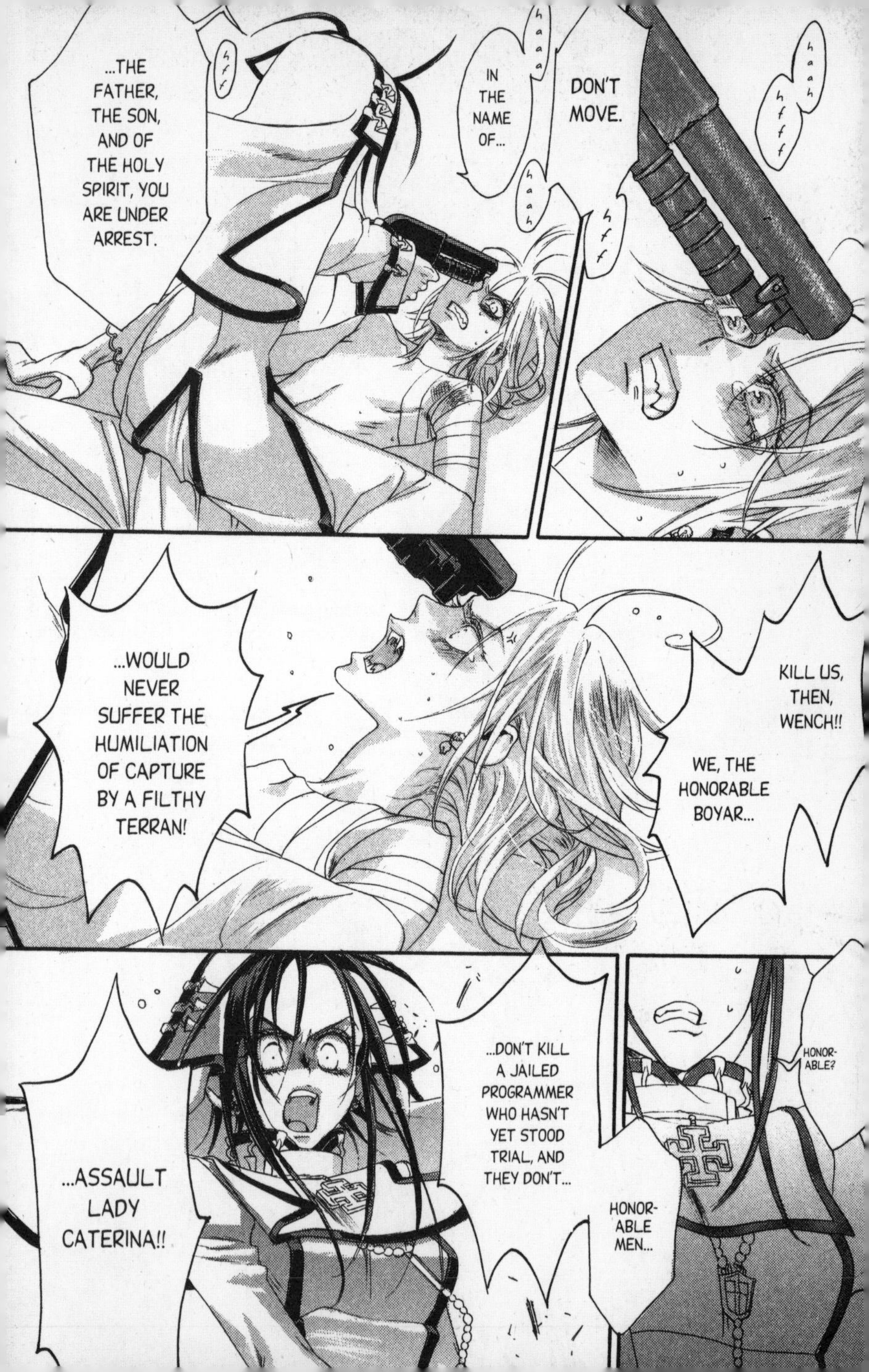
haah hfff
hff
DON'T MOVE.
haaa
IN THE NAME OF...
haah
hff
...THE FATHER, THE SON, AND OF THE HOLY SPIRIT, YOU ARE UNDER ARREST.
KILL US, THEN, WENCH!!
WE, THE HONORABLE BOYAR...
...WOULD NEVER SUFFER THE HUMILIATION OF CAPTURE BY A FILTHY TERRAN!
HONOR-ABLE?
HONOR-ABLE MEN...
...DON'T KILL A JAILED PROGRAMMER WHO HASN'T YET STOOD TRIAL, AND THEY DON'T...
...ASSAULT LADY CATERINA!!

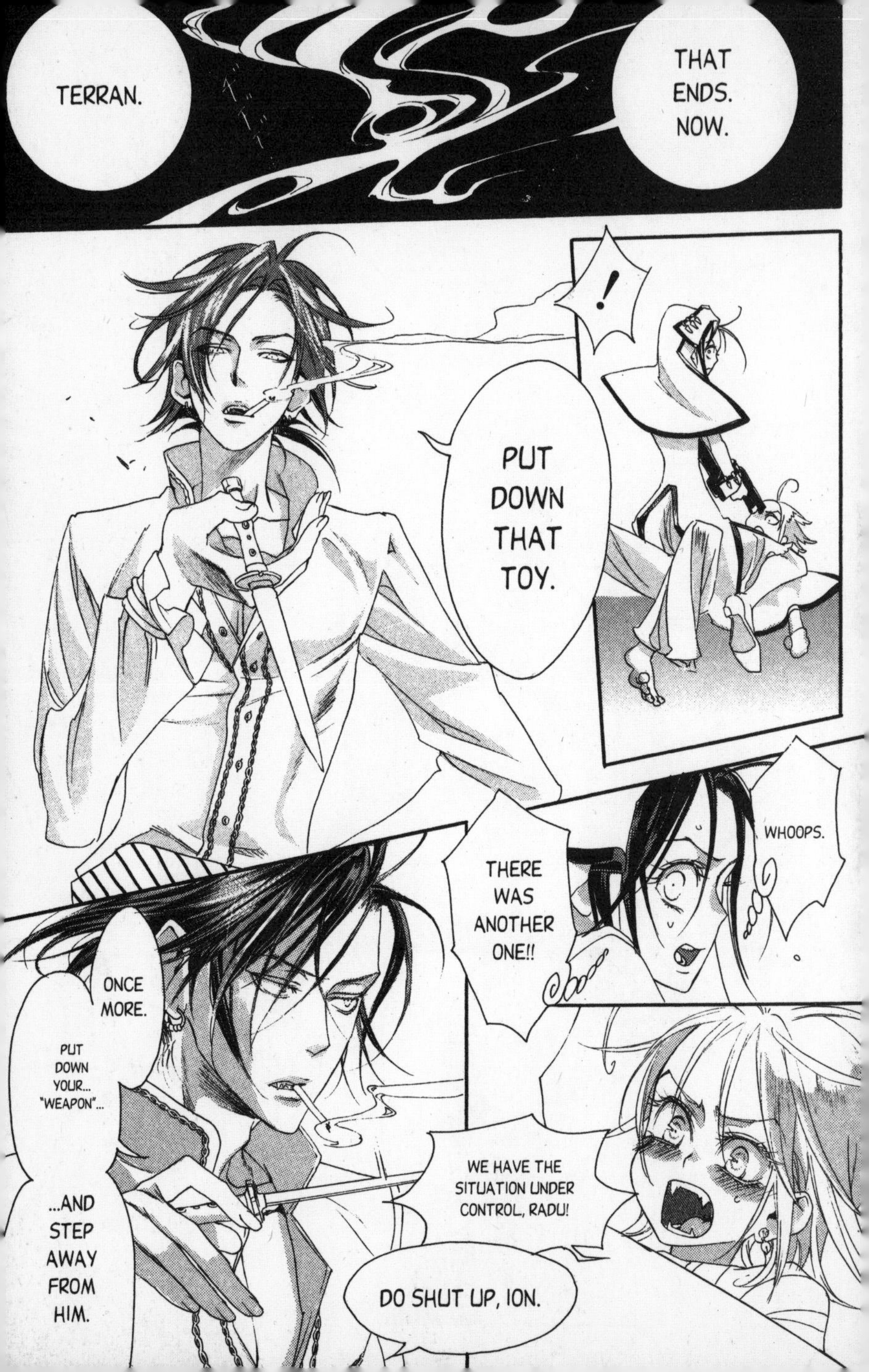
THAT ENDS. NOW.
TERRAN.
!
PUT DOWN THAT TOY.
WHOOPS.
THERE WAS ANOTHER ONE!!
WE HAVE THE SITUATION UNDER CONTROL, RADU!
DO SHUT UP, ION.
ONCE MORE.
PUT DOWN YOUR... "WEAPON"...
...AND STEP AWAY FROM HIM.

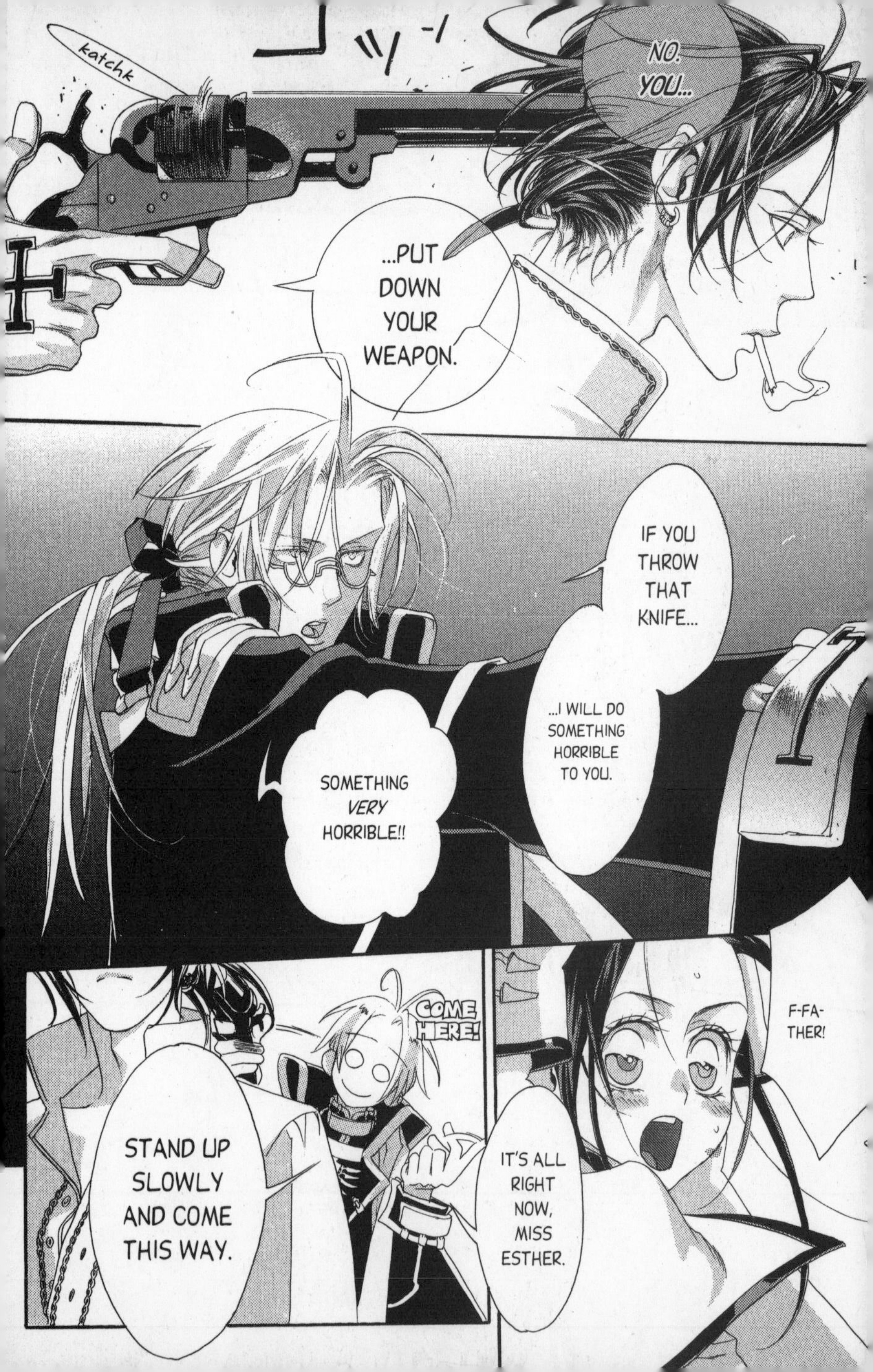
NO. YOU...
katchk
...PUT DOWN YOUR WEAPON.
IF YOU THROW THAT KNIFE...
...I WILL DO SOMETHING HORRIBLE TO YOU.
SOMETHING *VERY* HORRIBLE!!
F-FA-THER!
IT'S ALL RIGHT NOW, MISS ESTHER.
COME HERE!
STAND UP SLOWLY AND COME THIS WAY.

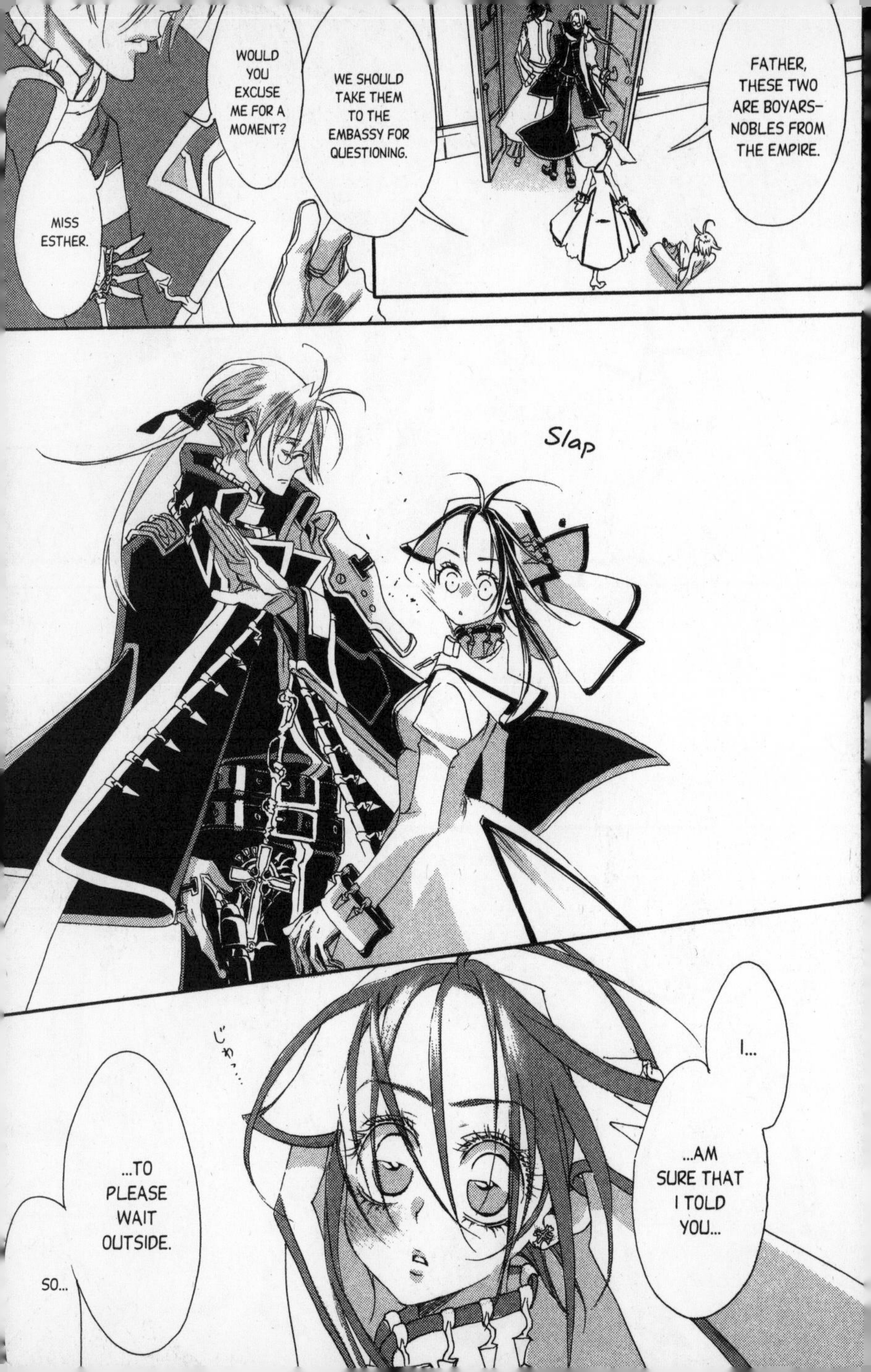
FATHER, THESE TWO ARE BOYARS— NOBLES FROM THE EMPIRE.
WE SHOULD TAKE THEM TO THE EMBASSY FOR QUESTIONING.
WOULD YOU EXCUSE ME FOR A MOMENT?
MISS ESTHER.
Slap
I...
...AM SURE THAT I TOLD YOU...
じわっ…
...TO PLEASE WAIT OUTSIDE.
SO...

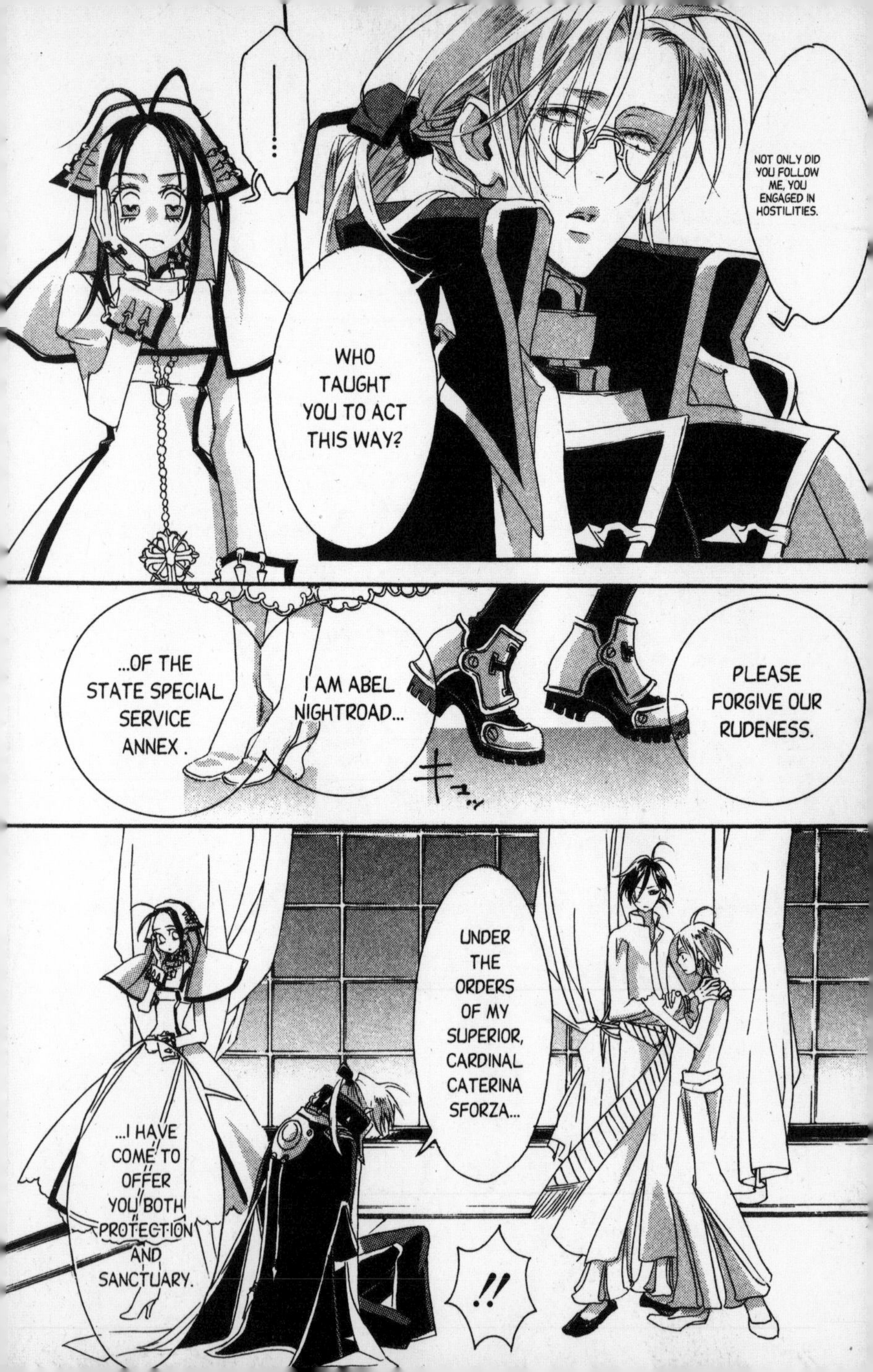
NOT ONLY DID YOU FOLLOW ME, YOU ENGAGED IN HOSTILITIES.
WHO TAUGHT YOU TO ACT THIS WAY?
……
PLEASE FORGIVE OUR RUDENESS.
キュッ
I AM ABEL NIGHTROAD...
...OF THE STATE SPECIAL SERVICE ANNEX .
UNDER THE ORDERS OF MY SUPERIOR, CARDINAL CATERINA SFORZA...
!!
...I HAVE COME TO OFFER YOU BOTH PROTECTION AND SANCTUARY.

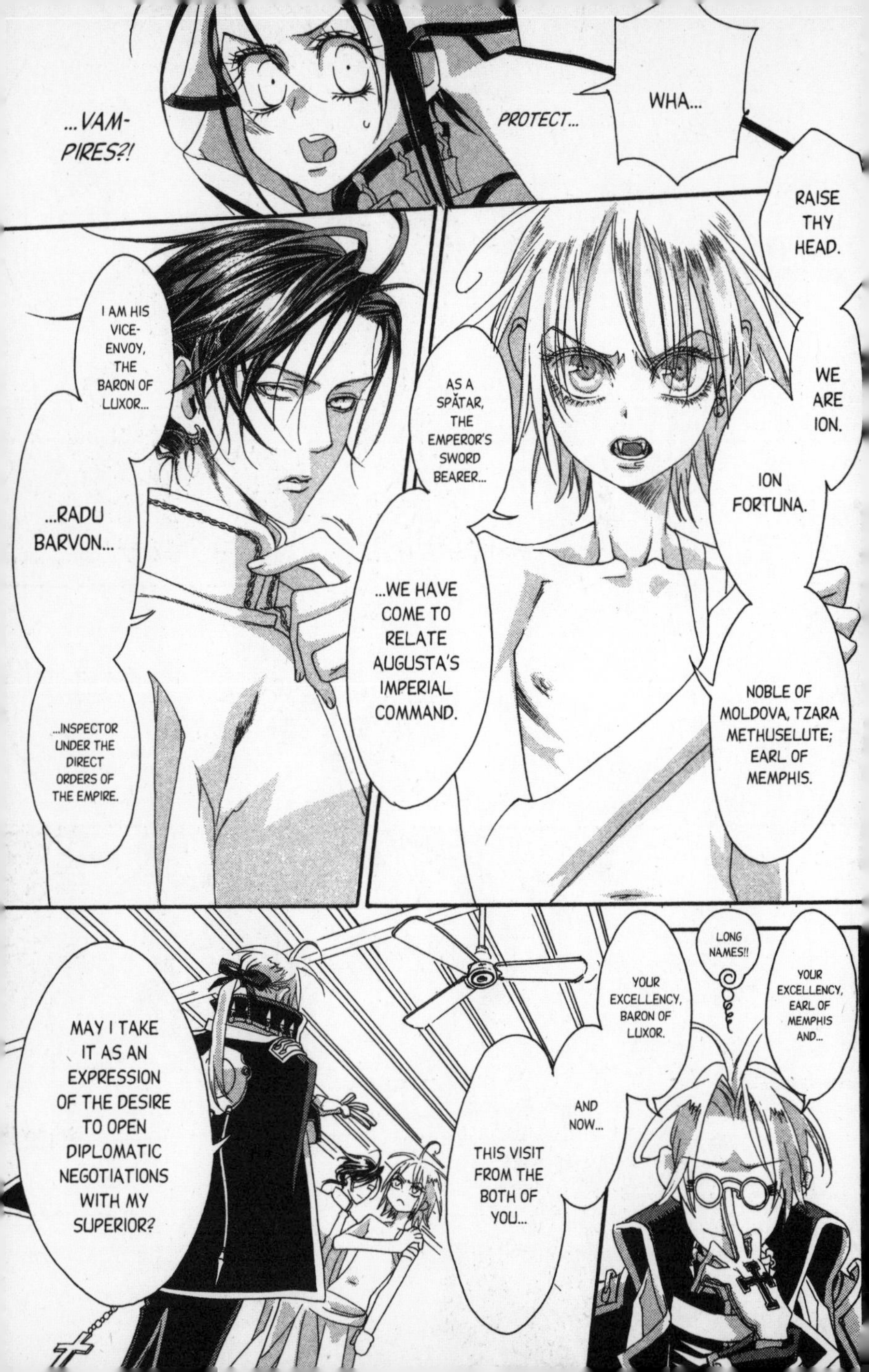
WHA...
PROTECT...
...VAM-PIRES?!
RAISE THY HEAD.
WE ARE ION.
ION FORTUNA.
NOBLE OF MOLDOVA, TZARA METHUSELUTE; EARL OF MEMPHIS.
AS A SPĂTAR, THE EMPEROR'S SWORD BEARER...
...WE HAVE COME TO RELATE AUGUSTA'S IMPERIAL COMMAND.
I AM HIS VICE-ENVOY, THE BARON OF LUXOR...
...RADU BARVON...
...INSPECTOR UNDER THE DIRECT ORDERS OF THE EMPIRE.
YOUR EXCELLENCY, EARL OF MEMPHIS AND...
LONG NAMES!!
YOUR EXCELLENCY, BARON OF LUXOR.
AND NOW...
THIS VISIT FROM THE BOTH OF YOU...
MAY I TAKE IT AS AN EXPRESSION OF THE DESIRE TO OPEN DIPLOMATIC NEGOTIATIONS WITH MY SUPERIOR?

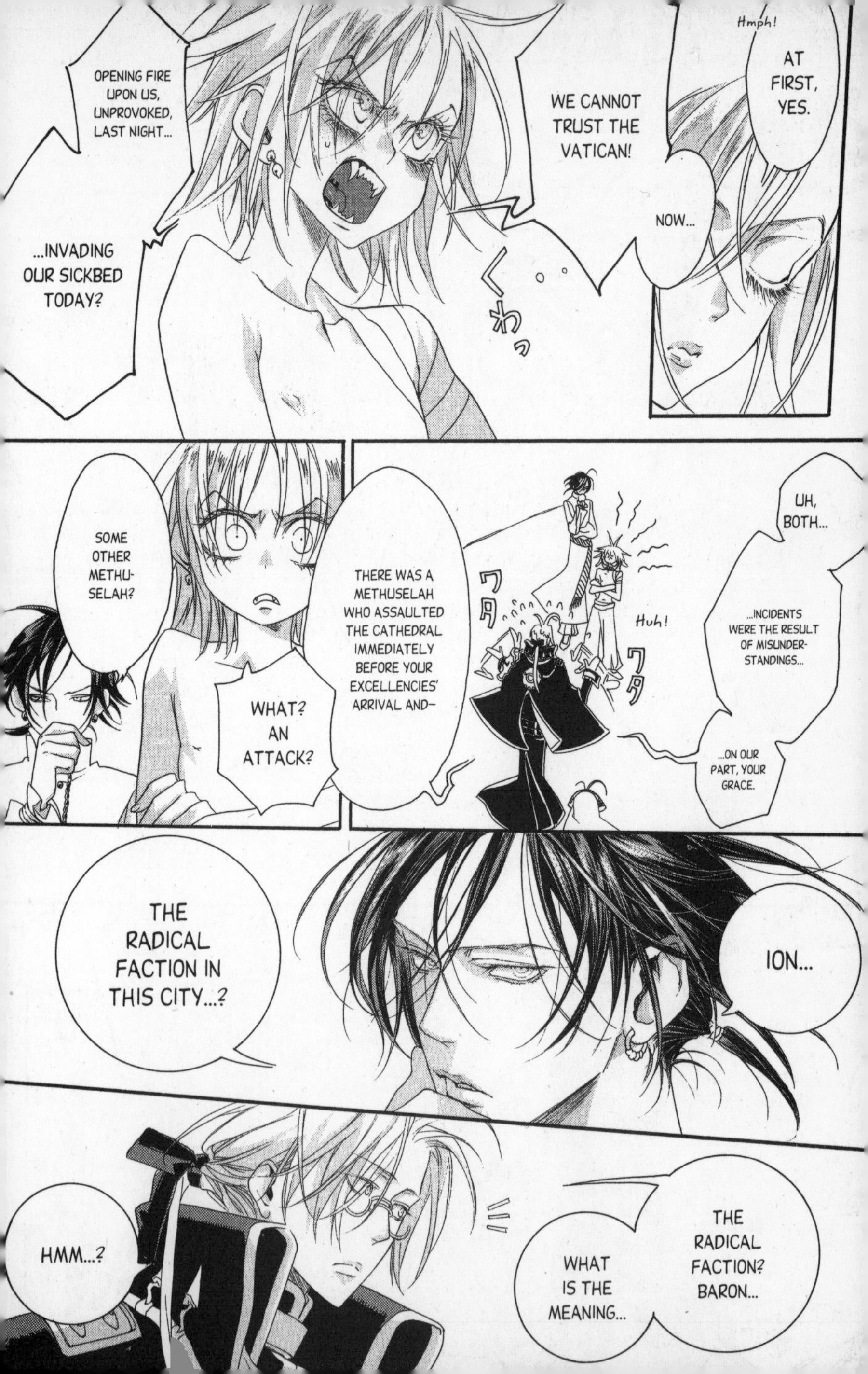
Hmph!
AT FIRST, YES.
NOW...
WE CANNOT TRUST THE VATICAN!
OPENING FIRE UPON US, UNPROVOKED, LAST NIGHT...
...INVADING OUR SICKBED TODAY?
くわっ
UH, BOTH...
...INCIDENTS WERE THE RESULT OF MISUNDER-STANDINGS...
...ON OUR PART, YOUR GRACE.
Huh!
ワタ
ワタ
THERE WAS A METHUSELAH WHO ASSAULTED THE CATHEDRAL IMMEDIATELY BEFORE YOUR EXCELLENCIES' ARRIVAL AND–
WHAT? AN ATTACK?
SOME OTHER METHU-SELAH?
ION...
THE RADICAL FACTION IN THIS CITY...?
THE RADICAL FACTION? BARON...
WHAT IS THE MEANING...
HMM...?

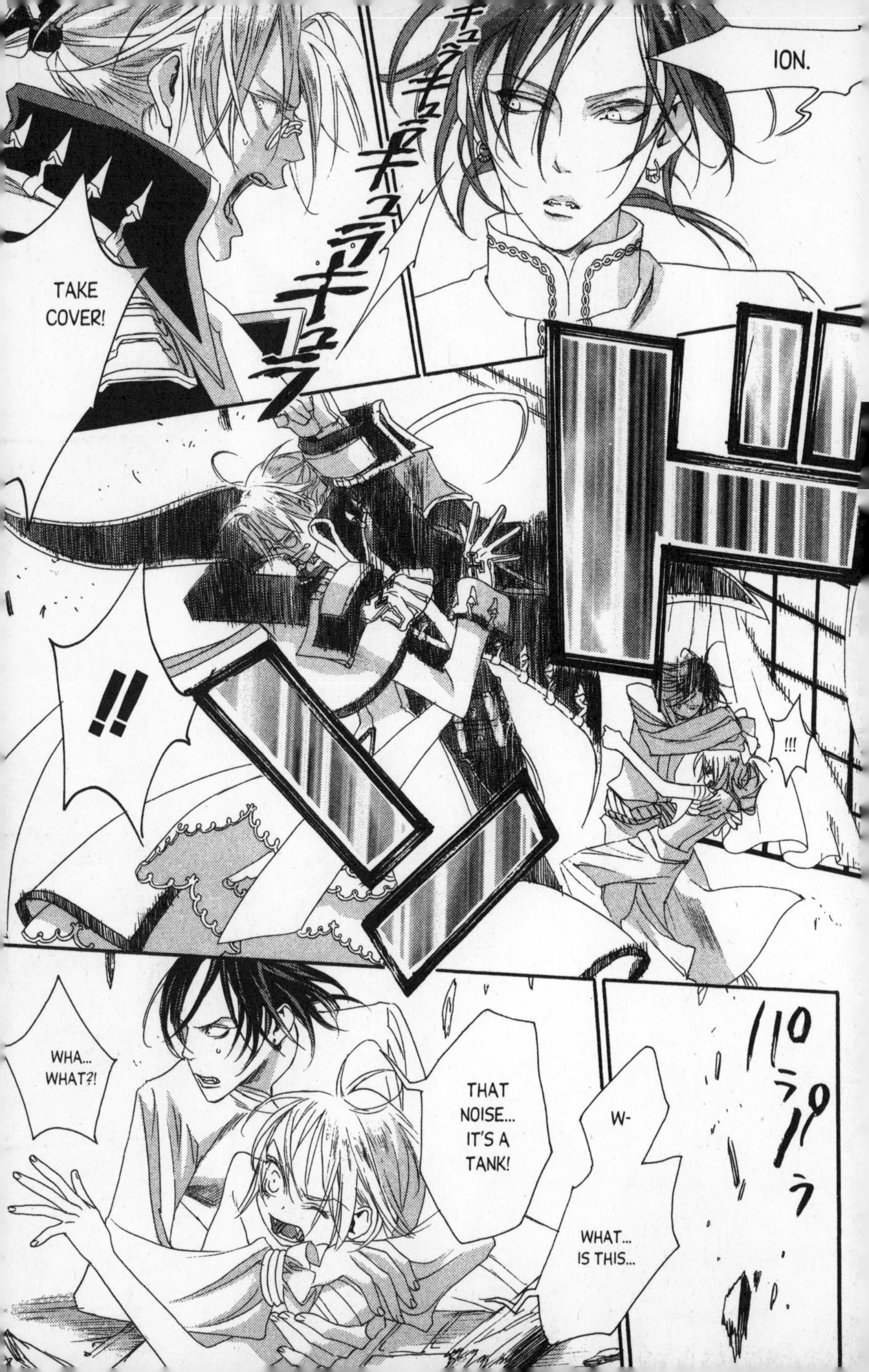
ION.
キュラキュラキュラキュラ
TAKE COVER!
!!!
!!
パラパラ
W-
WHAT... IS THIS...
THAT NOISE... IT'S A TANK!
WHA... WHAT?!

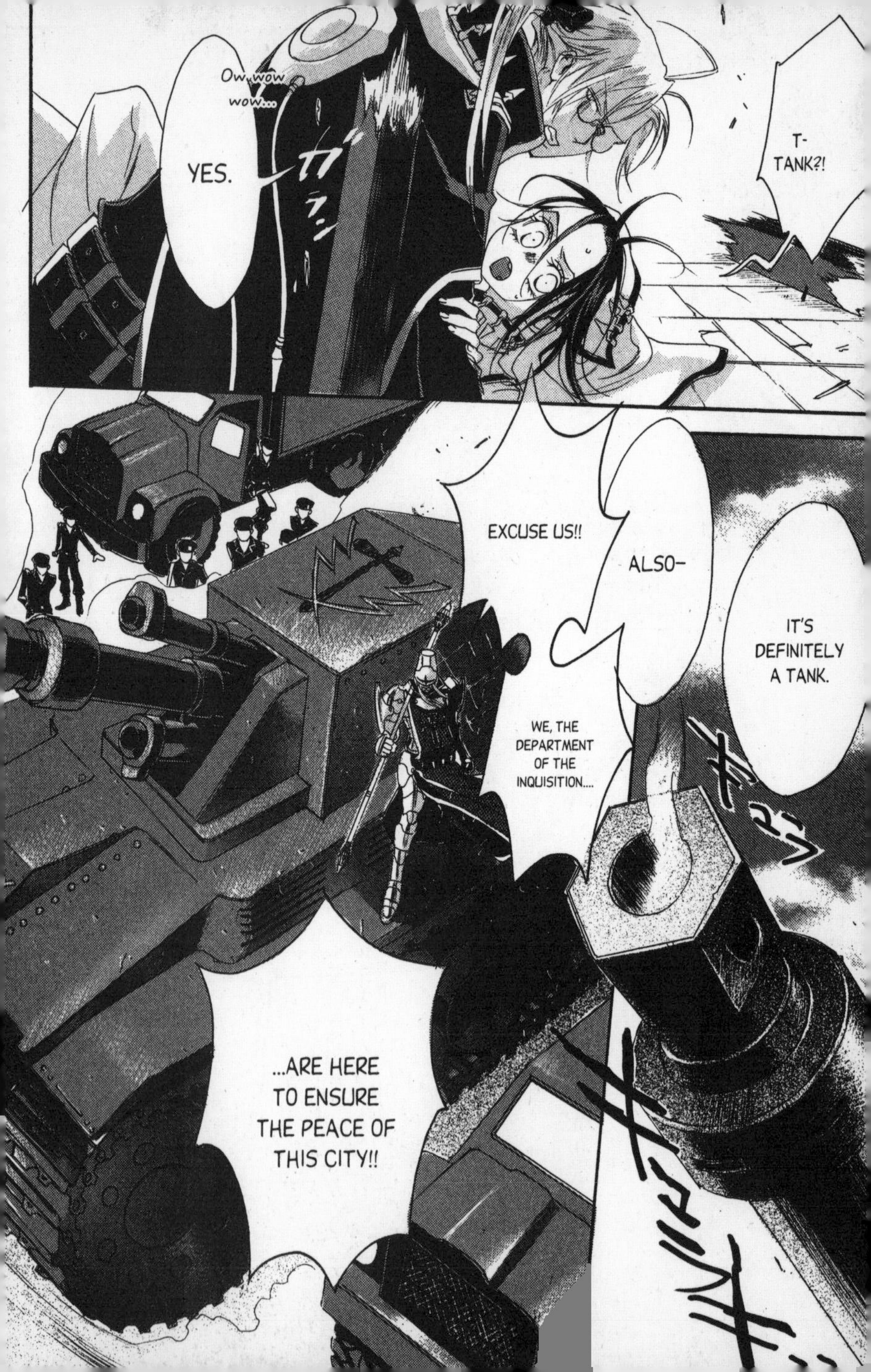
T-TANK?!
Ow wow wow...
YES.
IT'S DEFINITELY A TANK.
ALSO–
EXCUSE US!!
WE, THE DEPARTMENT OF THE INQUISITION....
...ARE HERE TO ENSURE THE PEACE OF THIS CITY!!

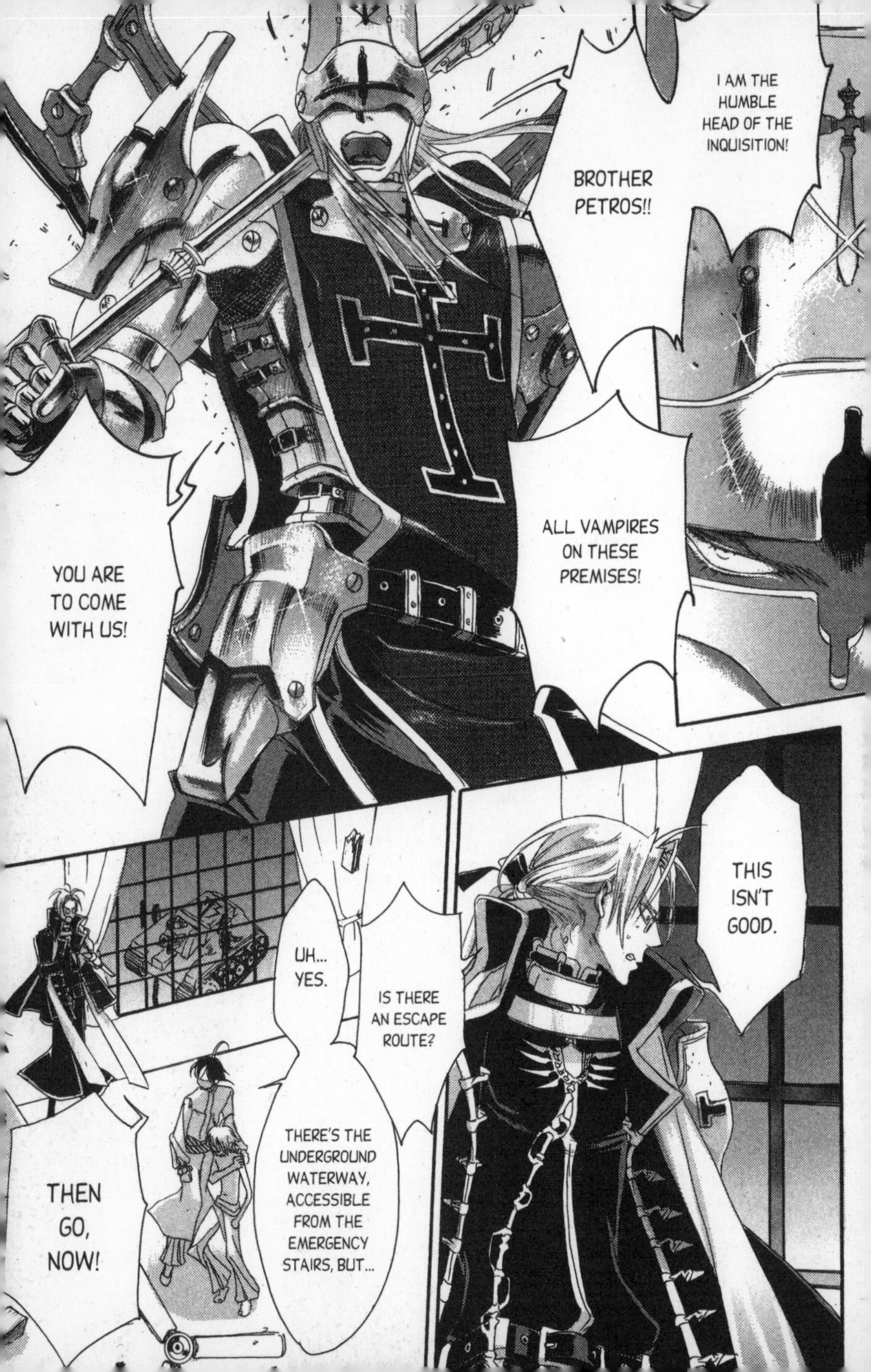
I AM THE HUMBLE HEAD OF THE INQUISITION!
BROTHER PETROS!!
ALL VAMPIRES ON THESE PREMISES!
YOU ARE TO COME WITH US!
THIS ISN'T GOOD.
IS THERE AN ESCAPE ROUTE?
UH... YES.
THERE'S THE UNDERGROUND WATERWAY, ACCESSIBLE FROM THE EMERGENCY STAIRS, BUT...
THEN GO, NOW!

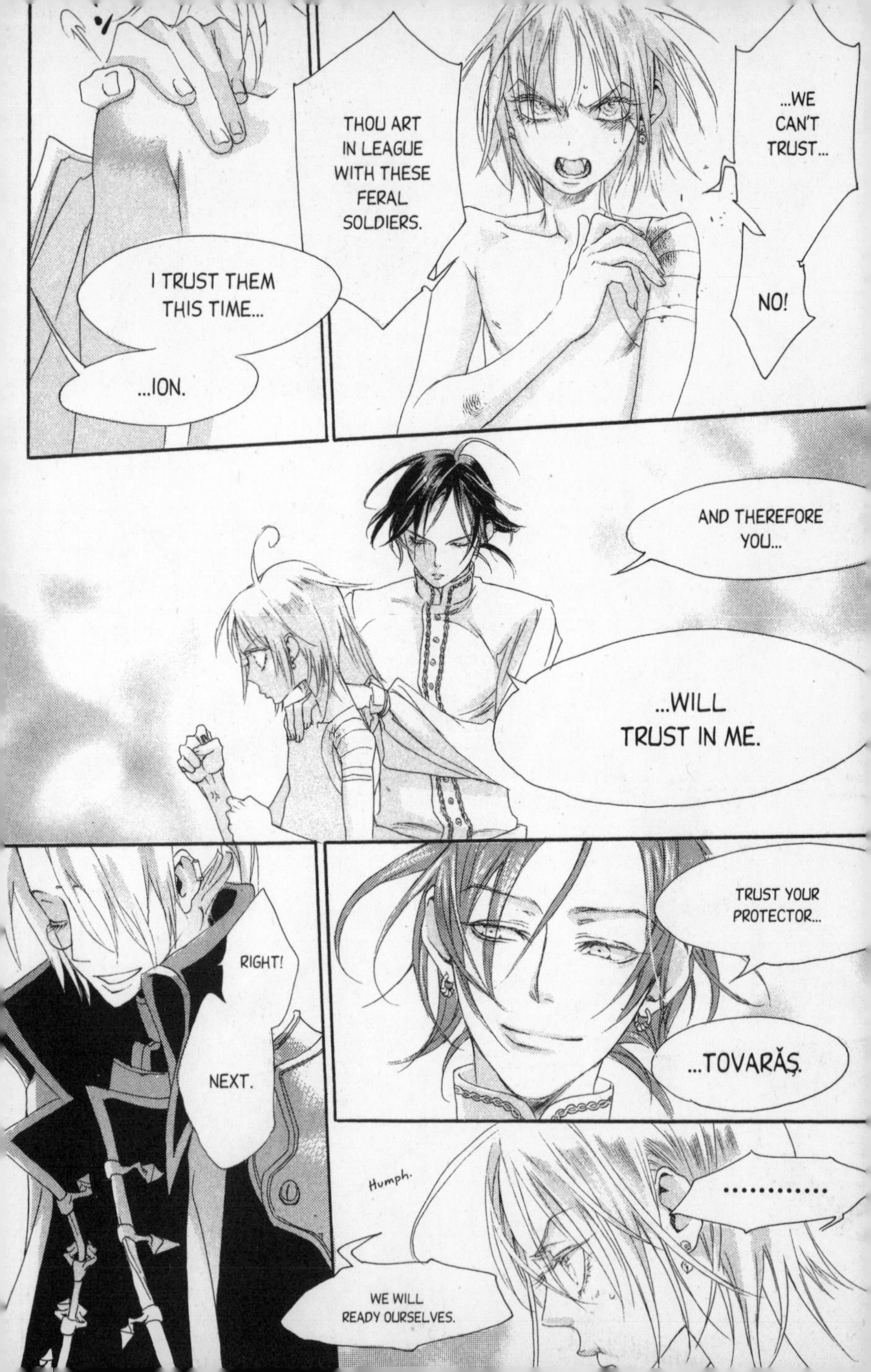
...WE CAN'T TRUST...
THOU ART IN LEAGUE WITH THESE FERAL SOLDIERS.
NO!
I TRUST THEM THIS TIME...
...ION.
AND THEREFORE YOU...
...WILL TRUST IN ME.
TRUST YOUR PROTECTOR...
...TOVARĂȘ.
....
Humph.
WE WILL READY OURSELVES.
RIGHT!
NEXT.

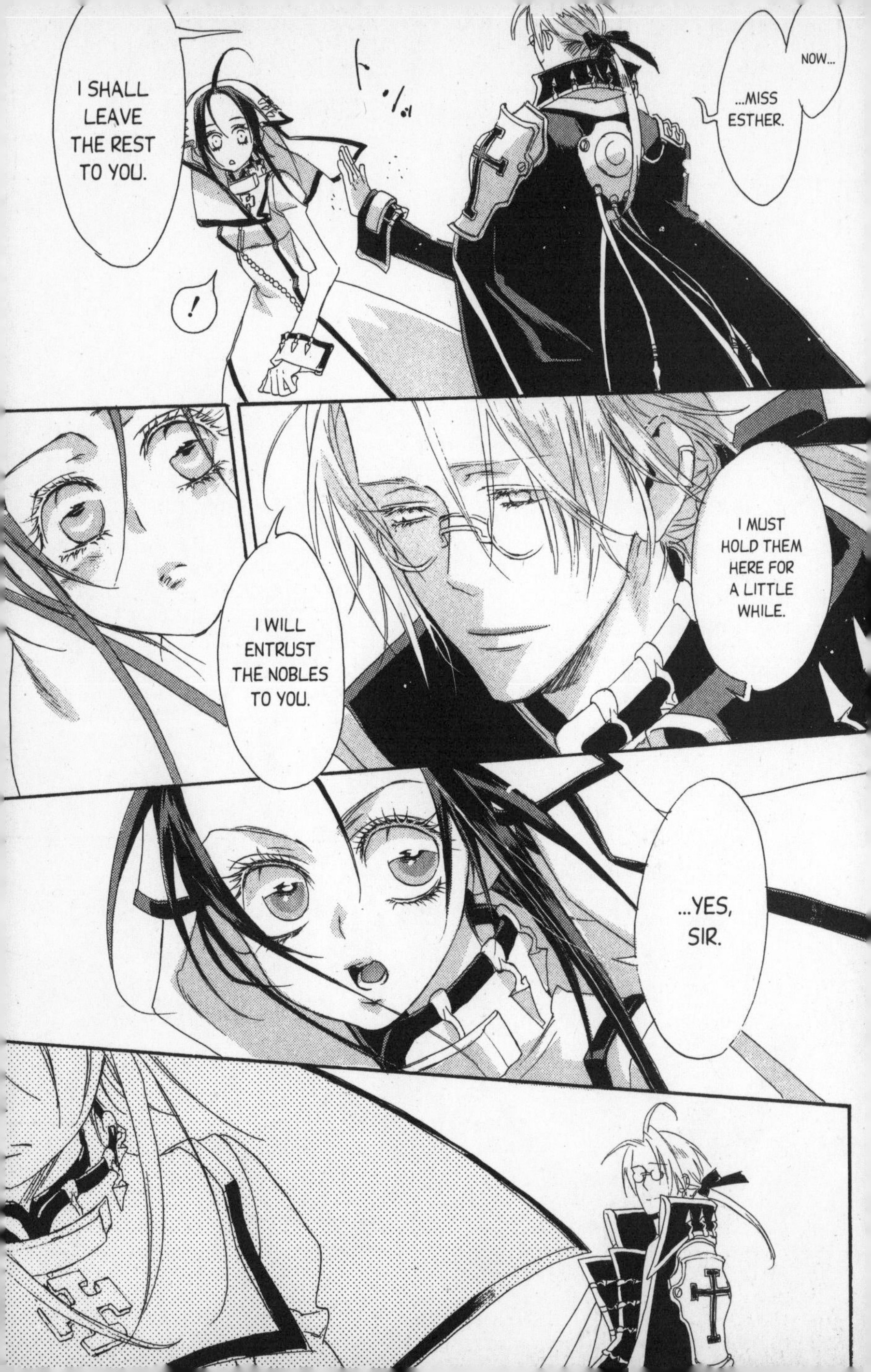
NOW...
...MISS ESTHER.
I SHALL LEAVE THE REST TO YOU.
!
I MUST HOLD THEM HERE FOR A LITTLE WHILE.
I WILL ENTRUST THE NOBLES TO YOU.
...YES, SIR.

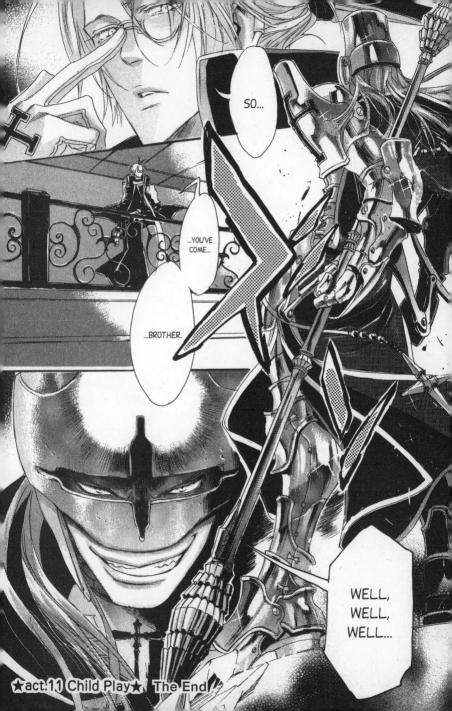

SO...

...YOU'VE COME...

...BROTHER.

WELL, WELL, WELL...

★act.11 Child Play★ The End

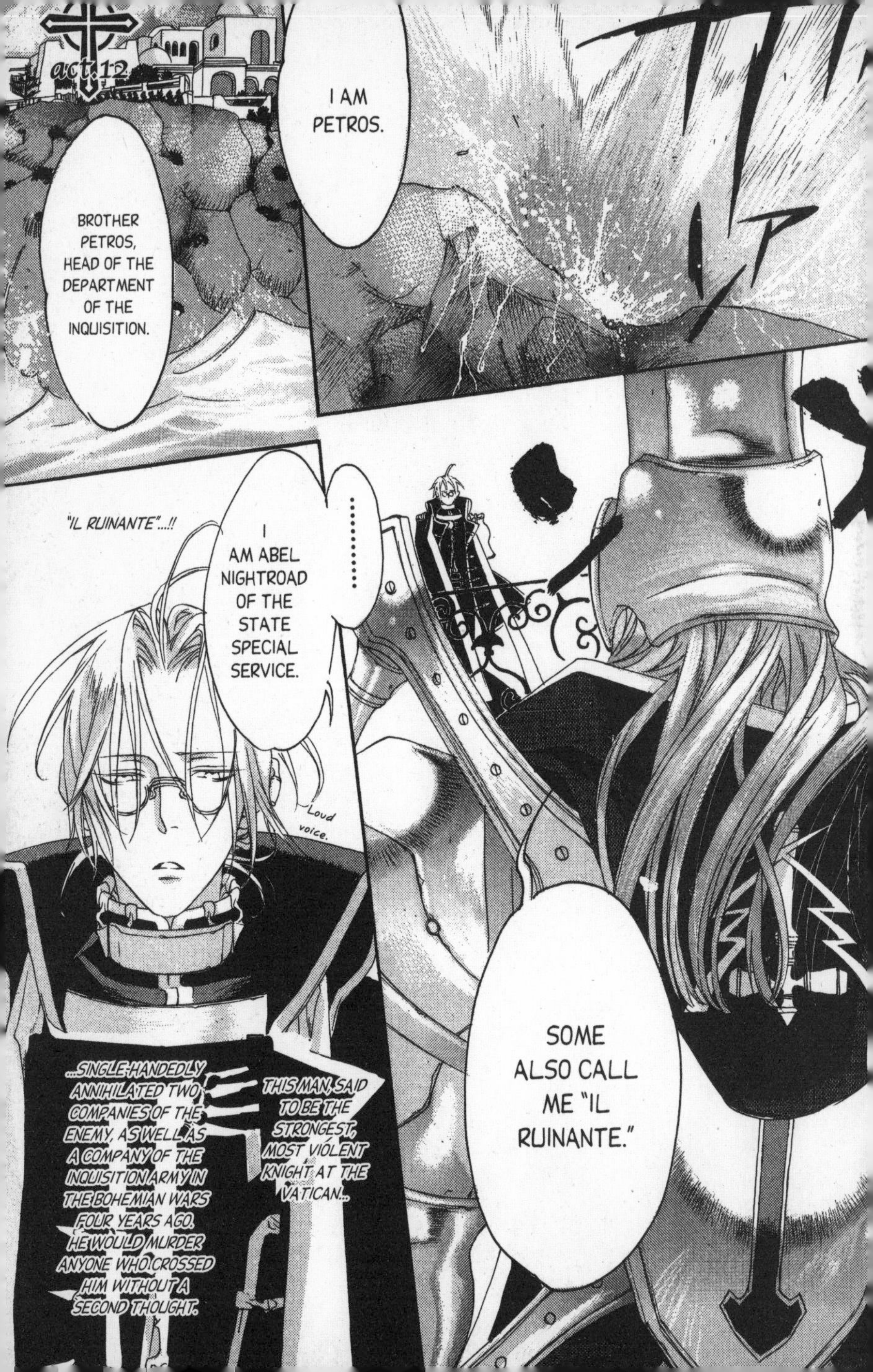
act.12
I AM PETROS.
BROTHER PETROS, HEAD OF THE DEPARTMENT OF THE INQUISITION.
......
SOME ALSO CALL ME "IL RUINANTE."
I AM ABEL NIGHTROAD OF THE STATE SPECIAL SERVICE.
"IL RUINANTE"...!!
Loud voice.
THIS MAN, SAID TO BE THE STRONGEST, MOST VIOLENT KNIGHT AT THE VATICAN...
...SINGLE-HANDEDLY ANNIHILATED TWO COMPANIES OF THE ENEMY, AS WELL AS A COMPANY OF THE INQUISITION ARMY IN THE BOHEMIAN WARS FOUR YEARS AGO. HE WOULD MURDER ANYONE WHO CROSSED HIM WITHOUT A SECOND THOUGHT.

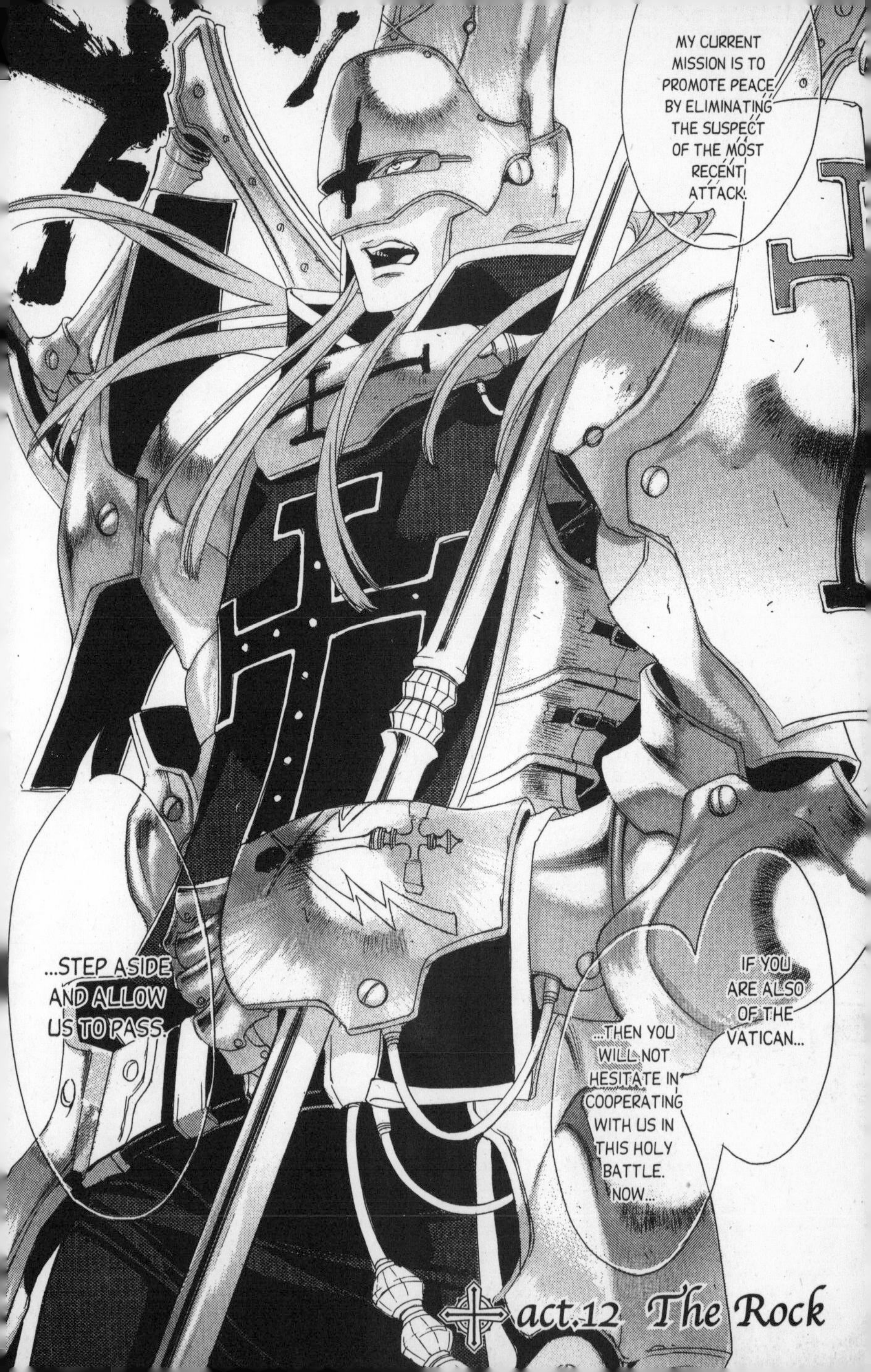
MY CURRENT MISSION IS TO PROMOTE PEACE BY ELIMINATING THE SUSPECT OF THE MOST RECENT ATTACK.
IF YOU ARE ALSO OF THE VATICAN...
...THEN YOU WILL NOT HESITATE IN COOPERATING WITH US IN THIS HOLY BATTLE. NOW...
...STEP ASIDE AND ALLOW US TO PASS.
act.12 The Rock

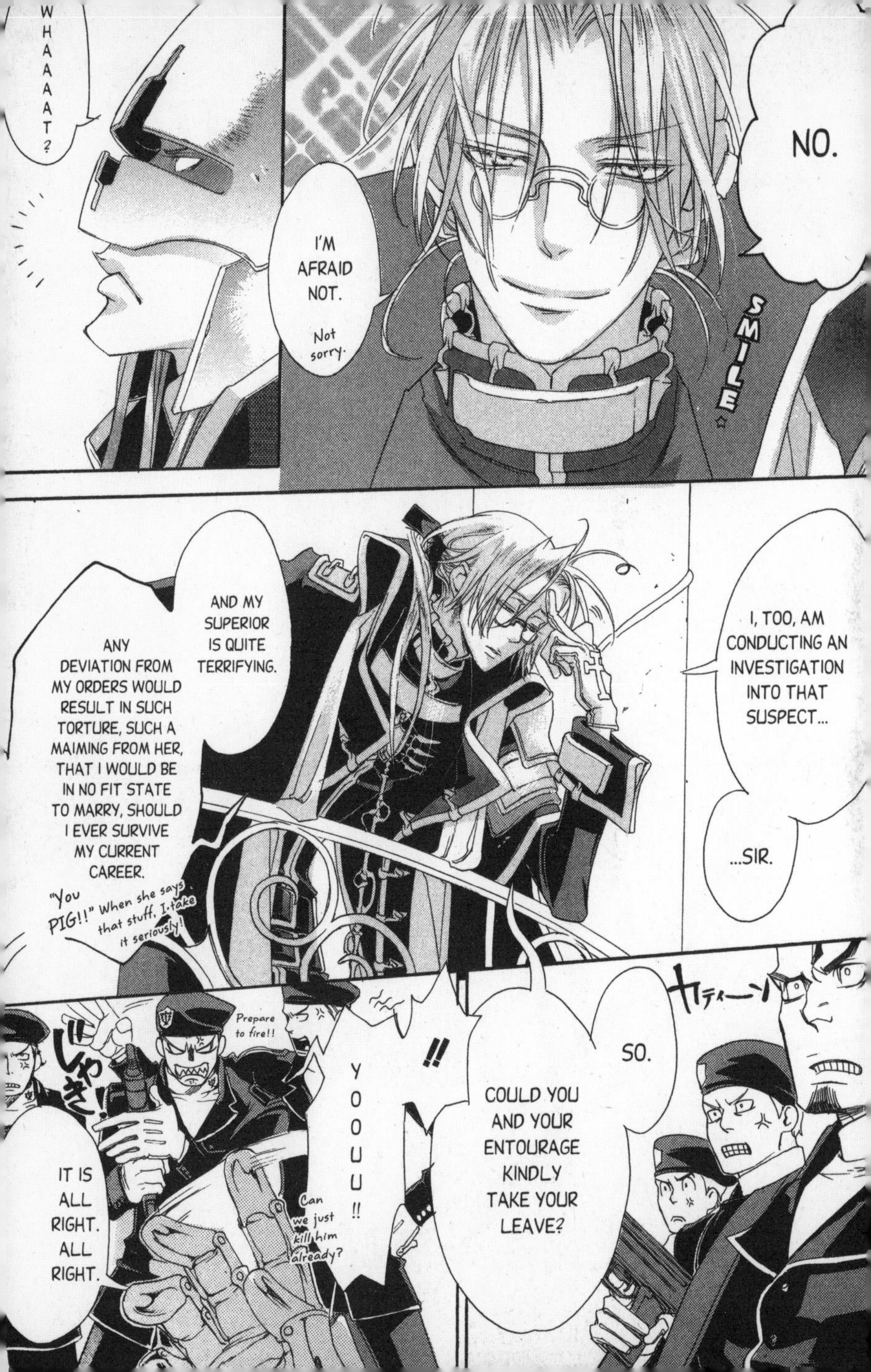
NO.
SMILE☆
I'M AFRAID NOT.
Not sorry.
WHAAAAT?
I, TOO, AM CONDUCTING AN INVESTIGATION INTO THAT SUSPECT...
...SIR.
AND MY SUPERIOR IS QUITE TERRIFYING.
ANY DEVIATION FROM MY ORDERS WOULD RESULT IN SUCH TORTURE, SUCH A MAIMING FROM HER, THAT I WOULD BE IN NO FIT STATE TO MARRY, SHOULD I EVER SURVIVE MY CURRENT CAREER.
"You PIG!!" When she says that stuff, I take it seriously!
SO.
COULD YOU AND YOUR ENTOURAGE KINDLY TAKE YOUR LEAVE?
!!
YOOUUU!!
Can we just kill him already?
Prepare to fire!!
じゃき!
IT IS ALL RIGHT. ALL RIGHT.

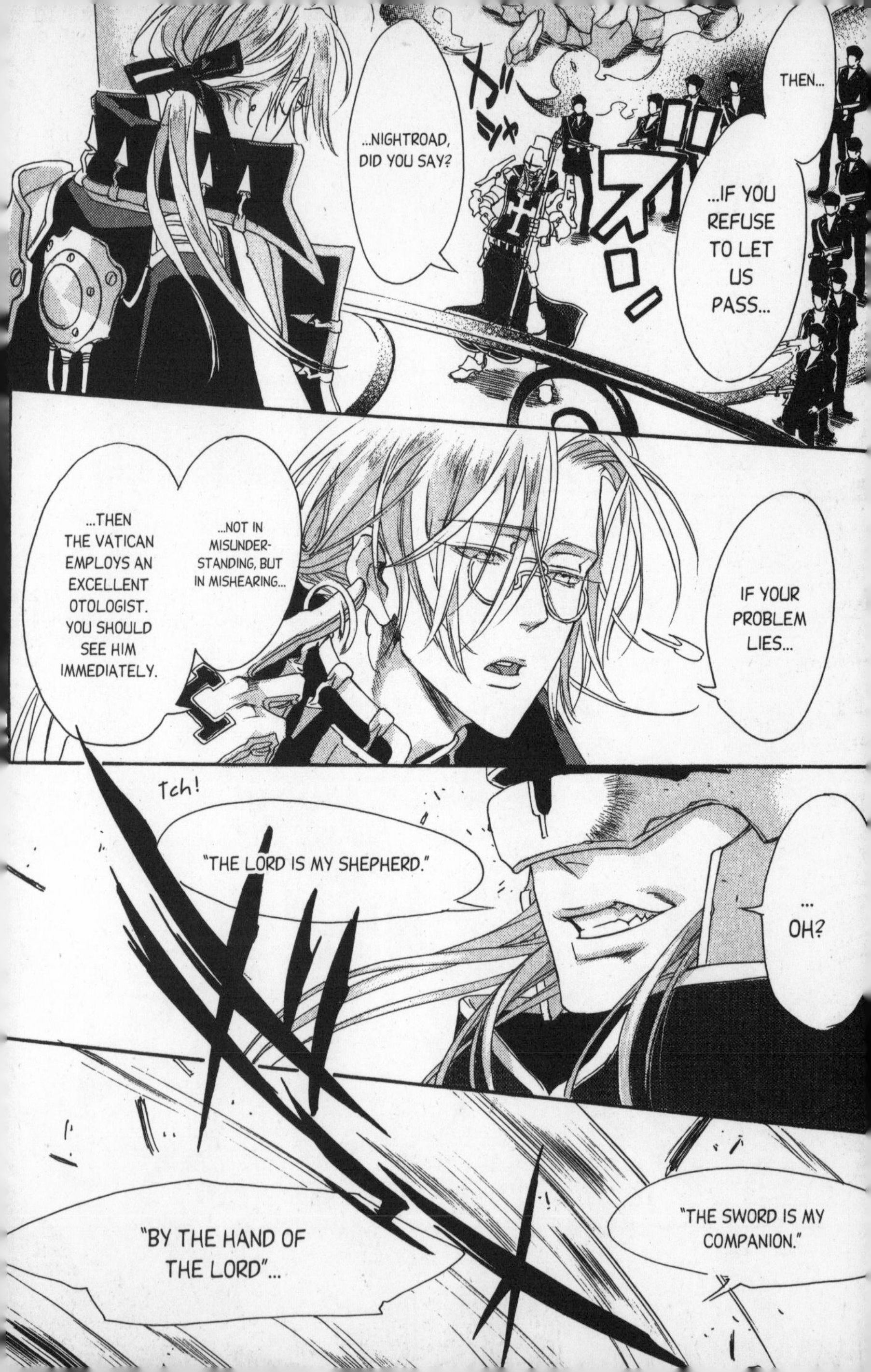
THEN...
...IF YOU REFUSE TO LET US PASS...
...NIGHTROAD, DID YOU SAY?
IF YOUR PROBLEM LIES...
...NOT IN MISUNDERSTANDING, BUT IN MISHEARING...
...THEN THE VATICAN EMPLOYS AN EXCELLENT OTOLOGIST. YOU SHOULD SEE HIM IMMEDIATELY.
... OH?
Tch!
"THE LORD IS MY SHEPHERD."
"THE SWORD IS MY COMPANION."
"BY THE HAND OF THE LORD"...

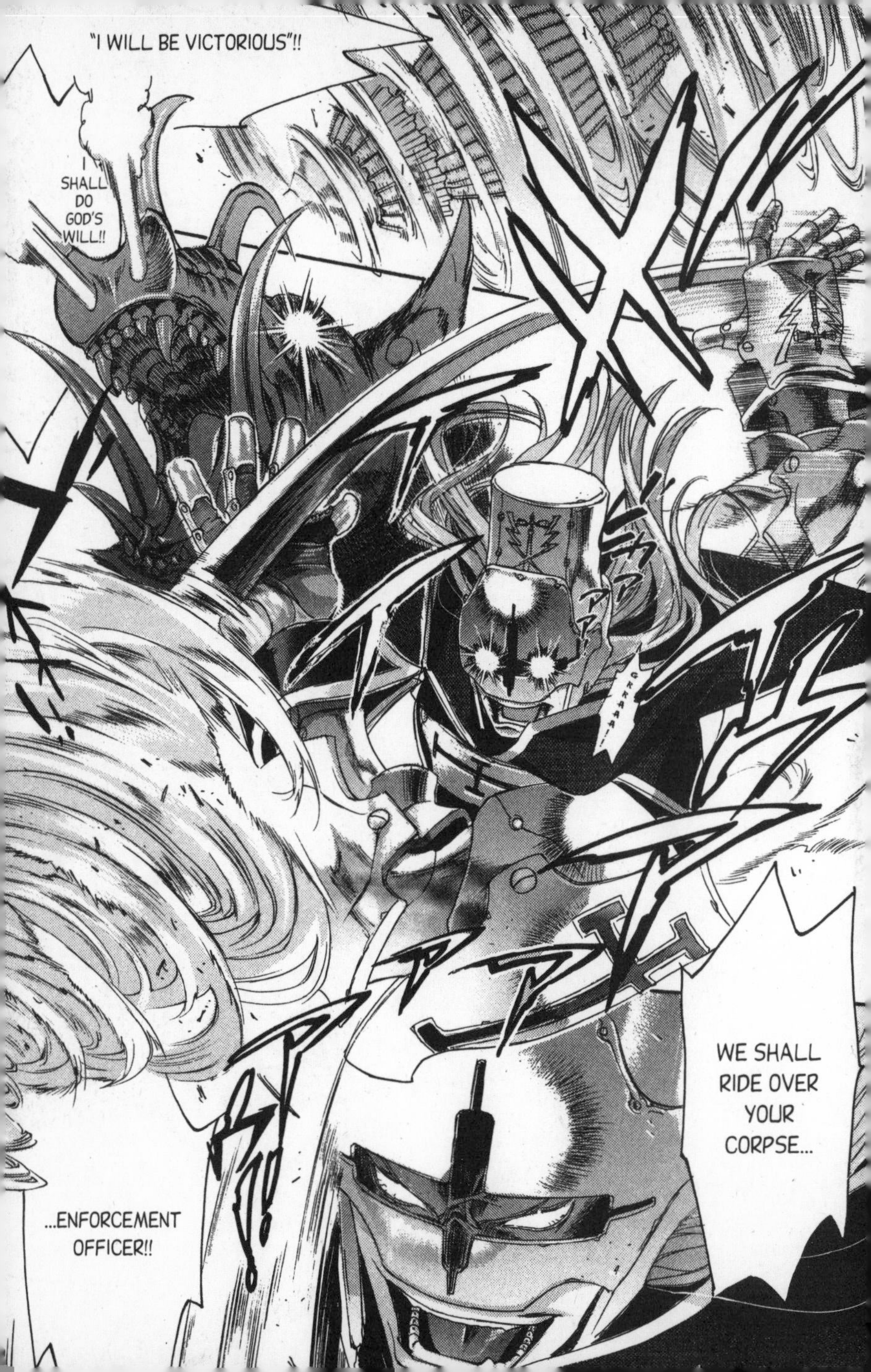
"I WILL BE VICTORIOUS"!!
I SHALL DO GOD'S WILL!!
GRRAAA...!!
WE SHALL RIDE OVER YOUR CORPSE...
...ENFORCEMENT OFFICER!!

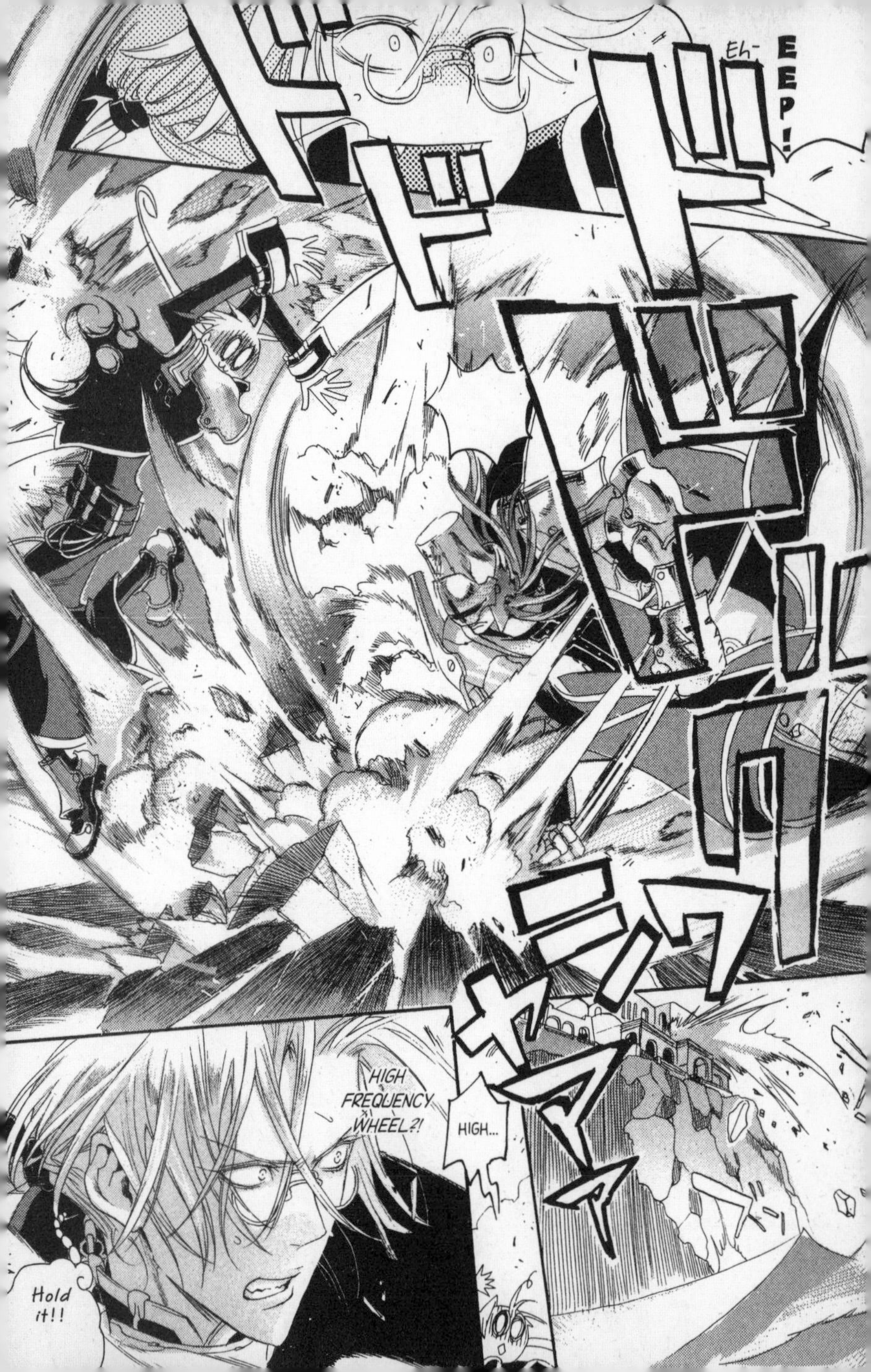
Eh-
EEP!!
HIGH...
HIGH FREQUENCY WHEEL?!
Hold it!!

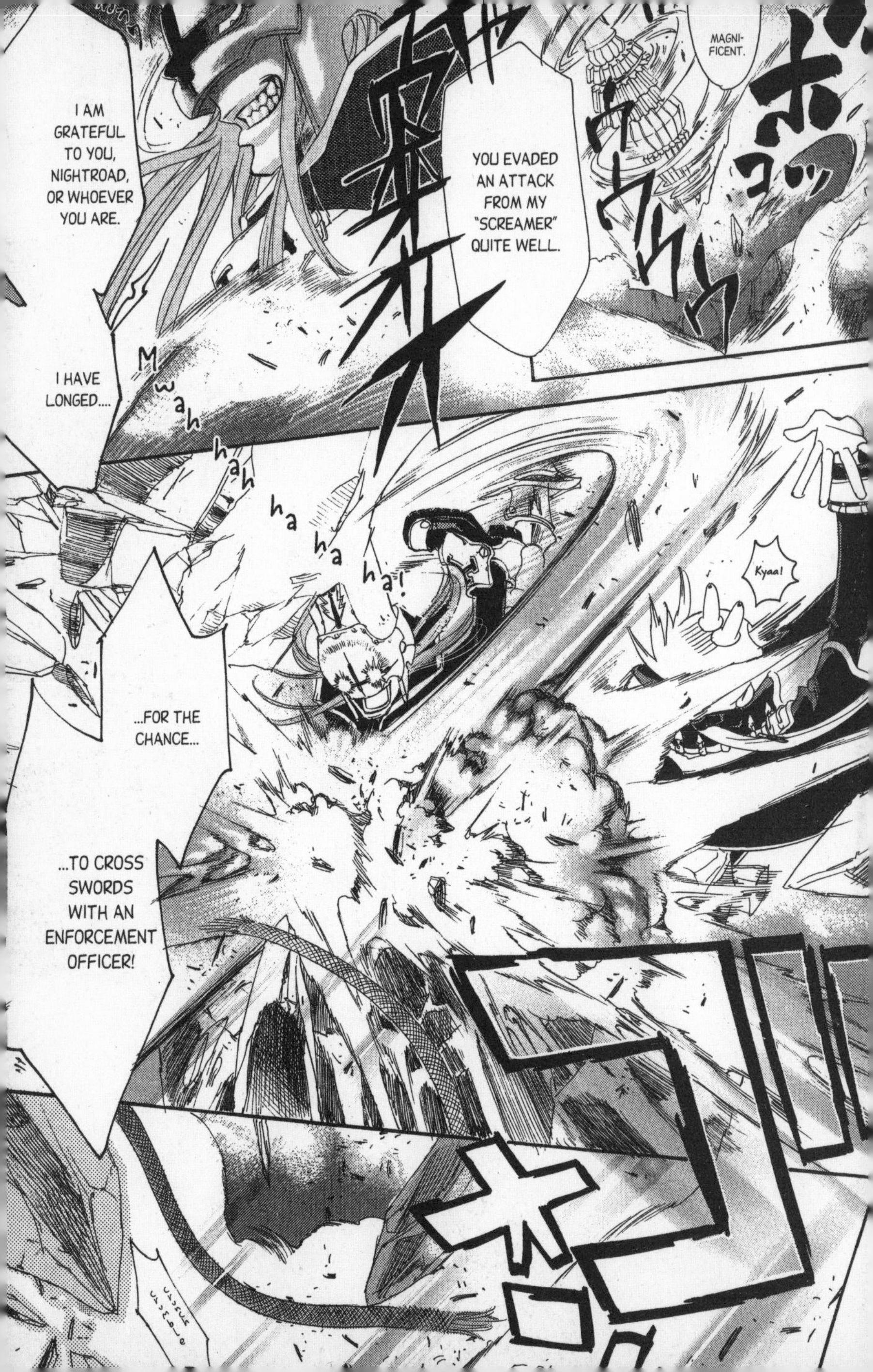
MAGNI-FICENT.
YOU EVADED AN ATTACK FROM MY "SCREAMER" QUITE WELL.
I AM GRATEFUL TO YOU, NIGHTROAD, OR WHOEVER YOU ARE.
I HAVE LONGED....
Mwahhahhahahaha!
Kyaa!
...FOR THE CHANCE...
...TO CROSS SWORDS WITH AN ENFORCEMENT OFFICER!

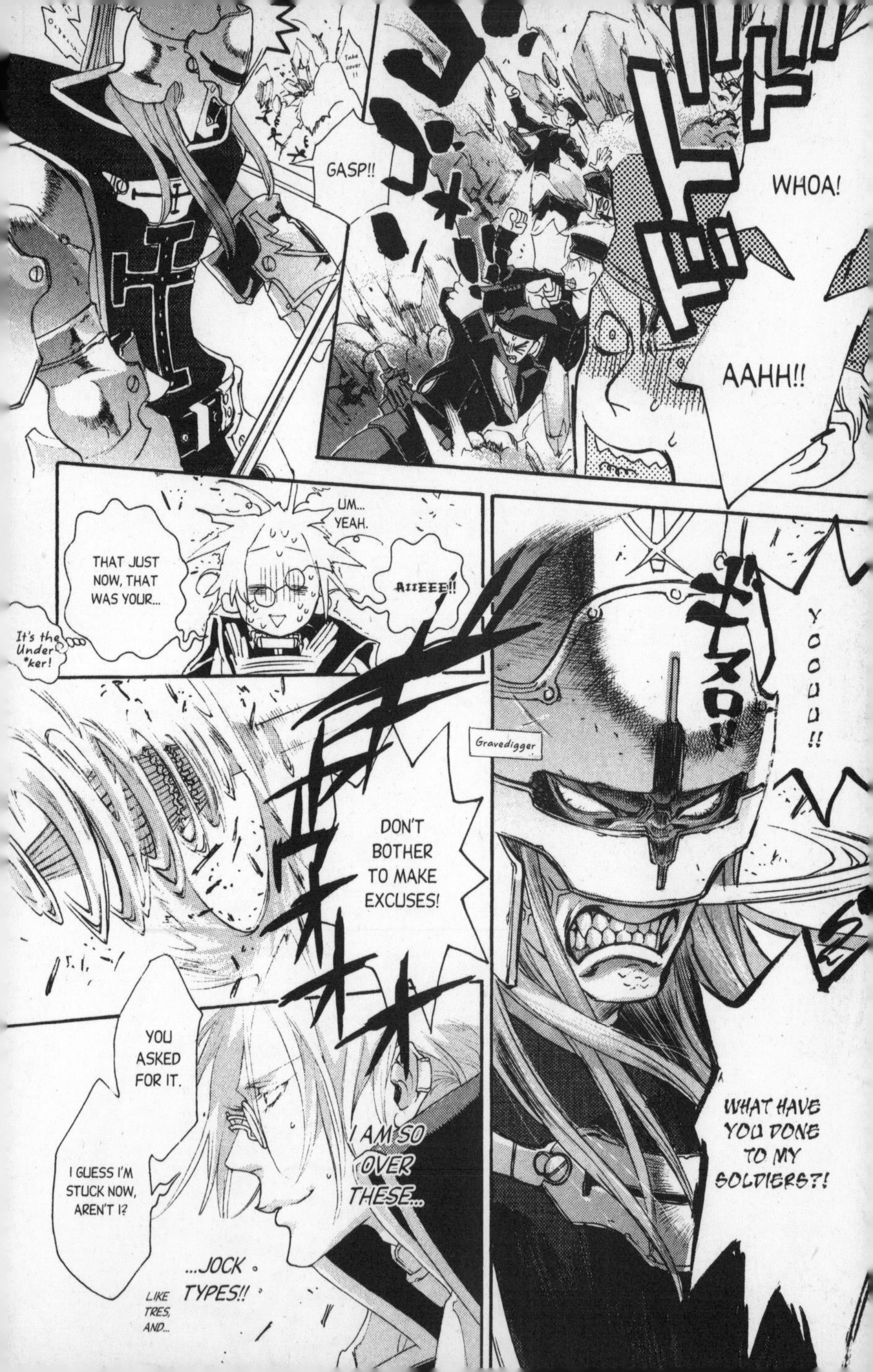
WHOA!
AAHH!!
GASP!!
Take cover!!
YOOUUU!!
Gravedigger
WHAT HAVE YOU DONE TO MY SOLDIERS?!
UM... YEAH.
AIIEEE!!
THAT JUST NOW, THAT WAS YOUR...
It's the Under*ker!
DON'T BOTHER TO MAKE EXCUSES!
YOU ASKED FOR IT.
I AM SO OVER THESE...
I GUESS I'M STUCK NOW, AREN'T I?
...JOCK TYPES!!
LIKE TRES, AND...

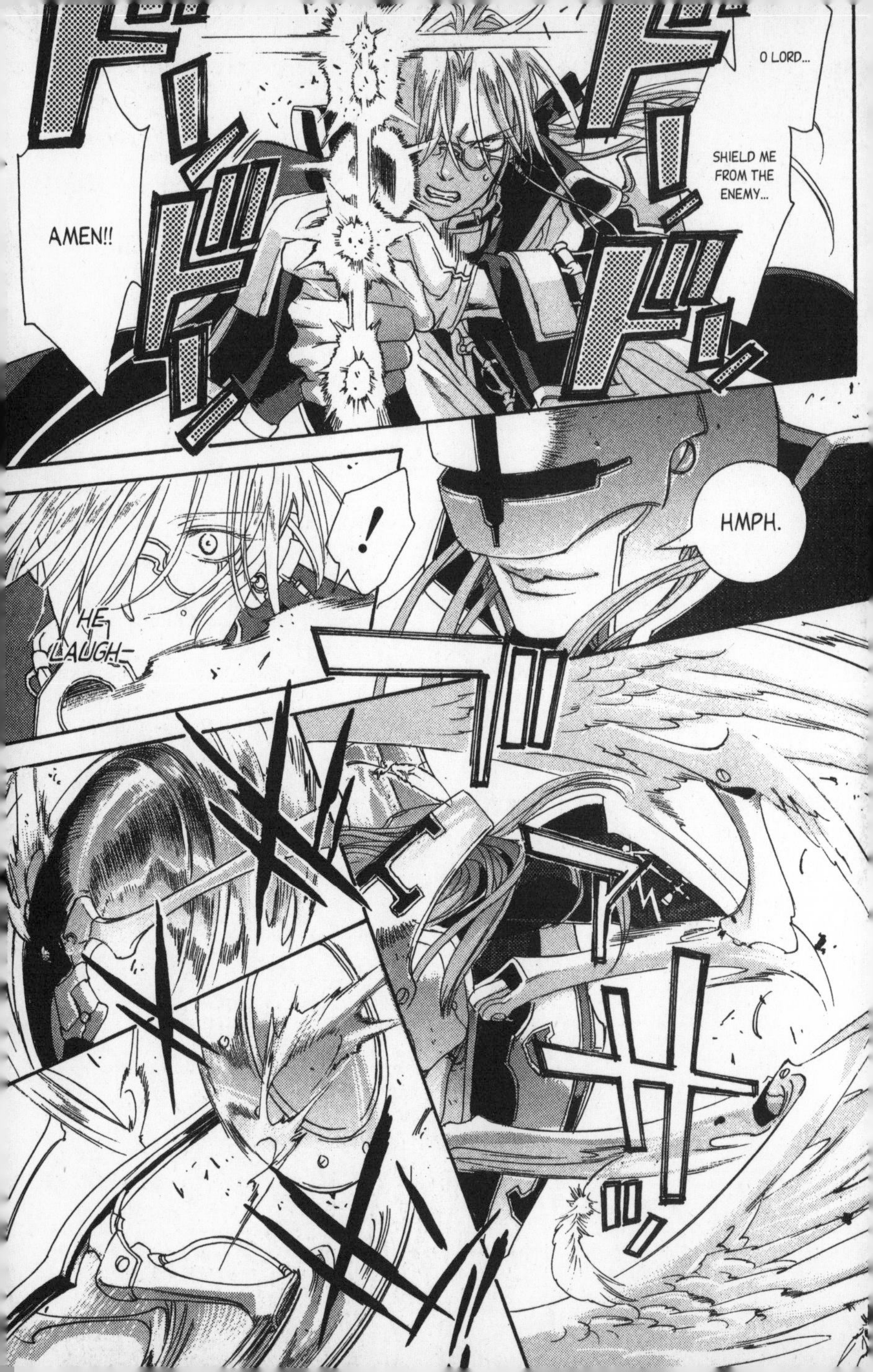
O LORD...
SHIELD ME FROM THE ENEMY...
AMEN!!
HMPH.
!
HE LAUGH-

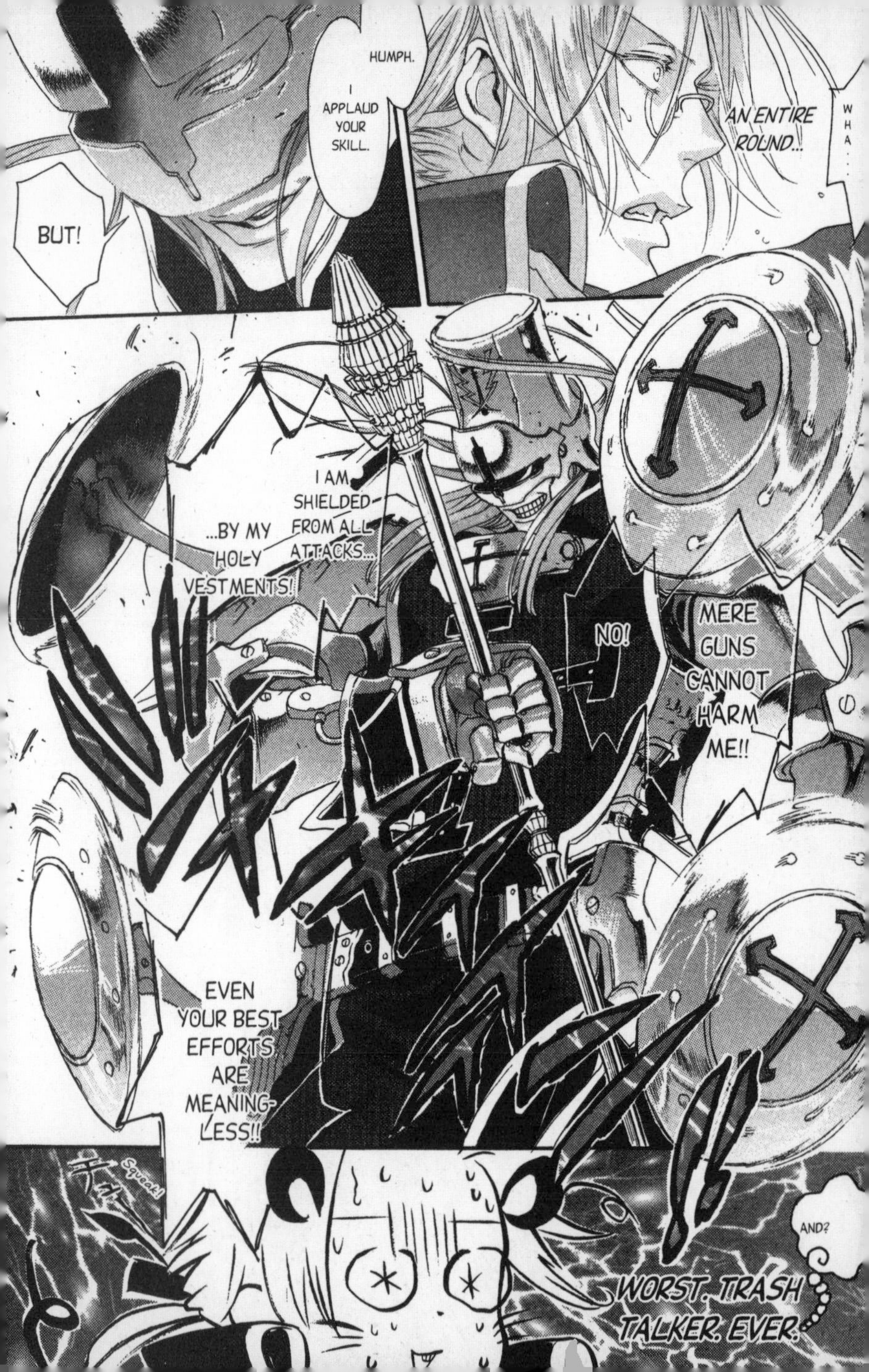
W H A . . .
AN ENTIRE ROUND...
HUMPH.
I APPLAUD YOUR SKILL.
BUT!
MERE GUNS CANNOT HARM ME!!
NO!
I AM SHIELDED FROM ALL ATTACKS...
...BY MY HOLY VESTMENTS!
EVEN YOUR BEST EFFORTS ARE MEANING-LESS!!
AND?
WORST. TRASH TALKER. EVER.
Squeak!

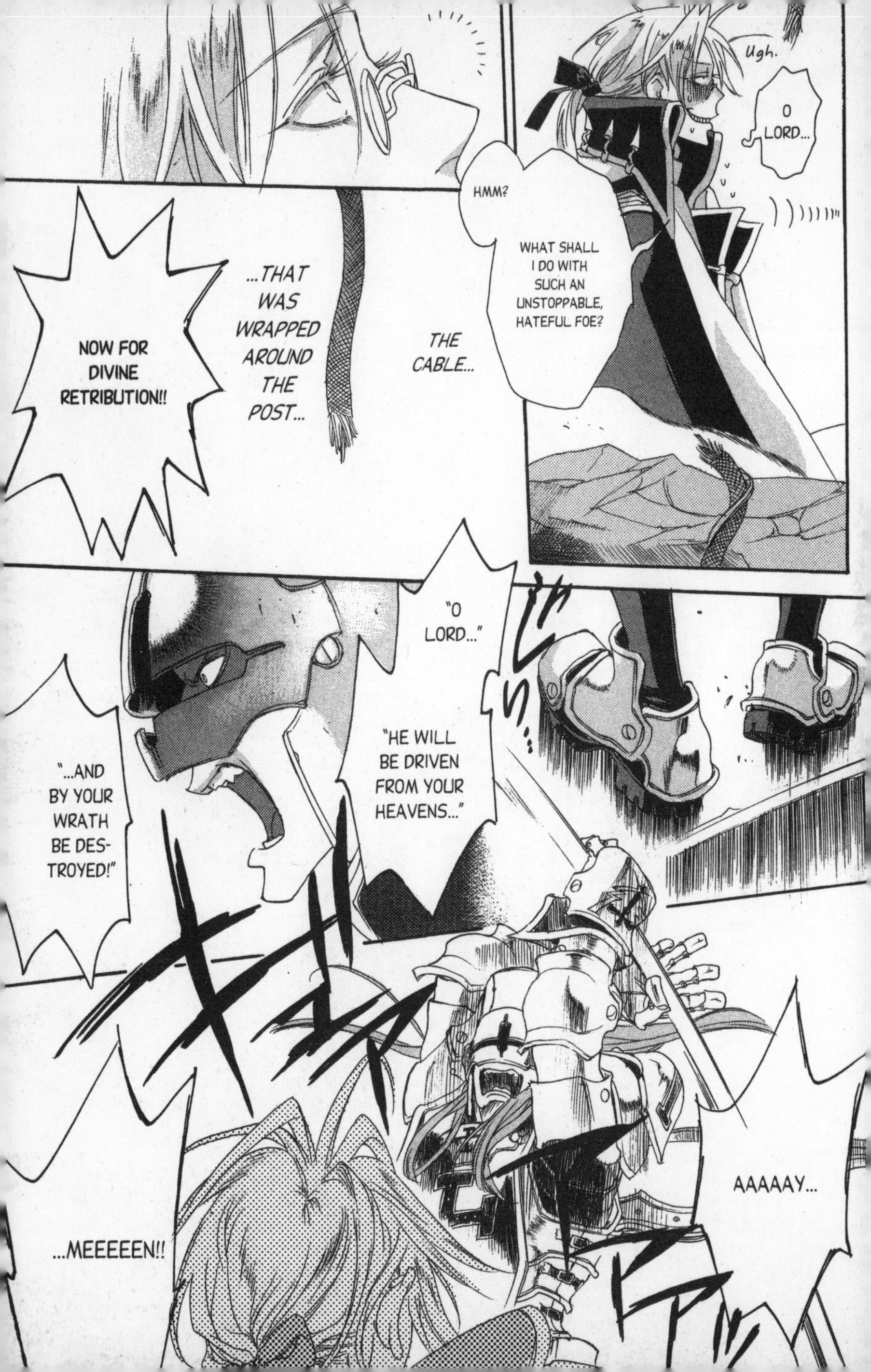

Ugh.
O LORD...
HMM?
WHAT SHALL I DO WITH SUCH AN UNSTOPPABLE, HATEFUL FOE?
THE CABLE...
...THAT WAS WRAPPED AROUND THE POST...
NOW FOR DIVINE RETRIBUTION!!
"O LORD..."
"HE WILL BE DRIVEN FROM YOUR HEAVENS..."
"...AND BY YOUR WRATH BE DES-TROYED!"
AAAAAY...
...MEEEEEN!!

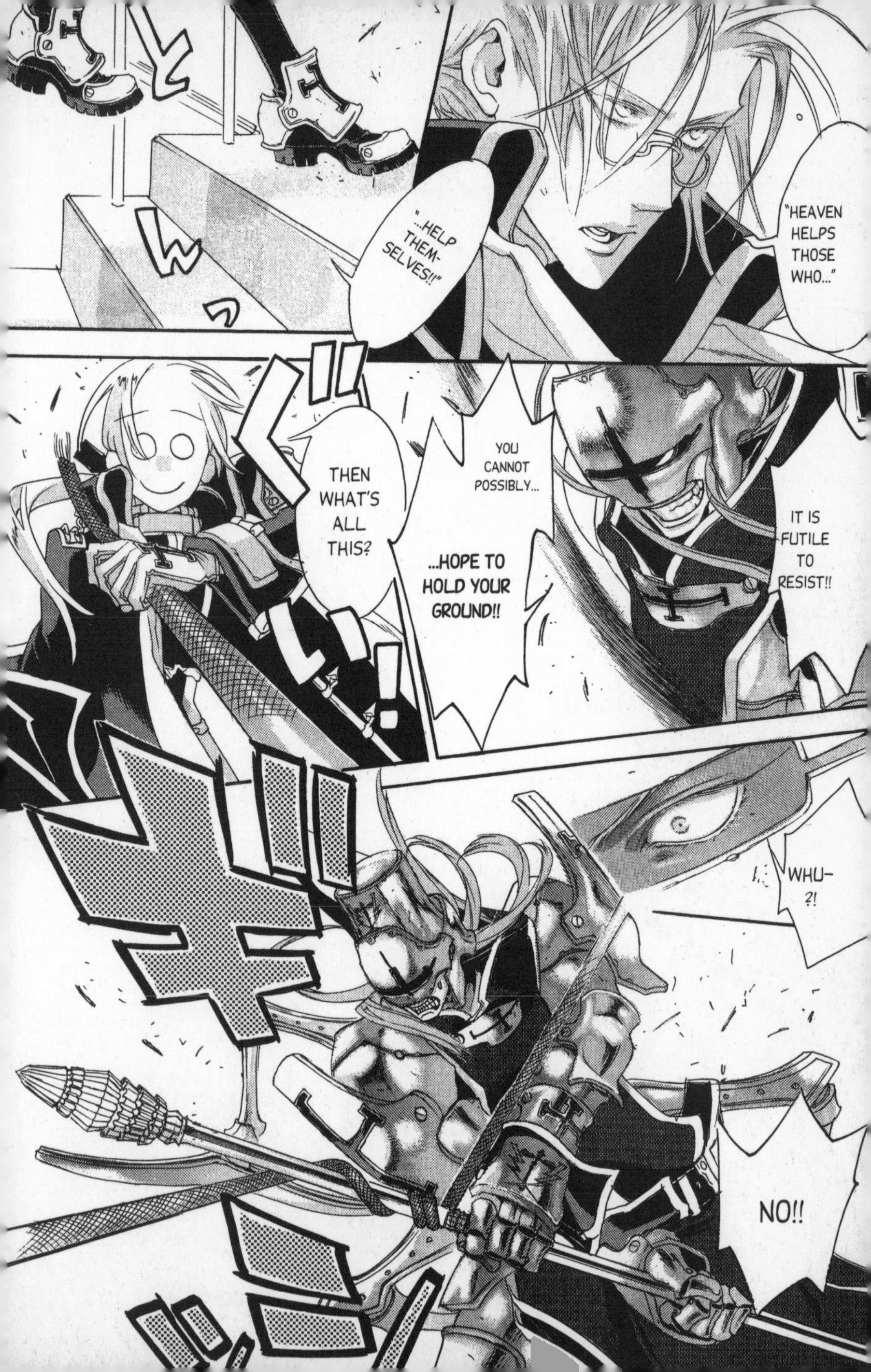
"HEAVEN HELPS THOSE WHO..."
"...HELP THEM-SELVES!!"
IT IS FUTILE TO RESIST!!
YOU CANNOT POSSIBLY...
...HOPE TO HOLD YOUR GROUND!!
THEN WHAT'S ALL THIS?
WHU- ?!
NO!!

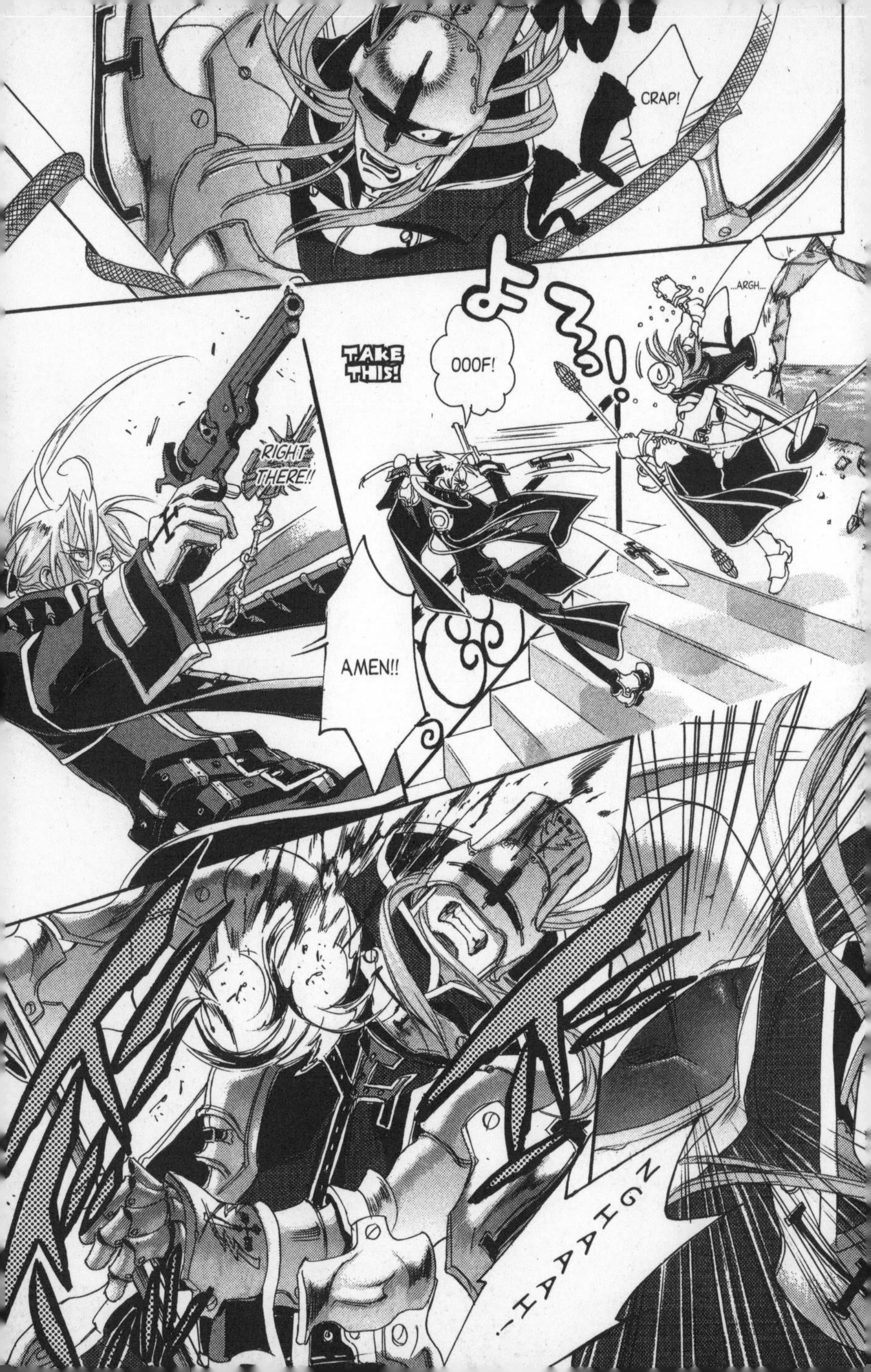

CRAP!
...ARGH...
OOOF!
TAKE THIS!
RIGHT THERE!!
AMEN!!
NGHAAAAH!

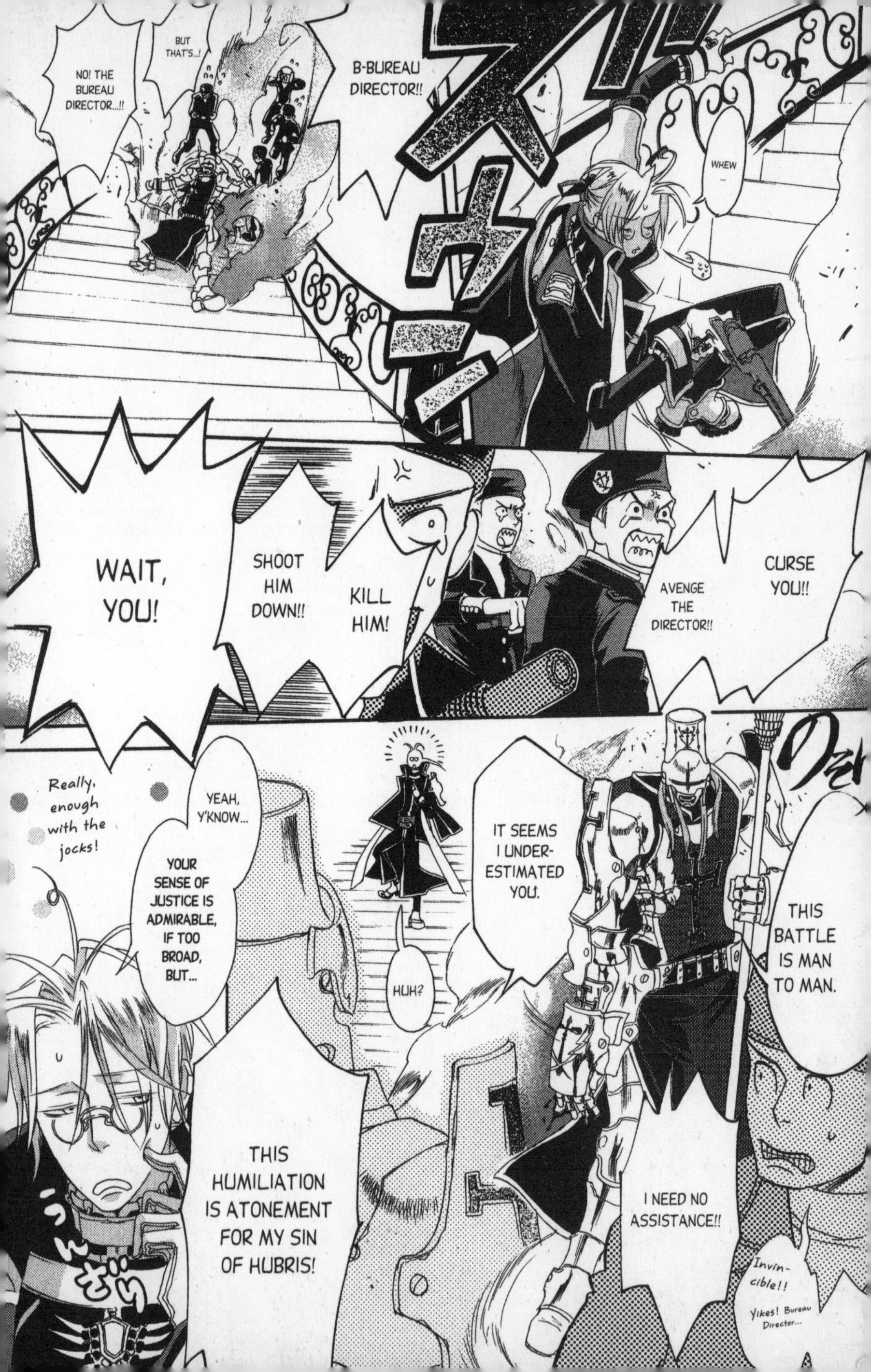

WHEW ...
B-BUREAU DIRECTOR!!
BUT THAT'S...!
NO! THE BUREAU DIRECTOR...!!
CURSE YOU!!
AVENGE THE DIRECTOR!!
KILL HIM!
SHOOT HIM DOWN!!
WAIT, YOU!
THIS BATTLE IS MAN TO MAN.
IT SEEMS I UNDER-ESTIMATED YOU.
I NEED NO ASSISTANCE!!
Invin-cible!!
Yikes! Bureau Director...
HUH?
YEAH, Y'KNOW...
YOUR SENSE OF JUSTICE IS ADMIRABLE, IF TOO BROAD, BUT...
THIS HUMILIATION IS ATONEMENT FOR MY SIN OF HUBRIS!
Really, enough with the jocks!

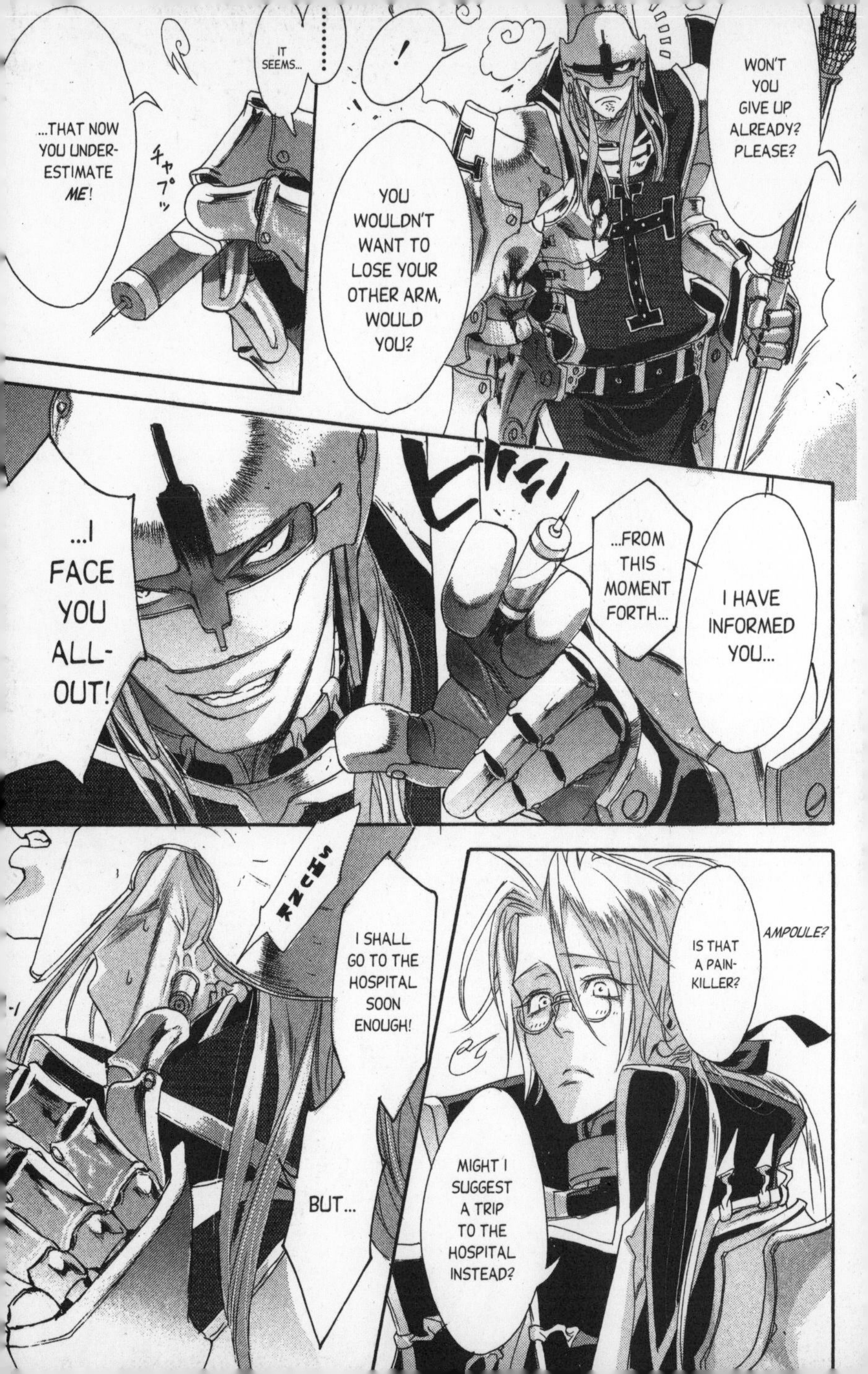
WON'T YOU GIVE UP ALREADY? PLEASE?
YOU WOULDN'T WANT TO LOSE YOUR OTHER ARM, WOULD YOU?
!
......
IT SEEMS...
...THAT NOW YOU UNDER-ESTIMATE *ME*!
チャプッ
I HAVE INFORMED YOU...
...FROM THIS MOMENT FORTH...
...I FACE YOU ALL-OUT!
AMPOULE?
IS THAT A PAIN-KILLER?
MIGHT I SUGGEST A TRIP TO THE HOSPITAL INSTEAD?
I SHALL GO TO THE HOSPITAL SOON ENOUGH!
BUT...

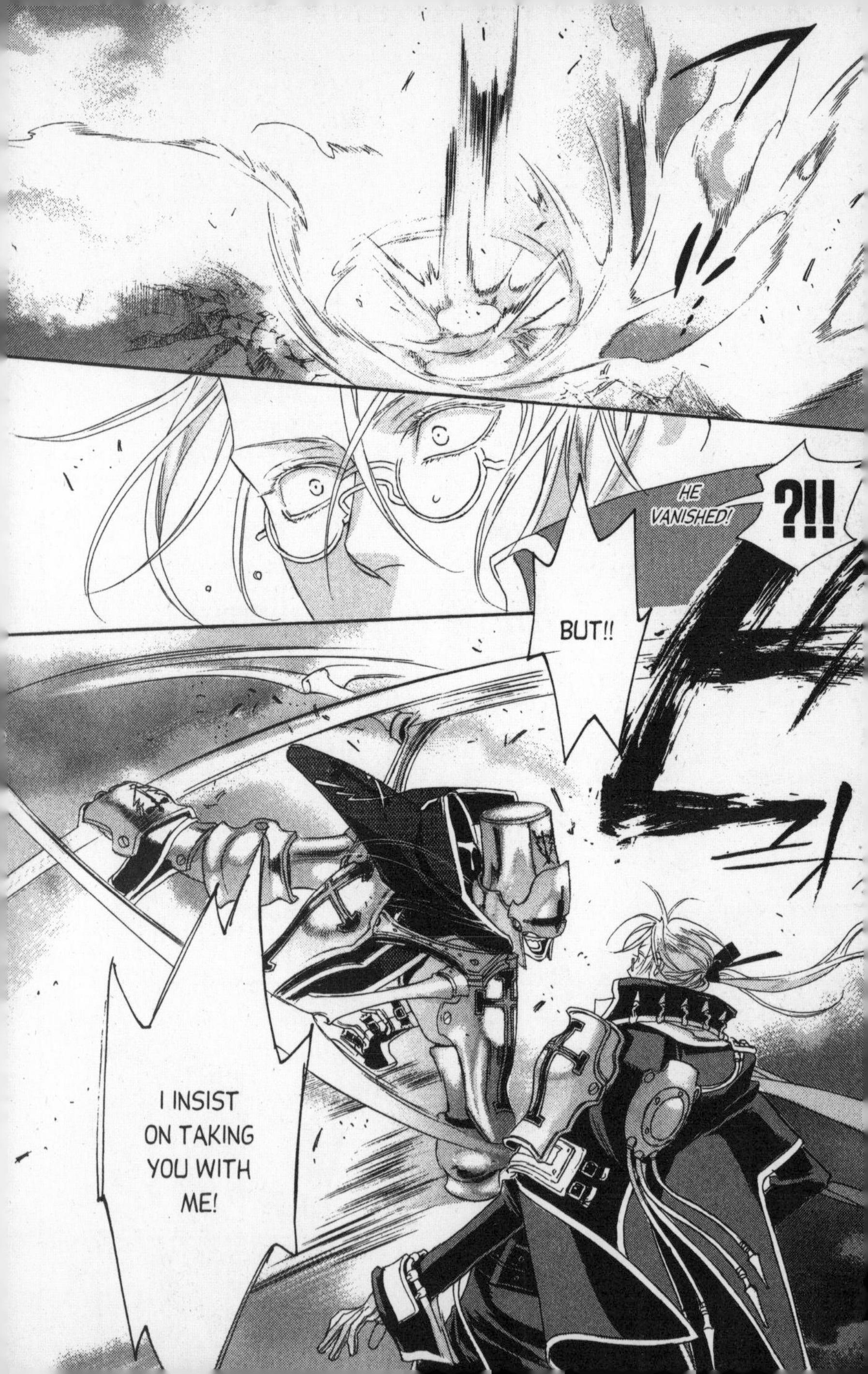
?!!
HE VANISHED!
BUT!!
I INSIST ON TAKING YOU WITH ME!

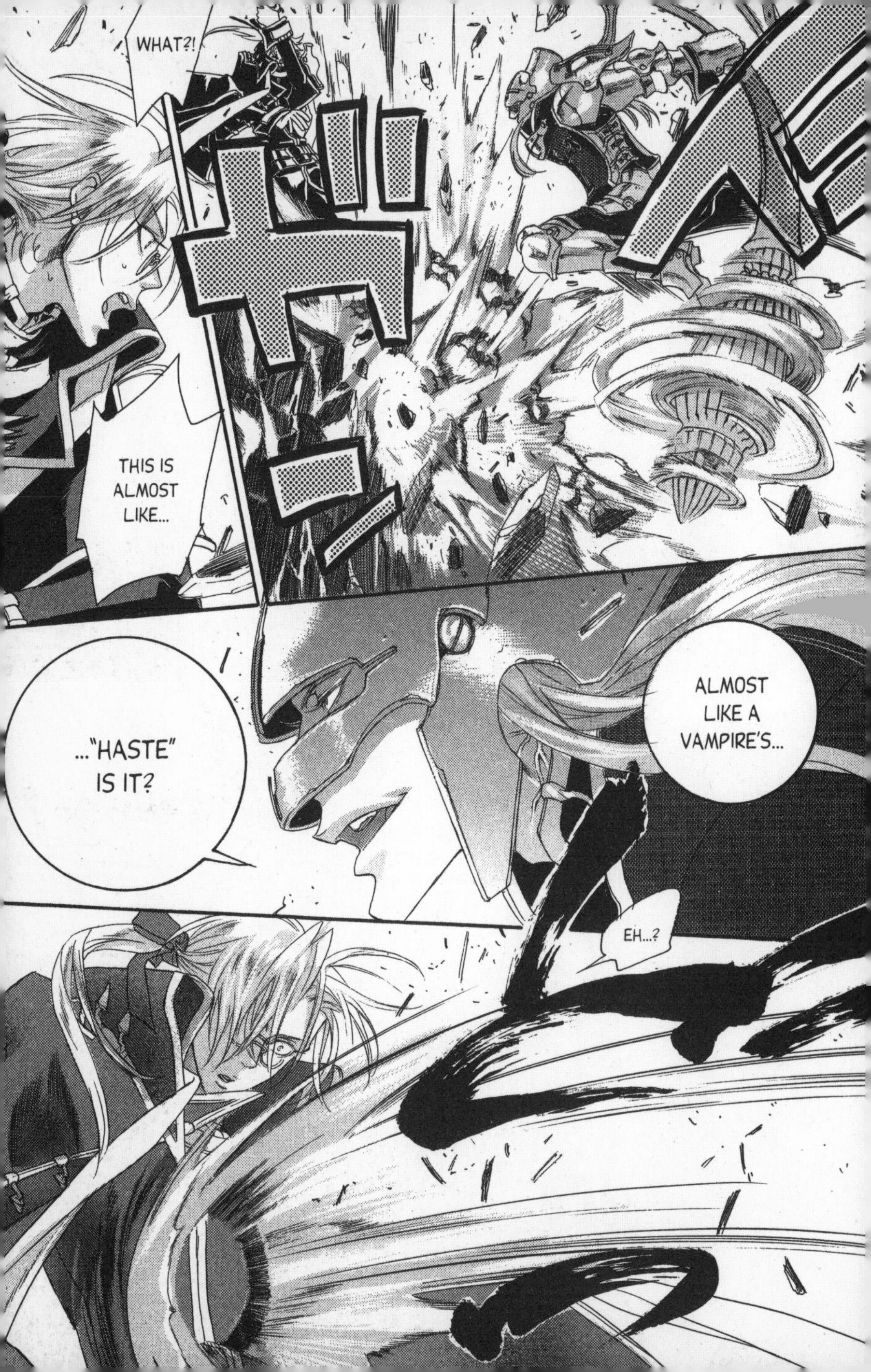
WHAT?!
THIS IS ALMOST LIKE...
ALMOST LIKE A VAMPIRE'S...
..."HASTE" IS IT?
EH...?

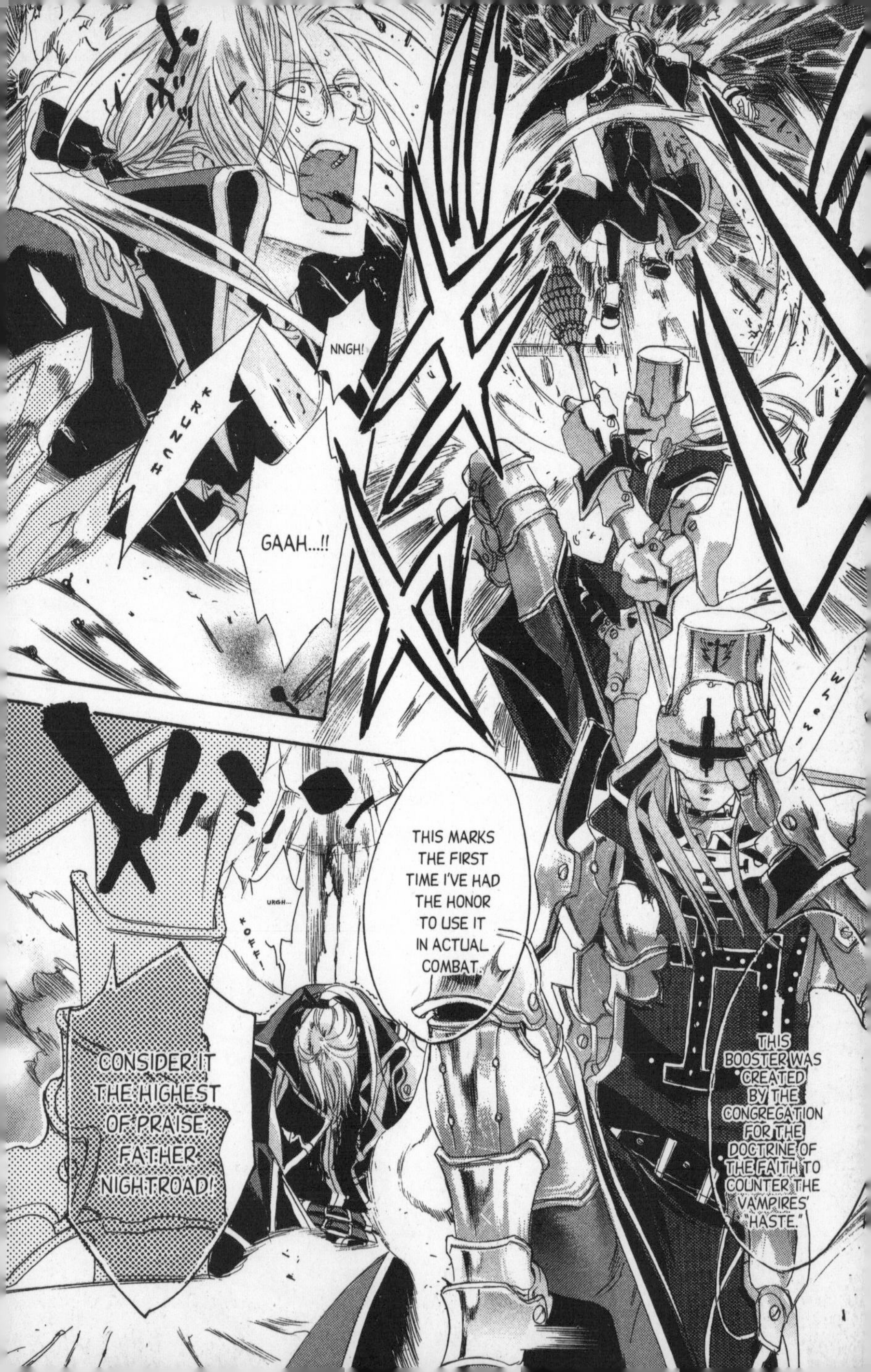
WHEW!
THIS MARKS THE FIRST TIME I'VE HAD THE HONOR TO USE IT IN ACTUAL COMBAT.
THIS BOOSTER WAS CREATED BY THE CONGREGATION FOR THE DOCTRINE OF THE FAITH TO COUNTER THE VAMPIRES' "HASTE."
KRUNCH
NNGH!
GAAH...!!
URGH...
KOFF!
CONSIDER IT THE HIGHEST OF PRAISE, FATHER NIGHTROAD!

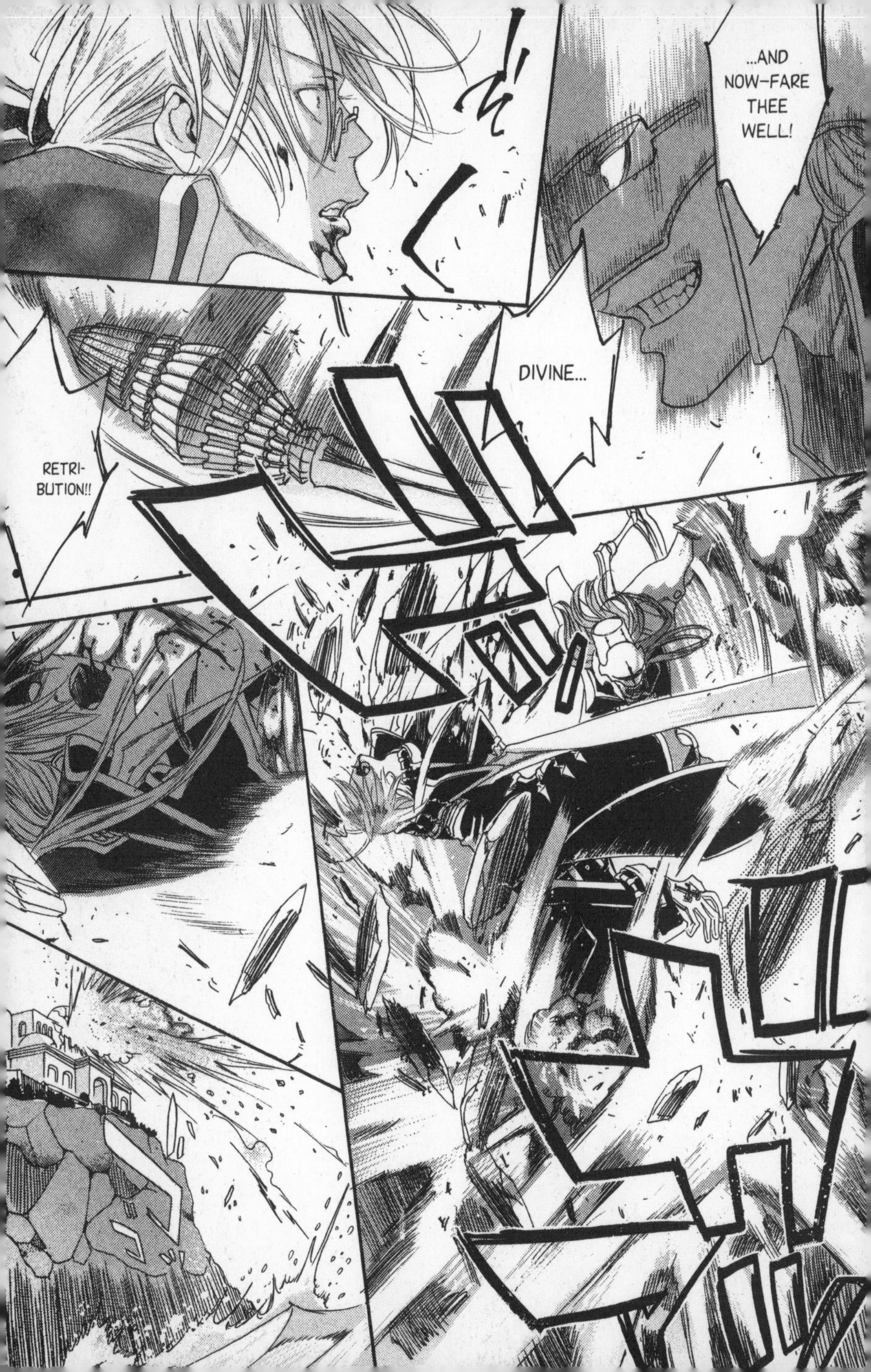
...AND NOW—FARE THEE WELL!
DIVINE...
RETRI-BUTION!!

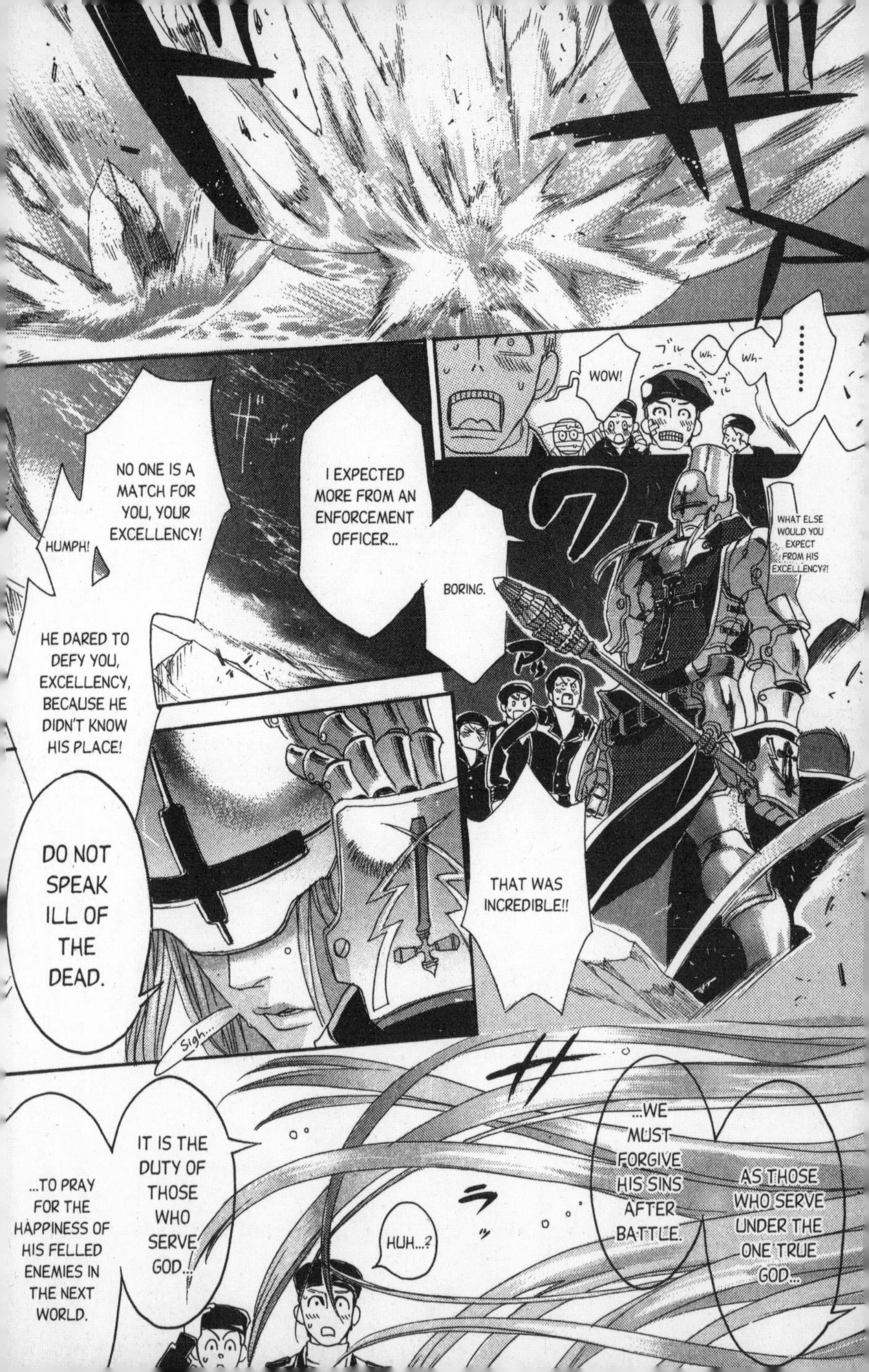
......
Wh-
Wh-
WOW!
WHAT ELSE WOULD YOU EXPECT FROM HIS EXCELLENCY?!
BORING.
I EXPECTED MORE FROM AN ENFORCEMENT OFFICER...
THAT WAS INCREDIBLE!!
NO ONE IS A MATCH FOR YOU, YOUR EXCELLENCY!
HUMPH!
HE DARED TO DEFY YOU, EXCELLENCY, BECAUSE HE DIDN'T KNOW HIS PLACE!
DO NOT SPEAK ILL OF THE DEAD.
Sigh...
AS THOSE WHO SERVE UNDER THE ONE TRUE GOD...
...WE MUST FORGIVE HIS SINS AFTER BATTLE.
HUH...?
IT IS THE DUTY OF THOSE WHO SERVE GOD...
...TO PRAY FOR THE HAPPINESS OF HIS FELLED ENEMIES IN THE NEXT WORLD.

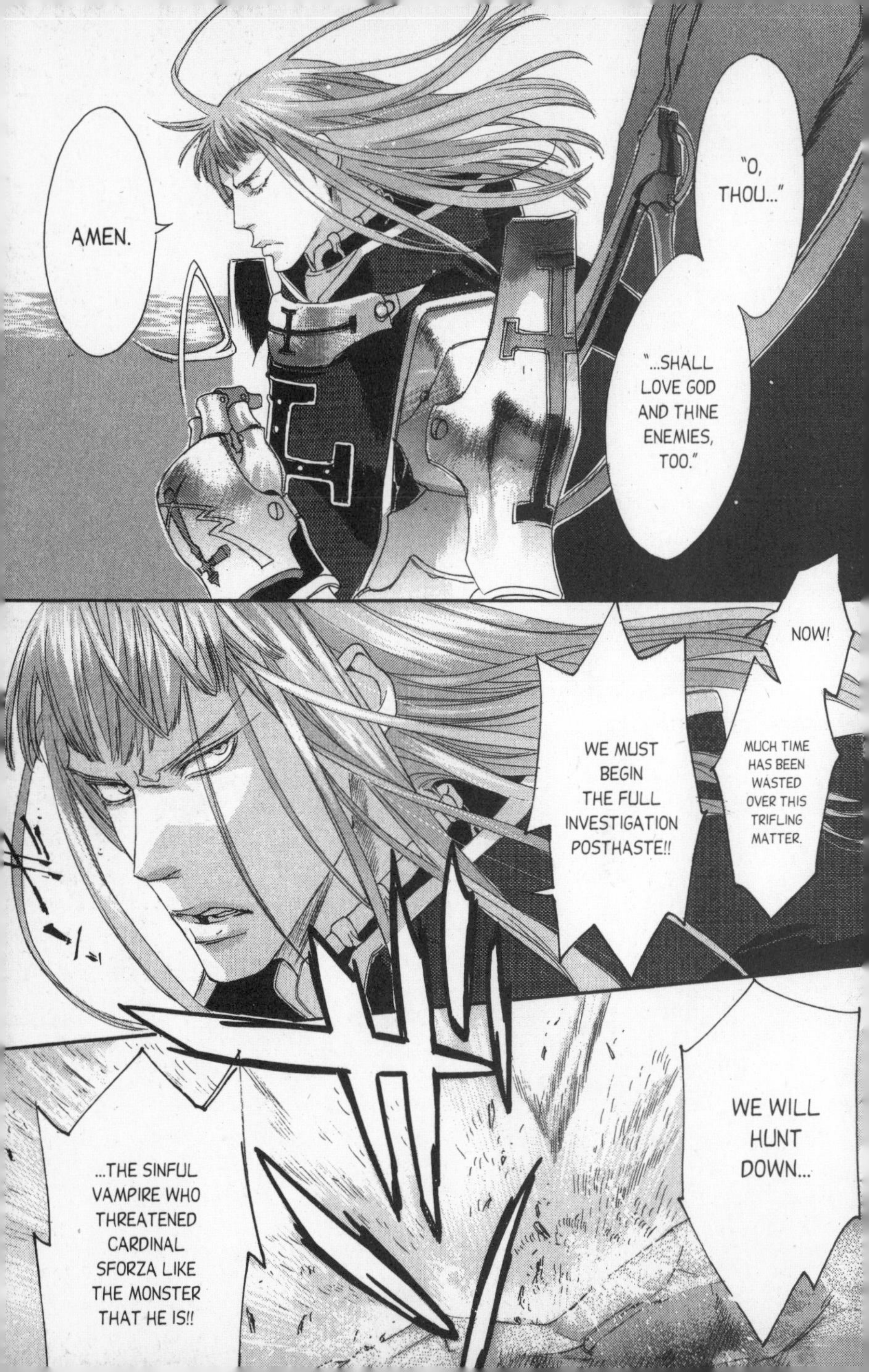
"O, THOU..."
"...SHALL LOVE GOD AND THINE ENEMIES, TOO."
AMEN.
NOW!
MUCH TIME HAS BEEN WASTED OVER THIS TRIFLING MATTER.
WE MUST BEGIN THE FULL INVESTIGATION POSTHASTE!!
WE WILL HUNT DOWN...
...THE SINFUL VAMPIRE WHO THREATENED CARDINAL SFORZA LIKE THE MONSTER THAT HE IS!!

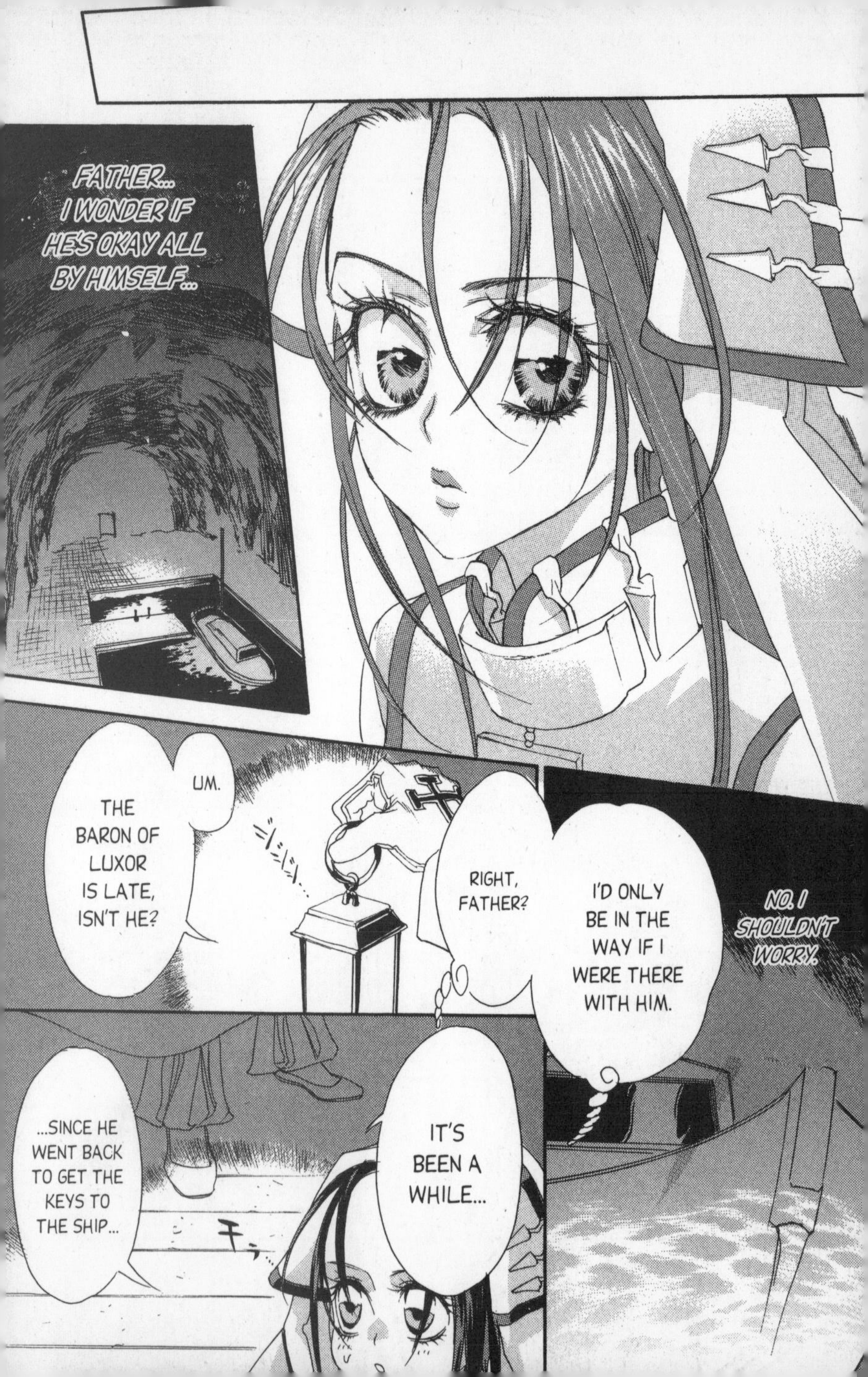
FATHER... I WONDER IF HE'S OKAY ALL BY HIMSELF...
NO. I SHOULDN'T WORRY.
I'D ONLY BE IN THE WAY IF I WERE THERE WITH HIM.
RIGHT, FATHER?
UM.
THE BARON OF LUXOR IS LATE, ISN'T HE?
IT'S BEEN A WHILE...
...SINCE HE WENT BACK TO GET THE KEYS TO THE SHIP...

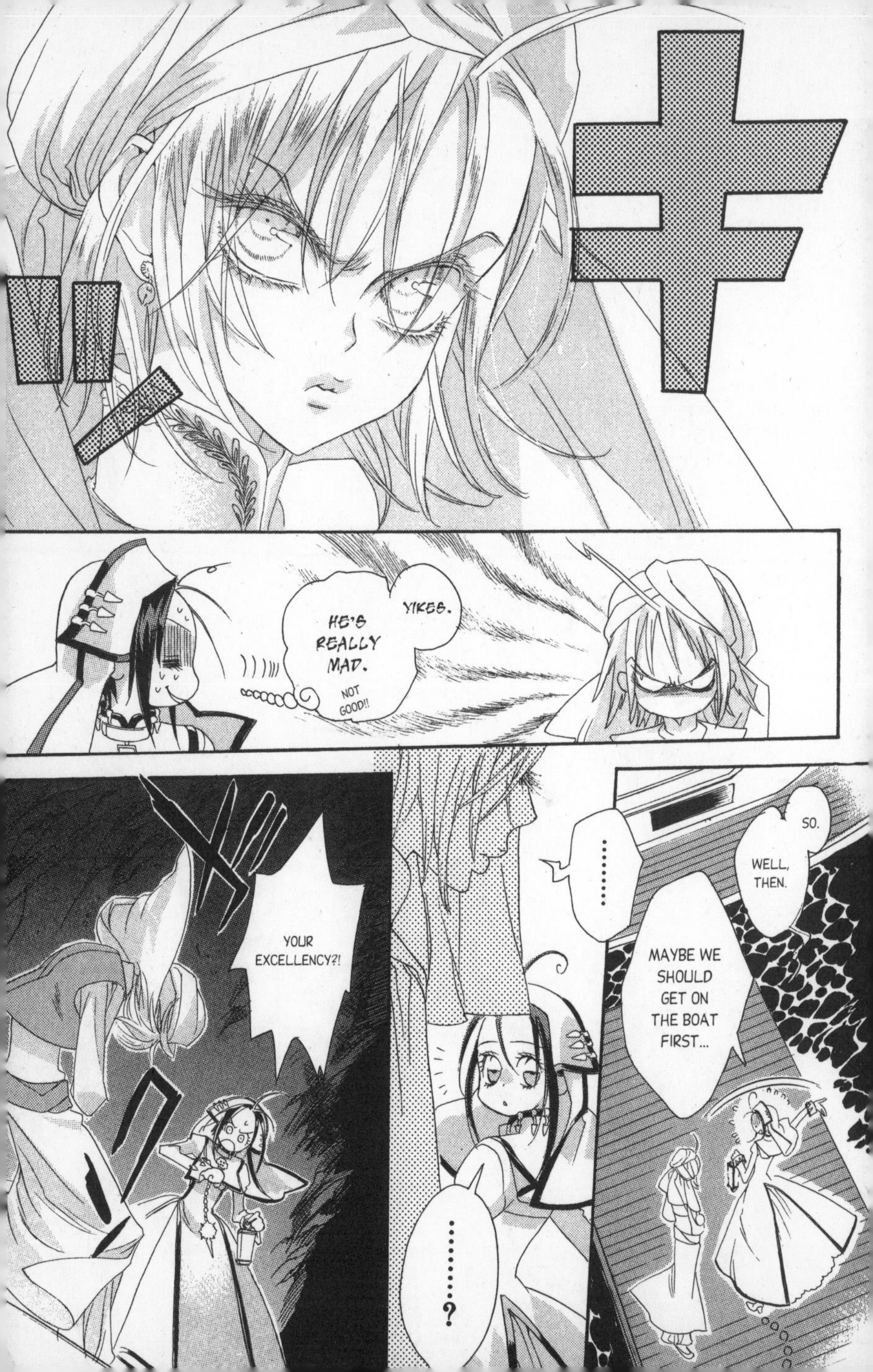

YIKES.
HE'S REALLY MAD.
NOT GOOD!!
SO.
WELL, THEN.
......
MAYBE WE SHOULD GET ON THE BOAT FIRST...
......?
YOUR EXCELLENCY?!

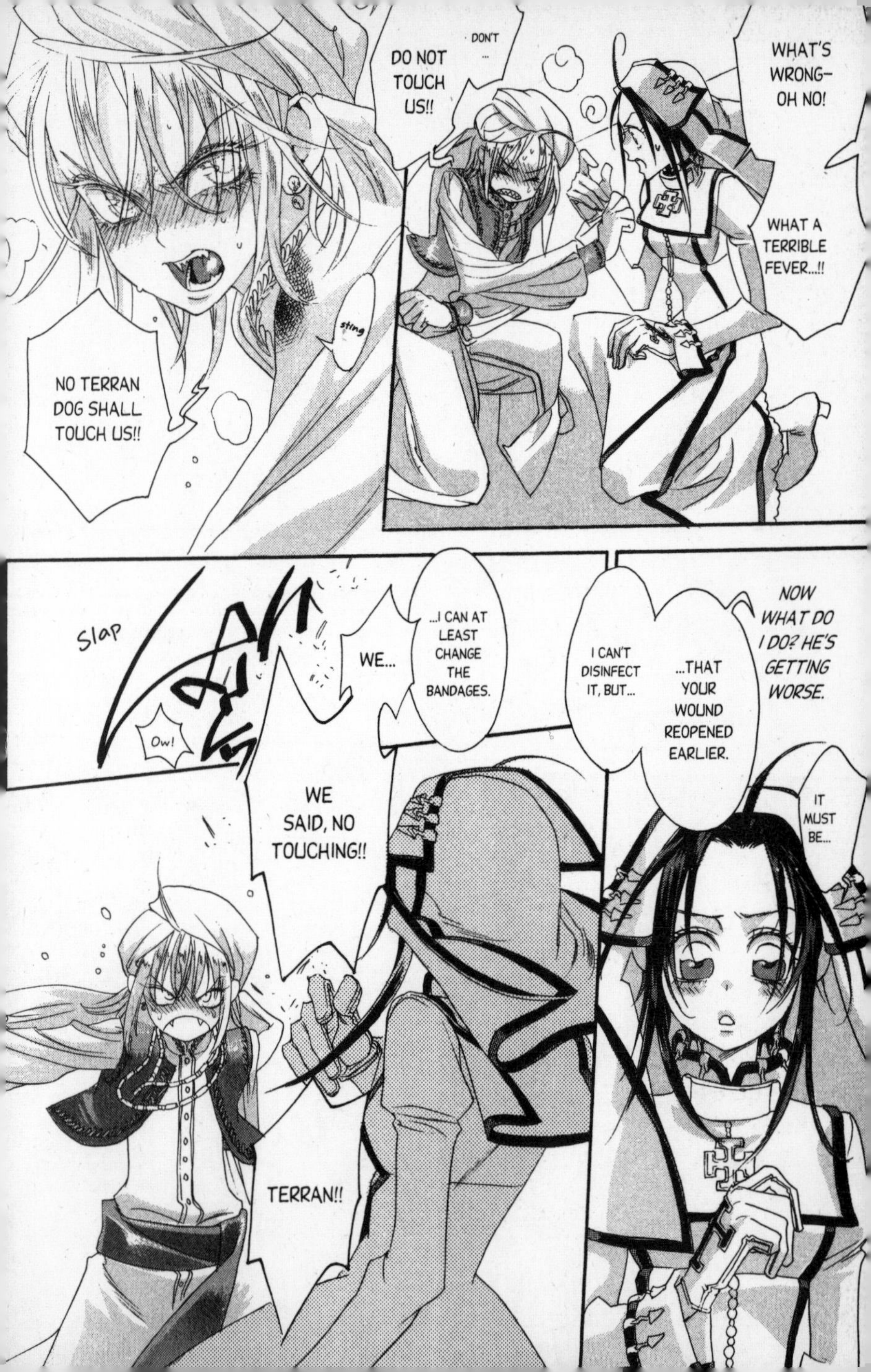
WHAT'S WRONG— OH NO!
DON'T ...
DO NOT TOUCH US!!
WHAT A TERRIBLE FEVER...!!
sting
NO TERRAN DOG SHALL TOUCH US!!
NOW WHAT DO I DO? HE'S GETTING WORSE.
IT MUST BE...
...THAT YOUR WOUND REOPENED EARLIER.
I CAN'T DISINFECT IT, BUT...
...I CAN AT LEAST CHANGE THE BANDAGES.
WE...
Slap
Ow!
WE SAID, NO TOUCHING!!
TERRAN!!

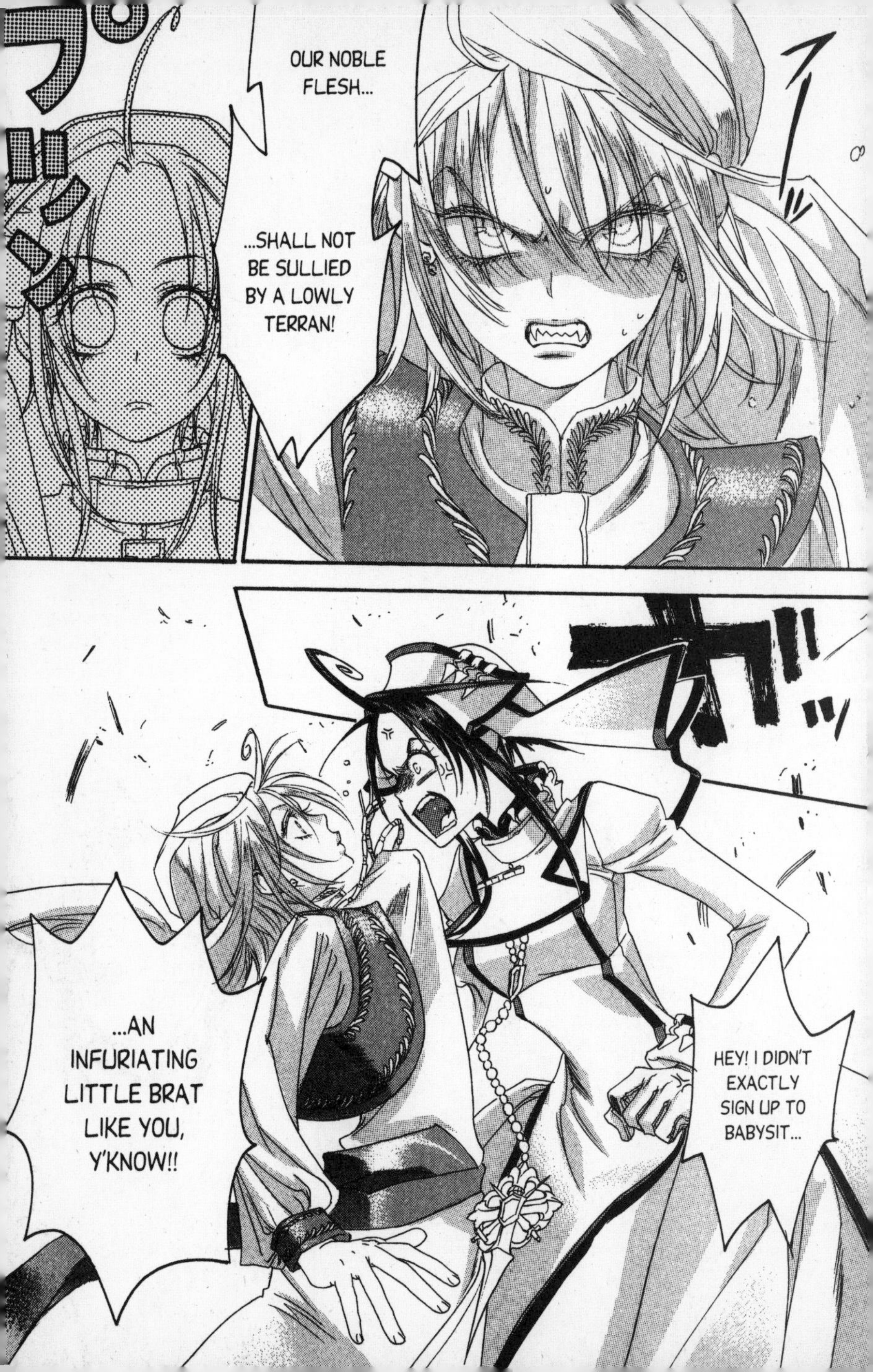
OUR NOBLE FLESH...
...SHALL NOT BE SULLIED BY A LOWLY TERRAN!
HEY! I DIDN'T EXACTLY SIGN UP TO BABYSIT...
...AN INFURIATING LITTLE BRAT LIKE YOU, Y'KNOW!!

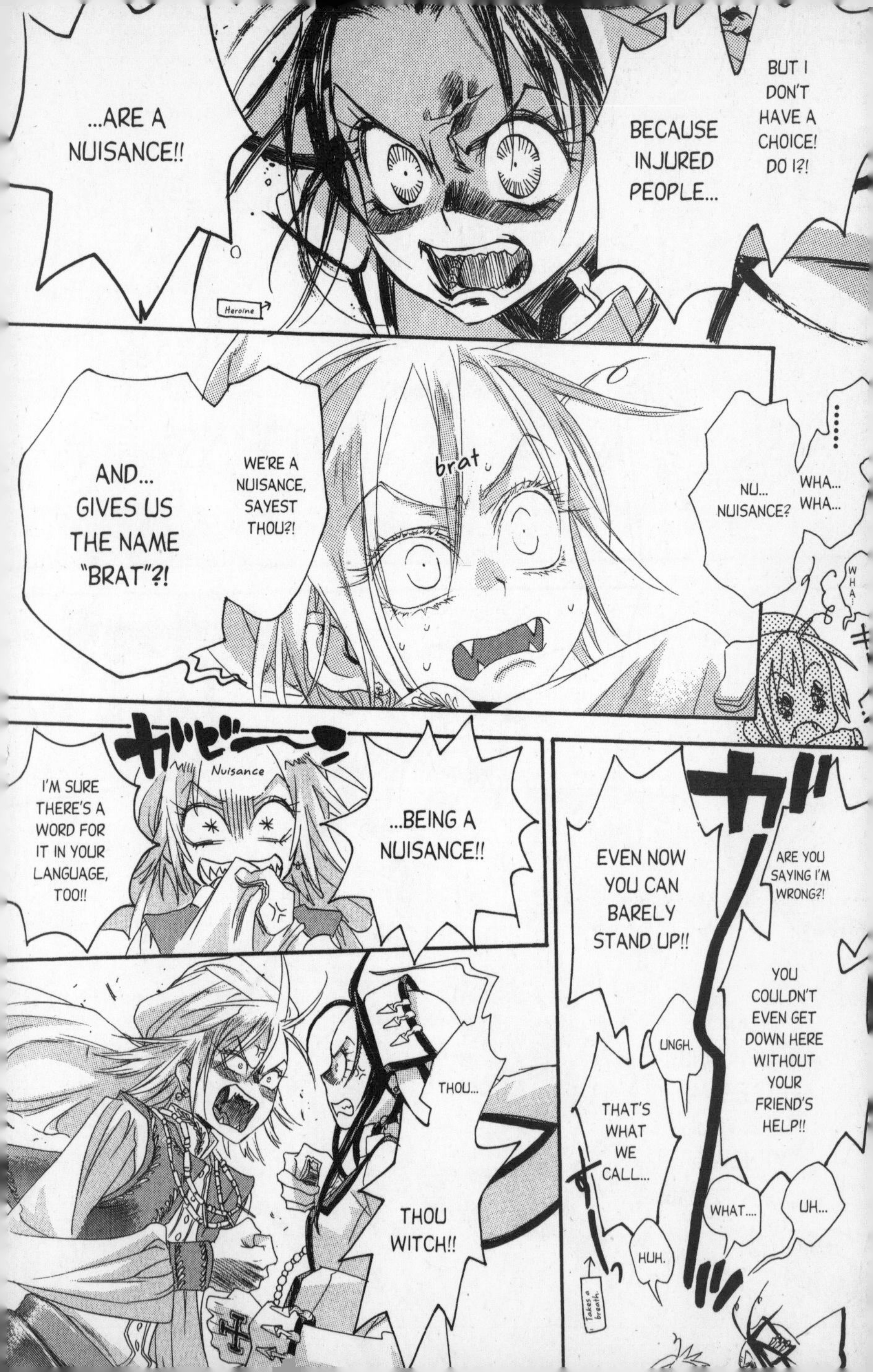
BUT I DON'T HAVE A CHOICE! DO I?!
BECAUSE INJURED PEOPLE...
...ARE A NUISANCE!!
Heroine
WHA... WHA...
NU... NUISANCE?
WHA...
brat
WE'RE A NUISANCE, SAYEST THOU?!
AND... GIVES US THE NAME "BRAT"?!
ARE YOU SAYING I'M WRONG?!
EVEN NOW YOU CAN BARELY STAND UP!!
YOU COULDN'T EVEN GET DOWN HERE WITHOUT YOUR FRIEND'S HELP!!
UNGH.
UH...
WHAT....
THAT'S WHAT WE CALL...
HUH.
Takes a breath.
Nuisance
...BEING A NUISANCE!!
I'M SURE THERE'S A WORD FOR IT IN YOUR LANGUAGE, TOO!!
THOU...
THOU WITCH!!

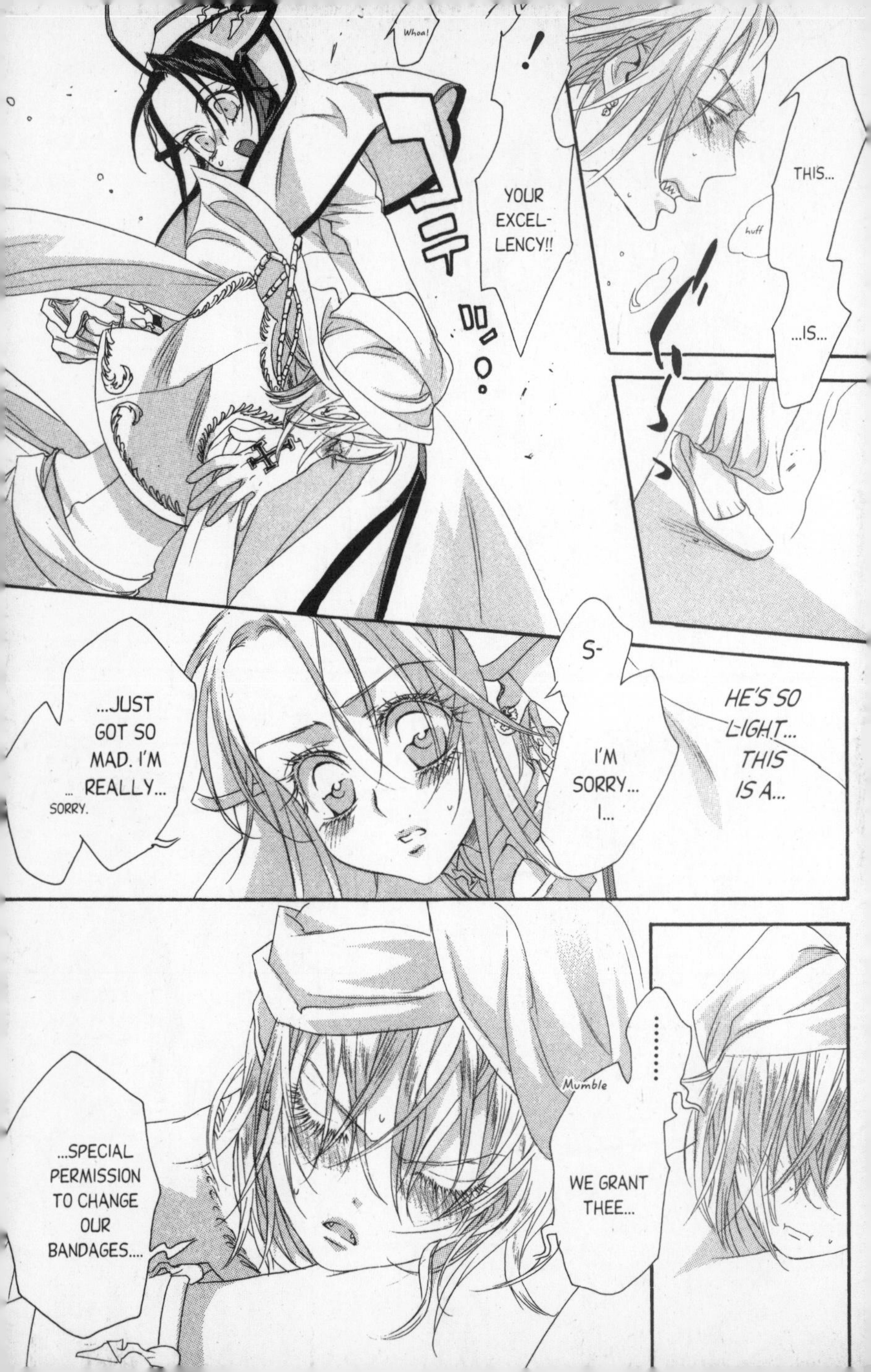
THIS...
huff
...IS...
Whoa!
YOUR EXCEL-LENCY!!
HE'S SO LIGHT... THIS IS A...
S-
I'M SORRY... I...
...JUST GOT SO MAD. I'M REALLY...
... SORRY.
......
Mumble
WE GRANT THEE...
...SPECIAL PERMISSION TO CHANGE OUR BANDAGES....

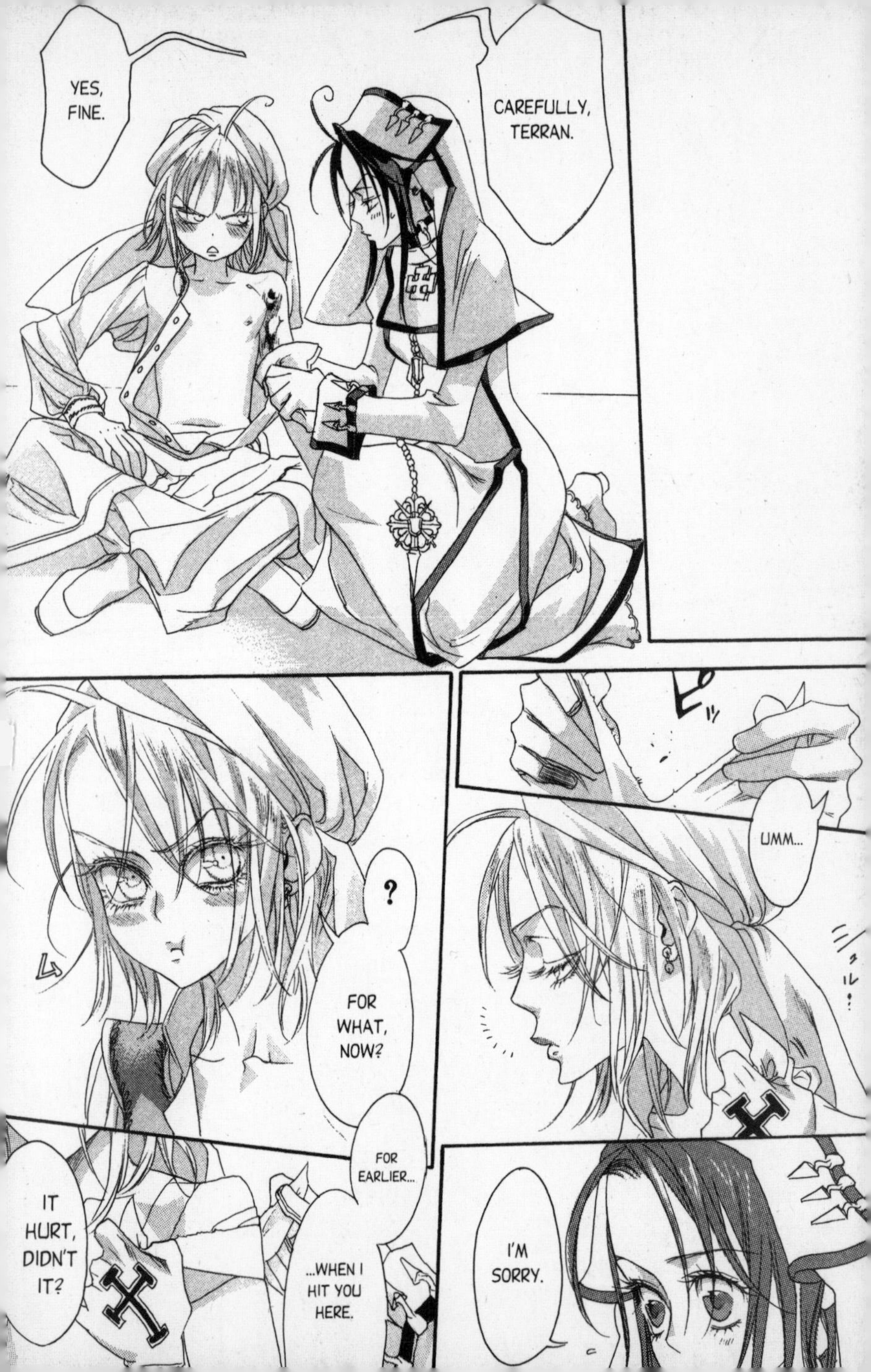

CAREFULLY, TERRAN.
YES, FINE.
UMM...
?
FOR WHAT, NOW?
I'M SORRY.
FOR EARLIER...
...WHEN I HIT YOU HERE.
IT HURT, DIDN'T IT?

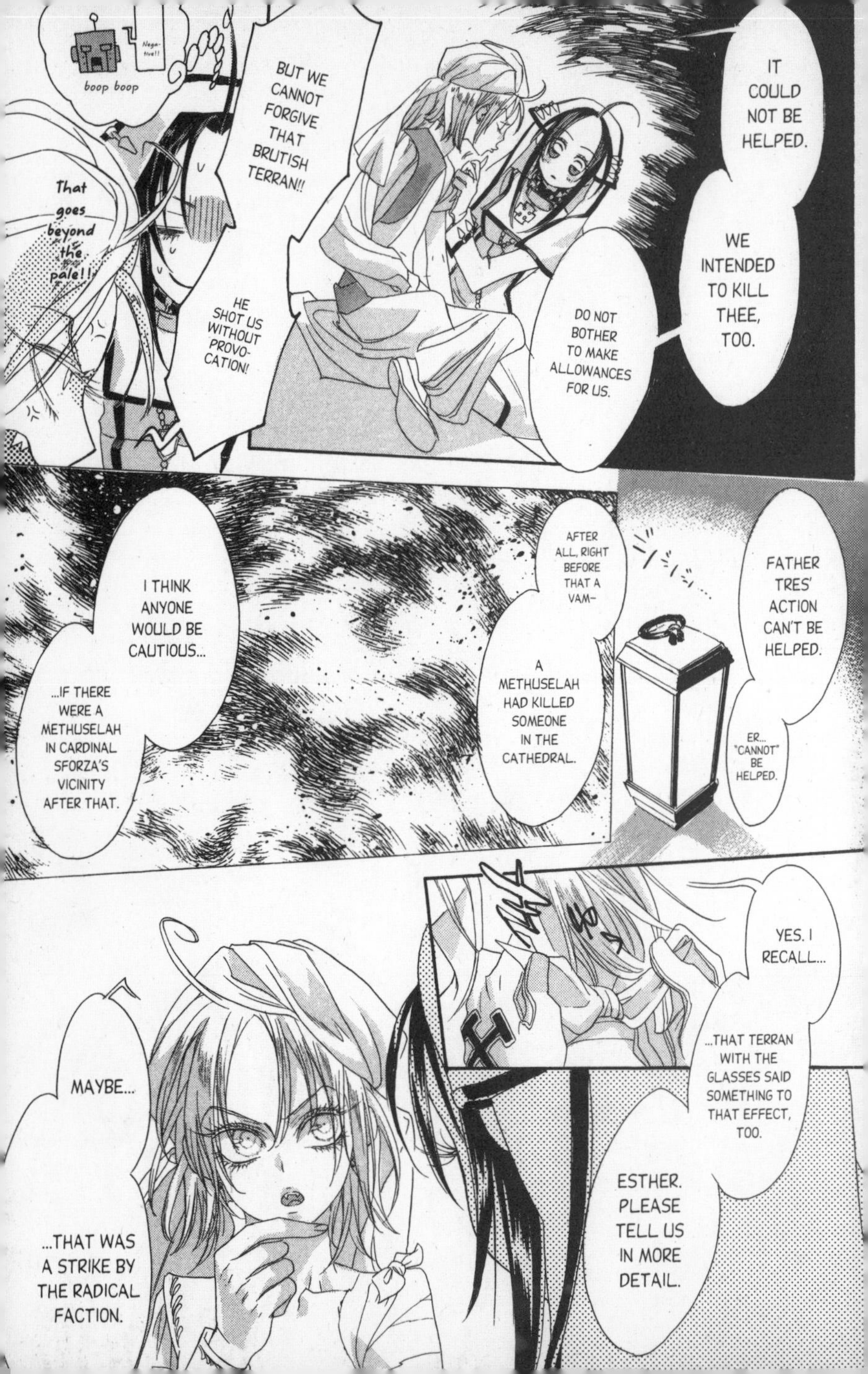
IT COULD NOT BE HELPED.
WE INTENDED TO KILL THEE, TOO.
DO NOT BOTHER TO MAKE ALLOWANCES FOR US.
BUT WE CANNOT FORGIVE THAT BRUTISH TERRAN!!
HE SHOT US WITHOUT PROVO-CATION!
Nega-tive!!
boop boop
That goes beyond the pale!!
FATHER TRES' ACTION CAN'T BE HELPED.
ER... "CANNOT" BE HELPED.
AFTER ALL, RIGHT BEFORE THAT A VAM—
A METHUSELAH HAD KILLED SOMEONE IN THE CATHEDRAL.
I THINK ANYONE WOULD BE CAUTIOUS...
...IF THERE WERE A METHUSELAH IN CARDINAL SFORZA'S VICINITY AFTER THAT.
YES. I RECALL...
...THAT TERRAN WITH THE GLASSES SAID SOMETHING TO THAT EFFECT, TOO.
ESTHER. PLEASE TELL US IN MORE DETAIL.
MAYBE...
...THAT WAS A STRIKE BY THE RADICAL FACTION.

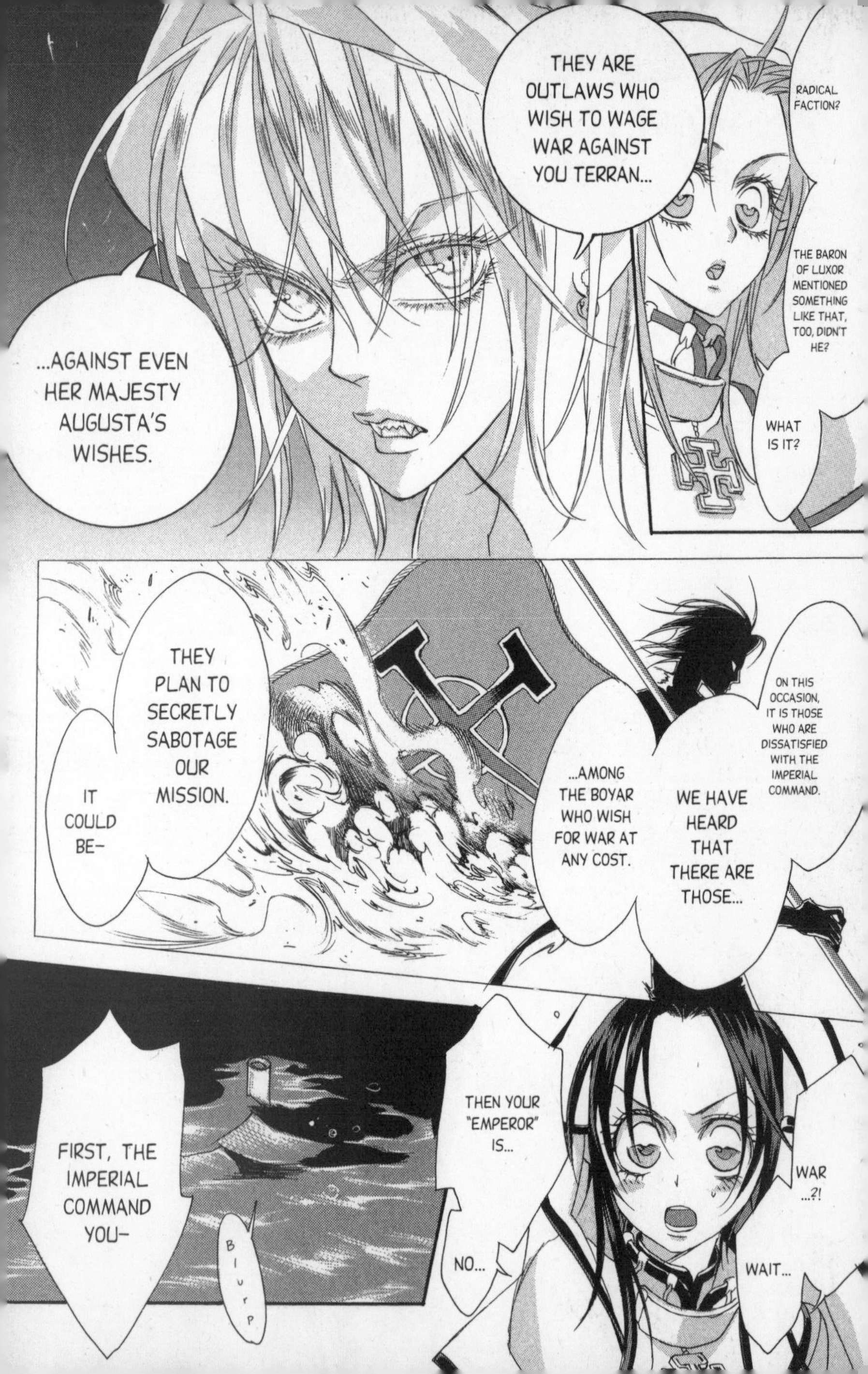

RADICAL FACTION?
THE BARON OF LUXOR MENTIONED SOMETHING LIKE THAT, TOO, DIDN'T HE?
WHAT IS IT?
THEY ARE OUTLAWS WHO WISH TO WAGE WAR AGAINST YOU TERRAN...
...AGAINST EVEN HER MAJESTY AUGUSTA'S WISHES.
ON THIS OCCASION, IT IS THOSE WHO ARE DISSATISFIED WITH THE IMPERIAL COMMAND.
WE HAVE HEARD THAT THERE ARE THOSE...
...AMONG THE BOYAR WHO WISH FOR WAR AT ANY COST.
THEY PLAN TO SECRETLY SABOTAGE OUR MISSION.
IT COULD BE-
WAR ...?!
WAIT...
THEN YOUR "EMPEROR" IS...
NO...
FIRST, THE IMPERIAL COMMAND YOU-
Blurp

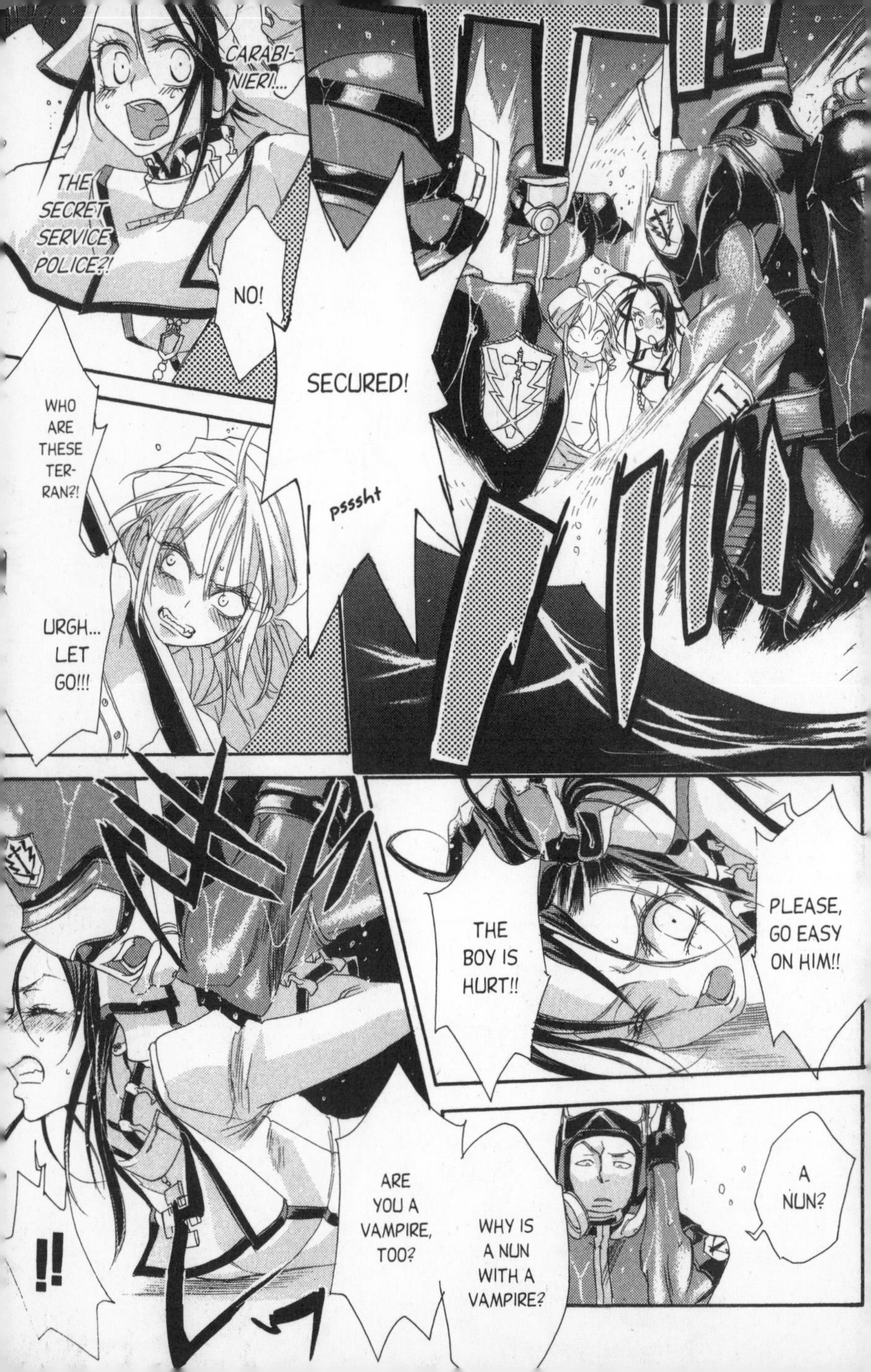
SECURED!
pssht
CARABI-NIERI!...
THE SECRET SERVICE POLICE?!
NO!
WHO ARE THESE TER-RAN?!
URGH... LET GO!!!
PLEASE, GO EASY ON HIM!!
THE BOY IS HURT!!
A NUN?
WHY IS A NUN WITH A VAMPIRE?
ARE YOU A VAMPIRE, TOO?
!!

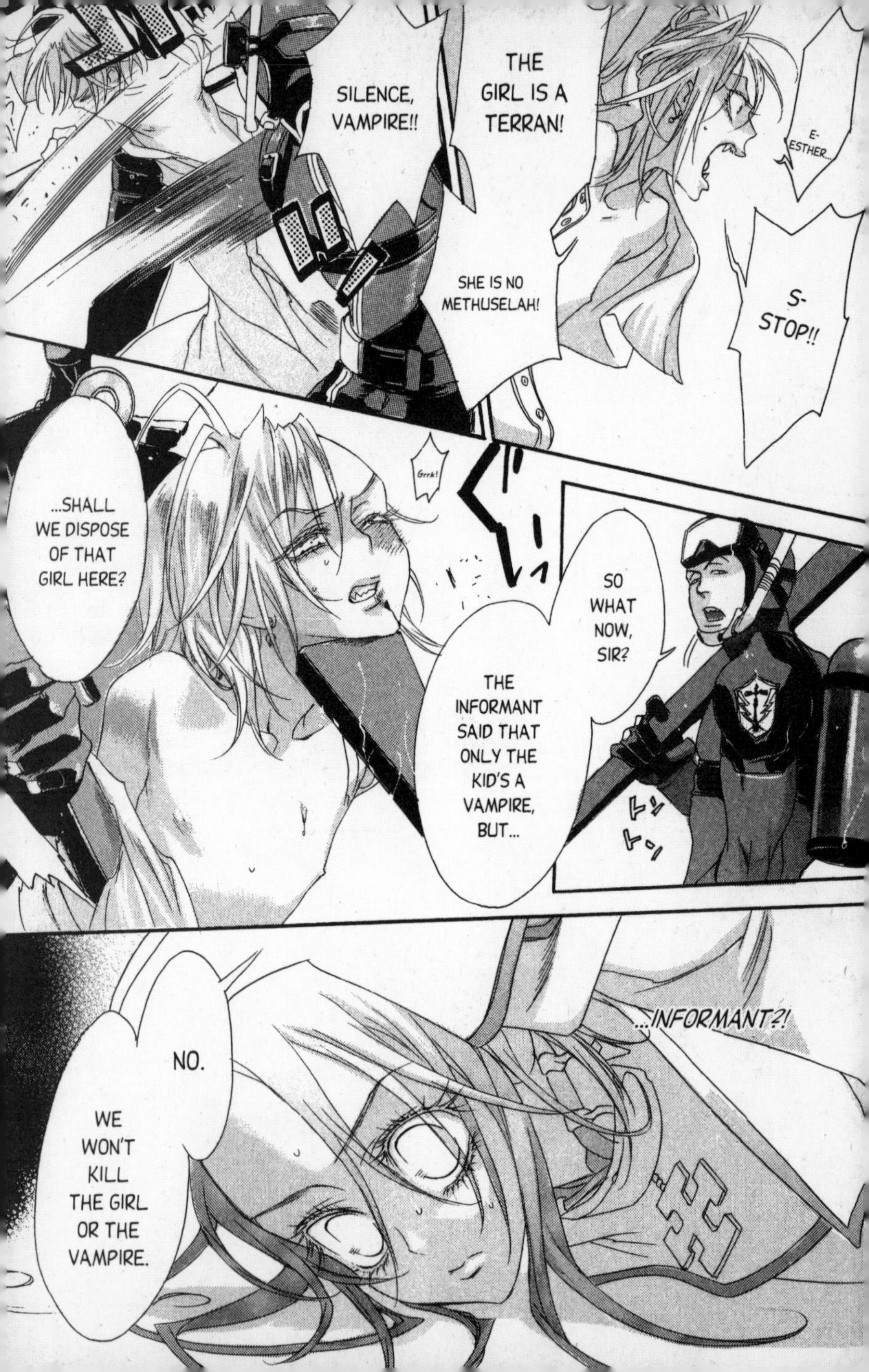
E-
ESTHER...
S-
STOP!!
THE GIRL IS A TERRAN!
SHE IS NO METHUSELAH!
SILENCE, VAMPIRE!!
SO WHAT NOW, SIR?
THE INFORMANT SAID THAT ONLY THE KID'S A VAMPIRE, BUT...
Grrk!
...SHALL WE DISPOSE OF THAT GIRL HERE?
...INFORMANT?!
NO.
WE WON'T KILL THE GIRL OR THE VAMPIRE.

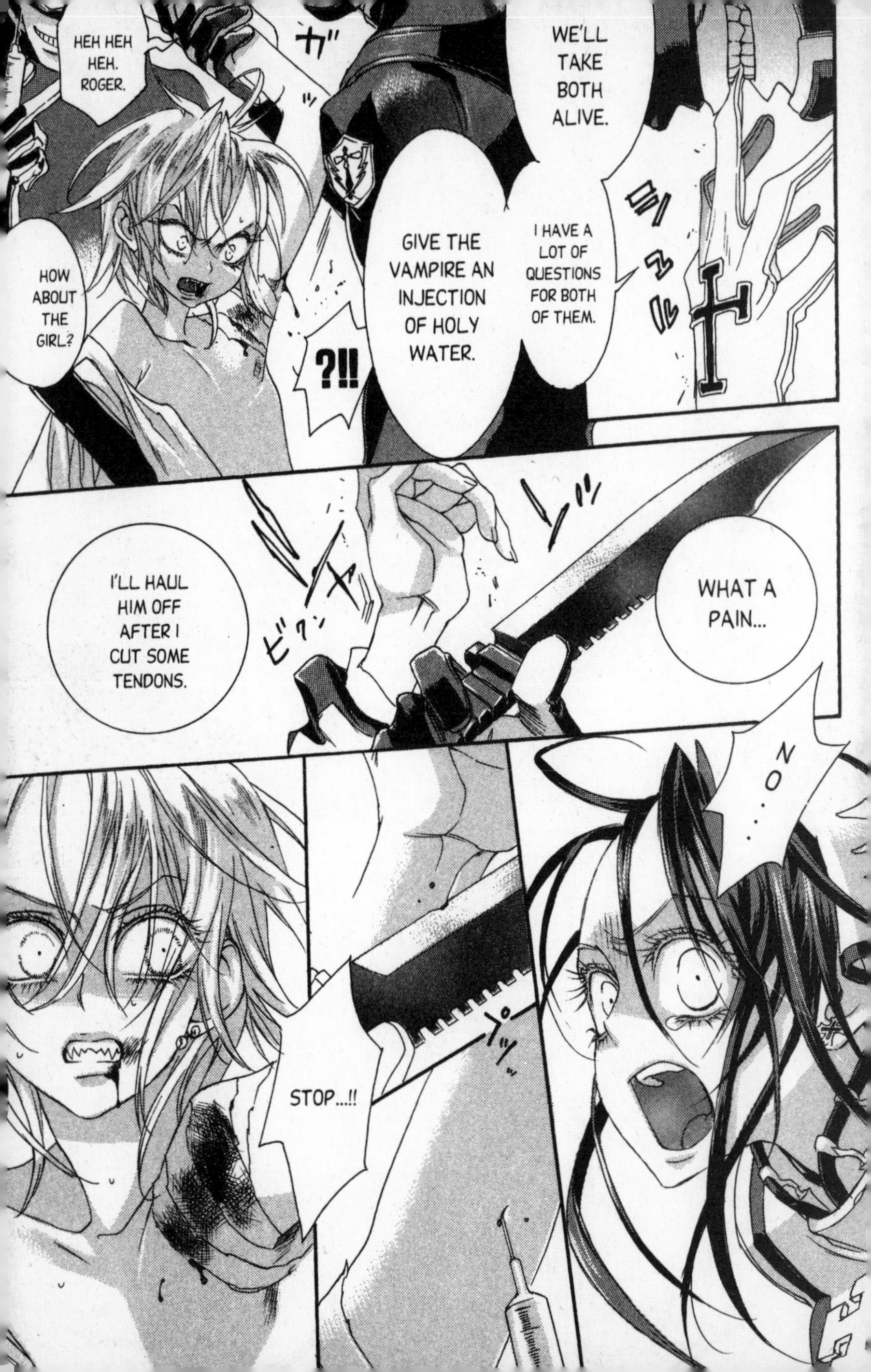
WE'LL TAKE BOTH ALIVE.
I HAVE A LOT OF QUESTIONS FOR BOTH OF THEM.
GIVE THE VAMPIRE AN INJECTION OF HOLY WATER.
?!!
HEH HEH HEH. ROGER.
HOW ABOUT THE GIRL?
WHAT A PAIN...
I'LL HAUL HIM OFF AFTER I CUT SOME TENDONS.
NO...
STOP...!!

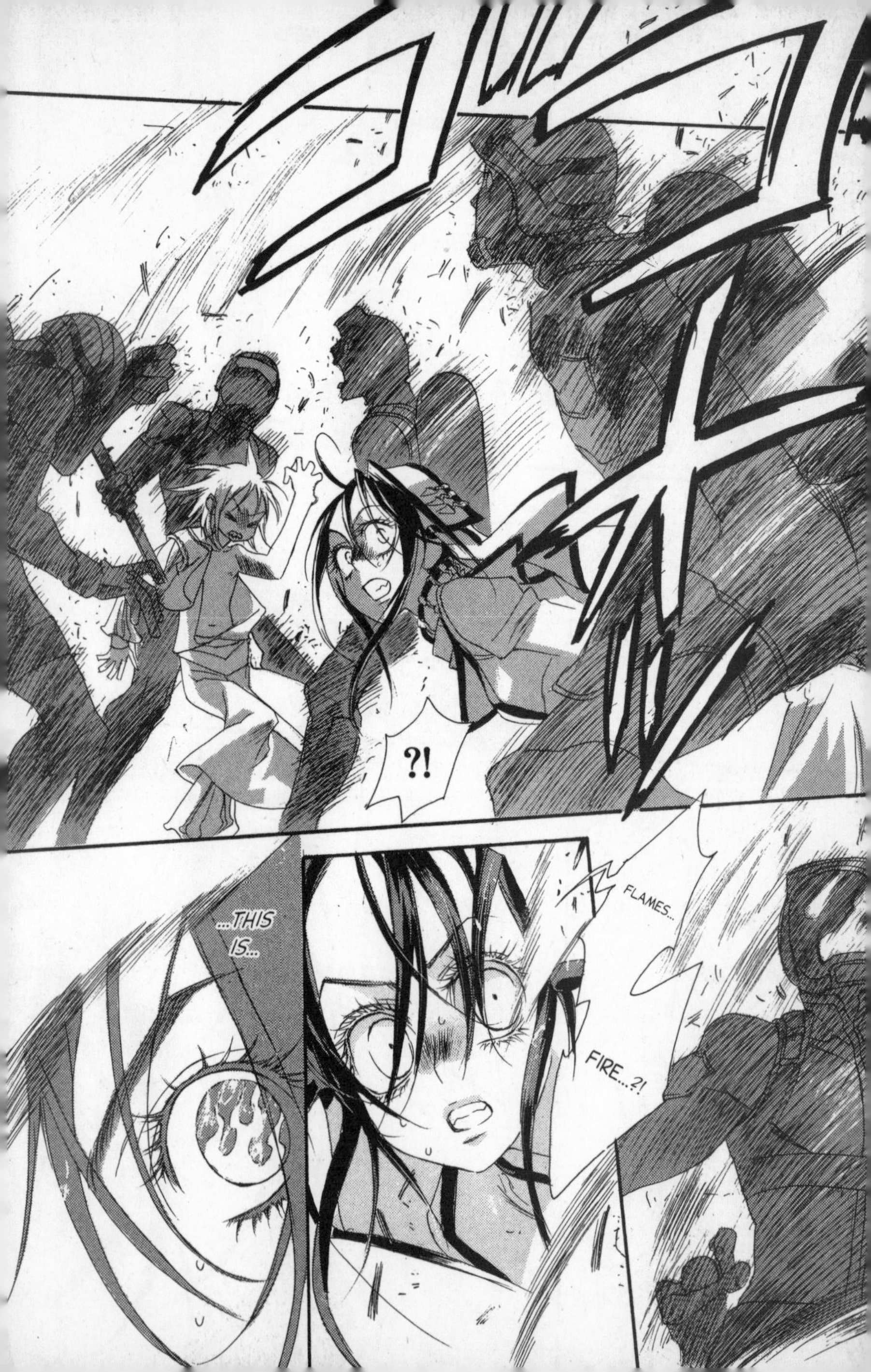
?!
FLAMES...
FIRE...?!
...THIS IS...

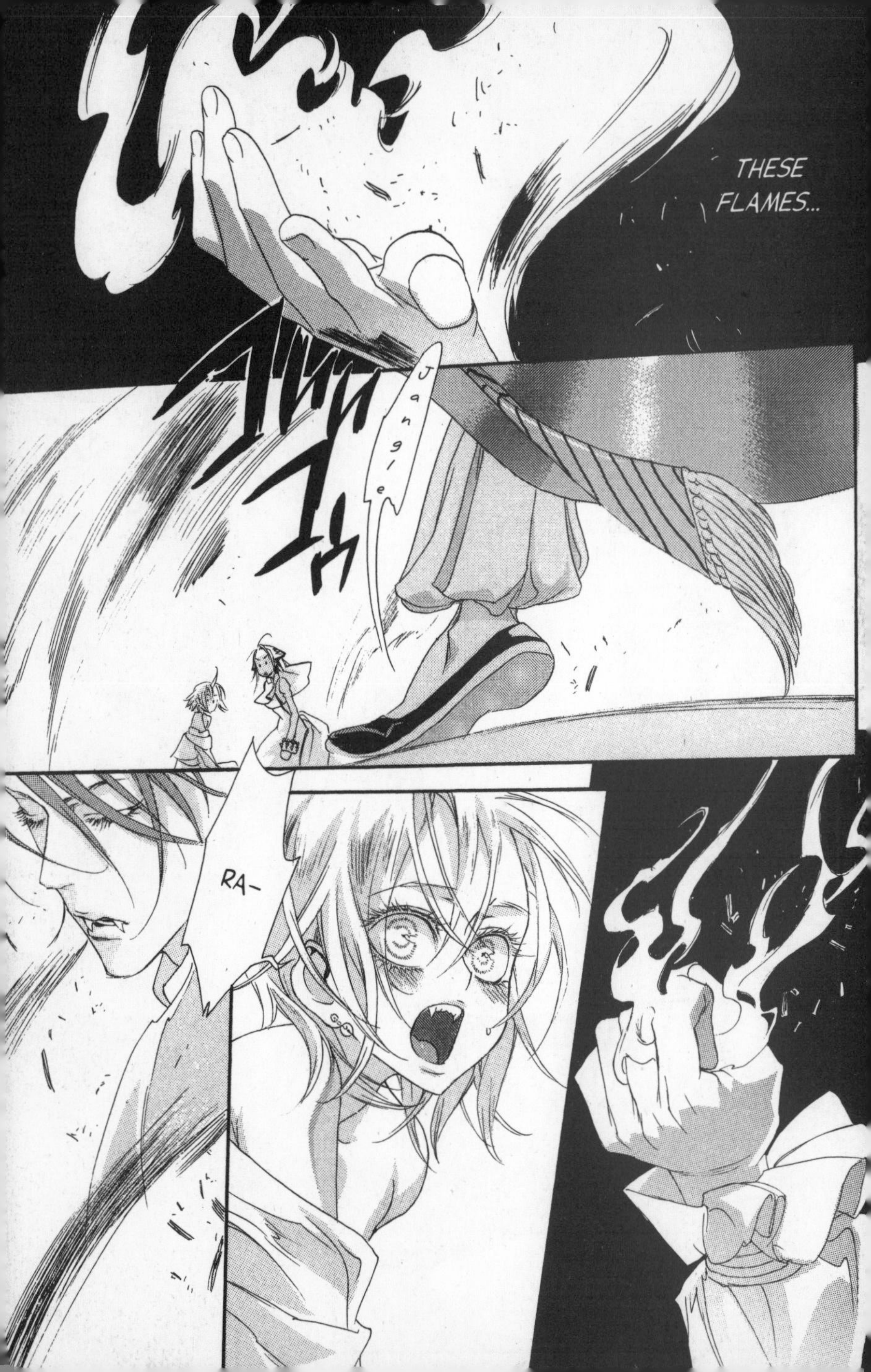
THESE FLAMES...
Jangle
RA-

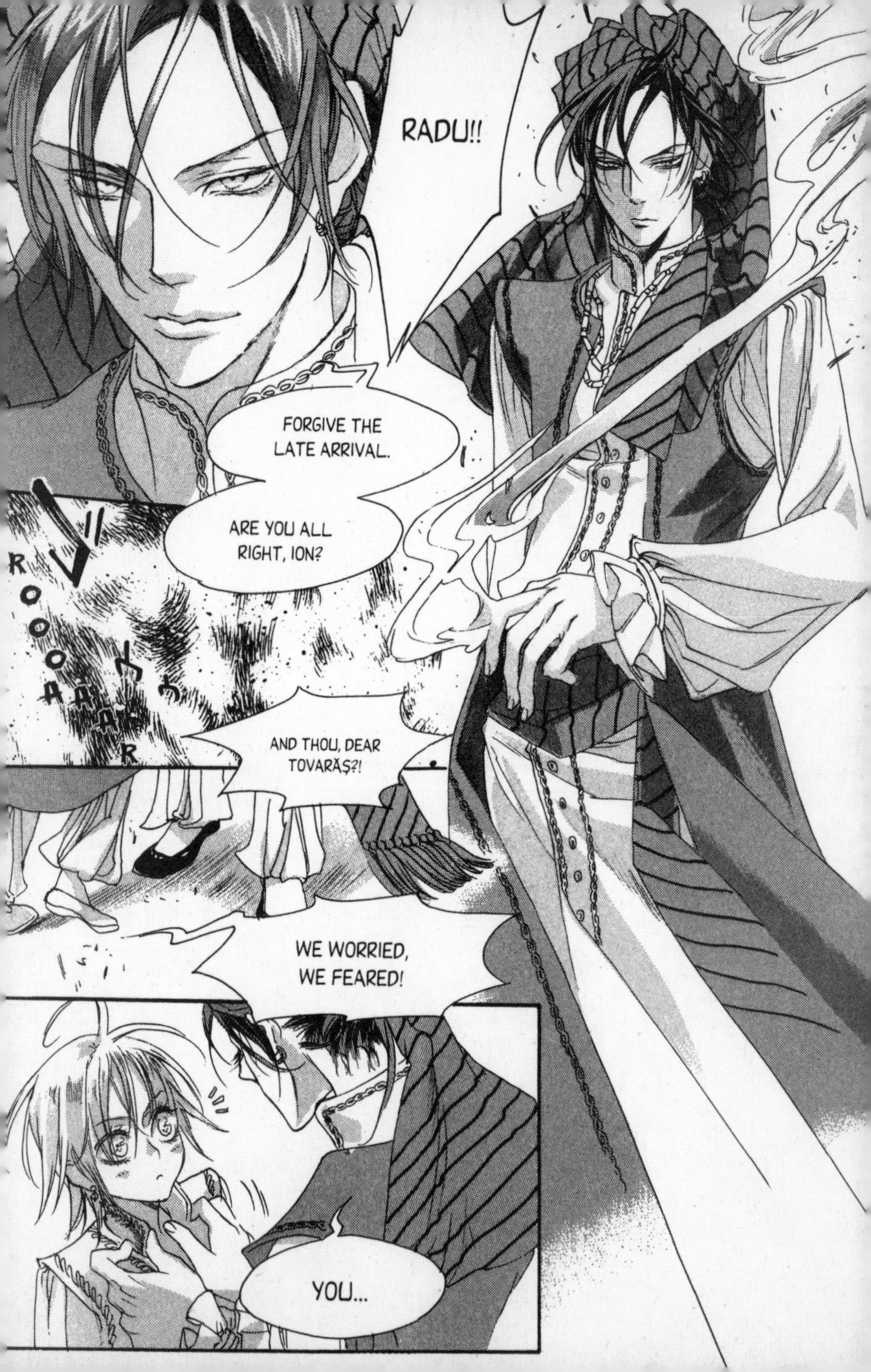
RADU!!
FORGIVE THE LATE ARRIVAL.
ARE YOU ALL RIGHT, ION?
ROOOOAAAR
AND THOU, DEAR TOVARĂŞ?!
WE WORRIED, WE FEARED!
YOU...

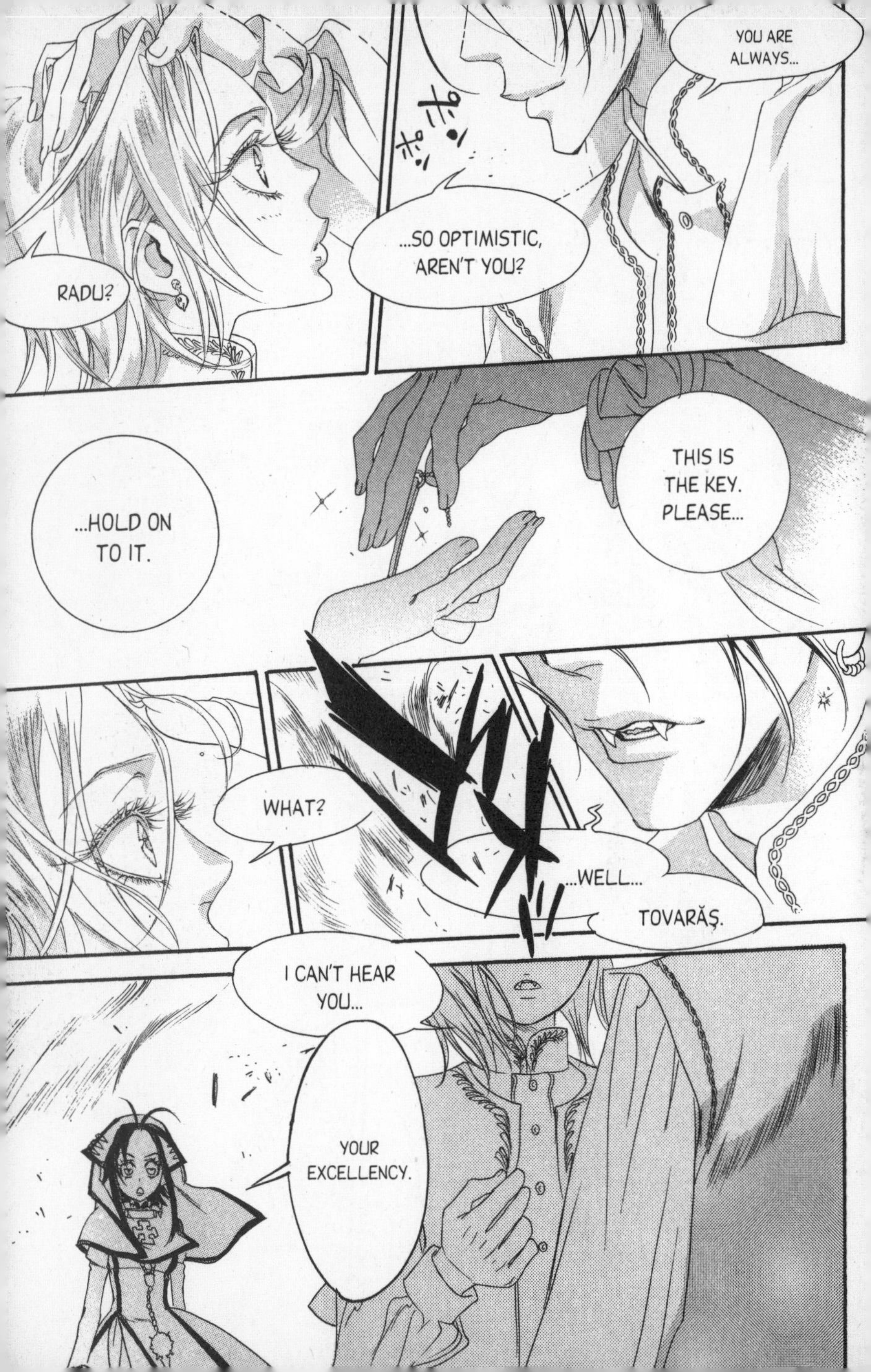
YOU ARE ALWAYS...
...SO OPTIMISTIC, AREN'T YOU?
RADU?
THIS IS THE KEY. PLEASE...
...HOLD ON TO IT.
...WELL...
TOVARĂȘ.
WHAT?
I CAN'T HEAR YOU...
YOUR EXCELLENCY.

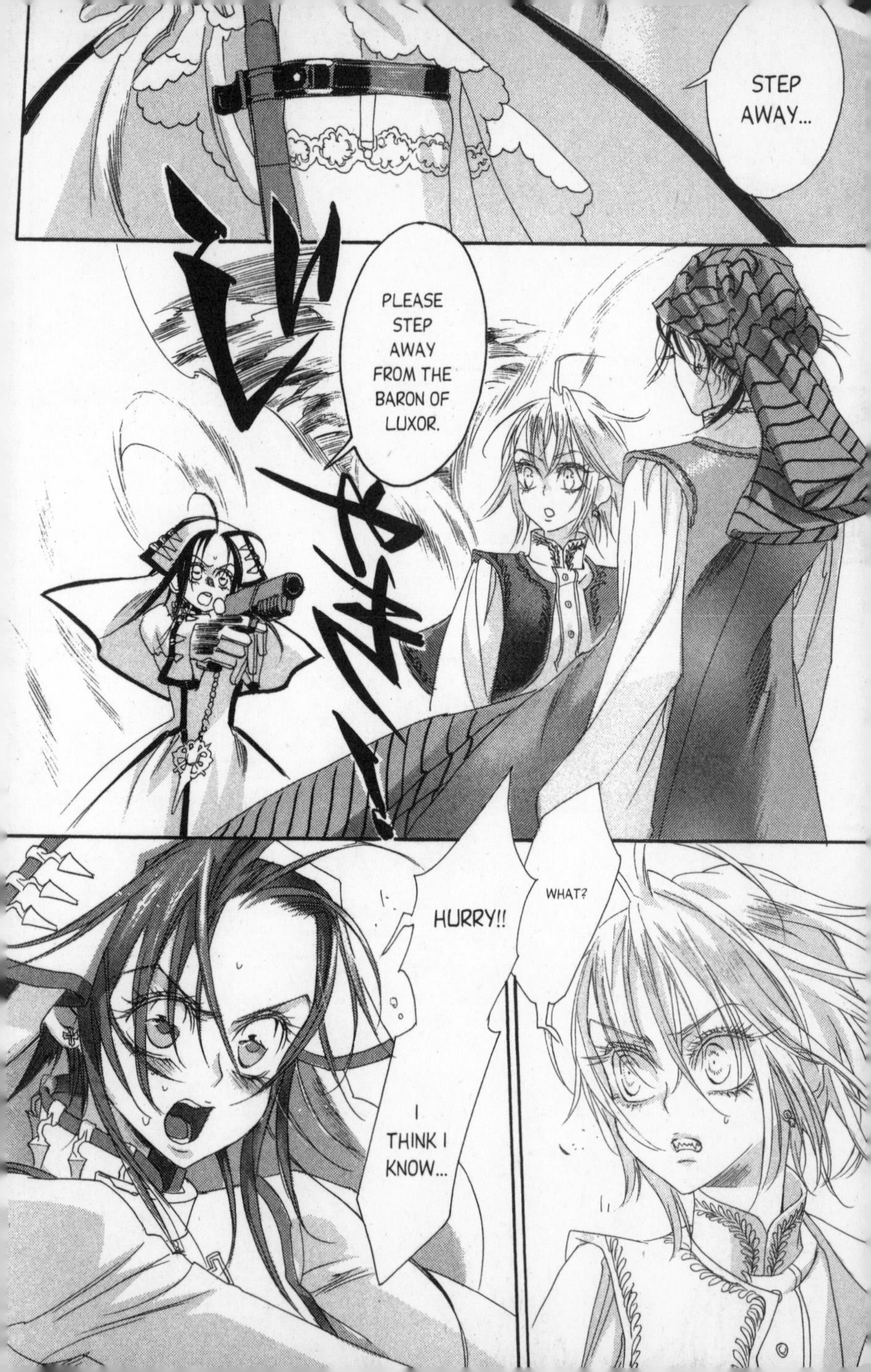
STEP AWAY...
PLEASE STEP AWAY FROM THE BARON OF LUXOR.
WHAT?
HURRY!!
I THINK I KNOW...

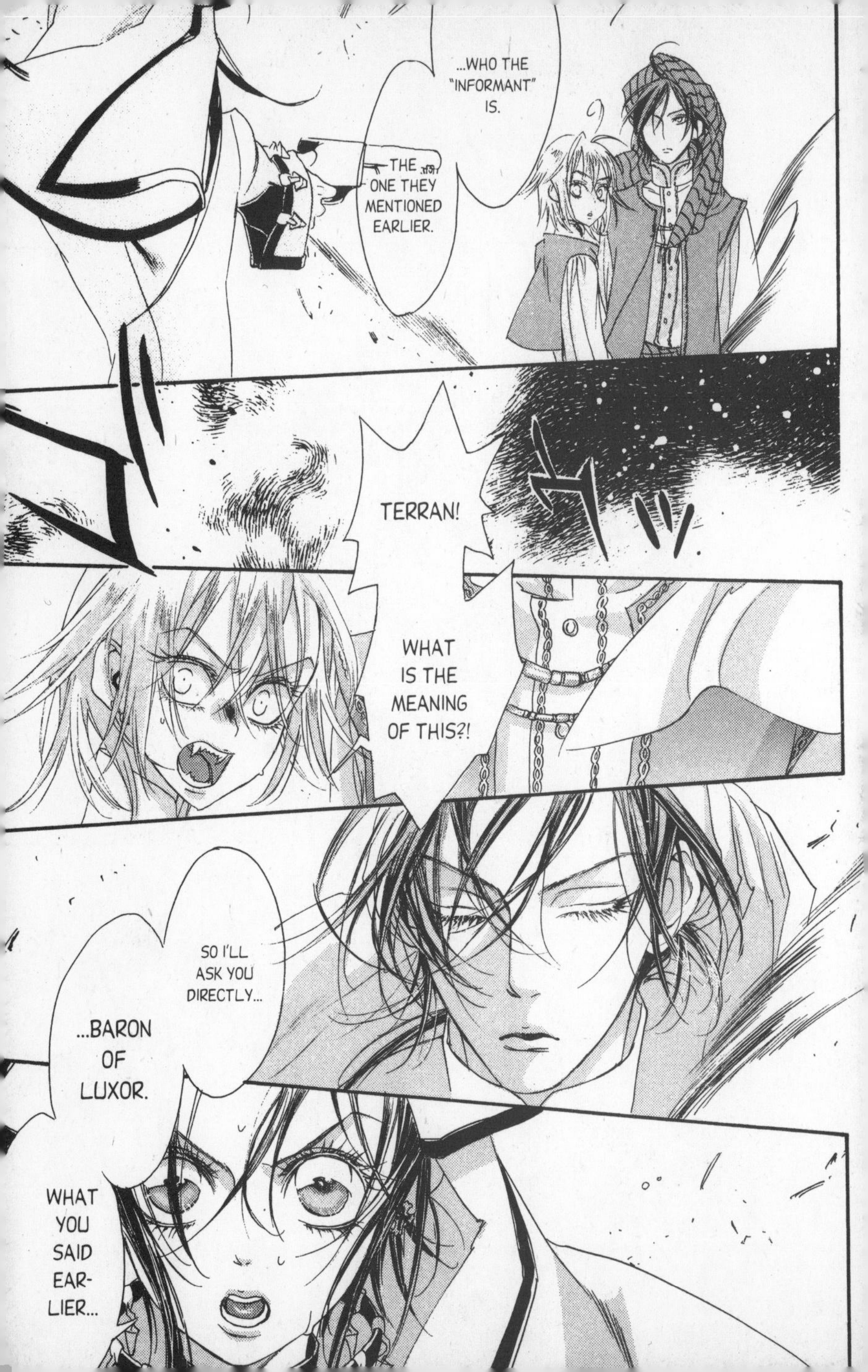
...WHO THE "INFORMANT" IS.
THE ONE THEY MENTIONED EARLIER.
TERRAN!
WHAT IS THE MEANING OF THIS?!
SO I'LL ASK YOU DIRECTLY...
...BARON OF LUXOR.
WHAT YOU SAID EAR-LIER...

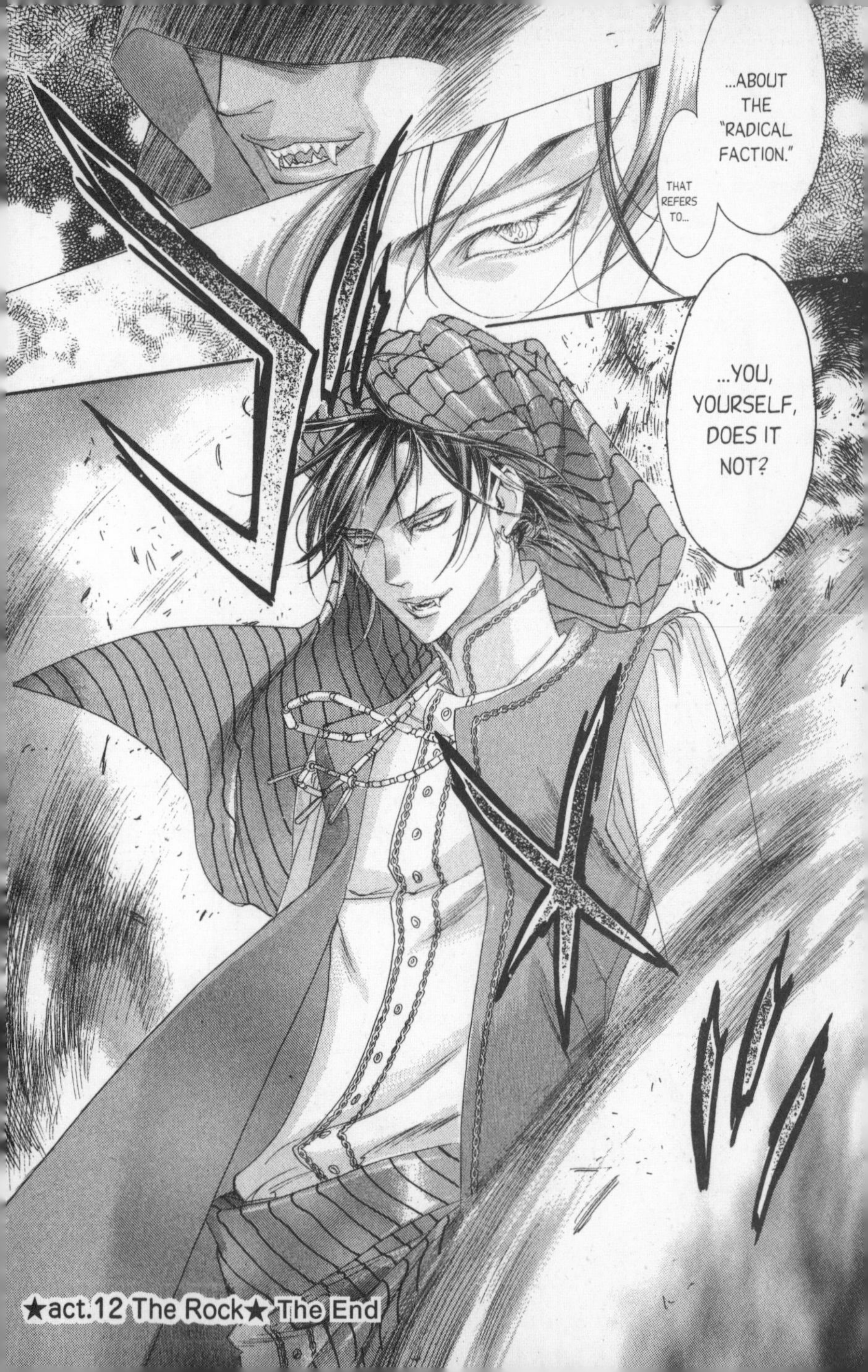
...ABOUT THE "RADICAL FACTION."
THAT REFERS TO...
...YOU, YOURSELF, DOES IT NOT?
★act.12 The Rock★ The End

Bloodshed: Where Death Rains Down

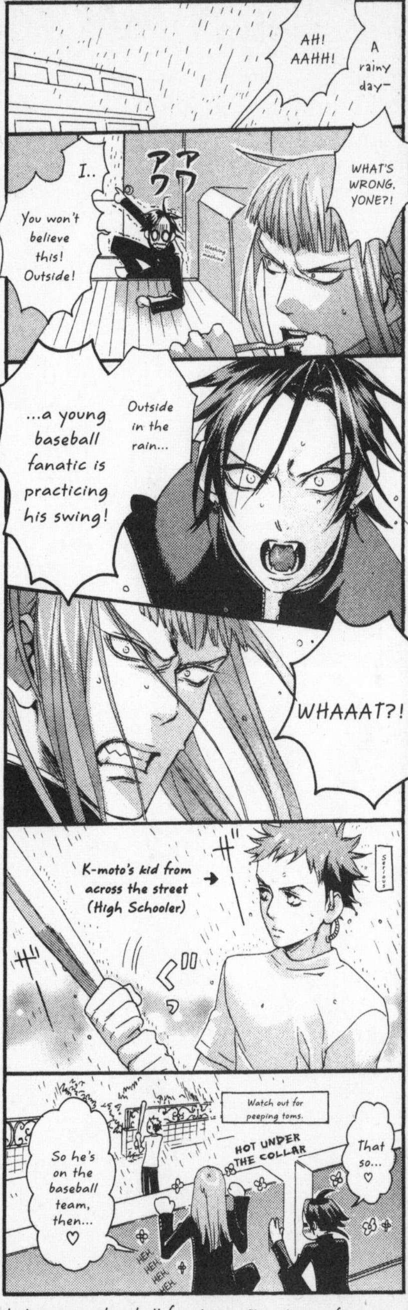
A rainy day—
AH! AAHH!
WHAT'S WRONG, YONE?!
I..
You won't believe this! Outside!
Washing machine
Outside in the rain...
...a young baseball fanatic is practicing his swing!
WHAAAT?!
Serious
K-moto's kid from across the street (High Schooler)
That so... ♡
HOT UNDER THE COLLAR
Watch out for peeping toms.
So he's on the baseball team, then... ♡
HEH, HEH, HEH, HEH.

We love young baseball fanatics.

The school uniforms are what they wear for work.

Bloodshed: Broad Daylight

Magician: Friend

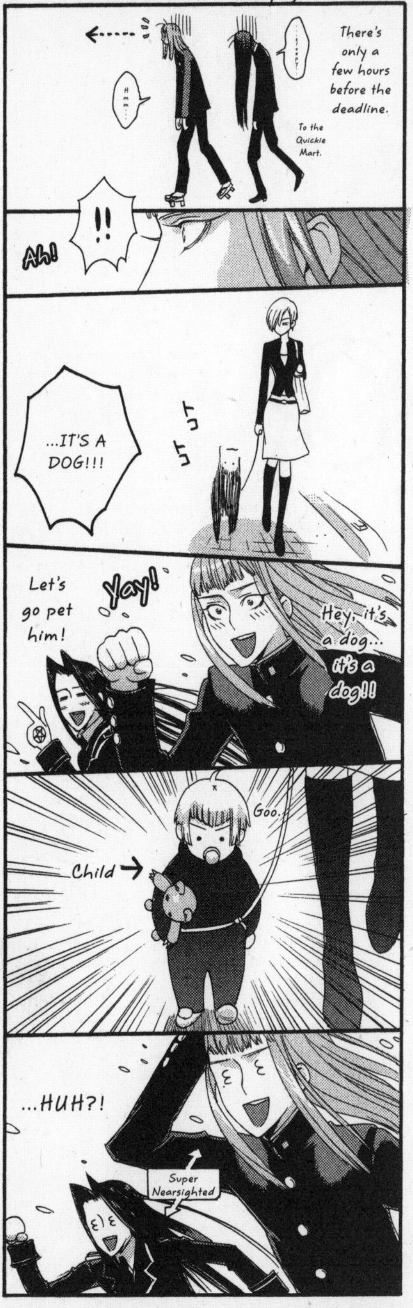
There's only a few hours before the deadline.
To the Quickie Mart.
Hmm...
!!
Ah!
...IT'S A DOG!!!
Hey, it's a dog... it's a dog!!
Yay!
Let's go pet him!
Goo..
Child →
...HUH?!
Super Nearsighted

We also love dogs.

Until recently I thought that Brother Andreas was Petros and Paulai's kid.

for this third volume, I began to think about the Toribura characters a little more seriously.

Petros

I play Honda in SFII, Jeffery in Virtua fighter, and Jack in Tekken, so if Toribura was a fighting game, then I would definitely pick Petros. I like ones with powerful builds. After all, even if you suck, you can still win...My editor, who had no interest whatsoever in Petros, said, "Draw him however you want to already," but lately it's, "Exaggerate him some more." Y-you like him after all, right?! Saori-san! That said, I don't have the skill. I want to draw him cooler. Or should I say, I really wish they'd make a fighting game out of Toribura...Max power in a Boar stance...or something.

Abel

I cut his bangs.
I have a friend who's 193 cm, but you could say that some tall people are more "long" than tall. But Naoya Ogawa (the pro wrestler) is 193 cm, too, huh? Woo hoo! Abel is the main character and I'm supposed to draw him the most, but he's the hardest to draw. I can't draw him so he looks cool at all. Plus, I don't get his personality. Is he a slacker? Is he kind? Is he cold? Is that character complete? Is he under construction? It's a mystery! People say the comic version of Abel is "so obviously a former juvenile delinquent," or "acts quiet but isn't" or "loose." Are they serious?

Ion

In the original work, he's written as oh-so-lovely this and oh-so-princess-like that and while drawing him I wondered how much of a pretty boy he was supposed to be. I have a feeling he's become even more of a heroine than Esther. I gave up all resistance and am trying my best to make him as lovely as possible. After all, every time he appears in the original work, he gets stuck in some kind of horrible situation. It's a dirty-the-pure-idol kind of thing, worthy of a Shinji Nojima drama. But he's got a really manly personality. Go, Ion!

Esther... ...secretly has massive boobage?!

I tried to keep her as close to the original as possible because she's the heroine, but she's become a totally different person. Tee hee. Rough, almost trashy, high tempered, drama queen...she gets branded with a lot of modifiers before "nun." I can't make her polite now, all of a sudden. Sorry. I bought a sawed-off shotgun as research material for her, but it's heavy! She probably has some amazing muscle-thighs, though. I think it'd be nice if I could draw her becoming more and more beautiful on the outside as she experiences inner growth. Probably.

Radu

"Blue hair that's as close to black as possible."...are we quoting R-Ryuu Murakami?! It's not like my editor's a naive little girl, but it seems she likes "Characters who smoke" and is partial to Radu. This side-part hairstyle is really hard to draw, but I also like how Radu is such a small, selfish person inside; kind of like...his theme song would be Simon and Garfunkel's "A Hazy Shade of Winter." He fails at being human!! Even so, "Radu Barvon" is such a powerful sounding name, isn't it?

Tres-kun

I saw "T2" for the first time in a long while, so...I guess that's my model...totally. Regardless, the comic version of Tres has been called, "sleepy looking," "shiba dog," "stupid looking," and "ear cleaner" and so I have to cry out in joy. EEK!!! I thought I was paying attention while drawing him, but... that's funny. I took another look at THORES-sensei's Tres and I was really surprised because that one's so cool. He's supposed to look like he's in his late teens to about early 20s, but that's so equivocal! Which part of him is?! Boys change so much at that age, don't they? After all it's the springtime of their lives, you know.

Ear cleaner

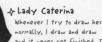

Dietrich

"A melancholy beauty." "If angels exist, then God would have made them look like him," so how beautiful is that supposed to be?!! I hold my head and think that when I draw him. A super good-looking guy who sticks out from all the good-looking guys of Toribura... I can't draw this...!! THORES-sensei said, "If you ask me, then Deet has sloping eyes," so I guess sloping eyes are correct...or should I say the refreshing Dietrich from the first half of volume 1 of the comics... I-I-I should have made him even more fresh then!!!

✤ Lady Caterina

Whenever I try to draw her normally, I draw and draw and it never get finished. Too bad!! "If it bothers you, then, come on down to the Vatican." Cold!!! But of all the female characters I like her personality and stuff the second best, right after Sister Paulai. She's really human. My editor said, "scary, scary," but... you told me to draw her scary!! But how do you draw a..."sickly woman"...I don't know...When I draw her, she looks like she'd come out victorious in battle, too.

...get serious and really think about this, self!!

OUTRO.

This is Toribura volume 3. ..It's because of you that I got this far. Thank you very much!!! This volume was aggravating in a lot of ways. It was the beginning of a new chapter, they'd decided to make an anime, and then there was something that shouldn't be forgotten... a lot was going on. Even with all that, the story must go on every month so I think I'll be okay no matter what happens from now on. After all, Brother Petros made his appearance. To me, who likes the Department of Inquisition the best of all the organizations that appear in Toribura, this was a big deal; like Obon and Christmas all at the same time. Woo hoo! B-but it seems like you need technique and determination in proportion to that tension, so just willpower alone isn't enough...Petros... Well, well. For now, willpower will have to do!! I will commit myself. I will go forth without doubt. I'll find out when I get there! By Inoki! Well, then! I'll be really happy if we meet again in the fourth volume!

Kyujyo

SPECIAL THANX

Kyoko "First ♡ Time" **Tarasawa** Reception Girl (ACT.11)
It was really an unexpected summer experience...sorry!! Come...again, okay?

Matthew "Hey, Impacted Tooth" **Masaki** Athlete (ACT.9)
Good luck on your senior thesis! I'm like acting like an upperclassman and all (but I haven't even graduated).

Kazutoshi "The Bloody Fist" **Masaki**
Corporal (Promoted)(ACT.10,12)
A lot happened again, huh...! You were crazy, barfing from the flu during the rough draft, but as the draft was done and K-1 came out you were well. What's up with that?! After all, **Masato** was in a necktie, right! And even helping with the move....questionable taste again?!

Mayuko "Boy Crazy Minami Asakura" **Wada**
I'm seriously glad I got to meet you...!! Thank you for the countless unforgettable lines like, **"If you got jelly, then something good'll happen!"** I'm gonna fill it chock full of jelly again, you know!!!

Yone "Full Tank of India Ink" **Sesshou** Catcher
Sorry for all the calling you over for emergencies that keep you up all night! By the way, when did you start counting your strike zone? At **4 years?!** 4 years old?

THORES "Meow!!!" **Shibamoto** Sensei
Thank you for everything at the "Remembrance Meeting"! I am happy that you taught me so much. Best regards.

Saori "Kadokawa's Caterina Sforza" **Yoshida**-sama
I make so much trouble for you all the time...!! I'm really sorry. And then the **Wood Carving of a Bear with a Salmon in His Mouth**...made me way happy!!!!!

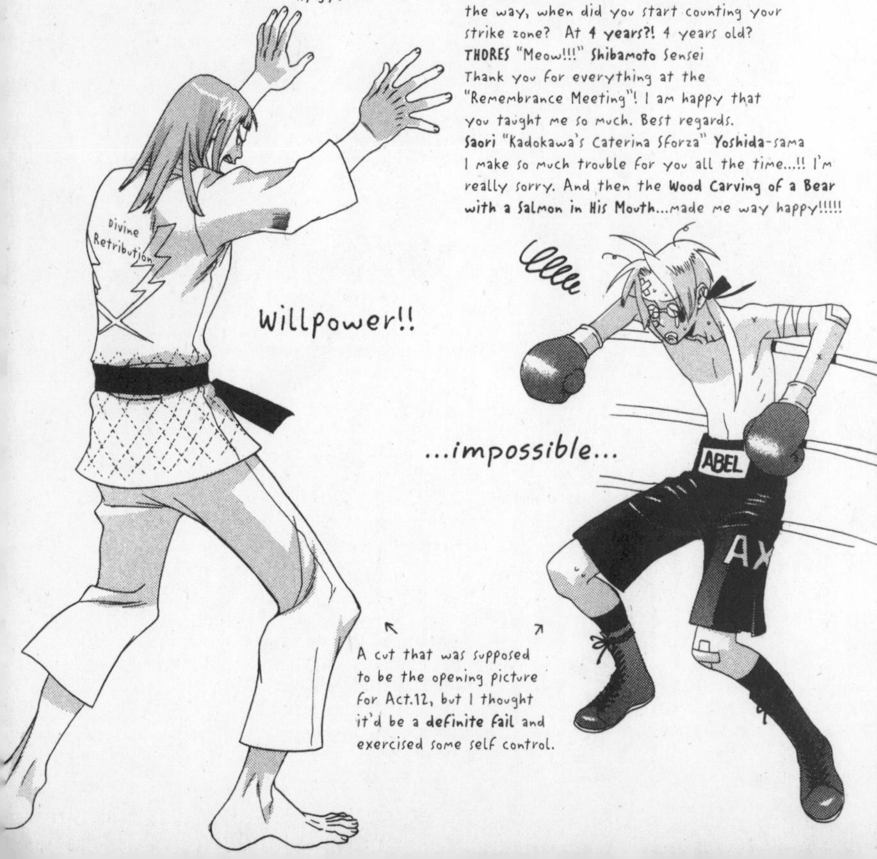

Divine Retribution
Willpower!!
...impossible...
ABEL
AX

A cut that was supposed to be the opening picture for Act.12, but I thought it'd be a **definite fail** and exercised some self control.

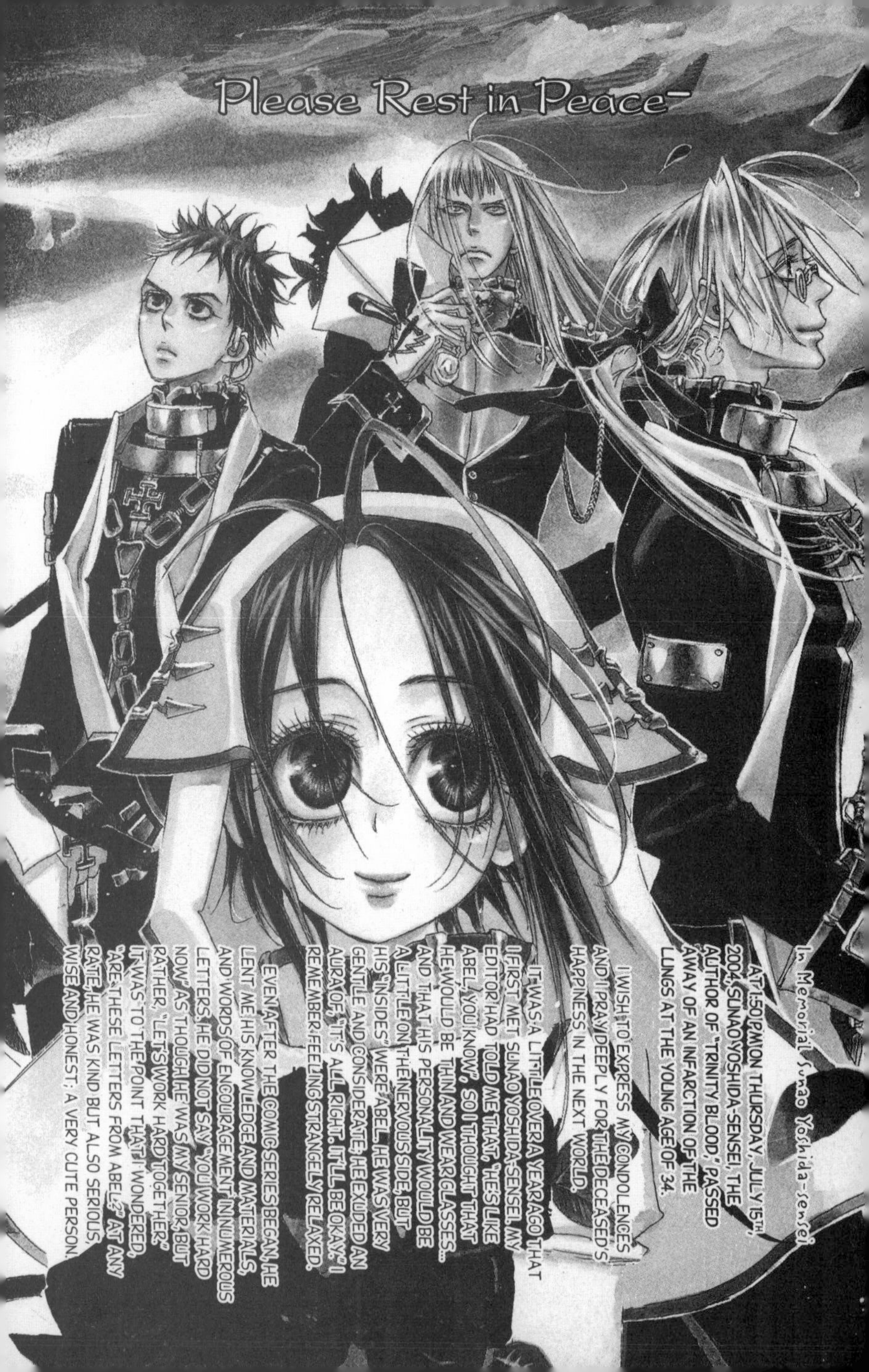
Please Rest in Peace-
In Memorial Sunao Yoshida-sensei
AT 1:50 P.M. ON THURSDAY, JULY 15TH, 2004, SUNAO YOSHIDA-SENSEI, THE AUTHOR OF "TRINITY BLOOD," PASSED AWAY OF AN INFARCTION OF THE LUNGS AT THE YOUNG AGE OF 34.
I WISH TO EXPRESS MY CONDOLENCES AND I PRAY DEEPLY FOR THE DECEASED'S HAPPINESS IN THE NEXT WORLD.
IT WAS A LITTLE OVER A YEAR AGO THAT I FIRST MET SUNAO YOSHIDA-SENSEI. MY EDITOR HAD TOLD ME THAT, "HE'S LIKE ABEL, YOU KNOW", SO I THOUGHT THAT HE WOULD BE THIN AND WEAR GLASSES... AND THAT HIS PERSONALITY WOULD BE A LITTLE ON THE NERVOUS SIDE, BUT HIS "INSIDES" WERE ABEL. HE WAS VERY GENTLE AND CONSIDERATE; HE EXUDED AN AURA OF, "IT'S ALL RIGHT. IT'LL BE OKAY." I REMEMBER FEELING STRANGELY RELAXED.
EVEN AFTER THE COMIC SERIES BEGAN, HE LENT ME HIS KNOWLEDGE AND MATERIALS, AND WORDS OF ENCOURAGEMENT IN NUMEROUS LETTERS. HE DID NOT SAY "YOU WORK HARD NOW" AS THOUGH HE WAS MY SENIOR, BUT RATHER, "LET'S WORK HARD TOGETHER." IT WAS TO THE POINT THAT I WONDERED, "ARE THESE LETTERS FROM ABEL?" AT ANY RATE, HE WAS KIND BUT ALSO SERIOUS, WISE AND HONEST; A VERY CUTE PERSON.

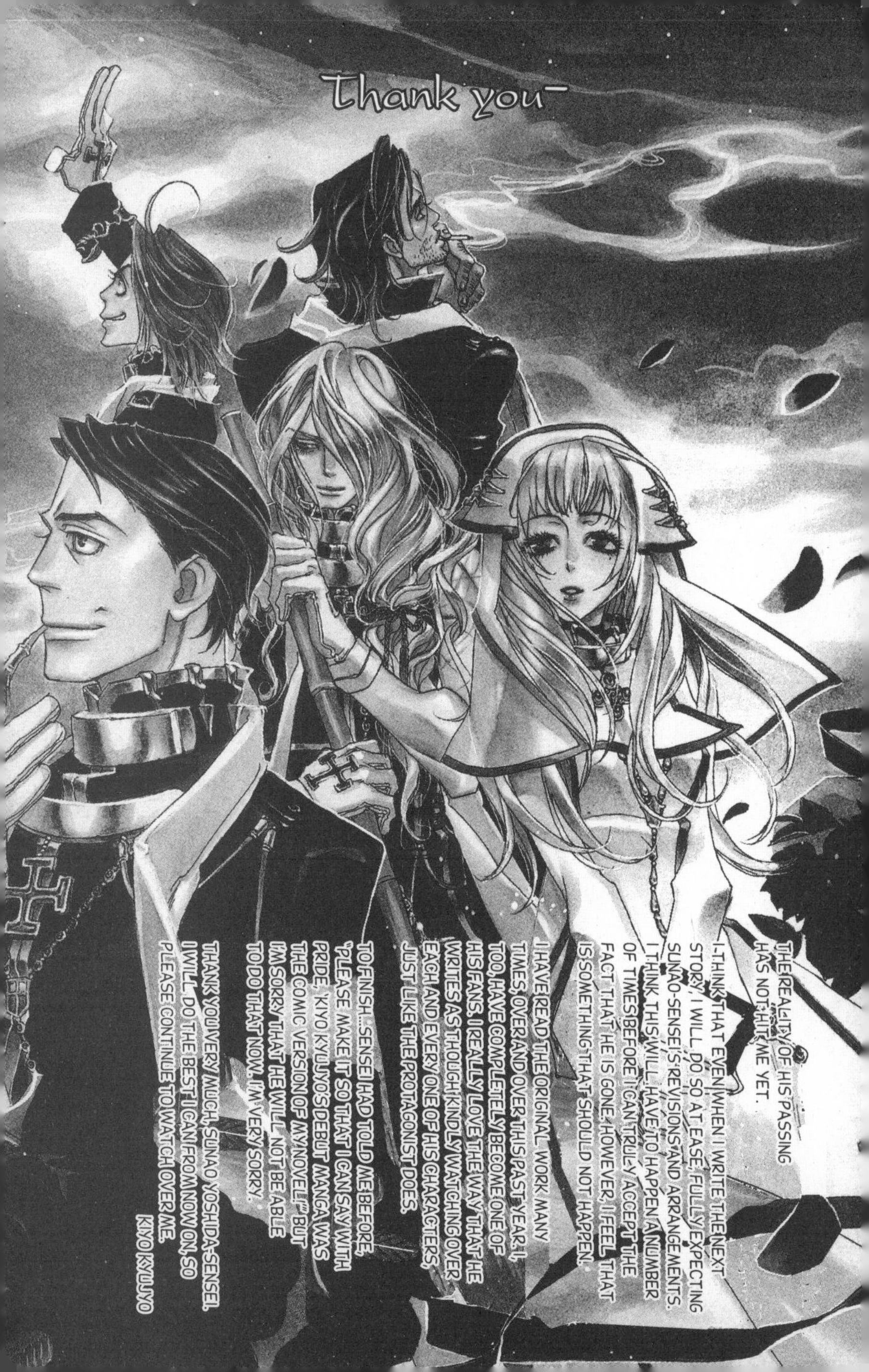
Thank you~
THE REALITY OF HIS PASSING
HAS NOT HIT ME YET.
I THINK THAT EVEN WHEN I WRITE THE NEXT
STORY, I WILL DO SO AT EASE, FULLY EXPECTING
SUNAO-SENSEI'S REVISIONS AND ARRANGEMENTS.
I THINK THIS WILL HAVE TO HAPPEN A NUMBER
OF TIMES BEFORE I CAN TRULY ACCEPT THE
FACT THAT HE IS GONE. HOWEVER, I FEEL THAT
IS SOMETHING THAT SHOULD NOT HAPPEN.
I HAVE READ THE ORIGINAL WORK MANY
TIMES, OVER AND OVER THIS PAST YEAR. I,
TOO, HAVE COMPLETELY BECOME ONE OF
HIS FANS. I REALLY LOVE THE WAY THAT HE
WRITES AS THOUGH KINDLY WATCHING OVER
EACH AND EVERY ONE OF HIS CHARACTERS,
JUST LIKE THE PROTAGONIST DOES.
TO FINISH, SENSEI HAD TOLD ME BEFORE,
"PLEASE MAKE IT SO THAT I CAN SAY WITH
PRIDE, 'KIYO KYUJYO'S DEBUT MANGA WAS
THE COMIC VERSION OF MY NOVEL!'" BUT
I'M SORRY THAT HE WILL NOT BE ABLE
TO DO THAT NOW. I'M VERY SORRY.
THANK YOU VERY MUCH, SUNAO YOSHIDA-SENSEI.
I WILL DO THE BEST I CAN FROM NOW ON, SO
PLEASE CONTINUE TO WATCH OVER ME.
KIYO KYUJYO

IN THE NEXT VOLUME OF
TRINITY BLOOD™

Ion is stunned by Radu's betrayal, and his memories of their childhood together are totally shattered. But in spite of Radu's connection to the mysterious and malevolent Rosenkreuz Orden, Ion isn't ready to accept the loss of his beloved friend. Abel and Esther struggle to escape Carthage with their precious cargo from the Empire in tow, fighting off both the Inquisition and Radu simultaneously, but how will Esther respond when Abel's darkest secret is revealed?

PEACE MAKER
ピースメーカー

IS GETTING REVENGE WORTH THE PRICE OF SACRIFICING YOUR OWN HUMANITY?

TOKYOPOP presents Nanae Chrono's original manga series that inspired the Peace Maker Kurogane anime

AFTER TETSUNOSUKE ICHIMURA SAW HIS PARENTS MURDERED BY A CHOUSHUU ASSASSIN, HE VOWS WITH ALL HIS HEART TO TAKE REVENGE ON THEIR KILLER. IT IS THE FIRST YEAR OF GENJI, AND TETSUNOSUKE HEADS TO THE HEADQUARTERS OF THE SHINSENGUMI WITH HIS OLDER BROTHER TATSUNOSUKE TO FULFILL HIS DREAMS OF GETTING REVENGE. BUT IN ORDER TO JOIN THE SHINSENGUMI, HE MUST FOREGO HIS HUMANITY AND BECOME A DEMON.

FOR MORE INFORMATION VISIT: WWW.TOKYOPOP.COM

STOP!

This is the back of the book.
You wouldn't want to spoil a great ending!

This book is printed "manga-style," in the authentic Japanese right-to-left format. Since none of the artwork has been flipped or altered, readers get to experience the story just as the creator intended. You've been asking for it, so TOKYOPOP® delivered: authentic, hot-off-the-press, and far more fun!

DIRECTIONS

If this is your first time reading manga-style, here's a quick guide to help you understand how it works.

It's easy... just start in the top right panel and follow the numbers. Have fun, and look for more 100% authentic manga from TOKYOPOP®!

1
2
3
4
5
6
7
8
9
10

THE MANGA REVOLUTION · LEADING · 漫画革命 · LEADING · THE MANGA REVOLUTION